T0235480

Human–Computer Interaction Series

HCI is a multidisciplinary field focused on human aspects of the development of computer technology. As computer-based technology becomes increasingly pervasive – not just in developed countries, but worldwide – the need to take a human-centered approach in the design and development of this technology becomes ever more important. For roughly 30 years now, researchers and practitioners in computational and behavioral sciences have worked to identify theory and practice that influences the direction of these technologies, and this diverse work makes up the field of human-computer interaction. Broadly speaking it includes the study of what technology might be able to do for people and how people might interact with the technology. The HCI series publishes books that advance the science and technology of developing systems which are both effective and satisfying for people in a wide variety of contexts. Titles focus on theoretical perspectives (such as formal approaches drawn from a variety of behavioral sciences), practical approaches (such as the techniques for effectively integrating user needs in system development), and social issues (such as the determinants of utility, usability and acceptability).

More information about this series at http://www.springer.com/series/6033

Pradipta Biswas • Carlos Duarte • Patrick Langdon
Luis Almeida
Editors

A Multimodal End-2-End Approach to Accessible Computing

Second Edition

Editors
Pradipta Biswas
Department of Engineering
University of Cambridge
Cambridge, UK

Carlos Duarte
Department of Informatics
University of Lisbon
Lisboa, Portugal

Patrick Langdon
Department of Engineering
University of Cambridge
Cambridge, UK

Luis Almeida
Centre of Computer Graphics
University of Minho
Guimarães, Portugal

ISSN 1571-5035
Human–Computer Interaction Series
ISBN 978-1-4471-7074-7 ISBN 978-1-4471-6708-2 (eBook)
DOI 10.1007/978-1-4471-6708-2

Springer London Heidelberg New York Dordrecht

Softcover reprint of the hardcover 2nd edition 2015

Printed on acid-free paper

Springer-Verlag London Ltd. is part of Springer Science+Business Media (www.springer.com)

Foreword from the First Edition

An explosion in the widespread public use of computers and the rapid deployment of digital delivery of entertainment means that very few citizens can now avoid having to use a variety of user interfaces in their everyday lives. We might need to access official government information which is only conveniently available via the web or we may wish to select our TV viewing from a myriad choice of programmes and channels and then to choose those programmes which have subtitling or audio description.

Historically, user interfaces (UIs) have typically been designed for an individual product or range of products in apparent isolation. Rarely, it seems, has much consideration been given to the complete system from service design, application and delivery to user interaction and essential real-time help functions including post-installation support. Designers have seldom taken a broad view of "digital literacy" when considering the full range of capabilities of their potential users. Thorough involvement of the entire user community at each stage of product or service development has been the exception rather than the rule. Where UI designers have paid any attention to the particular needs of elderly or users with disabilities, all too often the result has been a bespoke solution specific to one disability alone – an exclusive "ghetto" approach which has inevitably resulted in small markets, high unit costs and very short lifecycles. Alternative simplistic "one-size-fits-all" approaches have generally failed to offer a wholly satisfactory solution for any one user.

One direct consequence is that service users are often faced with an uncoordinated multiplicity of disparate UI styles and thus with a bewildering and dispiriting inconsistency in user experience between different products (even where these offer similar notional functionality). This would bc a challenge for anyone but is especially so for older people or those with some functional disability.

In addition to the moral imperative of inclusion and equal opportunity for all, consistent ease of use clearly brings strong commercial benefits for any manufacturer or service provider in terms of wider markets, improved brand reputation and brand loyalty plus a significantly reduced need for post-sales support. The importance of a coherent end-to-end strategy for "accessibility" is now becoming recognised by some individual manufacturers and service providers.

This book brings together research from a number of groups active in this field. It outlines a coherent framework for the design, development and maintenance of accessible interactive intelligent systems and in doing so makes a valuable contribution to our understanding of the wider context of accessibility.

Dorking, UK
2013

Nick Tanton
Head of Technology BBC Switchover Help Scheme 2007–2012

Editorial

Pradipta Biswas, Carlos Duarte, Patrick Langdon, and Luis Almeida

The second edition of the book *Multimodal End-to-End Approach to Accessible Computing* further broadens the scope of accessible computing with new chapters from researchers at Nippon Hōsō Kyōkai (Japan Broadcasting Corporation), Auckland University of Technology, New Zealand; Leuphana University, Germany; and Indian Institute of Technology, Madras. The book does not confine accessible computing only to computers and computer peripherals; rather, it presents a wide array of chapters ranging from designing accessible interactive television in China, Japan and Europe to mobile phone-based agriculture advisory system developed for Indian farmers. Authors of this book belong from 13 different countries spread over four different continents.

The new edition has the following 16 chapters divided into three sections:

1. **Design:** This section focuses on user-centred design process and discusses the challenges of meeting requirements of users with a wide range of abilities and a prospective solution through user modelling.
   (a) **Chapter 1 [What Technology Can and Cannot Offer an Ageing Population: Current Situation and Future Approach]** sets the scene up with a case study of an elderly family, points out requirements of inclusive design and advocates for adopting the 'design for all' approach.
   (b) **Chapter 2 [Survey on Inclusive Human Machine Interaction Issues in India]** takes forward the discussion of Chap. 1 in Indian context. It compares and contrasts HCI issues for elderly users between developing and developed countries.

P. Biswas • P. Langdon
Department of Engineering, University of Cambridge, Cambridge, UK

C. Duarte
Department of Informatics, University of Lisbon, Lisboa, Portugal

L. Almeida
Centre of Computer Graphics, University of Minho, Guimarães, Portugal

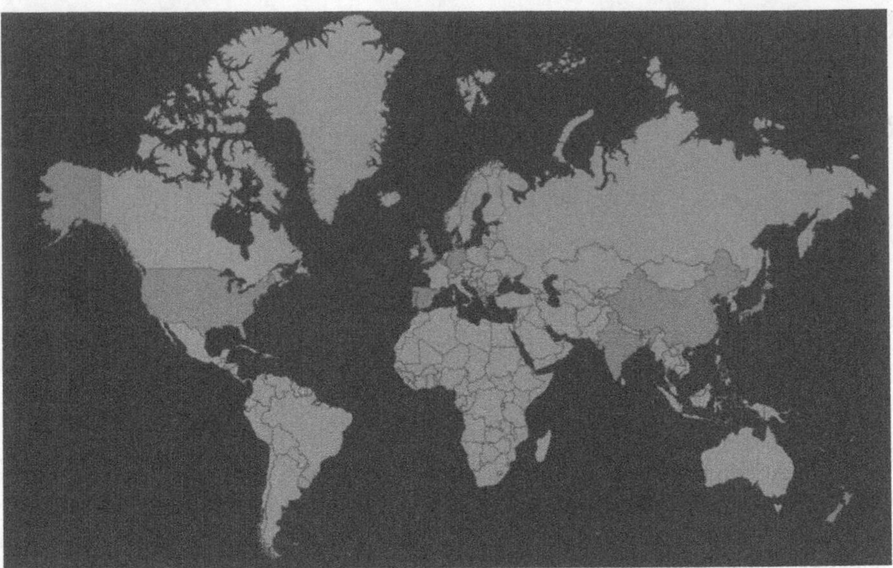

Geographic coverage of authors' countries

(c) **Chapter 3 [Developing an Interactive TV for the Elderly and Impaired: An Inclusive Design Strategy]** examines a user-centred design approach for inclusive populations, where capability ranges are wider and more variable than found in conventional design.
(d) **Chapter 4 [Designing TV Interaction for the Elderly – A Case Study of the Design for All Approach]** presents a case study of 'design for all' approach in the context of developing a multimodal inclusive digital TV framework and lists a set of technical requirements.
(e) **Chapter 5 [Inclusive User Modeling and Simulation]** presents the concept of user modelling, which formulates the user requirements into a statistical model that can be used to improve interface design and adapt interaction in run time.

2. **Development:** The development section looks at both research on multimodal systems and accessibility solutions for different platforms like computers, ubiquitous devices and digital televisions.

(a) **Chapter 6 [Intelligent Interaction in Accessible Applications]** presents assistive devices and interaction systems developed at North Carolina State University. It presents a tactile wearable system that aids people with vision impairment in locating, identifying and acquiring objects and helps them to explore maps and other forms of graphical information.
(b) **Chapter 7 [Interaction Techniques for Users with Severe Motor Impairment]** extends the discussion at Chap. 5 to more novel interactive sys-

tems involving eye gaze tracker, single-switch scanning system and brain-computer interfaces.

(c) **Chapter 8 [Embodied Virtual Agents as a Means to Foster E-Inclusion of Older People]** introduces virtual character (commonly known as Avatar) as a means of showing empathy to elderly users and discusses the state of the art of the Avatar technology.

(d) **Chapter 9 [Building an Adaptive Multimodal Framework for Resource Constrained Systems]** binds the previously discussed interaction technologies together through presenting a system that fuses multiple modalities of interaction and thus provides adaptation capability to nonadaptive systems.

(e) **Chapter 10 [A New Agricultural Advisory System-Personalized Interfaces and Interactions]** extends the principle of inclusive interfaces to Indian farmers presenting a system for early detection and remedy of diseases in crop.

(f) **Chapter 11 [Audio Games: Investigation of the Potential Through Prototype Development]** discusses a few prototype games developed in New Zealand for visually impaired users and analysed their acceptance for both visually impaired users and their able-bodied counterpart.

3. **Maintenance:** Development should always be followed by evaluation and deployment. The last section discusses case studies of evaluating accessible systems and developing international standards to maintain accessible solutions.

(a) **Chapter 12 [R&D for Accessible Broadcasting in Japan]** discusses various technologies to improve accessibility of broadcasting in Japan and the vision of accessible broadcasting in the future.

(b) **Chapter 13 [Evaluating the Accessibility of Adaptive TV Based Web Applications]** presents a system to evaluate dynamic web content.

(c) **Chapter 14 [Television Accessibility in China]** addresses the present status and the strategic options for making television accessible in China.

(d) **Chapter 15 [An Interoperable and Inclusive User Modeling Concept for Simulation and Adaptation]** extends the concept of user modelling presented in Chap. 4 to develop an international standard on user modelling.

(e) Finally **Chap. 16 [Standardization of Audiovisual Media Accessibility]** concludes by discussing existing issues in accessibility with respect to different stakeholders and sets up a vision for the near future.

Editorial for the First Edition

Modern research in intelligent interactive systems can offer valuable assistance to elderly and disabled population by helping them to engage more fully with the world. However, many users find it difficult to use existing interaction devices either for physical or ageing-related impairments, though researches on intelligent voice recognition; adaptable pointing, browsing and navigation; and affect and gesture recognition can hugely benefit them. Additionally, systems and services developed for elderly or disabled people often find useful applications for their able-bodied counterparts. A few examples are mobile amplification control, which was originally developed for people with hearing problem but helpful in noisy environment, audio cassette version of books originally developed for blind people, the standard of subtitling in television for deaf users and so on. Further many important technical achievements could not yet be implemented at the industrial level, mostly due to the lack of awareness among industrial developers and missing software and guideline support during design and development. Existing research and development on interactive systems often works for 'average' users and excludes a certain portion of the population who finds it difficult to use existing systems and may benefit from intelligent adaptation of the interface. There exists a gap between accessibility practitioners and other computing professionals; they often fail to understand each other and come up with wrong solutions. The lack of knowledge about the problems of disabled and elderly users has often led designers to develop non-inclusive systems. On the other hand, accessibility research often focuses on developing tailor-made products for a certain type of disability and lacks portability across different platforms and users. Existing literature on accessibility consists mainly of guidelines like Web Content Accessibility Guidelines (WCAG) and conference proceedings like ACM ASSETS proceedings, which are useful for a particular audience, but lacks a coherent picture of the challenges and vision for accessibility.

This book takes an end-to-end approach to illustrate the state of the art of technology and sketch a vision for accessibility in the near future by considering challenges faced by accessibility practitioners at research institutes, industries and legislative institutes like international standardization organizations in different parts of the world. The book looks at different phases of delivering accessible products or service starting from design, development, deployment and maintenance. It leverages the range of abilities of users through intelligent multimodal interfaces and aims to be a handbook for practitioners. It does not go into the details of individual research or work; rather, it provides a context for thoughts and vision for the future.

What This Book Is About

A Handbook for Researchers and Practitioners This book is different than existing conference proceedings and LNCS books on accessibility in terms of a coherent structure. It consists of only 11 chapters written by selected authors from 10 different countries spread over three continents who are working in the field of accessibility for many years. Each section is on a particular theme like design, development or maintenance. The chapters do not explore too much technical detail and statistical results; instead, they provide an assimilation of individual authors' work that can be accessible to people with a wide range of backgrounds.

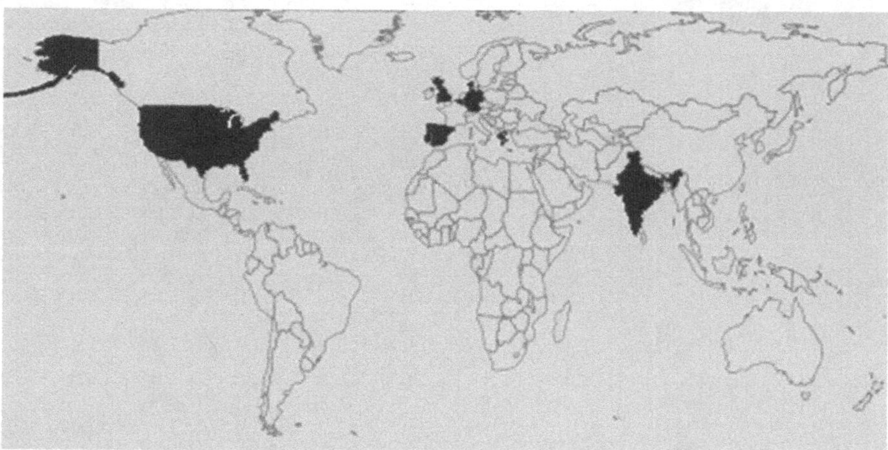

Geographic coverage of authors' countries

End-to-End Approach The book contains chapters from researchers, industrial developers and representatives from international standardization institutes. It aims to provide an end-to-end picture in terms of requirement analysis, accessible content development, evaluation and maintenance through regulation and legislation.

Unique Multimodal Approach to Accessibility Existing research or development on accessibility is often stigmatized as 'special' additional features for people with disabilities. Instead, this book leverages the range of abilities of users in different contexts through user modelling and multimodal interaction techniques like gesture-based system, virtual character, brain-computer interfaces or eye gaze tracker-based interaction techniques.

Acknowledgement

We would like to thank Miss Minh Chau Nguyen of Oxford Brookes University, UK, for doing the fantastic illustrations for this book.

Contents

Contributors

U. Rajendra Acharya Ngee Ann Polytechnic, Singapore, Singapore

Robert St. Amant Department of Computer Science, North Carolina State University, Raleigh, NC, USA

Sina Bahram Department of Computer Science, North Carolina State University, Raleigh, NC, USA

Jarosław Beksa School of Computer and Mathematical Sciences, Auckland University of Technology, Auckland, New Zealand

Pradipta Biswas Department of Engineering, University of Cambridge, Cambridge, UK

Luís Carriço Department of Informatics, LaSIGE/University of Lisbon, Lisboa, Portugal

Phil Carter School of Computer and Mathematical Sciences, Auckland University of Technology, Auckland, New Zealand

Arpan Chakraborty Udacity

Subhagata Chattopadhyay Camellia Institute of Engineering, Madhyamgram, India

José Coelho Faculty of Sciences, University of Lisbon, Lisboa, Portugal

Daniel Costa Faculty of Sciences, University of Lisbon, Lisboa, Portugal

David Costa Faculty of Sciences, University of Lisbon, Lisboa, Portugal

Carlos Duarte Department of Informatics, University of Lisbon, Lisboa, Portugal

Aitziber Etxaniz INGEMA, San Sebastian, Spain

Pedro Feiteira Faculty of Sciences, University of Lisbon, Lisboa, Portugal

Nádia Fernandes Department of Informatics, LaSIGE/University of Lisbon, Lisboa, Portugal

Sonia Fizek Gamification Lab, Centre for Digital Cultures, Leuphana University, Lüneburg, Germany

Linnea Frid INGEMA, San Sebastian, Spain

Alvaro García INGEMA, San Sebastian, Spain

Mari Feli Gonzalez INGEMA, San Sebastian, Spain

Tiago Guerreiro Faculty of Sciences, University of Lisbon, Lisboa, Portugal

Takayuki Ito NHK Engineering System Inc., Setagaya-ku, Tokyo, Japan

Ido A. Iurgel EngageLab, Centro Algoritmi, University of Minho, Guimarães, Portugal

Ashok Jhunjhunwala Department of Electrical Engineering, IIT Madras, Chennai, TN, India

Rohan Joshi Department of Industrial Design, Designed Intelligence Group, Eindhoven University of Technology, KU Leuven, Leuven, Belgium

Christophe Jung Fraunhofer IGD, Darmstadt, Germany

N. Kaklanis Information Technologies Institute, Centre for Research and Technology Hellas, Thessaloniki, Greece

Patrick Langdon Department of Engineering, University of Cambridge, Cambridge, UK

Iker Laskibar INGEMA, San Sebastian, Spain

Dongxiao Li College of Media and International Culture, Zhejiang University, Hangzhou, China

Teik-Cheng Lim SIM University, Singapore, Singapore

Peter Olaf Looms ECOM-ICOM Programme, University of Hong Kong, Hong Kong SAR, China

Y. Mohamad Fraunhofer FIT, Sankt Augustin, Germany

Dominic Noy Computer Graphics Center (CCG), University of Minho – Campus de Azurém, Guimarães, Portugal

M. Peissner Fraunhofer-Institut für Arbeitswirtschaft und Organisation IAO, Leiter Competence Center Human-Computer Interaction, Stuttgart, Germany

Srinath Ravindran Yahoo

Pedro Ribeiro Computer Graphics Center (CCG), University of Minho – Campus de Azurém, Guimarães, Portugal

D. Tzovaras Information Technologies Institute, Centre for Research and Technology Hellas, Thessaloniki, Greece

Jayalakshmi Umadikar RTBI, IIT Madras, Chennai, TN, India

Part I
Design

Chapter 1
What Technology Can and Cannot Offer an Ageing Population: Current Situation and Future Approach

Linnea Frid, Alvaro García, Iker Laskibar, Aitziber Etxaniz, and Mari Feli Gonzalez

Abstract Technological development and the growing older population are two phenomena which are both quickly increasing in the twenty first century. Ageing, in general, come with some inevitable changes in several areas such as our perceptual and cognitive functions and physical mobility. Technology is predicted to have a potential positive impact in terms of enhancing the older people's quality of life, helping them to adapt well to the new life situation. However many current technologies have great difficulties to reach this particular age group. This chapter is analyzing the current situation from an accessibility point of view and outlines some recommendations for near future.

1.1 Introduction

Older persons are experiencing today's information and technological society with some difficulties that is not always seen by the rest of society. The examples presented below are fictitious persons, taken from real life situations, aiming to portray some contexts this age group might encounter in everyday life.

1.1.1 Scenario

Al, now 73, retired from his work 12 years ago. He used to work in a small company for over 40 years. His job was to implement electrical installations in houses built by

---

L. Frid (✉) • A. García • I. Laskibar • A. Etxaniz • M.F. Gonzalez
INGEMA, San Sebastian, Spain
e-mail: linnea.s.frid@gmail.com; alvaro.garcia@matiainstituto.net; iker.laskibar@matiainstituto.net; aitziber.etxaniz@matiainstituto.net; mari.gonzalez@matiainstituto.net

P. Biswas et al. (eds.), *A Multimodal End-2-End Approach to Accessible Computing*, Human–Computer Interaction Series, DOI 10.1007/978-1-4471-6708-2_1

his company. He never needed to use a computer to execute his job, something that Al was happy about. From his point of view, all those devices are barriers impeding personal contact with other people.

Whenever Al needs money, he goes to the bank office and always tries to avoid the cash machine because he finds it cold and difficult to use. The font size is not big enough and the contrast of the screen is not good, which results in difficulties to see what's showing on the screen. Al is also uncomfortable to use the cash machine for safety reasons as he does not trust the electronic service. For example he worries that the solicited amount of money will not be delivered, but be withdrawn from the account. This is something that could be hard to prove afterwards.

Al also finds problems using his mobile phone. The font size is so small that he has difficulties to write and read messages, handle contacts when making a call etc. In addition it has too many options and he does not even know what half of them stand for. The large amount of possible options makes Al lost whenever he tries to perform an action. For this reason he only uses the mobile phone to receive calls, he rarely calls someone himself.

Al is married with Peg, 79 years old. Peg is a writer by profession, which she has dedicated more than 42 years to do. During this time Peg has gradually changed her tools, following the technological development in the society. At the beginning she wrote with a pen, then she started to use a typewriter and some years later she bought a computer. Peg recognizes the computer as something that facilitates her work.

Al is worried about Peg's state of health. Some years ago Peg started to forget things that she had never had problems to remember before. During the last years this has become worse and worse. A couple of years ago, Al observed for the first time that Peg spent plenty of time just looking at the computer screen without typing anything. In the beginning he thought that she was in deep thoughts finding new ideas for her new novel, but one day he saw her typing incoherent phrases that did not make sense. The couple decided to consult a neurologist and a neuropsychologist. After several examinations Peg was diagnosed with dementia. She began to receive treatment immediately but since then nothing is the same anymore. Two months ago, she went to a cash machine and took out a large amount of money that just disappeared. Al is constantly worried that Peg one day will forget to turn off the gas, the oven or that she will get out of the house and risk being involved in an accident. Al has to watch over and care for Peg every minute of day and night. He does not want Peg to move to a residence because he thinks that being a husband implies to take care of her and that they have to stay together. Due to this new situation, Al has not been able to do anything outside his home for a long time. For example go for a walk in the forest with his friend Jefferson, as he used to do every week.

Jefferson is 76 years old and visits Al every week in order to give him a hand with different everyday tasks during this difficult period. Jefferson is a former colleague to Al, who used to work in the same company. Jefferson had somewhat different work tasks than Al and was introduced to work with a computer so he has some experience with this type of technology. He has a positive attitude towards technological devices in general and has been using them, but now he feels that the development is running away from him. New technological devices are created so fast that he is not able catch up with the market.

Some years ago, Jefferson tried to teach Al how to use a computer and internet. Al liked the idea to be able to search and look for medical advices online, and how to purchase some food and get it home delivered as he is not able to leave the house for longer periods. But even if Al's intention was genuine, he was not able to succeed. It was too complicated and Al is concerned about the privacy of the data he enters on internet. He was very frustrated when wanting to use "such a bloody complex device" and decided to stop trying.

Even Jefferson, who has a positive attitude towards technology, finds it hard to learn how to use the new devices that are released. In addition to the learning aspect, there are other difficulties, for example the size of the buttons of his mobile phone. They are so small that he makes many mistakes when writing a SMS. Jefferson is not as accurate as he used to be with his hands anymore. Another problem is that Jefferson has some hearing difficulties, and the volume of his mobile phone is not loud enough so he does not always realize that someone is calling him. He has the same problem with the TV. He set the volume so loud when watching, that his neighbors complain.

Marcy, Jefferson's wife, is 73 and worked as a bus driver. She was diagnosed with diabetes some months ago. Every day, several times a day she measures the sugar level in the blood. Even if she is able to do so, she still does not know how to interpret the values she gets from the measurement which makes her worried. Jefferson and Marcy would like to be able to ask a doctor more frequently how to proceed once they have taken an assessment. But since there is no existing, simple enough option to do it online, they have to go to hospital every time.

1.2 Facts and Figures

Older adults are the fastest growing demographic group in many developed countries right now and the group is expected to increase in an even higher speed in future. In both absolute and relative terms this means that there will be more and more older people within our society. In 1995 the median age for the European Union (27 countries included) was 36.5 years, thereafter the population started to age in a relative rapid pace reaching 40.9 years in 2010. This number means that in 2010, 50 % of the population in EU was over 40.9 years and the tendency is predicted to follow the same pattern. The median age is predicted to establish at around 47.6 years in 2060. The whole EU population was estimated to 501.1 million persons in the beginning of 2010, of these, 87.1 million were aged 65 or over. This is an increase of 3.7 % in 20 years reaching a total percentage of 17.4 of the total population. Table 1.1 shows the age distribution in the European countries.

The increase of aging people varies between the member states but in general the pattern is the same for the whole EU [1–3].

Table 1.1 Population on 1 January 2012

Total	Total population (1,000)	% of total population		
		Aged 50–64	Aged 65–79	Aged 80+
EU-27	501101.8	19.1	12.7	4.7
BE	10839.9	19.3	12.2	4.9
BG	7563.7	20.8	13.7	3.8
CZ	10506.8	20.8	11.7	3.6
DK	5529.4	19.7	12.2	4.1
DE	81802.3	19.3	15.6	5.1
EE	1340.1	18.8	13.0	4.1
IE	4467.9	16.0	8.5	2.8
EL	11305.1	18.9	14.3	4.6
ES	45989.0	17.4	12.0	4.9
FR	64716.3	19.2	11.4	5.2
IT	60340.3	19.0	14.5	5.8
CY	803.1	18.0	10,.1	2.9
LV	2248.4	18.5	13.4	3.9
LT	3329.0	17.7	12.4	3.6
LU	502.1	17.8	10.3	3.6
HU	10014.3	20.3	12.7	3.9
MT	414.4	21.3	11.5	3.3
NL	16575.0	20.1	11.4	3.9
AT	8375.3	18.4	12.8	4.8
PL	38167.3	20.8	10.2	3.3
PT	10637.7	18.6	13.4	4.5
RO	21462.2	18.8	11.9	3.1
SI	2047.0	20.3	12.6	3.9
SK	5424.9	19.5	9.5	2.7
FI	5351.4	21.7	12.4	4.6
SE	9340.7	19.1	12.8	5.3
UK	62008.0	18.1	11.8	4.6
IS	317.6	17.1	8.7	3.3
LI	35.9	20.5	10.3	3.2
NO	4858.2	18.6	10.3	4.5
CH	7785.8	19.1	12.0	4.8
ME	632.9	17,9	10.6	2.3
HR	4425.7	20.2	13.7	3.5
MK	2052.7	18.0	9.8	1.8
TR	72561.3	12.4	5.8	1.2

Source: Eurostat – Key figures on Europe 2012

The reason that European countries are undergoing a significant change in its population structure is a consequence of many different factors. One of them being the fact that we live longer than ever before, which is a result of improved standards of living such as healthier lifestyle (nutrition and physical activity), big advances in health care and increased safety in general. People also suffer different kind of diseases nowadays than earlier days. Before development of modern healthcare, there were more acute and severe diseases which often led to a quick death. Diseases are today not life threatening in the same way but chronic and slow developing (further described in section "Older peoples benefits of ICTs" below [1]).

Another major cause of the significant change in the European population structure is the trend of decreased birth-rate. People wait longer to bear their first child and are sometimes not willing to, or considering themselves as unable to, raise children. Having children later is also one natural explanation to the trend of having fewer children per family. The fertility rate was 1.6 per family in 2008 which is considered relatively low. This phenomenon is also clearly shown in the statistics. There were 7.5 million new born children in the EU-27 in 1961, which fell briefly to 5 million during 2002, recovering a bit to 5.4 million 2010 [1].

Further the EU's population structure is also characterized by a particularly high number of individuals born two decades after the Second World War. This European baby-boom with high population cohorts born between 1940s and 1960s, are now entering the age of retirement. This group has also given birth to few children. Demographic changes take time to become apparent. Because of this, we now witness the effects by the relative large cohorts of baby-boomers progressively moving up the EU's population pyramid towards older age, contributing to a top-heavy population pyramid as show in Fig. 1.1 below.

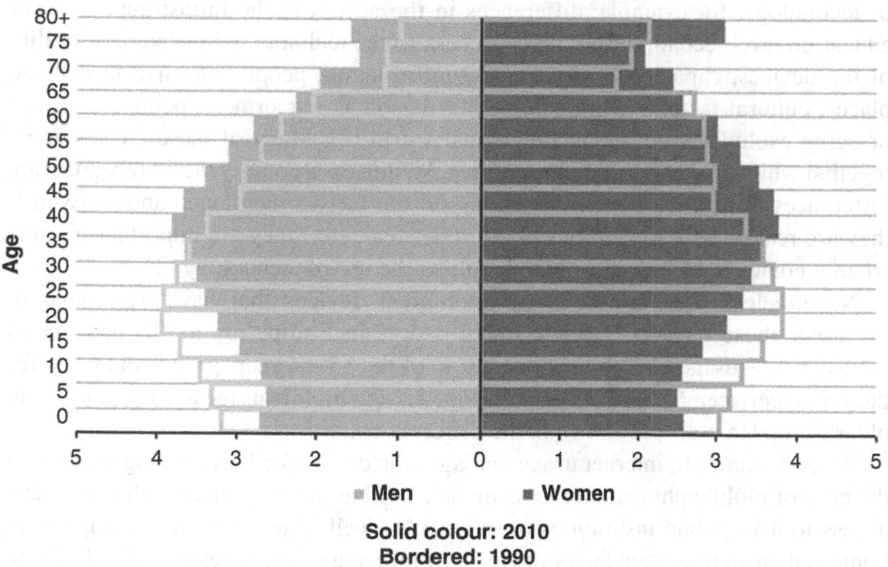

Fig. 1.1 The changing European population pyramid (Source: Eurostat – Key figures on Europe 2012)

The different factors described above make the natural change growing, that is, the difference between the number of births and the number of deaths is increasing. The extension of life expectancy is considered both blessing and a problem. Blessing because people in general want to live longer lives, and a problem as the rapidly growing older population will have major impacts from the perspective of society and their quality of life. This new demand will affect the society not only with new structural changes in the system and organization, but also in the aspect of how to finance the care and maintenance of the quality of life of the older [3]. One way to address the new demands of an ageing population is the introduction of different technological devices.

1.3 Older People and Technology – Digital Exclusion

During past years, technology development has expanded through all spaces of the human life and we can assume that the modern society is a "technological society". However, technology is having great difficulties to penetrate the field of ageing; and older people are far from taking advantage from the potential benefits of technology in terms of quality of life. The digital exclusion is one of the most common findings while studying the implementation of technology in society. It is a phenomenon that separates people those have the level and knowledge enough to control technology, from the ones who, for different reasons, do not. There are a lot of different reasons for the existing digital exclusion that generates a lower knowledge and usage of technology, for example: differences in the access to the infrastructure, lower education level, economical motives, access to the technology in general, usability of the devices, capacity to acquire new information, people who live in isolated places, cultural factors; or for some other reason as impairment, being immigrant or being excluded from the technological world [2]. Many of these factors come together which makes it difficult to combat. Within each country there are significant differences in technology use depending on the factors mentioned above. Even if they are real or only psychological (attitude, fear, etc.) they are important barriers when it comes to incorporate older people in the use of technology [2].

Nevertheless there are some technological devices that have been able to overcome these barriers. Among young people in Europe (up to 54) there is an almost 100 % usage of mobile phone, 80 % of the 55–64 years group, and 61 % for the group between 65 and 74 years. In Fig. 1.2 the mobile usage among young and older European users are shown in the different countries.

When it comes to internet usage and age, the difference becomes bigger than in the case of mobile phone. Internet is mainly used at home, even though some have access to it in public institutions or at work as well. The access to a computer at home is then an important factor related to internet use. The access to a good quality internet connection follows the same pattern as access in general. Scandinavian countries and Netherlands are the ones with most frequent internet use and are the ones with most developed internet infrastructure. The percentage of users between 65 and 74 those never used internet, is around 70 % with big variation among

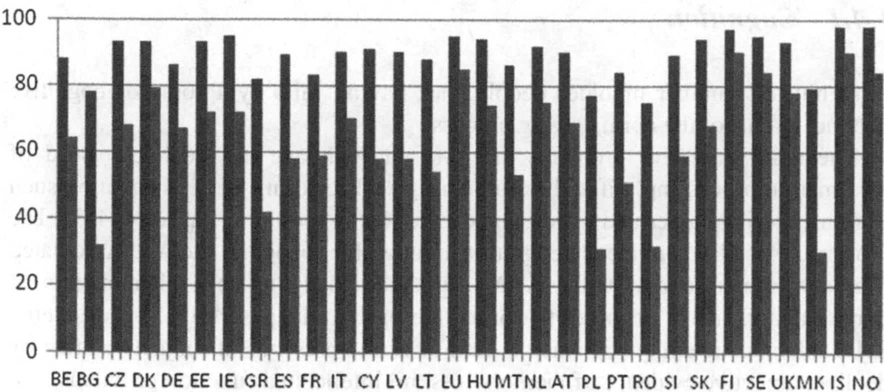

Fig. 1.2 Mobile phone usage in the different European countries. The whole population of the country (*blue* or dark grey) and elderly (*red* or light grey) between 55 and 64 years old (Source: http://epp.eurostat.ec.europa.eu/)

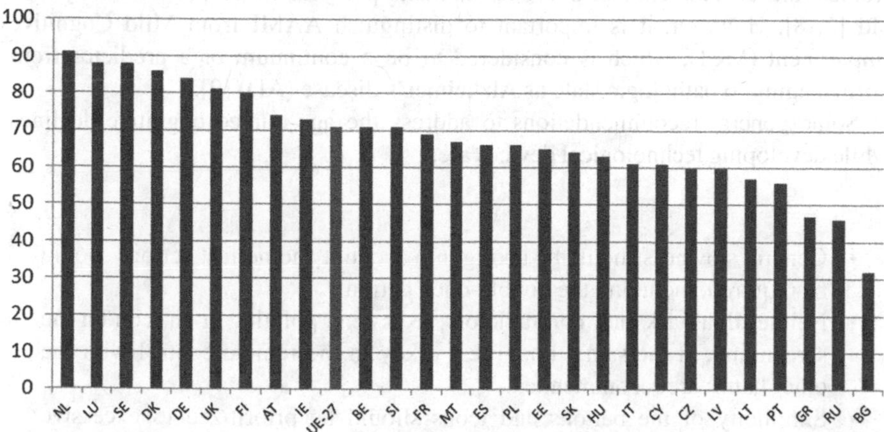

Fig. 1.3 Access to internet in the European homes (Source: http://epp.eurostat.ec.europa.eu/)

different European countries. Scandinavian countries, Netherlands and Luxemburg all have usage percentages for older people reaching over 50 % while the rest significant below [2] (Fig. 1.3).

1.4 The Aging Process Related to Technology

Ageing is commonly accompanied by different changes that can have an influence in the interaction between older people and technology. In the following paragraphs the most usual changes and pathologies related to ageing are described. In later sections, how these disabilities and pathologies affect the interaction with technological devices are explained.

1.4.1 Cognition

A significant number of older people start having mild symptoms of cognitive decline, as part of the normal aging process.

The main cognitive problems that worsen with age are declined speed of information processing, difficulties in storing and recalling new information such as remembering names and words, and difficulties in reasoning capacity [4, 5]. The most usual condition related to cognition among older people is the Age Associated Memory Impairment (AAMI). AAMI appeared likely to be a phenomenon of normal aging, and is attributed to normal biological changes. AAMI is considered to be a diagnostic entity [6] which is defined as the presence of subjective memory decline, objective evidence of memory loss, no intellectual function problems, and the lack of dementia or other memory disorder in a person 50 years or older.

Lane and Snowdon reported that there is a prevalence rate of 35 % for AAMI in subjects with 65 years and over. The prevalence increases with the age and some studies find an incidence of 54/1000 habitants per year in people over 75 years-old [7, 8]. However, it is important to distinguish AAMI from Mild Cognitive Impairment (MCI), which is considered to be a continuum or a predictor from normal aging to pathologic state as Alzheimer's disease (AD) [9].

Some general recommendations to address the age-related cognitive declines while developing technological devices are:

- General slowness should be taking into account and no fast actions should be required, including the double-click action.
- Neither dual tasks nor contradictory tasks (e.g. pointing at an icon on the screen and, at the same time, press a key in the remote control with the other hand) are recommended.
- Simplicity of the buttons and icons should be prioritized to excessive embellishment to help to focus the attention.
- Button labels, icons, text and graphics should be understandable enough without required a lot of extra explanations.
- Respect limits of the human working memory and the echoic store (approx. 3 to 4 elements) when designing menus.
- The process of learning how to use a system is also closely related with memory and attention capacities. In order to make easier and faster this process, the interaction with technology should be as easier as possible and the number of actions needed to carry out an operation should be reduced.
- It is advisable to reduce the memory load. For instance, for the elderly it can be more difficult to remember the verbal or gesture commands needed to carry out an action when speech or gesture recognition is used.
- In order to avoid memory load, allow the users to repeat some actions, for instance, repeat a message given by the system.

(continued)

- Visual and auditory feedback to confirm item selections should be provided.
- Provide both visual and auditory instructions simultaneously since it helps to better memorize the information
- Messages should be short, factual and informative. Minimize the amount of information by presenting only what is necessary.

It should be taken into account that the cognitive problems described in this chapter are the ones associated with the ageing process but more serious problems in the interaction with technologies can appear when pathologies like Alzheimer's disease is diagnosed.

1.4.2 Visual

At different stages in life, changes in external parts of the eye (cornea, lens and muscles) affect the visual transmission and the visual ability. Changes in the retina and in the nervous system begin to be significant between 55 and 65 years-old. Most frequent vision problems that appear with age are:

- Deterioration in visual acuity: the inability to accurately discriminate between two stimuli. For instance, an elderly person can have difficulties for discriminating between two similar traffic signs while driving.
- Presbyopia: Age-related condition affecting the ability to see close objects accurately.
- Glare: blinding effect produced by direct light.
- The eye's ability to adapt to changing light conditions is reduced.
- Reduced visual field capacity. This appears as the loss of peripheral vision, a phenomenon known as tunnel vision.

The decrease in the sensibility to contrast starts around 25 years-old, being more significant from 40 to 50 years-old on. Dazzle is a problem that might appear at any age, but it becomes more serious around 40 years old.

– More or less at the age of 30 years-old some problems distinguishing colors, specially green-blue, blue-violet, and pale colors appear.

The most usual pathologies related to vision that comes with age are:

- Cataracts. The amount of light reaching the cornea is diminishes because the lens becomes yellow with age [10]. Therefore, older people need more light for reading than the young.
- Glaucoma, which is the increase in intraocular pressure leading to optical nerve atrophy and visual field abnormalities [11].

The above mentioned changes and pathologies affect the interaction with technological devices, and should be taken into account in the following cases:

- Contrast:
  - Older people need more time to adapt their vision from a dark to a light environment.
  - Contrast should be adjustable by the user.
  - It is recommendable to put dark characters on a light background.
- Brightness
  - Due to the changes in the crystalline, a person who is 60 years-old needs three times more light than a person who is 20 years-old. So brightness should be reduced since it makes it difficult to perceive images and also produce visual fatigue.
- Dazzle
  - The screen should be free of glare and reflections.
- Color
  - Light colors reflect more amount of light than dark colors. Dark colors provoke more visual fatigue.
  - Bold or semi-bold letters are preferred over normal ones.
- Distance between the icons
  - The system should provide the zoom option to have the possibility to increase the icons and buttons size
  - Text lines should be separated enough.

1.4.3 Hearing

Most hearing loss in old age is mainly due to degenerative changes of the cochlea, the main receptor for the hearing nerve. After 75 years, the hearing deficit occurs to many people and it more frequently appears among men than women. In a recent study, Hannula and colleagues [12] found that 37.1 % of older adults had hearing difficulties and 43.3 % had difficulties following a conversation in a noisy environment.

Another common hearing problem that appears with age is presbycusis. Presbycusis appears when sensitivity to tones of higher frequencies diminished [13]. At higher frequencies, men generally have poorer hearing sensitivity than women, a difference that increases with age. This increase has been related to different levels of noise exposure [14].

Older people with hearing problems can have normal low frequency hearing with loss of mid and high frequencies. This leads to problems with understanding speech especially in noisy or echoing environments [15]. Sometimes affected people are unaware of the loss.

A general classification of the degree of the hearing loss [16] affirms that a normal degree of hearing loss is the range from −10 to 15 dB HL hearing loss.

Age related hearing loss affects interaction with technological devices in following cases:

- A user can listen to 150–160 words per minute comfortably. But in the case of the older people it is advisable to reduce this speed since they have a slower speed of processing [17]. Speech output should be intermediate, not too fast but not too slow and the gap between items should be kept fairly short (0.5–1.0 s).
- Avoid the use of homonyms (words which sound similar). Use single words, or common (perhaps also jargon) word pairs.
- The language used should be simple, easy to understand and without using technical terms. Unnecessary information should not be presented since this can cause and overload the cognitive functions.
- Where possible provide a volume control so that users can adjust the loudness of signals and tones. Abrupt changes of volume should be avoided.
- Use a different sound than a real sound (e.g. telephone), to avoid confusion. Take advantage of the associations between a concrete sound and a situation (e.g. emergency situation and the ambulance sound) learnt throughout life. These associations are also found in older people and also people with dementia.
- Users generally prefer natural recorded speech to synthetic speech
- Messages should be presented in a serial mode, not at the same time [18].

1.4.4 Mobility

Around 40 % of older people have some degree of activity limitation due to health problems. It is found that around 20 % of those aged 76 years and older have a walking speed around 0.4/s, which is considered to be a severe limitation in mobility [19]. There findings suggest that 10 % of the non-institutionalised older population have one or more limitations in activities of daily living while 17 % of them report one or more limitations in instrumental activities of daily living. Besides that The Survey of Health, Ageing and Retirement in Europe [20] reported approximately 17 % of the men and 23 % of the woman aged 65 and over have physical limitations (e.g. Arthritis, Parkinson, etc . . .) that also cause difficulties performing activities of daily living (e.g. dressing, getting in/out bed, eating, preparing a meal, shopping). National Center for Health Statistics (NCHS) reported that the presence of one or more physical limitations increases with age. This lead to a higher probability in adults aged 80 and over, who are 2.5 times more likely to have one or more physical limitations compared to adults aged 50–59 (43 % and 17 %). Whereas only 8 % of the adults in the range of age from 50 to 59 have three or more physical limitations, 27 % of the adults aged 80 and over have three or more physical limitations [21]. In this study, the presence of eight possible physical limitations were studied: walk a quarter of a mile; walk up 10 steps without resting; stand or be on your feet for about 2 h; sit for about 2 h; stoop, bend, or kneel; reach up over your head; use your fingers to grasp or handle small objects; lift or carry something as heavy as 10 pounds.

Another finding from NCHS, postulated that women are more prone than men of the same age to suffer one or more physical limitations.

One of the most usual pathologies related to mobility that comes with age is arthritis. Arthritis is a painful condition that can strike the spine, neck, back, shoulder, hands and wrists, hip, knee, ankle, and feet. It can be immobilizing, and it comes in many forms.

Mobility problems per se, and the pain derived of the health condition that causes the mobility problems, can complicate interaction with technologies. For example, pointing devices need 0.3–0.6 N of force which may not be possible for older adults due to the weakness. Another problem that can appear is tremor. In this case, the action with pointing devices requiring the hand movements should be adequate to this problem and the area for selecting, for instance, an icon, should be larger. These problems should be taken into account when designing technological devices for older people. For people with severe mobility problems alternative modalities of interaction (e.g. speech) are recommended.

Chapter 5 on Inclusive User Model presents a rule based system, where we actually implemented these rules in a software framework to personalize applications.

1.5 Benefits of ICTs

Information and Communication Technological solutions in developed societies are changing to adapt to new user needs. Technological solutions are vertiginously evolving in TV, mobile phones, personal computers, cooking instruments, washing machines and so on. Technology is getting more and more complex to offer better services and more specific features to target users. However older people, especially the ones having no experience with technology during their working lives are not involved in this societal change. They often fail to develop necessary abilities to interact with technological devices and several solutions have not been designed to being used for this group.

As previously stated, the ageing process implies several biological, societal and behavioral changes that could lead to impairment, illness, dependency, pain, social mistreatment, isolation and in worst of the cases, hospitalization and death. Technology should not be a need by itself but a developing contribution to society, and in this case be accessible to the requirements, desires and needs of the older people. Accessibility can be defined as: “The Possibility that places, products and services can be satisfactorily used by the greatest possible number of people, independent of their personal limitations or those limitations that arc dcrivcd from their surroundings” [22]. To be able to implement accessibility, older people’s special capacities and needs has to be taken into account which adds extra emphasis on smart interface solutions.

Technology can benefit users in two main ways: fostering positive or minimizing negative. In both cases there are several fields where technology can support older people with their most frequent problems or just empowering them to improve their quality of life, independency, autonomy, leisure time, and thus, improving their lives. These fields, within a bio-psycho-social model, can be broadly separated in three categories: cognitive, physical and societal benefits.

1.5.1 Cognitive Functions

At the cognitive level, technology can offer support through customized software of self-management, exercise or stimulation to improve general cognitive functionalities, such as memory, attention, monitoring capabilities, and so on.

1.5.1.1 Self-Management

Self-management applications are being broadly developed for different platforms. These applications can include agendas, reminders, organization applications, task checklists, etc. The idea is to translate pen and paper strategies for organization in daily life into an automated, easy to use on-screen solutions with audio-visual feedback.

1.5.1.2 Exercise and Rehabilitation

Even in severe impairment resulting from neurodegenerative diseases like traumatisms or stroke, there is a chance to improve the cognitive status due to the effect of neural plasticity [23–25]. This implies that new neural structures can be developed with exercise through life. Older people could benefit exercising their cognitive abilities, not only to make up for degeneration caused by ageing, but as a way to engage with society or just to enjoy leisure time.

Technologies aim to bring accessible, usable and adapted training to older people in order to make them cognitively active throughout the life course. Currently the scientific community is researching the benefits of the Cognition supporting

Software. Although evidence is still unknown, studies point in the direction that technological support offer moderate benefits in cognitive abilities or at least a slower decline and maintenance [26, 27].

1.5.2 Physical Abilities

As we age, our perceptual, cognitive and motor performance levels tend to decline, however the incidence and prevalence of chronic diseases increase. Chronic diseases like cardiovascular disease, chronic obstructive pulmonary disease (COPD), and diabetes are the leading cause of death in developing countries. Technology can support medical treatments, pharmacological and psychological therapy for people with disabilities or illness. These solutions are constantly being developed to cope with the impairments associated with age.

1.5.2.1 Monitoring and Direct Interaction

The increasing economic burden of chronic disease on health care requires a fundamental change in the model of care-giving. The approach taken by reference entities and recommended by national and international policies is to provide care directly at home. This ensures appropriate monitoring and treatment of patients while reducing cost involved in the process. It is not envisaged as a substitute of long term hospitalization or physician contact, but a more economic and usable provision of care directly to the patient. To this end, ICTs are being pointed out as the best option. Tele-health technologies, by means of smart home environments, adapted structures and home and tele-monitoring is a way of responding to the care of the ageing population.

Monitoring of chronic diseases could bring a more direct and efficient system to support and control diseases like Diabetes Mellitus, COPD, Heart Failure, Alzheimer's disease and other similar chronic or degenerative illnesses. The aims of this technology are:

- Monitoring changes in the vital constants: lung capacity, airflow limitation, oxygen saturation, blood pressure, blood glucose levels, heart rate, retinal imaging, etc.
- Measuring behavioral and psychological indicators: Number of medical visitations, number of nurse calls, quality of life, emotional wellbeing, activities performance, physical exercise, etc.
- Alarm: fast reaction to predefined risk values in the measurements allowing the user to make a video call to a formal or informal caregivers, call an ambulance or raise an automatic alarm at the professional health record.
- Stimulation and feedback: to react to the user comments, alarms or physiological measurements giving the user information, guidelines of action, or providing the

user with reminders to take medication, to visit the physician or to take the own measurements.

- Patient information: as primary and secondary prevention, the system could provide the user with counseling, nutritional support, healthy activities, behavioral and psychological coping strategies, etc.

Thus, monitoring could bring several advantages to the user such as more safety, specific control of his medication and vital measurements, updated information about his health status, less burden, risk situations quick management and information, and on the other hand could bring several advantages to the healthcare system as more efficiency and reduced costs.

1.5.2.2 Supporting Perception, Basic and Instrumental Activities of Daily Living

One of the main objectives for supporting technologies is to keep the autonomy and the independency as much and as long as possible. Older people in state of dependency use to have cognitive, perceptive or motoric impairment which prevents them to carry out on the one hand the basic activities of daily living (BADL) such as: eating, brushing, washing up, going to the WC, walking, sitting down or getting up, and on the other hand the more complex Instrumental Activities of Daily Living (Calling, by phone, go shopping, cleaning the house, washing clothes, taking medication, management of the own economic aspects, etc.). People with no cognitive impairment nor motor or perceptive disability should not need direct technological support with BADL, but people that do would benefit from, reminders, stepwise activity definition, alarms, stimulation or direct physical robotic support. Regarding perception supporting technology, several devices or functionalities address a broad range of impairments: glasses, hearing aids are very frequent too, accessibility visual customizable features for different devices (features such as brightness, light, font shape and size, contrast etc.) or haptic.

ICT for IADL, however, have a broader field of support for older people. Several solutions are being currently developed to improve the quality of life of the older people by means of supporting the instrumental activities of daily living, activities that make the person able to interact with the environment:

- Accessible phones with bigger screens, bigger keys, less options, easy to customize, with amplified sound options and braille.
- Help for shopping. As the older users are a great part of the target users, and they will be more with the ageing of the population, stores webpage are getting more accessible adopting several standards for accessibility and making more users able to interact and shop by internet. On the other hand, several solutions to support shopping in place are being developed as intelligent trolleys, robots, RFID accessible information, pervasive environments, virtual supermarkets, etc. Both in site or at home solutions by means of more accessible systems would support people with shopping and making them needing less cognitive and

perceptive resources (memorizing less, stop reading little labels, supporting with searching for products for special needs), or physical resources (carrying the bags, moving the trolleys, etc.).

- Housework (cooking, washing clothes, tidying the room ...): People with motor impairment stated that they want support with this task [28] as they would do with a vacuum cleaner, dishwasher, or kitchen robot. Electrical devices should be designed more accessible to make all the users able to carry out the tasks. Several projects are including supporting functionalities to cooking activities (recipes, cooking suggestions, cooking step by step videos), intelligent fridges, robots to help with grabbing and moving items, etc.
- Managing money: People with cognitive impairment associated to Alzheimer's disease have problems managing their own money. Technological aids with a visual easy-to-understand representation of money organization could help, shopping help and accessible websites to facilitate shopping too.

The basic and instrumental activities of daily living consist of several behavioral and cognitive interactions with the environment to achieve basic goals relevant to keep living actively, independently and autonomous. Technology should be adapted in order to facilitate achieving these goals.

1.5.2.3 Rehabilitation and Training

Technology has an important part in rehabilitation for last 20 years. For example, neuropsychological technologies has already lead to computer based prosthetics and orthotics, cognitive probes with millisecond accurate links to functional imaging, virtual reality managed ecological assessments, cognitive retraining, assistive devices, and online, "real-time" database-driven evaluations [29], robotics, brain computer interfaces or rehabilitation techniques based in biofeedback are some of the procedures and instruments in which technology supports rehabilitation of motor control (gait, balance, fine and broad motor control), and some other more specific abilities.

1.5.3 Societal Benefits

Between others, one of the European Commission social aims is to foster social inclusion. The information and communication technologies are involved in the concept of e-inclusion. E-inclusion aims to achieve that "no one is left behind" in enjoying the benefits of ICT [30].

In 2000 the Lisbon Council agreed to make a decisive impact on the eradication of poverty and social exclusion by 2010. Concrete steps in the National Action Plans against poverty and social exclusion and to improve access to the new ICTs and opportunities new technologies can provide were encouraged. In 2006 The Riga

Ministerial Declaration on e-Inclusion identified six themes which the European Commission should use to foster e-Inclusion:

1. E-Accessibility – make ICT accessible to all, meeting a wide spectrum of people's needs, in particular any special needs.
2. Ageing – empower older people to fully participate in the economy and society, continue independent lifestyles and enhance their quality of life.
3. E-Competences – equip citizens with the knowledge, skills and lifelong learning approach needed to increase social inclusion, employability and enrich their lives.
4. Socio-Cultural e – Inclusion – enables minorities, migrants and marginalized young people to fully integrate into communities and participate in society by using ICT.
5. Geographical e-Inclusion – increase the social and economic wellbeing of people in rural, remote and economically disadvantaged areas with the help of ICT.
6. Inclusive e-Government – deliver better, more diverse public services for all using ICT while encouraging increased public participation in democracy [30].

By means of the e-inclusion policy and other similar initiatives (Ambient Assisted Living (AAL) Joint Program or e-Accessibility), to eliminate the technological gap and to include elderly people in the technological society is envisaged. Solving this gap would have direct effect into the elderly people needs, making them able to access to different ways of support the technology can bring. Being able to use ICTs' would guarantee access to information, support tools, education and learning, skills development, illness management, medical support and monitorization, increasing autonomy and independency, increasing social network and avoiding isolation, increasing quality of life and social participation and, summarizing, making elderly people able to live full life and with all the opportunities to do it integrated in the society.

1.6 Looking Towards Future-Design for All

It turns evident now that the future points towards Design for All approach that makes products and services accessible to everybody. The basic principles for achieving Design for All are the following:

- Simplicity: superfluous elements and operations must be reduced to a minimum. The devices are supposed to be as simple as possible for the user to interact with them. The hardware should include the minimal amount of buttons to avoid confusion and avoid the risk of erroneous choices. The same regarding the software, there should be a trade-off between amounts of available choices without losing complexity. For example having a well-organized interface where users intuitively know what options are available and how to interact in the best way.

- Flexibility: the design must adapt to the users' abilities to interact with it. Its use will therefore have to be flexible enough to adapt to its users' characteristics. All kind of users should be able to use the device, with no importance regarding gender, age, culture background, previous knowledge or physical condition. The interface has to be adjustable and customizable to users' different capacities and needs. For example if a user with lower vision is about to read a text, the font size should be adjustable to fit the users preferences, as a zoom function or something equal.
- Quick information: the system must enable users to perceive quickly and unequivocally what it is and how they should start using it. The necessary information should be available and precise.
- It must respond to a conceptual model of functioning that adapts to users' previous experience and expectations. It is important that the users feel familiar with the device even if it is new. Well known concepts and analogs should be used constantly. For example if something is to be rotated the button should rotate at the same direction as the clock which is a well-known standard. Other well-known analogs as using a stylus pen as an input device on a tablet, is a good choice for older users as it is a well-known analog for a normal pen a paper situation [31].
- There must be a clear relationship between the activation systems at users' disposal and the results that they generate. The latency should be as low as possible, when the user makes a choice the system should react immediately. Also if a button/icon indicates something, the reaction must be the expected.
- It must contain a feedback system that keeps users permanently informed about the product condition and what it is doing. Receiving relevant feedback is very important when interacting with a technological device. We need to know that the device has received our command and the response the system is generating should be clear. That way the dialog between the human being and the device is fluid.
- Error prevention and handling: users may misunderstand or use the product for a purpose other than the one for which it is intended, without this causing any harmful consequences. The system must provide mechanisms for the user to solve this situation. There should always be an option to "go back" or regret ones input.
- Ensuring that the users take part in the product design and evaluation process. This is the second main criteria when applying design for all, broadly accepted in research and development projects as a methodological procedure named User Centered Design. The approach is applied to ensure that for a representative sample of potential users, the product or service will suit their anthropometric and functional characteristics. This will also in its turn be compatible with their habits and culture.

The starting point of the concept of Design for All is the principle that all potential users can use the product or service correctly and that people find the product easy to use. User participation in the design process provides direct information about how people use products. Nevertheless, direct contact between users and designers can be risky if it is not properly structured. Designers can use interviews to strengthen their own ideas or collect piles of unstructured data. User participation should be structured and systematic, starting by formulating the specific aims of involving the users in the design process. The information provided by the user participation is often very profitable and necessary for constructing objective arguments for the decisions that are made during the design process, although the evidence may be costly. The next chapter elaborates the concept of user centred design and Chap. 3 presents a case study of Design for all approach.

References

1. Eurostat. (2011). *Active ageing and solidarity between generations. A statistical portrait of the European Union 2012*. Statistical books. Publications office of the European Union, Luxembourg.
2. Los mayores ante las TIC (Fundación Vodafone España) – EN2011. http://www.scribd.com/doc/47992310/Los-mayores-ante-lasTIC-Fundacion-Vodafone-Espana-EN2011. Accessed 13 July 2012.
3. European Commission. (2009). *Emerging trends in socio-economic sciences and humanities in Europe*. http://ec.europa.eu/research/social-sciences/books05_en.html. Accessed 13 July 2012.
4. Willis, S. L., Tennstedt, S. L., Marsiske, M., et al. (2006). Long-term effects of cognitive training on everyday functional outcomes in older adults. *Journal of the American Medical Association, 296*(23), 2805–2814.
5. Juncos-Rabadán, O., Pereiro, A. X., Facal, D., Rodriguez, N., Lojo, C., Caamaño, J. A., Sueiro, J., Boveda, J., & Eiroa, P. (2012). Prevalence and correlates of cognitive impairment in adults with subjective memory complaints in primary care centres. *Dementia and Geriatric Cognitive Disorders, 33*(4), 226–232.
6. Crook, T., Bartus, R. T., Ferris, S. H., Whitehouse, P., Cohen, G. D., & Gershon, S. (1986). Age-associated memory impairment: proposed diagnostic criteria and measures of clinical change – report of a national institute of mental health work group. *Developmental Neuropsychology, 2*(4), 261–276.
7. Morris, J. C., & Cummings, J. (2005). Mild cognitive impairment (MCI) represents early-stage Alzheimer's disease. *Journal of Alzheimer's Disease, 7*(3), 235–239; discussion 255–262.
8. Bischkopf, J., Busse, A., & Angermeyer, M. C. (2002). Mild cognitive impairment– a review of prevalence, incidence and outcome according to current approaches. *Acta Psychiatrica Scandinavica, 106*(6), 403–414.
9. Petersen, R. C., & Morris, J. C. (2003). Clinical features. In R. C. Petersen (Ed.), *Mild cognitive impairment: aging to Alzheimer's disease* (pp. 15–19). New York: Oxford University Press.
10. Weale, R. (1998). The eye within the framework of human senescence: biological decline and morbidity. *Ophthalmic Research, 30*(2), 59–73.
11. Schaie, K. W., & Willis, S. L. (2002). *Adult development and aging*. New York: Prentice Hall.
12. Hannula, S., Bloigu, R., Majamaa, K., Sorri, M., & Mäki-Torkko, E. (2011). Self-reported hearing problems among older adults: prevalence and comparison to measured hearing impairment. *Journal of the American Academy of Audiology, 22*(8), 550–559.
13. Lethbridge-Cejku, M., Schiller, J.S., & Bernadel, L. (2004). Summary health statistics for U.S. adults: National Health Interview Survey, 2002. *Vital and Health Statistics, 10*(222), 1–151.
14. Cruickshanks, K. J., Wiley, T. L., Tweed, T. S., Klein, B. E., Klein, R., Mares-Perlman, J. A., & Nondahl, D. M. (1998). Prevalence of hearing loss in older adults in Beaver Dam, Wisconsin. The epidemiology of hearing loss study. *American Journal of Epidemiology, 148*(9), 879–886.

15. Birren, J. E., & Schaie, K. W. (2001). *Handbook of the psychology of aging*. San Diego: Academic.
16. Clark, J. G. (1981). Uses and abuses of hearing loss classification. *ASHA, 23*(7), 493–500.
17. Salthouse, T. A. (2010). Selective review of cognitive aging. *Journal of International Neuropsychological Society, 16*(5), 754–760.
18. Pereiro, A. X., Juncos, O., & Rodríguez, M. S. (2001). Memoria operativa, atencion selectiva y velocidad de procesamiento. Una aportacion al debate sobre el deterioro del funcionamiento cognitivo en la vejez Working memory, selective attention and speed processing. A contribution to discuss cognitive decline in aging. *Cognitiva, 13*(2), 209–225.
19. Nicholas, S., Huppert, F. A., McWilliams, B., & Melzer, D. (2003). Physical and cognitive function. In M. Marmot, J. Banks, R. Blundell, C. Lessof, & J. Nazroo (Eds.), *Health, wealth and lifestyles of the older population in England: the 2002 English Longitudinal Study of Ageing* (pp. 249–271). London: IFS.
20. Alcser, K. H., Avendano, M., Börsch-Supan, A., Brunner, J. K., Cornaz, S., Dewey, M., et al. (2005). *Health, ageing and retirement in Europe. First results from the Survey of Health, Ageing and Retirement in Europe*. Mannheim: Mannheim Research Institute for the Economics of Aging (MEA).
21. Holmes, J., Powell-Griner, E., Lethbridge-cejku, M., & Heyman, K. (2009). Aging differently: physical limitations among adults aged 50 years and over: United States, 2001–2007. *NCHS Data Brief, 20*, 1–8.
22. Ministerio de Industria, Turismo y Comercio. (2009). *Digital terrestrial television (DTT) accessibility recommendations*. www.inteco.es/file/snb-6ZR2I2DaXKiMJlkT_g. Accessed 13 July 2012.
23. Greenwood, P. M. (2007). Functional plasticity in cognitive aging: review and hypothesis. *Neuropsychology, 21*(6), 657–673.
24. Kleim, J. A. (2011). Neural plasticity and neurorehabilitation: teaching the new brain old tricks. *Journal of Communication Disorders, 44*(5), 521–528.
25. Burke, S. N., & Barnes, C. A. (2006). Neural plasticity in the ageing brain. *Nature Review Neuroscience, 7*(1), 30–40.
26. Wenisch, E., Cantegreil-Kallen, I., De Rotrou, J., Garrigue, P., Moulin, F., Batouche, F., Richard, A., De Sant'Anna, M., & Rigaud, A. S. (2007). Cognitive stimulation intervention for elders with mild cognitive impairment compared with normal aged subjects: preliminary results. *Aging Clinical and Experimental Research, 19*(4), 316–322.
27. González-Abraldes, I., Millán-Calenti, J. C., Balo-García, A., Tubío, J., Lorenzo, T., & Maseda, A. (2010). [Accessibility and usability of computer-based cognitive stimulation: telecognitio]. *Revista Española de Geriatría y Gerontología, 45*(1), 26–29.
28. García, A., Facal, D., & Ansorena X. (2012). *DELIVERABLE D1.4.1: Requirement specification of future remotely control service robot for home care*. Instituto Gerentologico Matia, Spain: SRS "Multi–role Shadow Robotic System for Independent Living".
29. Chute, D. L. (2002). Neuropsychological technologies in rehabilitation. *The Journal of Head Trauma Rehabilitation, 17*(5), 369–377.
30. European Commission. (2012). Europe's Information Society Thematic Portal. In: European Commission. Europe's Information Society Thematic Portal. e-Accessibility. http://ec.europa.eu/information_society/activities/einclusion/index_en.htm. Accessed 18 July 2012.
31. Dewsbury, G., Rouncefield, M., Sommerville, I., Onditi, V., & Bagnall, P. (2007). Designing technology with older people. *Universal Access in the Information Society, 6*(2), 207–217.

Chapter 2
Survey on Inclusive Human Machine Interaction Issues in India

Pradipta Biswas

Abstract This chapter takes forward the discussion of the previous chapter in Indian context. It compares and contrasts HCI issues for elderly users between developing and developed countries. Our study found that there is a significant effect of age on hand strength of elderly users limiting their use of standard computer peripherals. It is also found that European elderly users tend to score higher in cognitive tests than their Indian counterpart and for Indian population and there is a significant correlation between education level and cognitive abilities. We also pointed out a set of guidelines for interface designers to develop inclusive systems.

2.1 Introduction

The previous chapter presented a survey on users' perceptual, cognitive and motor capabilities and also their experience and attitude towards technology in three different European countries. This chapter takes forward that survey in a developing country by presenting a short survey on the human computer interaction (HCI) issues of elderly and disabled users in India. It may be noted that by the term HCI, we did not confine ourselves only to computers but also considered other electronic interactive devices like mobile phones and Television sets. We have initially identified functional parameters [3, 4] that can affect users' interaction with electronic devices and combined both objective metrics on functional parameters and subjective attitude towards technology. Previous surveys either concentrated on ergonomics or demographic details of users in European countries [8, 11, 12, 15] or focused on a particular device like digital TV or mobile phones [13, 14]. There is not much reported work on capabilities and attitude towards technology of older Indian population, especially from a HCI point of view [8, 12, 15].

P. Biswas (✉)
Department of Engineering, University of Cambridge, Trumpington Street, Cambridge, Cambridgeshire CB2 1PZ, UK
e-mail: pb400@hermes.cam.ac.uk

P. Biswas et al. (eds.), *A Multimodal End-2-End Approach to Accessible Computing*, Human–Computer Interaction Series, DOI 10.1007/978-1-4471-6708-2_2

Our study found that there is a significant effect of age on hand strength of elderly users limiting their use of standard computer peripherals. It is also found that European elderly users tend to score higher in cognitive tests than their Indian counterpart and for Indian population and there is a significant correlation between education level and cognitive abilities. We also found that elderly people acknowledge the need of using new technologies though they prefer to use TV and mobile phones than computers. The paper also points out the implication of the findings for designers in Sect. 2.4.

2.2 Survey

We have conducted a survey to estimate users' perceptual, cognitive and motor capabilities and also their experience and attitude towards technology. Previous surveys either concentrated on ergonomics or demographic details of users or focused on a particular device like digital TV or mobile phones. We have initially identified functional parameters [3, 4, 6] that can affect their interaction with electronic devices and combined both objective metrics on functional parameters and subjective attitude towards technology.

2.2.1 Place of Survey

The survey was conducted at Mandi, Himachal Pradesh, Kolkata, West Bengal and Bangalore, Karnataka. The survey was conducted at old-age homes and participants volunteered for the study. We also collected data from nine young people with physical impairment at an Orthopedic Hospital in Kolkata.

For comparative analysis with European population, we used results from a previous survey (presented in the previous chapter and [9]) conducted in UK, Spain and Germany.

2.2.2 Participants

We collected data from 33 users. Figure 2.1 shows an age histogram while 10 users were female and 23 were male. Nine users were younger but had physical impairment as listed in Table 2.1.

We have also used results from a previous survey conducted on approximately 30 people at Spain, UK and Germany. We used that data to compare performance and attitude of Indian population to their European counterpart.

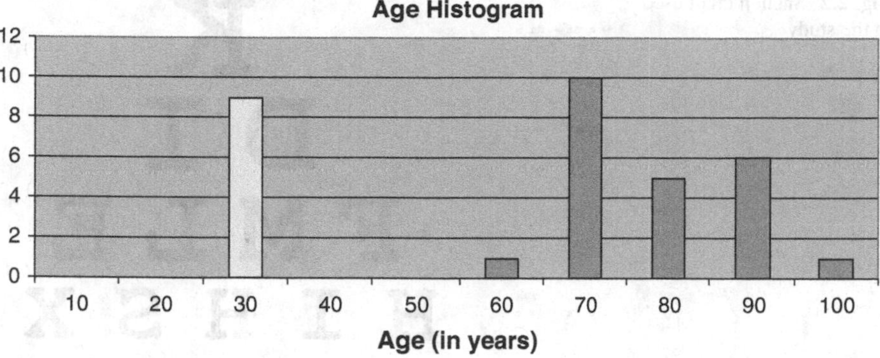

Fig. 2.1 Age histogram of Indian sample

Table 2.1 Description of younger users

Age	Sex	Disability
26	F	Polio
30	F	Polio
25	F	Polio
26	M	Polio
27	F	Birth defect
26	M	Birth defect
27	M	Lost one hand in accident
28	M	Lost one hand in accident

2.2.3 Functional Parameters Measurement

We measured objective parameters about perceptual, cognitive and motor abilities of users using standard test batteries. We have measured the following parameters based on our previous studies which identified them as relevant for interaction with electronic devices.

Minimum Font Size (FS) We measured it using a Snellen chart (Fig. 2.2) calibrated for a 1024 × 768 display screen and recorded the last line users can read correctly from 3 ft distance using identical screen for all users. Based on that we can calculate the minimum visual angle required for different users and can convert it into different units of specifying font size like point, pixel or em.

Colour Blindness (CB) We measured the presence and type of colour blindness using the plates 16 and 17 of Ishihara Test [7] (Fig. 2.3). People with dichromatic colour blindness can only read one digit – people with Protanopia can only read the left hand side digit while with Deuteranopia can only read right hand side digit.

Grip Strength (GS) measures how much force a person can exert gripping with the hand. We measured it using a mechanical dynamometer (Fig. 2.4).

Fig. 2.2 Snellen chart used in the study

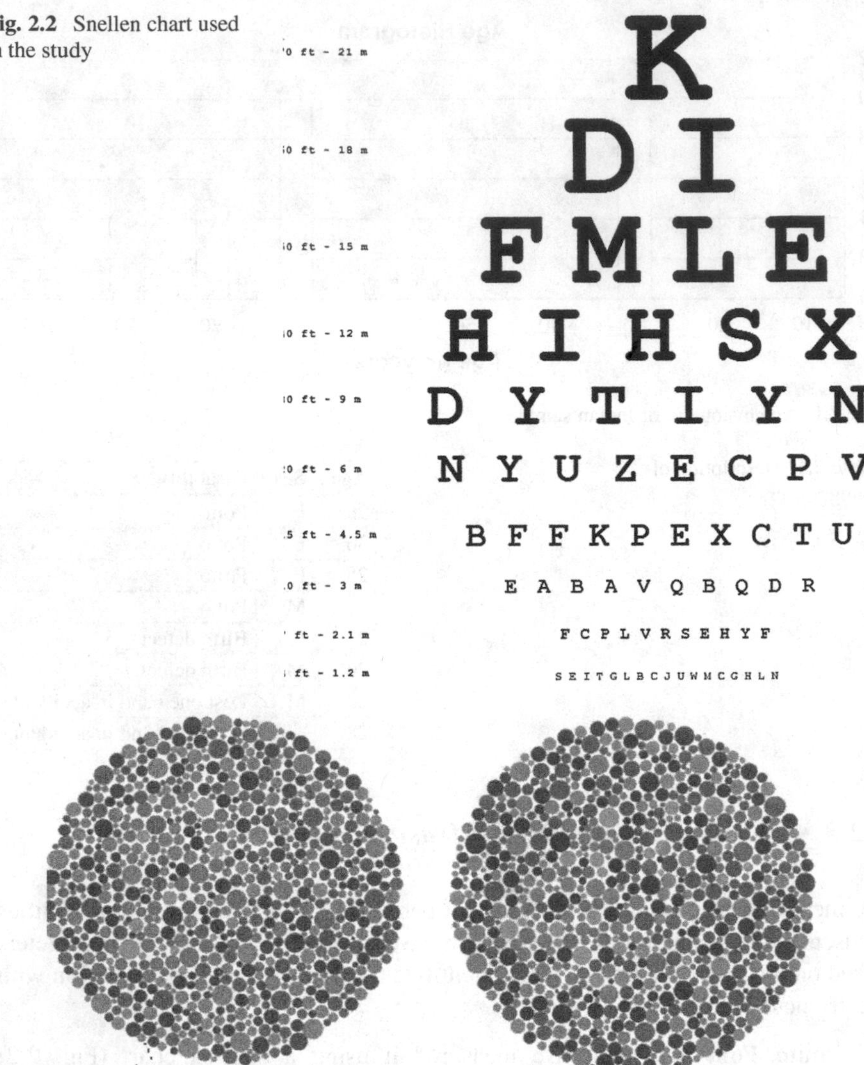

Fig. 2.3 Plates 16 and 17 of Ishihara test

Active Range of Motion of Wrist (ROMW) is measured as the summation of Radial and Ulnar deviation. Radial deviation is the motion that rotates the wrist away from the midline of the body when the person is standing in the standard anatomical position [10]. When the hand is placed over a table with palm facing down, this motion rotates the hand about the wrist towards the thumb. Ulnar deviation is the motion that rotates the wrist towards the midline of the body when the person is standing in the standard anatomical position. When the hand is placed over a table with palm facing down, this motion rotates the hand about the wrist towards the little finger. We measured the deviations with the goniometer (Fig. 2.5).

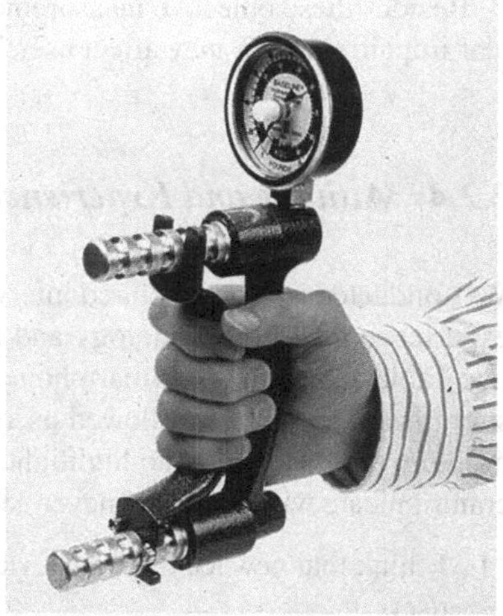

Fig. 2.4 Measuring grip strength

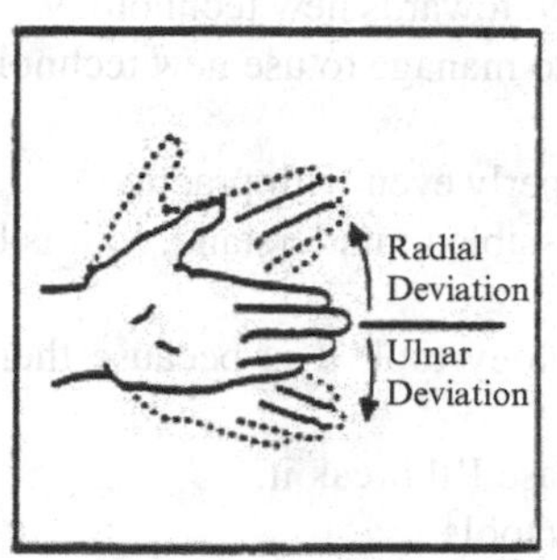

Range of Motion of wrist (Palm facing down)

Measuring Radial Deviation

Measuring Ulnar Deviation

Fig. 2.5 Measuring active ROM of wrist

Trail Making Test (TMT) The Trail Making Test [2] is a neuropsychological test of visual attention and task switching. It consists of two parts in which the subject is instructed to connect a set of 25 dots as fast as possible while still maintaining accuracy. It can provide information about visual search speed, scanning, speed of processing, mental flexibility, as well as executive functioning. It is also sensitive to detecting several cognitive impairments such as Alzheimer's disease and dementia.

Digit Symbol Test (DST) It is a neuropsychological test [2] sensitive to brain damage, dementia, age and depression. It consists of (e.g. nine) digit-symbol pairs (e.g. 1/-,2/⊥ ... 7/Λ,8/X,9/=) followed by a list of digits. Under each digit the subject should write down the corresponding symbol as fast as possible. The number of correct symbols within the allowed time (90 s) is measured.

Besides these objective measurements, we also recorded presence of any particular impairment that may affect users' interaction with electronic interfaces.

2.2.4 *Attitude and Experience Towards Technology*

We conducted a semi structured interview and discussion with each user about their experience of using technology and their attitudes toward new electronic devices like Tablet Computers or Smartphone. We used the following set of questionnaire to start discussion but also allowed users to speak freely about any particular issue or problem they would like to highlight. We took help from local language experts to communicate with users whenever needed.

1. I think that new technology devices are developed mainly to be used by young users.
2. I think that I need to use new technology.
3. I consider it important to try to be open-minded towards new technology.
4. I consider myself having the necessary skills to manage to use new technology tools.
5. I have problems to use these technologies properly even with practice.
6. The problems of technology devices are impossible to understand, so it is hard to find a solution.
7. When there is a problem with a new technology tool, it is because there is something wrong with that device.
8. I'm afraid to touch a new technology tool in case I'll break it.
9. I don't get advantage of using new technology tools.
10. I prefer to use an old fashion tool with fewer functions than a new one.
11. Do you use
    (a) Computer
    (b) Tablet
    (c) Kiosks, at railway station, community centre
    (d) TV
    (e) Mobile phone
    (f) Smartphone
12. Peripherals used with Computer/Tablet/TV
13. Problems with Computer/Laptop
14. Problem with mobile phone
15. Do you have experience with any 'special' device
16. Problem with any other electronic device

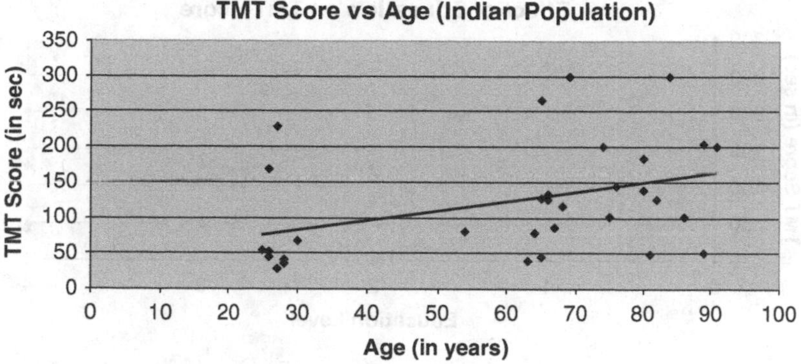

Fig. 2.6 Comparing TMT score with age

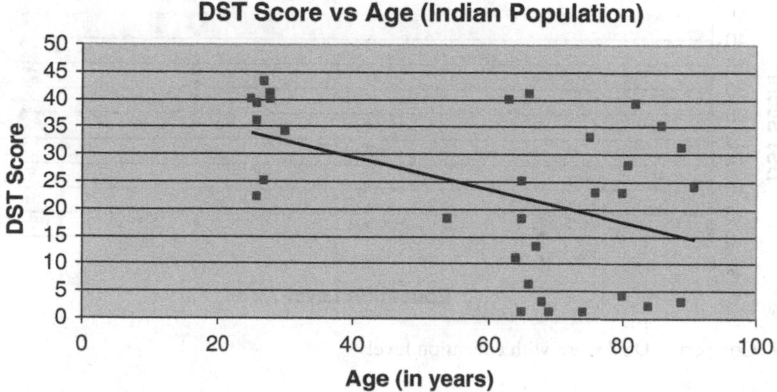

Fig. 2.7 Comparing DST score with age

2.3 Results

2.3.1 Cognitive Data Analysis

We analyzed the effect of age and education on cognitive scores of participants. For Indian population we found a moderate correlation between age and TMT score ($\rho = 0.38$) and DST Score ($\rho = -0.46$) (Figs. 2.6 and 2.7). However we did not find age to be correlated with TMT and DST scores considering only elderly population, instead education level significantly correlated with TMT ($\rho = -0.68, p < 0.01$) and DST scores ($\rho = 0.79, p < 0.01$) (Figs. 2.8 and 2.9). The graphs used the following coding scheme for Education level (Table 2.2)

We compared the cognitive scores of Indian population with their EU counterpart. We found both TMT and DST scores are significantly different between EU and India samples – European people took less time in completing the Trail Making Task and scored more in the Digit Symbol Task than their Indian counterpart. (Tables 2.3 and 2.4)

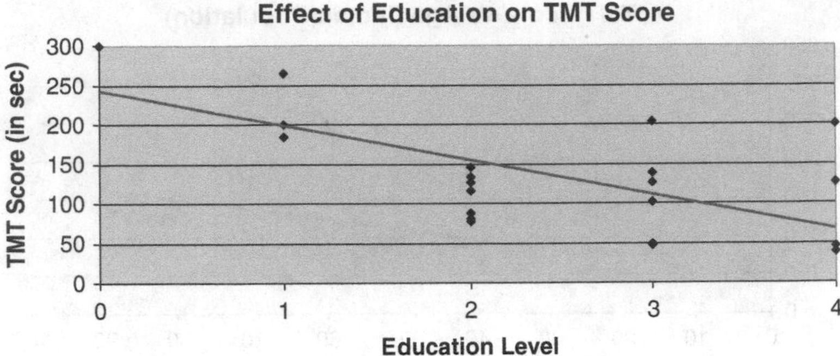

Fig. 2.8 Comparing TMT score with education level

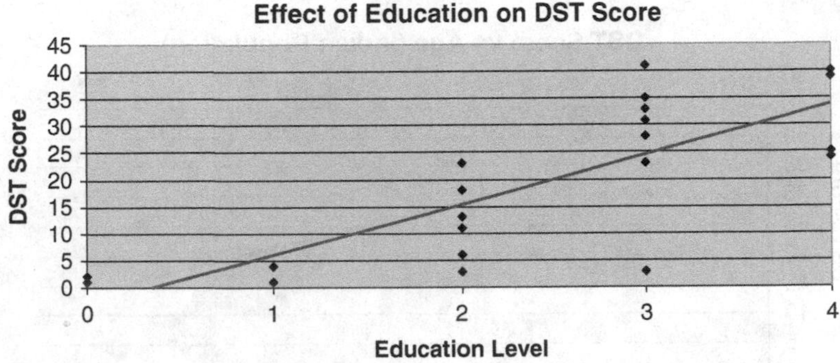

Fig. 2.9 Comparing DST score with education level

Table 2.2 Coding scheme for education level

Education level	Code
Illiterate	0
PreSchool	1
School	2
Graduate	3
PostGraduate	4

Table 2.3 T-test result on TMT score

	EU_TMT	India_TMT
Mean	66.95	122.44
Variance	1,713.74	6,181.93
df	43	
t Stat	−3.65	
P(T<=t) two-tail	0.001	
t Critical two-tail	2.02	

We also did not find any significant correlation between age, education level and TMT, DST scores for European population (Figs. 2.10 and 2.11).

Table 2.4 T-test result on DST score

	EU_DST	India_DST
Mean	39.84	23.22
Variance	249.23	215.99
df	70	
t Stat	4.74	
P(T < =t) two-tail	1.08E-05	
t Critical two-tail	1.99	

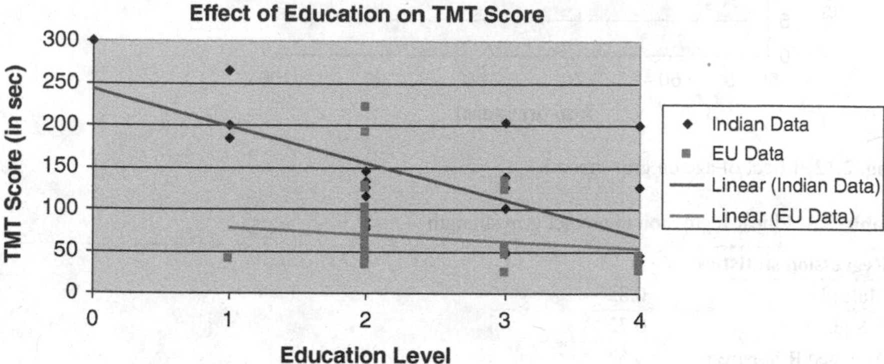

Fig. 2.10 Comparing effect of education level on TMT score between Indian and EU population

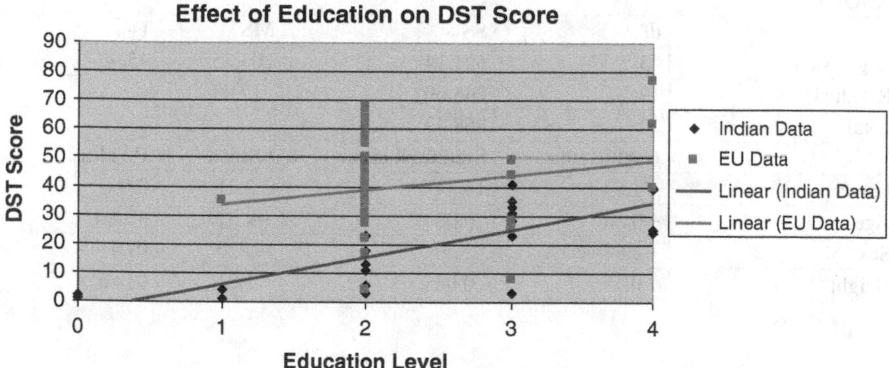

Fig. 2.11 Comparing effect of education level on DST score between Indian and EU population

2.3.2 *Hand Strength Data Analysis*

We found that age (Fig. 2.12), gender and height have a significant effect on grip strength for Indian population. Table 2.5 shows result from a linear regression to predict Grip Strength from age, gender and height.

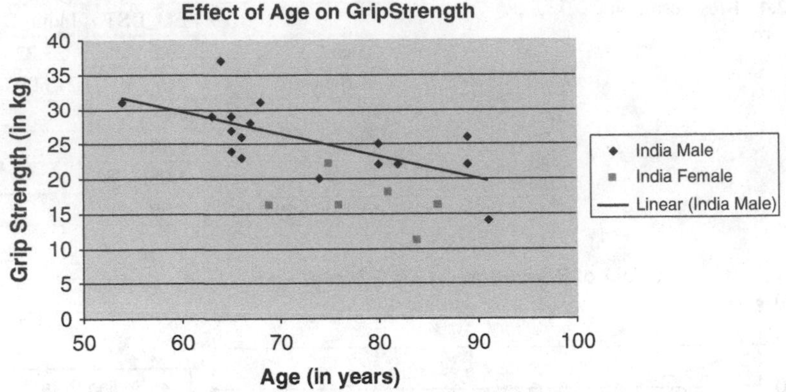

Fig. 2.12 Effect of age on grip strength

Table 2.5 Linear regression to predict grip strength

Regression statistics				
Multiple R	0.85			
R Square	0.72			
Adjusted R Square	0.67			
Standard error	3.60			
Observations	23			
ANOVA				
	df	**SS**	**MS**	**F**
Regression	3	621.74	207.25	15.96
Residual	19	246.69	12.98	
Total	22	868.43		
	Coefficients	**Standard error**	**t Stat**	**P-value**
Intercept	31.69	14.34	2.21	0.04
Age	−0.36	0.08	−4.37	3E-04
Sex	−4.84	2.20	−2.20	0.04
Height	0.15	0.08	1.81	0.086

However, we did not find significant effect of gender and height on a similar linear regression analysis on Active Range of Motion of Wrist (ROMW), only age is significantly correlated with ROMW (Fig. 2.13 and Table 2.6).

We compared the hand strength between Indian and EU population. A few European elderly people had grip strength higher than their Indian counterpart, but the ROMW did not have significant difference (Figs. 2.14 and 2.15).

We have found that for female EU elderly people, grip strength moderately correlate with their age ($\rho = -0.43$) though age was not found to be correlated with Range of Motion of Wrist (Figs. 2.16 and 2.17).

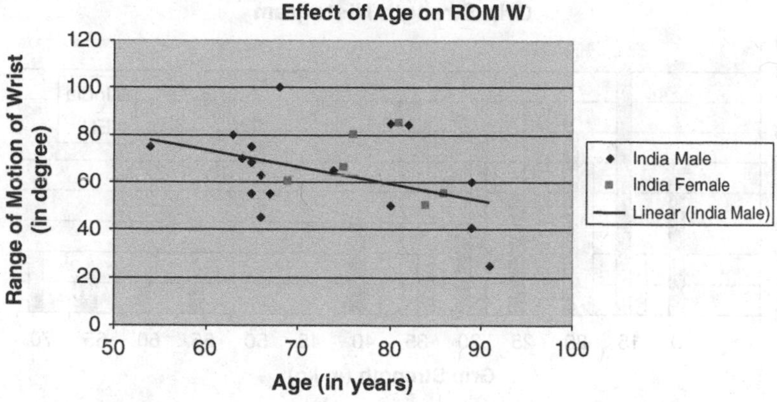

Fig. 2.13 Effect of age on ROMW

Table 2.6 Linear regression to predict active Range of Motion of Wrist (ROMW)

Regression statistics				
Multiple R	0.50			
R Square	0.25			
Adjusted R Square	0.14			
Standard error	15.91			
Observations	23			
ANOVA				
	df	**SS**	**MS**	**F**
Regression	3	1,639.68	546.56	2.16
Residual	19	4,810.93	253.21	
Total	22	6,450.61		
	Coefficients	**Standard error**	**t Stat**	**P-value**
Intercept	17.63	63.32	0.28	0.78
Age	−0.88	0.37	−2.39	0.03
Sex	14.79	9.71	1.52	0.14
Height	0.58	0.37	1.57	0.13

2.3.3 *Visual Data Analysis*

Among the Indian population, approximately one-third of the sample needed bigger font size than the standard level. They could not read the 3 m line in a Snellen chart from 3 m distance from screen. A few users who can read the 3 m line from a 3 m distance commented that they will be benefitted with a bigger font size in mobile keypad. We found 8 among 33 users could not read the plates 16 and 17 of Ishihara colour blindness test properly, 5 of them seemed to have Protanopia type of colour blindness as they could only read the left hand digit correctly, the rest three could not read any number at all.

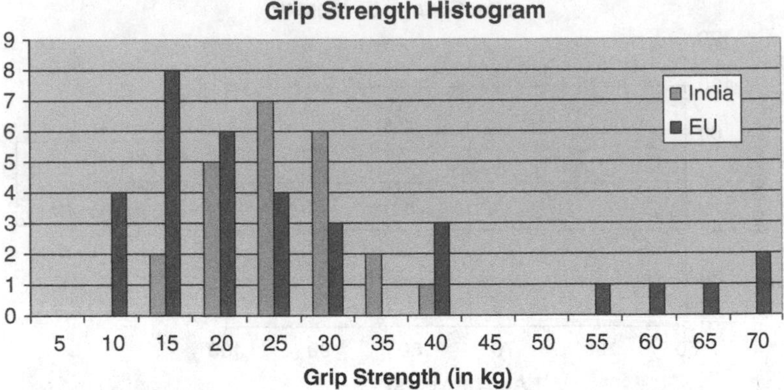

Fig. 2.14 Comparing grip strength histogram between Indian and EU population

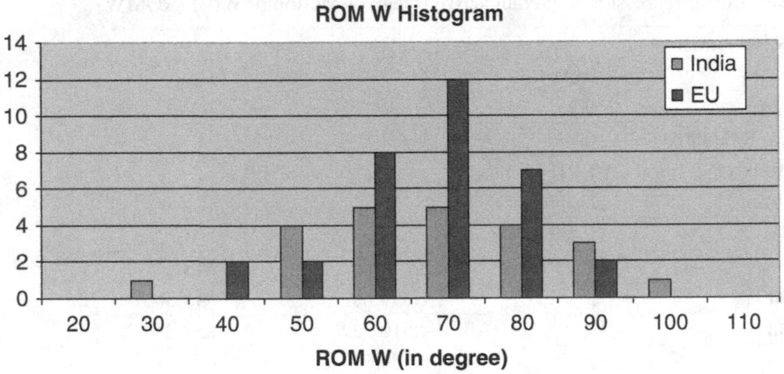

Fig. 2.15 Comparing ROMW histogram between Indian and EU population

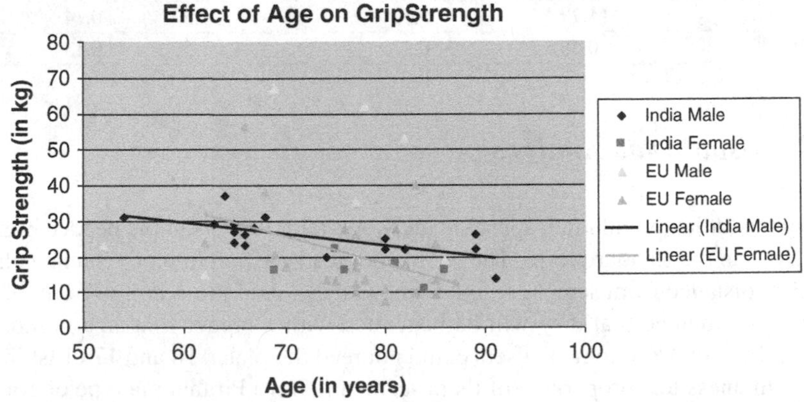

Fig. 2.16 Comparing effect of age on grip strength between EU and Indian population

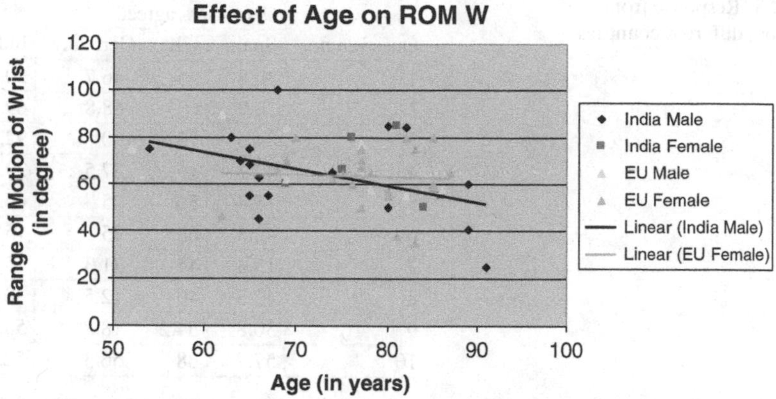

Fig. 2.17 Comparing effect of age on ROMW between EU and Indian population

Table 2.7 List of questions used to assess attitude towards technology

1. I think that new technology devices are developed mainly to be used by young users.
2. I think that I need to use new technology.
3. I consider it important to try to be open-minded towards new technology.
4. I consider myself having the necessary skills to manage to use new technology tools.
5. I have problems to use these technologies properly even with practice.
6. The problems of technology devices are impossible to understand, so it is hard to find a solution.
7. When there is a problem with a new technology tool, it is because there is something wrong with that device.
8. I'm afraid to touch a new technology tool in case I'll break it.
9. I don't get advantage of using new technology tools.
10. I prefer to use an old fashion tool with fewer functions than a new one.

2.3.4 *Attitude Towards Technology Data Analysis*

Table 2.7 reports the questions used to understand attitude towards technology while Table 2.8 reports report the response of people from different countries. Each question had three possible response – Agreed, Disagreed and Neutral.

We did not find any significant difference among elderly people from Spain, UK, India and Germany regarding their attitude towards technology through a single factor ANOVA (Fig. 2.18, Table 2.9). The subjective attitude is discussed in more detail in Sect. 2.4.4.

2.3.5 *Technology Exposure Data Analysis*

We found that none of the Indian users ever used Tablet computer, Kiosk or smart TV, only a couple of users uses Smartphone, while all users can use basic call

Table 2.8 Response from users from different countries

Question no.	% of users agreed			
	Spain	UK	Germany	India
1	30.8	56	46.7	30.43
2	26.9	60	68.8	69.23
3	84.6	72	100	92.31
4	42.3	16	37.5	39.13
5	15.4	56	25	46.15
6	42.3	68	75	15.38
7	15.4	44	31.3	15.38
8	42.3	40	12.5	30.43
9	30.8	54.2	18.8	53.85
10	57.7	68	56.3	52.17

Question no.	% of users agreed			
	Spain	UK	Germany	India
1	69.2	20	40	65.22
2	46.2	28	0	23.08
3	7.7	4	0	0
4	23.1	48	31.3	47.83
5	61.5	28	56.3	30.77
6	30.8	12	12.5	46.15
7	42.3	32	50	53.85
8	38.5	40	68.8	65.22
9	61.5	37.5	68.8	30.77
10	23.1	28	25	47.83

making and receiving facilities of mobile phone and can view their favourite channel in Television. Most of the younger people with physical impairment use computers regularly while three to four elderly users used computer before though none of the elderly users use computer regularly. They reported that they found computers complicated to use, could not remember functionalities and could not find it useful. However a few users wanted to use computers for emailing their sons or daughter or pursuing their hobbies like cookery, knitting etc.

2.4 Discussion

The aim of this survey was to understand effect of age on capability and attitude towards technology, in particular electronic interactive devices like computer, TV, mobile phone and so on. The study has pointed out some interesting insights as pointed below.

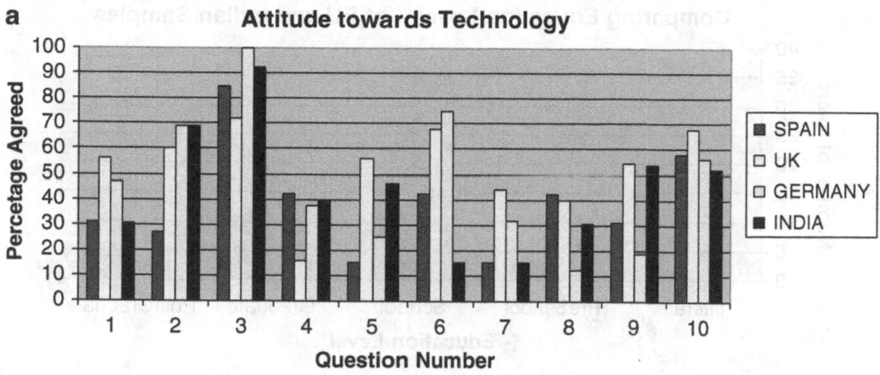

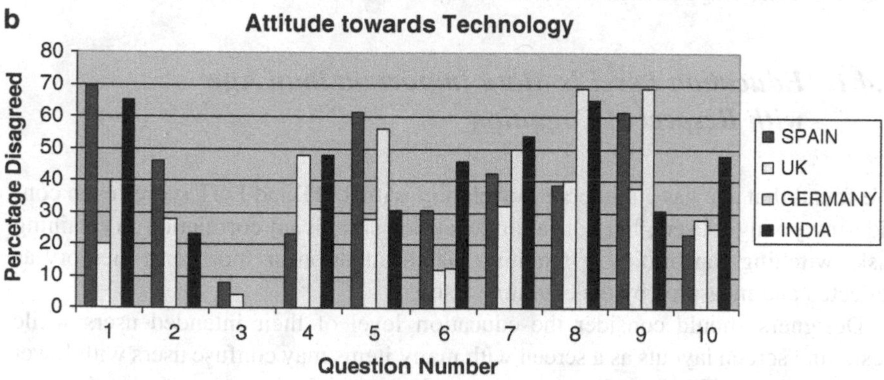

Fig. 2.18 Comparing attitudes towards technology for different users. (**a**) Comparing users agreed to question statements. (**b**) Comparing users disagreed to question statements

Table 2.9 ANOVA results on users' response

ANOVA summary					
Source	SS	df	MS	F	P
(a) ANOVA on users agreed to question statements					
Group	1,100.08	3	366.69	0.71	0.55
Error	18,480.70	36	513.35		
Total	19,580.78	39			
(b) ANOVA on uses disagreed to question statements					
Group	1,135.35	3	378.45	0.92	0.44
Error	14,793.70	36	410.94		
Total	15,929.04	39			

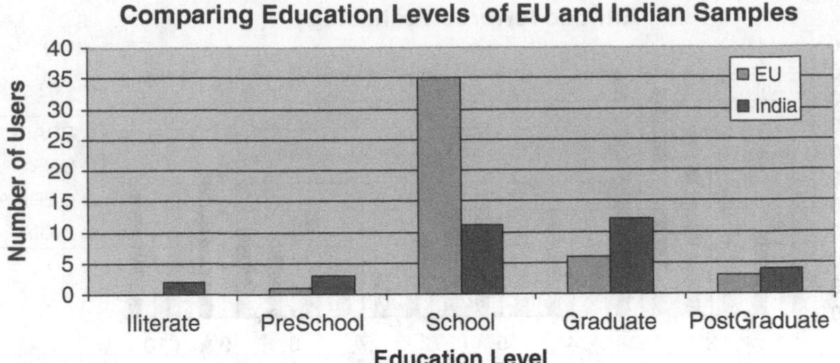

Fig. 2.19 Comparing education level of Indian and EU samples

2.4.1 Education Level Is More Important than Age with Respect to Cognition

We found that age has a moderate correlation with TMT and DST scores even considering younger users, but education level has significant correlation in retaining task switching capabilities or retaining visual attention or short term memory as reflected and measured by the cognitive tests.

Designers should consider the education level of their intended users while designing screen layouts as a screen with many items may confuse users with lower education level. This issue becomes more relevant while designing applications for illiterate or neo-literate people in India.

We also found that the average scores in cognitive tests are higher in European population. One possible reason may be most European users had a minimum school level of education while that was not true for their Indian counterpart (Fig. 2.19).

2.4.2 Age Reduces Hand Strength in Turn Capability of Using Computer Peripherals

Our previous study [3, 4] found that Grip Strength and Active range of motion of wrist is indicative of users' pointing performance with a variety of pointing devices like mouse, trackball, touchscreen and stylus. We found that both Indian and EU population reduce their grip strength with age that effectively make their use of standard computer peripherals inefficient. The reduced hand strength also makes it difficult to use touchscreen or keypads which was also explicitly mentioned by a few participants.

Designers and interface developers should explore use of hands free control for elderly users. Eye gaze tracking [5] or Brain Computer interfaces [5] can offer valuable alternative to standard keyboard, mouse and touchscreen interfaces.

Our analysis also developed a model to predict grip strength from age, height and gender of participants which was reported earlier in Ergonomics literature [1] but not probably validated on Indian population.

2.4.3 Bigger Font Size and Buttons Are Good

We found that one-third of users had reduced visual acuity even with a corrective glass. However most elderly users used glasses and a few of them more than one for near and far vision. It is likely that they may use TV or mobile phone without their glasses or with the wrong glasses on. Their reduced visual acuity compounded with reduced hand strength limits usability of standard mobile or remote keypad as well standard computer or TV interfaces.

Designers should provide bigger buttons and font sizes for elderly people. They should also adjust colour contrast for users with colour blindness.

2.4.4 Elderly Users Will Use It if It Is Interesting and Easy-to-Use

Most of our elderly users use the basic functionalities of mobile phone and TV as they find it easy-to-use and useful. However that does not hold true for computers as they find it complicated and serving no useful purpose for them. Some elderly users relied on others to send emails to their distant relatives. However more than 60 % users in India and Spain believed that new technology was not only meant for young users and more than 80 % of them felt themselves open-minded to use new technology. More than 60 % of Indian, British and German elderly users wanted to use new technology. However the opinion about braking a new too or using old-fashion tool is not very obvious as on average 50 % users agree or disagree to it and a few of them have no opinion regarding it. Many users especially younger ones with physical impairment emphasized the need of training in learning new technology.

Application developers should think about reducing complexity of applications intended for elderly users. Applications like email, video-chat may be found to be interesting among elderly users if they are easy to use. Similarly application deployed on low-end mobile phones or set top box has more chance to be acceptable by elderly users as they are already accustomed to those devices.

2.5 Conclusions

This chapter reports results from a survey on capability and attitude towards technology of elderly users conducted at three different geographic locations in India. The paper also compares results of a similar survey conducted in Spain, Germany and UK. The survey finds important results in terms of hand strength and cognitive abilities of users. It proposes a model to predict grip strength from age, sex and height of Indian elderly people while also reports a significant effect of education on scores of cognitive tests. Comparative analysis with European elderly people shows European people tend to sustain better cognitive abilities with age though their attitude towards new technology is not significantly different from their Indian counterpart. Finally it reports subjective view of elderly people about technology and proposes guidelines for future interface designers in developing countries. Following chapters have utilized the survey in developing a user model and proposing new interfaces and interaction techniques.

References

1. Angst, F., et al. (2010). Prediction of grip and key pinch strength in 978 healthy subjects. *BMC Musculoskeletal Disorders, 11*, 94.
2. Army individual test Battery. (1944). *Manual of directions and scoring*. War Department, Adjuvant General's Office, Washington, D.C.
3. Biswas, P., & Langdon, P. (2012). Developing multimodal adaptation algorithm for mobility impaired users by evaluating their hand strength. *International Journal of Human-Computer Interaction, 28*(9), 576–596. Print ISSN: 1044–7318.
4. Biswas, P., & Robinson, P. (2009). *Predicting pointing time from hand strength, Usability & HCI for e-Inclusion*. In: 5th symposium of the Austrian Computer Society (USAB 2009).
5. Biswas, P., Joshi, R., Chattopadhyay, S., Acharya, U. R., & Lim, T. (2013). Interaction techniques for users with severe motor-impairment. In: P. Biswas et al. (Eds.), *A multimodal end-2-end approach to accessible computing*. London: Springer.
6. Biswas, P., Robinson, P., & Langdon, P. (2012). Designing inclusive interfaces through user modelling and simulation. *International Journal of Human-Computer Interaction, 28*(1), 1–33. Print ISSN: 1044–7318.
7. Ishihara, S. (1917). *Tests for color-blindness*. Handaya: Hongo Harukicho.
8. Dalstra, J. A. A., Kunst, A. E., Borrell, C., Breeze, E., Cambois, E., Costa, G., et al. (2005). Socioeconomic differences in the prevalence of common chronic diseases: an overview of eight European countries. *International Journal of Epidemiology, 34*(2), 316–326.
9. GUIDE D7.1 Initial user study. Available at: http://www.guide-project.eu/includes/requestFile.php?id=129&pub=2. Accessed 18 June 2013.
10. Kaplan, R. J. (2006). *Physical medicine and rehabilitation review*. New York: McGraw-Hill.
11. Langdon, P., & Thimbleby, H. (2010). *Inclusion and interaction: Designing interaction for inclusive populations* (Editorial for special edition of interacting with computers, Vol 22, pp. 439–448). Amsterdam: Elsevier.
12. Mackenbach, J. P., et al. (1997). Socioeconomic inequalities in morbidity and mortality in Western Europe. *Lancet, 349*(9066), 1655–1659.

13. Making mobile phones and services accessible for persons with disabilities. Available at: http://www.itu.int/ITU-D/sis/PwDs/Documents/Mobile_Report.pdf. Accessed 18 June 2013.
14. Making television accessible report, G3ict-ITU, November 2011. Available at: http://www.itu.int/ITU-D/sis/PwDs/Documents/Making_TV_Accessible-FINAL-WithAltTextInserted.pdf. Accessed 18 June 2013.
15. Siegrist, J., & Marmot, M. (2004). Health inequalities and the psychosocial environment – two scientific challenges. *Social Science & Medicine, 58*(8), 1463–1473.

Chapter 3
Developing an Interactive TV for the Elderly and Impaired: An Inclusive Design Strategy

Patrick Langdon

Abstract Combining the development of multimodal technology with research exposes the weaknesses of conventional approaches when the target users are elderly or impaired. This chapter examines the antecedents, implementation and evaluation of a User Centered approach to the design of interactive technology such as iDTV and mobile devices that takes into account the variability and extraordinary capabilities of users and how to design for them. It describes the strengths and weaknesses of the new Inclusive Interaction Design approach and compares a usage case with another separate project with the same goals.

3.1 Why a User Centered Design Strategy? An Overview for Researchers or Practitioners

Why is it necessary to say more about User Centred Design in the context of inclusion? The answer is that Inclusive design strategy accommodates a greater range of users than normative usability or extreme accessibility approaches. Designing for this mid-range of capabilities extends design to mainstream groups who have been limited by the digital divide.

Inclusion refers to the quantitative relationship between the demand made by design features and the capability ranges of users who may be excluded from use of the product because of those features. By 2020, almost half the adult population in the UK will be over 50, with the over 80s being the most rapidly growing sector. These "inclusive" populations contain a great variation in sensory, cognitive and physical user capabilities, particularly when non-age related impairments are taken into account. Establishing the requirement of end users is intrinsically linked to the User centered Design process. In particular, a requirements specification is an important part of defining and planning the variables to be varied and measured and the technology use cases to be addressed during the interactions during user

P. Langdon (✉)
Department of Engineering, University of Cambridge, Trumpington Street, Cambridge, Cambridgeshire CB2 1PZ, UK
e-mail: pml24@eng.cam.ac.uk

P. Biswas et al. (eds.), *A Multimodal End-2-End Approach to Accessible Computing*, Human–Computer Interaction Series, DOI 10.1007/978-1-4471-6708-2_3

trials. This chapter looks at the background and motivation for this approach, some methods and methodology and uses the GUIDE iDTV project (www.guide-project.eu) as a case study of operationalising the approach. Finally, a comparison is made with a related EU project, spring-boarding a discussion of key issues raised and future scope.

3.1.1 Relation to Inclusive Design

Rather than consider impairment as synonymous with a disability or medical condition, the casting of impairment as a set of interrelated functional capabilities is an approach that has been introduced in the context of designing information technology. The idea here is that dysfunction due to ageing and other causes can be divided, as part of an inclusive user-centred design process, into various qualitative types of capability and the quantitative ranges for them that can be found in the population [28].

Research in the field of Inclusive design has developed the theory and practice of calculation of exclusion for product design. This is based on the fundamental concept of the capability-demand relationship and aims to quantify the number of people in the disabled population who would be excluded from use of a product as a result of the functional demand made by the product interface interacting with their function capabilities [35, 47, 48]. Inclusive Design aims to make products and services accessible to the widest range of users possible irrespective of impairment, age or capability. To do this, a substantial research effort has been directed towards developing the underlying theory and practice of design analysis in order to develop and provide tools and guidance to designers and those commissioning designs that they can use to improve the inclusion of a resulting product [6, 22]. This approach may be contrasted with that of Universal Design or "Design for All" as a main distinctive feature is that it does not advocate producing single products that satisfy a range of impairments. Instead it proposes widening the scope of designs deliberately to include more people with marginal capabilities.

3.1.2 Relation to Accessibility

Accessibility interventions frequently address specific well established disabilities in society. Only in recent years has this included age related impairments. Not all functional disability results from ageing. Some common examples of non age-related impairment include specific conditions such as stroke and head injury, which may affect any or all of perception, memory and movement, depending on the location and extent of damage to the brain.

Other conditions are generally associated with movement impairment. For example, Parkinson's disease is a progressive loss of motor control causing weakness, tremor and physical atrophy; Cerebral palsy is a non-progressive condition causing effects such as spasms, dynamic coordination difficulties and language and speech production impairment. Of course, many other conditions such as Down's syndrome and multiple sclerosis (MS) may affect cognitive capability either directly, through language learning and use, or indirectly through its effects on hearing, speech production and writing.

Of all the sources of variations discussed, many differentially affect normal population ranges of capability. They may be rapidly changing and vary in intensity both within and between individuals, leading to a demanding design environment that requires close attention to conflicting user requirements and a better understanding of user capability. Again, this confirms that interaction design for future generations of products must be inclusive. The relationship between the user's capabilities and their environment has long been considered in the context of assistive technology [30]. Newell (1995), for example, considers the equivalence of ordinary interactions impaired by extreme situations and impaired individuals in ordinary situations. Design should focus on the extra-ordinary or impaired first, accommodating mainstream design in the process [31].

3.1.3 Relation to Usability

Many products today are laden with a host of features which for the majority of users remain unused and often obscure the use of the simple features of use for which the product was devised. For example, since the target cognitive capabilities anticipated by the designers are often similar to their own demographic and largely not affected by age-related cognitive impairment, the cognitive demands made by such products are frequently high.

Since designers often anticipate that the cognitive capabilities of users will be similar to their own demographic and largely not affected by age-related cognitive impairment, and while the experimental literature seems to support this, the cognitive demand made by products is frequently high [21, 22]. Usability standards and methods [26] use statistical distribution assumptions to cater for the assumed "normal population". However, an alternative analysis of inclusive populations provided by Newell (2006) discusses the normal distribution formed by the proportion of population with differing degrees of functionality [28]. Rehabilitation engineering, for a start, specifically works with extremely low ranges of functionality; while accessibility design involves accessibility innovations offered as options on standard design and cater for low functionality and low to medium functionality groups. Inclusive design is identified as addressing the mainstream and extending the scope of design to accommodate greater numbers of lower functionality users. The standard normative approach to usability prevalent at the present and ubiquitous in both standards and pedagogical material is therefore likely to be inadequate for informing design in the future, where wider capability ranges are anticipated, and would certainly be inadequate for informing inclusive design of the GUIDE iDTV user interfaces.

3.1.4 Background to Inclusive Design and Antecedent Work

Inclusive Design aims to make products and services accessible to the widest range of users possible irrespective of impairment, age or capability. To do this, a substantial research effort has been directed towards developing the underlying theory and practice of design analysis in order to develop and provide tools and guidance to designers that they can use to improve the inclusion of a resulting product [6]. This research has principally been motivated by changes in national and International demographics evident in recent years leading to increasing numbers of older and reduced numbers of younger product users. The problems that arise from this include increased prevalence of impairment, which has led to legislative requirements for greater inclusion at home, at leisure and in the workplace. For the purpose of the GUIDE project, with intended end users encompassing the elderly and the mild to moderate impairments, this is an advantageous approach.

3.1.5 Brief History of Inclusion Research

Inclusive design is a user-centered approach that examines designed product features with particular attention to the functional demands they make on the perceptual, thinking and physical capabilities of diverse users, particularly those with impairments and ageing. It is known, for example, that cognitive capabilities such as verbal and visuospatial IQ show gradually decreasing performance with aging. Attending to goal-relevant, task features and inhibiting irrelevant ones is important in product interaction and this is known to be affected by ageing. Attentional resources may also be reduced by ageing, such that more mistakes are made during divided attention, dual task situations [29, 32, 36, 39, 41].

The elements of the population that should be considered by research in inclusive design were addressed by Keates and Clarkson (2003) who identified the loci of sub-populations within a theoretical space bounded by the severity of perceptual, cognitive and movement capability dimensions [18]. They illustrated the shortfalls apparent in usability approaches to design that propose normative methods that do not take into account sufficient variability across the population and hence cannot give rise to designs that are accessible and also cater for functional impairments at differing levels [26]. Keates et al. identified three sub-populations:

1. Special purpose design that caters for specialised products for specific impairment needs;
2. Modular or customisable designs where one product or multiple products can be configured to user needs and preferences; and
3. User aware design that aims to extend the design of mainstream products to accommodate as many users as possible.

Another related design approach that embraces social context, is that of universal design. This design approach advocates designing specific products so that they are usable for the widest possible range of capabilities. For example, buildings should be suitable for all possible end users regardless of functional capabilities, age, or social contexts [34]. Although illustrated by numerous architectural examples, this approach falls short of the detailed quantitative analysis required for interaction design. The rationale and underlying theory connecting the principles is not apparent. A further category is that of ordinary and extraordinary design that aims to improve design for older, impaired users of low functionality while at the same time enhancing design for the mainstream and ordinary users in extreme environments [29]. On this basis, design should focus on the extraordinary or impaired first, accommodating mainstream design in the process [31]. This issue has been pursued further in the context of understanding the properties of user populations from disability survey data [47, 48].

3.1.6 Why Do Trials or Experiments?

In Inclusive design, this sort of analytic approach to the evaluation of designs is intended to mitigate the need for extensive observational trials or experiments with products in use by selected samples of people. Instead, data about the prevalence of capability is used holistically in conjunction with a categorisation and task analysis of product properties and features, in order to quantify the numbers of users and sub-populations of users, who can use a design without mental or physical failure or difficulty. Such an inclusion task analysis requires:

1. A data set of the distribution of capability in the population, and
2. Methods for characterising and measuring the products' demands in different functional areas; sensory, cognitive and physical [35].

However, it is also clear that it must also take into account situational and cultural factors such as the social, physical and economic context of use. Importantly, this latter consideration is a novel research development related to design for all and universal design [43] that focuses on the exclusion of individuals from using products as a result of difficulties of use or failure of interaction resulting from the product's demands exceeding users' capability. The quantification of this capability-demand relationship is therefore referred to as a calculation of product inclusion.

3.1.7 Sampling Strategies: What Is a User?

In order to manifest this Inclusive design approach into the design and technical development of an interactive TV for older people such as the GUIDE system the GUIDE project pursued a user-centred design approach at the level of end-user interaction. A separate analysis was carried out for Developer interactions, assuming developers as users. This is described in GUIDE documentation. End user requirements for ageing and for those people with impairments were collected using a mixed methods approach based on the advantages of triangulation of data sources [9, 20]. In essence, this approach does not commit to a single source of data or a single data collection approach. The studies employed, contributed to the empirical triangulated approach that employed a range of methods that were capable of independent results. This allowed findings to be cross-checked against each other, helped to balance the advantages and disadvantages of the individual methods, and obtained a spectrum of views at different levels of objectivity [9, 20]. In the case of GUIDE, the framing of the project as a design problem for a set-top box prototype constrained the triangulation and assists it by directing the focus of comparison on the design of the final interactions between user, system, technology, and usage context.

Establishing the requirements of end users is intrinsically linked to the User Centred Design (UCD) process. In particular, requirements specification is an important part of defining and planning the variables to be varied and measured and the technology usage cases to be addressed during the interactions in the user trials.

For the purpose of devising a working sampling strategy for early pilot trials it was necessary to adopt a stratified sampling strategy, screening participants who took part in the GUIDE user Survey and allocating them to age and capability ranges of interest and that were required for analysis. GUIDE initially grouped participants into groups with respect to the severity of their perceptual, cognitive and motor capabilities [See Sect. 3.5.4 of GUIDE D2.1, The screening criteria are exemplified for Gender in table 10–3].

The relative proportions of participants in sampling categories were initially decided by opportunistic sampling but this process was informed by the Inclusion and disability analysis [Sect. 4.3.3, D2.1] based on the exclusion calculations of proportion of an exemplar EU population (UK GB) who might be expected to fall into the categories of high, medium and low impairment, and who consider themselves disabled in some capability area (Table 3.1).

For example, the gender balance for the population age ranges and proportion of individuals experiencing some impairment for each gender were also calculated using the exclusion estimation form the UK inclusive design exclusion calculator [47, 48]. Because the sampling strategy of older and impaired users in the age groups of interest was, by necessity opportunistic, these calculations were used

Table 3.1 Gender balance for each of the age ranges and populations included for all impairments

Overall impairments (UK 1997)	Age range	Male (Pop size) [Exclusion]	Female (Pop size) [Exclusion]	Both (Pop size) [Exclusion]
	49–60	21.84 % [3.91 m]	19.51 % [3.97 m]	20.67 %[7.88 m]
	60–90	42.53 % [4.65 m]	41.39 % [5.89 m]	41.89 % [10.54 m]

as a broad indication of an estimate of the relative sizes of the samples required in each category. This meant, for example, that roughly twice as many individual would be sampled in the older age group compared with the younger age group and that the sample should be biased towards larger numbers of female rather than male participants. In the actual sampling these proportions were only partially achieved, the predominant population being older female, although the age group sampling was partially successful. The extent which this reflects the sample specific to Northern Spain is unknown but comparisons with other populations in the UK and Germany were carried out in the analysis of year 2 user trials. However, the resulting distribution was at this point only an approximation to the ideal. Although the distribution is biased to the older 60–90 age group, within that the impairments are concentrated on the low impairment groups with less in the medium and high impairment groups. This is the result of the opportunistic sampling but fortunately is broadly consistent with the proportions suggested by the estimates and also presents some face validity in that this is the distribution one would expect from daily experience of working with older populations. In the UK there are 0.76 Males to each female in the 65+ age group [11]. There was a strong bias towards female rather than male participants and this exceeds that which was estimated. The smaller number of participants in the 40–60 age groups reflects the lower generally lower frequencies of impairments in this age range. The concentration of high impairments in the age range may reflect small sample bias. The nature and definition of impairments however, is a matter of definition.

3.1.8 Models of Disability

Non-age-related impairment is frequently associated with disability, although a number of models of the notion of disability exist and different sectors, such as engineering or medicine may disagree as to which are more useful and appropriate. For example, the World Health Organization's International Classification of Impairment, Disability and Handicap, [46], model provides a standardised language, but its framework is medical and categorises disability as the functional performance consequences of impairment, which in turn is caused by loss or abnormality of bodily structure or function. This categorisation is widely used in gerontology and assistive technology. The model mixes medical conditions, terminology and philosophy with objective performance. The revised ICIDH2 avoids some of the original negative connotations by terminological improvements, but the aim remains to support caregivers rather than designers [46]. Nevertheless, the ICIDH irretrievably confounds medical conditions, jargon and philosophy, with objective performance. Petrie, for example, notes this weakness and proposes a purely functionally based classification of disability as a basis for the design of ICT interfaces [36]. In contrast, socially-motivated models emphasise the role of society in classifying people as disabled and focus on its obligations in providing the resources and interventions to prevent exclusion of individuals from full participation in society [33]. A hybrid model, combining the biological and social models, emphasises the complexity of impairment in functional and social terms, and focuses on its variability over time and within the individual. This model of disability encompasses both the interactions between multiple functional impairments and the consequent effects when these in turn interact with the detailed social effects of impairment, such as lack of empathy or negative attitudes. This model is adopted by GUIDE and embraces social psychology, social-economic, psychiatric and statistical considerations, as well as being consistent with developing fields, such as well-being [2].

3.1.9 Development Versus Research

The GUIDE project requires the simultaneous development of a software system capable of running on a set-top box, and also the carrying out of User centered design of the interface features and designed adaptions. This is necessary to support the end-user: the elderly and mildly impaired iDTV user with appropriate and effective adaptions compensating for perceptual, cognitive and physical impairments. Both forms of development are required for successful software outcomes; however the effectiveness of the GUIDE interventions requires both processes concurrently. This leads to a design environment based on overlapping sets of requirements. Development is usually alternated in an iterative cycle with evaluation. Evaluation can be cast as formative or summative evaluation [42]. In the former evaluation of change proceeds during development, while in the latter an evaluation is made at the end of a development. For example, good software development uses user trials in a formative way to evaluate new development and modify the design iteratively as the design proceeds towards completion. On the other hand, user centered design requires intervals of stringent and summative experimental examinations of the proposed adaptions for their effectiveness at improving interaction with representative samples of impaired populations. These two processes are not necessarily conflicting but require different levels of standardisation and fidelity of conditions. Current practice in engineering software design is appropriate for development and formative evaluation but frequently lacks rigor and experimental power. In particular, usability approaches are inappropriate for UCD of elderly and impaired populations who may possess higher incidences and variability of impairments and this necessitates accurate stratified sampling for user trials. Conversely, high fidelity prototyping is required for effective testing of elderly peoples' responses to proposed adaptions, necessitating advanced development techniques.

3.1.10 Some Problems with Normative Methods and Usability

The goal of an inclusive design "exclusion" analysis is that a proposed product design is subjected to capability-demand analysis in order to identify whether it can be used by people with specific quantified impairments. In order to develop system and interface designs that improve general human performance it will also be necessary to go outside of the boundaries of "normative" human capability and deal with extra-ordinary human capability in ordinary settings. To date, research underlying CTA approaches has focused on ordinary users in extra-ordinary situations of workload or physical context, such as air traffic control, piloting modern aircraft, or medical diagnosis. However, as pointed out by Newell (1995), individuals with capability impairments may be faced with the need to interact with designs intended for normal capabilities in everyday situations whilst possessing variable and unusual rages of capability [30, 31]. Hence, the user of a product may be excluded or disabled from effective use of it by poor design of its interface features, as for example when a key-pad is unusable in a low lighting situation.

On this basis, a novel and key requirement criterion of the framework GUIDE aims to develop is that it should be capable of accommodating an extra-ordinary range of capabilities, such as those presented by older and disabled people [30, 31]. However, these capabilities and their patterns of occurrence are not well understood, particularly for the engineering and technical backgrounds, so we turn next to summarise them for developers and non-practitioners.

3.1.11 The Elderly User

Age related impairments are associated with a variety of causes and conditions. For example, between the ages of 45 and 75 there may well be significant loss of static and dynamic visual acuity and contrast sensitivity, colour vision, focusing and adaptation to dark. Hearing loss increases with age, initially in the high, and later in the high to middle frequency ranges. Initial mild to moderate losses of strength and aerobic capability often progresses to slowing of movement and stiffness due to conditions such as arthritis. Movement and coordination are affected by ageing, particularly in the accuracy and speed of the dexterous movements required by mobile products and user interfaces. There are reductions of taste, smell and touch, and general health may be affected as a result of increased frequency of impairing chronic conditions such as hypertension, dementia and arthritis [7]. With respect to the interaction of product users with designed features, a number of mental or cognitive age-related variations have been clearly identified in the literature. There is a general slowing of cognition and response times. Attentional and split attention capability is reduced and automated responses may be slow to learn and more difficult to suppress. On the other hand, users maintain well-learned skills and abilities such as reasoning, well into old age [13]. This form of memory is stored for the long term and corresponds to so-called crystallized intelligence, whereas the immediate perceptual and instantaneous reasoning capability, identified as fluid intelligence, is more impaired with increasing age, [29]. This is particularly true of memory for procedures and episodes or events but not for semantic memory regarding the meaning of objects. Fluid intelligence is strongly related to the functions and capacity of working memory and its related processes such as executive function, which are thought to simultaneously retrieve, hold and use short-term information during an interaction. These capabilities are likely to be heavily involved during novel or unfamiliar tasks, such as the first use of interactive products like GUIDE IDTV. Pre-dementia impairment is also distinguishable in itself and is compatible with normal ageing, identified as Age-related Memory Impairment (AAMI). Some specific conditions that are strongly associated with cognitive ageing are dementia and Alzheimer's disease. Although these conditions are increasingly prevalent with age, they also involve physical changes in brain structure than can affect perception, memory and movement. Dementia and Alzheimer's are associated with general degradation of short-term memory (STM), particularly memory for personal experience. Long-term memories may be unaffected but the ability to retrieve these and deal with them in the short term is impaired, particularly when a structured interaction such as a dialogue is required. Dementia also affects verbal and visual spatial abilities, such as the perception of coherence in pictorial layouts and icons, or in the appreciation of metaphorical meanings. The understanding and production of speech is often impaired through specific aphasias [5, 13, 29].

While acknowledging that individuals differ in their cognitive profile of capabilities, and despite considerable intra-personal and inter-personal variability, the general trend is for increasing impairment and increasing variation over age, with some notable exceptions relating to crystallized general intelligence [5, 29, 36, 39]. The GUIDE requirements analysis was configured for cognitive impairment as well as perceptual and physical impairment with data collected during rigorous trials with cognitively impaired users on standardised cognitive tests.

3.1.12 *Disability and Mild to Moderate Impairment*

Not all functional disability results from ageing. Some common examples of non age-related impairment include specific conditions such as stroke and head injury, which may affect any or all of perception, memory and movement, depending on the location and extent of damage to the brain. This impairment would impact such users' interactions with the GUIDE system.

Other conditions are generally associated with movement impairment and, for example might affect peoples' ability to hold and point a handheld controller or to gesture and point using GUIDE's Visual Human Sensing input mechanism. For example, Parkinson's disease is a progressive loss of motor control causing weakness, tremor and physical atrophy, while cerebral palsy is an early acquired but non-progressive condition resulting from brain damage causing effects such as spasms, dynamic coordination difficulties and language and speech production impairment. Autism and Asperger's Syndrome are associated with impairment in the development of social communications capabilities and interaction skills such as non-verbal communication. In autism, these social dysfunctions are also accompanied by other general effects of reduced cognition, while in Asperger's other functions are unaffected. Problems using GUIDE were anticipated in the case of these impairments through the introduction of an "Avatar" or Virtual human being as an output modality during use. Of course, many other conditions such as Down's syndrome and multiple sclerosis (MS) may affect cognitive capability either directly, through language learning and use, or indirectly through its effects on hearing, speech production and writing.

Of all the variations discussed, many differentially affect normal population ranges of capability. They may be rapidly changing and vary in intensity both within and between individuals, leading to a demanding design environment that requires close attention to conflicting user requirements and a better understanding of user capability. Again, not only does this confirm that interaction design for future generations of ICT products for ageing must be inclusive, but also that, as in the case of GUIDE, the difficulties of specifying requirements for multiple conflicting conditions must be mitigated by a risk reduction strategy. This involved reducing the range and intensity of impairments accommodated by GUIDE and a focus on user data generated by trials with the actual prototype interfaces as they were developed.

3.1.13 Inclusion from an Analytical Functional Perspective

An analytic approach to the evaluation of designs mitigates the need for observational trials with products by relating data about the prevalence of capability ranges in the population with an analysis of the demand made by product properties and features. This enables a quantification of the number of users who can use a specific design. To date, there has been some success in identifying data sets and appropriate impairment and capability models for perception and movement in this novel "inclusive" research context. However, previous attempts to do so for cognitive aspects of product feature interaction have encountered a lack of suitable data and models.

3.1.14 Measuring the Capability-Demand Relationship in Interaction

Inclusive design, as developed by this approach, examines designed product or interface features with particular attention to the functional demands they make on the perceptual, thinking and physical capabilities of diverse users [10, 18, 35, 45]. Other related approaches, for example, use a single comprehensive data set from 100 people containing anthropometric and behavioural data but omit cognitive information. This latter HADRIAN system allows designers to query the data base for numerical and personal information [37] and the SAMMIE development allows the data to be used in a task analysis with trials of fit between virtual human figures and interfaces [38].

Initial research has focused on the only known complete set of data on capability variation for the population publically available through the UK Office of National Statistics [18]. This representative national data was from a UK disability follow-up (DFS) survey of over 7,000 individuals carried out in 1997 and was intended to establish the prevalence and severity of quality of life problems arising from functional impairments [8], (1997). It used a methodology devised for a number of partial surveys of Family resources and disability carried out by the UK Office of Population Censuses and Surveys [12]. The 1996–1997 survey used a self-report scaling approach, where respondents answered question items that were intended to locate their levels of functional impairment on a set of scales that were then used to calculate an overall index of severity of disability. The scales used included specific question items addressing functional capabilities, such as vision, hearing, dexterity, reaching and stretching, locomotion, intellectual function and communication. A number of less relevant scales related to areas such as continence, digestion and scarring were deemed more indirectly related to product interaction. Despite a mismatch between these disability-based scales and the requirements of functional capability analysis, recent research developments have successfully deconstructed this data set enabling derived values to be used in a psychological scaling approach to a product audit procedure. Hence, visual demand can be ascertained by asking designers to estimate the visual demand of the product feature on a visual scale with anchor points describing viewing text of different sizes [47]. Similarly, physical demand may be estimated by making comparison judgments with question items involving picking up pins or lifting objects and walking set distances. These judgments are indexed to the survey items of the original data set to yield estimates of numbers of individuals excluded at a given scale level [48]. In GUIDE these quantitative estimates have been used to estimate proportions of impairment as capability ranges in the older age groups.

However, despite their utility, the DFS survey scale items were compiled from sets of items devised by a chosen set of knowledgeable judges. One weakness of this approach, however, was the poor match of the Intellectual function survey items with cognitive capability. In particular, the survey scales were defined by judges who were practitioners and therapists, and focused on complex everyday tasks requiring intellect, rather than on current theories of cognitive function [24]. Furthermore, the resulting lack of correlation between items and scales and between individual judges led the survey designers to construct a scale that simply summed the numbers of intellectual problems selected form a undifferentiated list. An analysis of the requirements for analytical inclusive design scales carried out by Persad et al. highlighted this weaknesses of the survey scale functional assessment approach and discussed the requirements for improved capability measures [35]. For example, the survey's visual scale gave estimates of the individual's global level of visual functioning along a visual capability dimension. This was done by combining the responses to graded sets of items that addressed particular functions selected by practitioners, such as reading and person recognition. Persad hypothesised that a more accurate approach would be to use objective measures of low-level functional capability, in conjunction with a model relating these low-level capabilities and their combination. This would be used to predict high-level task performances, such as recognising a screen display setting, selecting a button or menu item.

An alternative approach would be to use psychological scaling as a method of obtaining precise estimates of visual and motor functional demand from specific product features. This has been investigated in more recent development of the inclusive design scales in order to quantify sensory and physical functions [48]. However, an further alternative, used in GUIDE core and framework, described in this book, takes a different starting point: namely, that of using accurately collected user data to developing a predictive model in the functional domain. The antecedents of this theoretical approach were outlined by Langdon et al. (2010) [23], and are described elsewhere in the light of associated empirical findings.

3.2 User Models vs. Usability

A model can be defined as "a simplified representation of a system or phenomenon with any hypotheses required to describe the system or explain the phenomenon, often mathematically". The concept of modelling is widely used in different disciplines of science and engineering ranging from models of neurons or different brain regions in neurology to construction model in architecture or model of universe in theoretical physics. Modelling human or human systems is widely used in different branches of physiology, psychology and ergonomics. A few of these models are termed as user models when their purpose is to design better consumer products. By definition a user model is a representation of the knowledge and preferences of users [1].

There is therefore a case for the development of frameworks that synthesise theories, models and findings from other fields into integrated approaches. This is instead of local theories that tend to identify contradictory hypotheses in a constrained theoretical context and test for these in a specific experimental domain. The creation of such frameworks fall more naturally to engineering and clinical communities [40] and this is consistent with the trends in computer science od software development. Also, the accompanying hybrid methodologies that are developed combine rigorous observation, quantification and computational modelling, often drawing on techniques from natural observation and qualitative research.

A good example of this general approach is the earlier work of Jacko and Vitense (2001) who justify the development of a novel conceptual framework directed towards user profile modelling that takes into account disability [17]. Taking the ability to access information as a fundamental requirement, they assembled a number of elements based on a comprehensive review of existing literature. Using this they then developed two classifications of functional ability and impairment in order to supplement conventional user profiles for the ultimate purpose of constructing a user model for accessible ICT design of handheld and wireless devices. Arguing that designers must have an understanding of impairments and associated functional abilities, the framework describes an approach based on the use, in the first instance, of impairment classification to drive an outline of capability with reference to specific cognitive, perceptual and physical abilities. This is accompanied by a mapping of functional abilities to current technologies with a focus on the cost-benefits analysis of whether specific technologies can benefit impaired users. Finally, they propose that this information is used to enhance conventional individual user profiles that may contain further rich information on needs, skills, preferences and habits and could be used adaptively in a user model. A case study example relates to a common impairment of vision, that of age-related degeneration of the retina. Since central vision loss is common in this case, they identify abilities such as near visual acuity, depth perception, night vision and colour discrimination that are likely to be degraded. A general user profile could be constructed from this information that may then be utilised by a user model. This, in turn, could make assumptions about the effects of degradation of these abilities in order to identify a number of adaptive configurations and styles. These would then impact GUI design variables, such as font size, colours and the use of speech input and output. This rationale is entirely consistent with the HCD development strategy of GUIDE.

However, one issue not completely addressed by this conceptual framework is the variability of pathology, impairment and abilities within the context of the unique individual. The authors proscribe adaption but the means for specifying the nature and configurations of adaption for success at the individual level are unclear. In particular, for example, the complexities of the interaction between perceptual, cognitive and movement cognition are not fully understood, as is exemplified by consideration of how learning takes place during the development of skills with newly experienced interfaces and how this relates to prior experience and performance.

Other researchers have attempted the rigorous modeling of inclusive human performance and tested this by using a detailed quantification of a range of human capabilities. Perhaps the best example is Kondraske's Elemental Resources Model (ERM) of human performance [19]. This is based on a calculation of compatibility by utilising resource-demand constructs such as visual acuity, contrast sensitivity, working memory capacity, force generation and movement capabilities, for a set of basic functions. Over a number of studies, Kondraske explored the relationships between high-level measurements of performance and low-level performance resources such as specific perceptual, cognitive and motor abilities. In conclusion, warning that correlations and regressions cannot capture the complexity of such relationships, he proposed a resource economic system performance model based on the likelihood of limitations in specific resource utilisations and the common non-linear thresholds that resulted from combining the measured variables [19].

The aim of such techniques has been to find the variables that have the highest correlations to higher level constructs. This is to say, which variables are mostly responsible for performance. This is a conventional approach in human factors and ergonomics for creating predictive models. However, its practice requires large enough numbers of cases to achieve statistical significance for multiple regressions [35]. Alternatively, as is described in more detail in Chap. 4, representative samples of specific impairment groups can be tested in capability tasks and the resulting values used to calibrate a user model capable of user simulation using hidden Markov algorithms and perceptual models. Such an approach was developed and implemented in the GUIDE framework as the GUIDE Simulator and User Model. This approach is dependent on validation using the statistical similarity of the model's performance and the originally sampled groups' capability performance.

3.2.1 How User Models Can Help

The GUIDE framework for adaption of its interface to specific users is based on user modelling. This is based on the principal that detailed interaction of demand with variable levels of reduced capability in extra-ordinary interactions [30] may be quantifiable using simplified approaches tested using user modeling techniques such as GOMS and ACT/R. This could give rise to a better understanding of the design principles applicable to designing interfaces for variable cognitive capability.

Models such as ACT-R will be essential to address the effectiveness of the proposed inclusive models for quantification as predictive tools for analytical exclusion auditing of alternative designs for inclusive populations. It is acknowledged that such an approach may not capture unique or idiosyncratic variation in capability due to other aspects of ageing or impairment. For example, as has been already mentioned that Newell et al. argue that it may not be possible for modeling to distinguishing the relative effectiveness of two Augmented communication (AAC) input interfaces [27]. It may not be possible to operationalise all the user's responses during an interaction although modeling can be used to instantiate various alternatives. The value of the quantitative accuracy in cognitive modeling may lie in its generality. This is not conducive to modeling the high variability found in impairment in the wider population but models could be varied to characterise different types of user. Specific or extreme users may require specially structured models and these can be accommodated by the modeling approach. Complex architectures such as ACT-R are capable of modeling errors, parallel processing and ranges and clusters of performance capability [16]. On the other hand, insights from the validation of the modeling process may yield better models of impaired interaction, particularly if cognitive impairment is considered explicitly. It is unclear whether alternative approaches to theorising about individual capability and performance would be more accurate or successful. The unknown or additional unconsidered factors such as specific cognitive impairments, social and emotional factors or communication disorders may affect the ways in which demand from design features can exclude users. These are not predicted by conventional user models [27]. However, in principle, these factors would be made more salient by the qualitative and quantitative mismatch between the model set-up, the specific predictions made and the observed user behaviour during experimental product trials with ageing and impaired users. Insights gained from these mismatches would then be used to develop better models.

The principal difference between conventional user modeling and modeling for inclusive demand is the necessity to deal with extraordinary ranges of perceptual, cognitive and movement capability in the prediction of performance with product interfaces. An important consequence of successful development of the framework and development of interactive software based on the sort of cognitive model intended, will be that developers need not have a detailed understanding of impairment in order to find out where aspects of their designs may exclude users with a certain level of capability. Nor, it is intended, will it be necessary for them to carry out expensive and time-consuming user trials with numerous participants. However, the importance of also relating the model to the knowledge and information that comes from health practitioners, the clinical and therapeutic disciplines, and design practice, cannot be underestimated. These will need to be incorporated into any tools developed using analytical inclusive design. Hence, user information and indexed knowledge, in the form of personas, video and presentation of key design and user capability issues, should be provided in documentation to contextualise the development process. In particular, the importance of variability in capability, within individuals and within the population should be stressed, in order to capture the diversity of older and impaired populations. Information about the social and economic context of interaction should also be available and linked to the adaption analysis. Ultimately, the utility of the framework will be judged by the developers' experimental tests of the effectiveness of inclusion resulting from the system adaptions with users, and levels of user satisfaction.

3.3 Case Study: Interactive Digital TV

The GUIDE project pursued a user-centred design (UCD) approach on the level of end-user interaction. End user requirements for ageing and those people with impairments have been collected using a mixed methods approach based on the advantages of triangulation of data sources [9, 20]. In essence, this approach does not commit to a single source of data or a single data collection approach. Instead data is collected from multiple approaches, for example: literature review, quantitative data analysis of data from forums, user trials, user surveys, and questionnaires, qualitative analysis of observational data from user forums or interviews, video from user trials and usage ethnography. A triangulated approach then seeks to establish the predominant weight of evidence on the basis of agreement or disagreement between sources knowing the strengths and limitations of the methods and methodologies. The studies employed, contributed to the empirical triangulated approach, employing a range of methods that are capable of independent results. This allowed findings to be cross-checked against each other, helped to balance the advantages and disadvantages of the individual methods, and obtained a spectrum of views at different levels of objectivity [9, 20]. In the case of GUIDE the framing of the project as a design problem constrains the triangulation and assists it by directing the focus of comparison on the design of the final interactions between user, system, technology, and usage context.

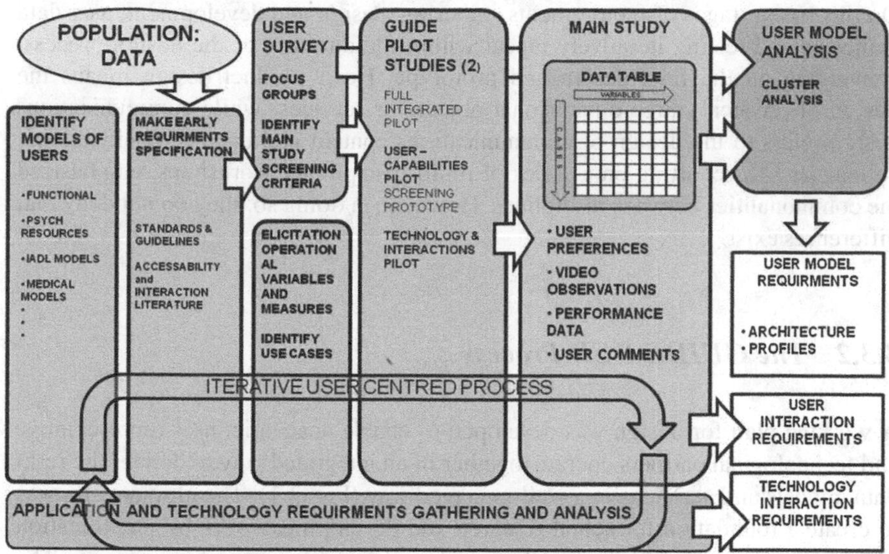

Fig. 3.1 The iterative basis of the user centered design process in GUIDE

An overview of the particular methods used is shown in Fig. 3.1. The sampling strategy employed was opportunistic, and stratified, choosing data sources according to convenience and resource limitations. In particular, much of the work took advantage of empirical and observational trials. However, the combination of multiple sources permits triangulation and thus increased validity and reliability of qualitative findings. In the case of GUIDE, the framing of the project as a design problem constrains the triangulation and assists it by directing the focus of comparison on the design of the final interactions between user, system, technology and usage context. Establishing the requirements of end users is intrinsically linked to the User Centred Design (UCD) process. In particular, requirements specification is an important part of defining and planning the variables to be varied and measured and the technology use cases to be addressed during the interactions in the user trials.

3.3.1 Engineering Design vs Human Centered Design

There is a great deal of variation between design disciplines, particularly between the main disciplines: engineering, product and communications design. Engineering Design generally adopts a highly prescriptive sequence of stages including requirements analysis, now current in Standards such as those of the DIN or VDI. Modern rapid-prototyping approaches such as that adopted by GUIDE utilize a spiral iterative design stages rather than a waterfall or concurrent stage model.

On this basis, stages of requirements gathering, design and development, user data gathering and testing iteratively repeat within the duration of the design process, converging on the final design and prototype. Here, product design means the design of physical, three-dimensional objects or services, while communications design refers to the design of communications content and media. Blackwell and colleagues [4], reporting on a series of multi-disciplinary workshops, emphasized the commonalities between disciplines. However, in doing so, they do not deny that differences exist.

3.3.2 The GUIDE UCD Process

A working plan for design was developed to enable academic, user-representative and technological partners operate together in an integrated way to deliver the right data, models and activities in a well-managed way (Fig. 3.1). The ultimate aim was to create a foundation for actual research and development work by identification of requirements from users as well as application and framework developers. The goal was the elements and components of the GUIDE framework and applications, specifically, the User Model in the form of clustered personas and profiles along with an algorithm and data structure that would support its use in the GUIDE framework. This plan was formulated during the first months of the project and adopted as it integrated iterative cycles of both design and the trials extra-ordinary user capability that were expected. The use of the proposed iDTV interfaces for testing usage cases of interaction and adaptions also conveniently provided test conditions for experimental trials.

3.3.3 User Requirements in Design Decisions at Development – Some Lessons Learnt

The GUIDE development approach is based on the concurrent requirements management process described in more detail in the next chapter. The basis of this is that requirements established during the user centered design process are incorporated into the software design in parallel with the collection of data from users regarding the efficacy of the interventions made in the latest cycle of design development. This process, permits continuing continuous updating of requirements after development cycles, requirements coverage can be seen as a metric for validation for the system development and design effort.

The primary aim of early stages in the process depicted in Fig. 3.1 required literature review and collection of user data from current interaction and accessibility literature. This was accompanied by early paper or PowerPoint based focus groups and small scale low-fidelity studies using elderly users. The main study and subsequent iterations of user trials were based on experimental trials combined with video analysis and retrospective protocol analysis. The initial data was aggregated and used to specify the items for a user survey carried out over the entire GUIDE user sample. The aim was to make accurate objective and subjective measures of perceptual, cognitive and physical capability of each user enabling selection of users based on a stratified sampling strategy. Furthermore this approach allowed comparisons of survey results with trial performance. Details of the survey, results and other HCD outcomes in GUIDE are available on the GUIDE website. The original aim of the process was to create a table of technical requirements for development, however due to the large volume of usability issues generated by the first pilot trials this was annotated with all requirements including those generated by UCD and usability considerations. This then unified the technical and UCD process as it was found to be necessary for developers to consider usability issues such as: speed of system response during controller manipulation and gesture detection, and lack of system feedback. The aim was to ensure programmers would prioritise elderly usability in their continuing development.

Two major issues emerged during the iterations of design and user trial cycles. First, the recruitment and management of older users for trials, especially in a number of different countries (UK, Germany, Spain) required considerably more resources than were specified for software development alone. Secondly, sampling required a stratification of users into groups to represent the proportions of specific impairments. This was managed using an analysis based on a combination of type of impairments and their severity required for a complete sample along with predicted disability levels from Inclusive design data sets. The survey was used as a selection and filtering tool. Significant numbers of users were required leading to strain on resources and time. A parallel difficulty with technical development was the lack of fidelity of the experimental system due to the early stages of development. The Low fidelity of the GUI and interactions used in trials were directly associated with poor usability outcomes in that speed of response was slow and accessibility features were not fully implemented. This reduced the usefulness of the trial results for improving usability and adaption. Because of this, the requirements generated by the UCD process were generally prioritised lower than development as the primary goal was seen as making the system more robust and faster in response in order to satisfy basic usability requirements for older users. Furthermore it was assumed by developers that implementation of adaptions and multimodal channels would solve the interaction problems that elderly and impaired users were experiencing. However, this was not the case, as was confirmed by a strict no-intervention usability study carried out on the system at a later stage. It may therefore be that linking UCD and development process in the manner described in GUIDE (Fig. 3.1) creates both advantages and disadvantages. The main issue may be that developers are generally reliant on validation studies at the end of a development phase rather than iterative evaluation during development. This then decouples usability and accessibility issues from development making it harder to ensure requirements are satisfied.

3.4 HCD and Validation

There is a complex relationship between the level of detail of validation against its generality. Unfortunately this implies that full validation is very often beyond the resource of a project such as GUIDE, as for example, it was attempted to validate the GUIDE system for all European countries. The cost in time and resources increase with increasing levels of validation required: For example, as part of their simulator model development for the GUIDE framework, Cambridge carried out detailed Simulator validation studies of disabled users, performance at specific tasks. Such trials were very costly and time consuming but valuable for predicting specific circumstances through their input into general models [3, 22].

The GUIDE HCD trials attempt to predict the performance of a large number of potential users from a minimal sample. This corresponds to weak generalisation but ensures good design, based on mild and moderately impaired users, with optimal cost. If the results achieved for the anticipated user groups can be validated as good, it will anticipate the results future projects like ICT-PSP which aims to validate technologies already developed with samples about 5,000 users in different European countries.

3.4.1 Guide Specific Requirements

GUIDE aimed to apply iterative user centered design in order to yield a good design representing users' needs, wants and preferences. A realistic goal was a framework implementations that will be generalisable and effective for EU "mild to moderately impaired users", particularly the elderly. Users will require an overall interaction experience that they want, find agreeable and feel is effective. Guide has adopted an inclusive user centered design method to address many of these issues, such as that of representing users' needs and wants, as well as to ensure an iterative improvement of design during the development process. By necessity this required tradeoffs to allow technology development decisions and to make it possible to define the sample of users who may be included. It should also be remembered that GUIDE had incorporated into it a user modelling approach that enables generalization of the frameworks responses beyond the original user validation sets. GUIDE adaption further permits the system to adjust its generality. The accuracy of these approaches is unknown. For example, the model is dependent on the validity of the user modelling process and adaption also is subject to the same constraints.

Because of the resulting uncertainty, in order to measure validity, further techniques are necessary, including: the establishment of Face validity from accessibility system researchers and reviewers as well as developers and end users; the measurement of metrics of user performance taken with, without GUIDE interventions; the qualitative and observational gathering of societal and ecologically valid factors to assess the impact of the system on end-users in their natural home environments or with developers at work. The effectiveness of such validation partially depends on procedures for changing the systems performance in response to metrics that are used. One further way of validating GUIDE's approach and findings would be a comparison between the GUIDE development and HCD process and that of a similar project with the same overall goals. Serendipitously, such a comparison was possible with the EU MyUI project also aimed at developing a self adapting interface based on a completely different user modelling approach [25].

3.5 Comparison with MyUI Project

3.5.1 Evaluation of Adaptive Systems

The GUIDE & MyUI Collaboration on End User Validation: A Joint validation plan document describes the details of joint validation. Van Velsen et al. reviewed 63 experimental studies where adaptive systems were evaluated. Most concerned personal computer applications that were not intended for use by older or impaired populations [44].

With respect to 'personalised systems' and referring to previous researchers findings [14, 15] their criticisms centre on the following specific design implications:

- The weakness of the widespread use of a non-personalised system as a comparison condition
- User bias towards personalised systems
- Experimenter effects (users may guess hypothesis or play "good subject")
- Shortness of experimental trials when measuring the full effect of adaption
- Irrelevance to overall usability
- Lack of Ecological validity of lab-based trials
- Status resulting from use of varying fidelity prototypes
- Pitfalls of using quantitative and data log analysis
- Lack of compatibility of expert review with user data

On the other hand they report positive assessment for various evaluative methods such as:

- Questionnaires
- Interviews and focus groups
- Thinking aloud protocols (concurrent protocol analysis)
- The use of triangulated data (e.g. quantitative measures plus questionnaires plus expert review)

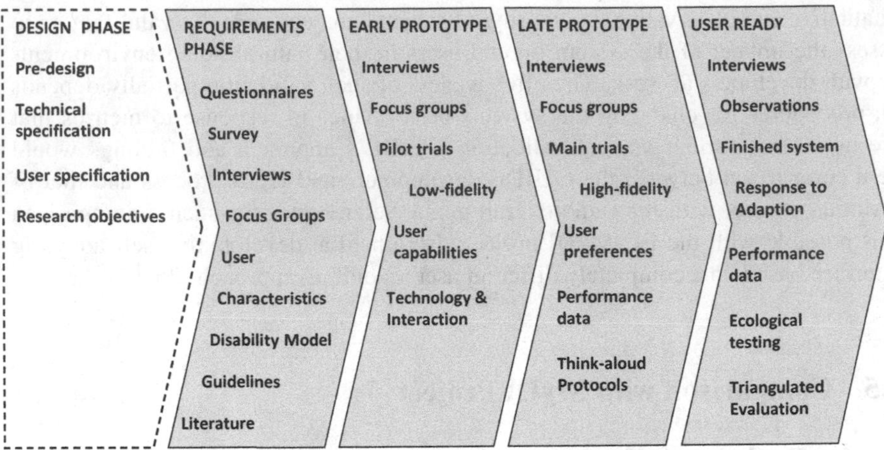

Fig. 3.2 Proposed appropriate approaches at differing iterative design stages based on GUIDE and MyUI (After Van Velsen et al. [44])

3.5.2 Discussion – Applicability to Research and Development

These considerations of Evaluation and other literature cited above suggests that a triangulated approach [9] combining multiple methods may be most effective and that this should include protocol analysis, observation over long durations in ecologically valid context. Justifications are given for the use of various qualitative measures in a previous section. In addition, as discussed above, the goal of evaluation is not equivalent to that of validation, although many of the conclusions in terms of operationalisation of studies may be the same. The rationale for validation in GUIDE, detailed above, reached similar conclusions to the Van Velsen review and proposes methodological approach based on triangulation (Fig. 3.2).

The testing or validation of adaption for ageing and impairment, rather than personalisation is not subject to the same criticisms as it is possible to conceive of and technically present a non-adapted interface that is not simply a weaker version of the adapted interface. In fact, it may be qualitatively and quantitatively different but there is no reason to suppose that it is somehow ‘weaker’. On the contrary, it is assumed in the GUIDE/MyUI adaption approaches that the adapted interface may not look attractive or superior to others than that for which its adaptations apply. This may be due to the enlargement of buttons and inter-button spacing’s, the use of colours to combat colour blindness; the use of input adaption to combat physical movement problems, and the modification of sound for hearing issues. Finally, the approach to the suitability of particular methods to design stages is presented in Van Velsen et al. [44] with a simplistic account that does not take into account the complexity of iterative user-centered design. As the GUIDE approach describe above illustrates, evidence from differing stages of prototyping can be fed back to the design process continuously, its value being assessed on the basis of the quality of the data resulting from various levels of prototyping. Different approaches and considerations will be most effective at each progressive design stage. The criteria for the effectiveness of sampling is discussed above in the context of an Inclusive Design approach, further illustrating the difficulties arising from the diversity of capability and the introduction of inaccuracies in obtaining quantitative measures as a result of sampling. This underlines the necessity for triangulated mixture of qualitative, usability and quantitative measures. For this reason GUIDE has employed a number of measures including usability, retrospective protocol analysis and quantitative controlled trials of adaption. It also planned ecologically valid trials of long term use on people's homes.

3.6 Future Scope

A new approach to interaction design is required when the anticipated users are elderly or impaired and the system to be developed is adaptive to these impairments. This new Inclusive Interaction Design should be based on the approaches discussed including yoking of technical requirements to user centered design requirement and the use of a triangulated approach to data collection with trials at different stages and as the design stages proceed through iterations of the design process.

Future research on adaptive interfaces can take advantage of the findings of the GUIDE and MyUI studies in order to maximize the effectiveness of UCD combined with Development trials. This should take the form of triangulated studies aggregating and interpreting data from questionnaires, experimental trials, and retrospective protocol analysis during the design cycle, and evaluating in the light of users' degree of acceptance in daily use in their own homes.

References

1. Benyon, D., & Murray, D. (1993). Applying user modeling to human computer interaction design. *Artificial Intelligence Review, 7*(3–4), 199–225.
2. Bichard, J., Langdon, P., & Coleman, R. (2007). 'Does my stigma look big in this?' Considering acceptability and desirability in the inclusive design of technology products. In *Coping with Diversity, 4th international conference on universal access in human-computer interaction, UAHCI 2007, Beijing, China, 4554* (pp. 622–631). Springer, Berlin/Heidelberg.
3. Biswas, P., Robinson, P., & Langdon, P. (2012). Designing inclusive interfaces through user modelling and simulation. *International Journal of Human-Computer Interaction, 9(1)*.
4. Blackwell, A. D., Eckert, C. M., Bucciarelli, L. L., & Earl, C. F. (2009). Witnesses to design: a phenomenology of comparative design. *Design Issues, 25*(1), 36–47.
5. Charness, N., & Bosman, E. A. (1992). Human factors and age. In F. I. M. Craik & T. A. Salthouse (Eds.), *The handbook of aging and cognition* (Ch 10, pp. 495–551). Hillsdale: Erlbaum.
6. Coleman, R. (2001). Designing for our future selves. In W. F. E. Preiser & E. Ostroff (Eds.), *Universal design handbook* (pp. 4.1–4.25). New York: McGraw-Hill.

7. Czaja, S. J., & Lee, C. C. (2008). Information technology and older adults, Chapter 39. In A. Sears & J. A. Jacko (Eds.), *The human-computer interaction handbook: Fundamentals, evolving technologies, and emerging applications human factors and ergonomics* (2nd ed., Section 5, Designing for Diversity, pp. 811–82). CDC, Taylor & Francis.
8. DFS-SN4090. (1997). *Disability follow-up to the 1996/97 [FRS] Family Resources Survey*. http://www.esds.ac.uk/findingData/snDescription.asp?sn=4090. Accessed 29 Jan 2013.
9. Flick, U. (2006). *An introduction to qualitative research*. London: Sage.
10. Freudenthal, T. D. (1998). *Learning to use interactive devices; age differences in the reasoning process*. PhD thesis, Eindhoven University of Technology, Eindhoven.
11. Gender Ratio. http://en.wikipedia.org/wiki/List_of_countries_by_sex_ratio. Accessed 29 Jan 2013.
12. Grundy, E., Ahlburg, D., Ali, M., Breeze, E., & Sloggett, A. (1999). *Disability in Great Britain: results from the 1996/97 disability follow-up to the family resources survey*. London: UK Department of Social Security, Corporate Document Services. ISBN 1-84123-119-3.
13. Haigh, R. (1993). The ageing process: a challenge for design. *Applied Ergonomics, 24*(1), 9–14.
14. Höök, K. Evaluating the utility and usability of an adaptive hypermedia system. SICS, Box 1263, 164 28 Kista, Sweden.
15. Höök, K. (2000). Steps to take before intelligent user interfaces become real. *Interacting with Computers, 12*(4), 409–426.
16. Horstmann, H. M., & Levine, S. P. (1990). Modeling of user performance with computer access and augmentative communication systems for handicapped people. *Augmentative and Alternative Communication, 6*, 231–241.
17. A review and reappraisal of information technologies within a conceptual framework for individuals with disabilities. *Universal Access in the Information Society (UAIS), 1*,56–76.
18. Keates, S., & Clarkson, J. (2003). *Countering design exclusion – an introduction to inclusive design*. London: Springer.
19. Kondraske, G. V. (2000). A working model for human system-task interfaces. In: J. D. Bronzino (Ed.), *The biomedical engineering handbook* (2nd ed., Vol. 2, pp. 147–141 – 147–118). CRC Press.
20. Langdon, P., Aurisicchio, M., Clarkson, P. J., & Wallace, K. (2003). *An integrated ethnographic and empirical methodology in a study of knowledge searches in aerospace design*. In International conference on engineering design.
21. Langdon, P. M., Lewis, T., & Clarkson, P. J. (2007). The effects of prior experience on the use of consumer products. *Universal Access in the Information Society*, *6(2)*, 179.
22. Langdon, P. M., Lewis, T., & Clarkson, P. J. (2010). Prior experience in the use of domestic product interfaces. *Universal Access in the Information Society*, *9(3)*, 209. ISSN:1615–5289.
23. Langdon, P., Persad, U., & Clarkson, P. J. (2010). Developing a model of cognitive interaction for analytical inclusive design evaluation. *Interacting with Computers*, *22(6)*,510–529.
24. Martin, J., & Elliot, D. (1992). Creating an overall measure of severity of disability for the office of population census and surveys disability survey. *Journal of the Royal Statistical Society Series A, 155*(1), 121–140.
25. MyUi Project. http://www.myui.eu/. Accessed 30 Jan 2013.
26. Neilson, J. (1993). *Usability engineering*. San Francisco: Morgan Kaufmann. ISBN 0-12-518406-9.
27. Newell, A. F., Arnott, J. L., & Waller, A. (1992). On the validity of user-modeling in AAC: comments on Horstmann and Levine (1990). *Augmentative and Alternative Communication, 8*, 89–92.
28. Newell, A. F. (2006). Older people as a focus for inclusive design. *Gerontechnology, 4*(4), 190–199.
29. Newell, A. F., Carmichael, A., Gregor, P., Alm, N., & Waller, A. (2008). Information Technology for cognitive support, Chapter 41. In A. Sears & J. A. Jacko (Eds.), *The*

human-computer interaction handbook: Fundamentals, evolving technologies, and emerging applications human factors and ergonomics (2nd ed., Section 5, Designing for Diversity, pp. 811–882). CDC, Taylor & Francis.

30. Newell, A. F. (1995). Extra-ordinary human computer operation. In A. D. N. Edwards (Ed.), *Extra-ordinary human-computer interactions*. Cambridge: Cambridge University Press.
31. Newell, A. F., et al. (1997). Human computer interfaces for people with disabilities. In M. Helander, T. K. Landauer, & P. Prabhu (Eds.), *Handbook of human computer interaction* (pp. 813–824). ISBN: 0-444-1862-6.
32. Nichols, T. A., Rogers, W. A., & Fisk, A. D. (2006). Design for aging. In G. Salvendy (Ed.), *Handbook of human factors and ergonomics* (3rd ed., pp. 1418–1445). Hoboken: Wiley.
33. Oliver, M. (2004). If I had a hammer: the social model in action. In J. Swain, S. French, C. Barnes, & C. Thomas (Eds.), *Disabling barrier; enabling environments* (2nd ed.). London/Thousand Oaks: Sage. ISBN 07619 42645.
34. Ormerod, M., & Newton, R. A. (2005). Moving beyond accessibility: the principles of universal (inclusive) design as a dimension in nD modelling of the built environment. *Architectural Engineering and Design Management, 1*(2), 103–110.
35. Persad, U., Langdon, P., & Clarkson, J. (2007). Characterising user capabilities to support inclusive design evaluation. *Universal Access in the Information Society, 6*(2), 119–135.
36. Petrie, H. (2001). Accessibility and usability requirements for ICTs for disabled and elderly people: a functional classification approach. In C. Nicolle & J. G. Abascal (Eds.), *Inclusive guidelines for human computer interaction*. London: Taylor & Francis. ISBN 0-748409-48-3.
37. Porter, J. M., Case, K., Marshall, R., Gyi, D. E., & Sims, R. E. (2004). 'Beyond Jack and Jill': designing for individuals using HADRIAN. *International Journal of Industrial Ergonomics, 33*(3), 249–264.
38. Porter, J. M., Marshall, R., Freer, M., & Case, K. (2004). SAMMIE: a computer aided ergonomics design tool. In N. J. Delleman, C. M. Haslegrave, & D. B. Chaffin (Eds.), *Working postures and movement tools for evaluation and engineering* (pp. 454–462). Boca Raton: CRC Press LLC.
39. Rabbitt, P. M. A. (1993). Does it all go together when it goes? The Nineteenth Bartlett Memorial Lecture. *The Quarterly Journal of Experimental Psychology, 46*(3), 385–434.
40. Reason, J. (1990). *Human error*. Cambridge/New York: Cambridge University Press.
41. Schaie, K. W. (1988). Variability in cognitive functions in the elderly: implications for societal participation. *Basic Life Sciences, 43*, 191–211.
42. Scriven, M. (1967). The methodology of evaluation. In R. W. Tyler, R. M. Gagne, & M. Scriven (Eds.), *Perspectives of curriculum evaluation* (pp. 39–83). Chicago: Rand McNally.
43. Story, M. F., Mueller, J. L., & Mace, R. L. (1998). *The universal design file*. Raleigh: North Carolina State University, The Centre for Universal Design.
44. Van Velsen, L., Van der Geest, T., Klaassen, R., & Steehouder, M. (2008). User-centered evaluation of adaptive and adaptable systems: a literature review. *The Knowledge Engineering Review, 23*(3), 261–281.
45. Vanderheiden, G. C., & Vanderheiden, K. (1992). *Guidelines for the design of consumer products to increase their accessibility to people with disabilities*. Madison: Trace R & D Center.
46. World Health Organization. (2001). *International classification of functioning, disability and health (ICF)*. Geneva: Author.
47. Waller, S. D., Williams, E. Y., Langdon, P. M., & Clarkson, P. J. (2010). Understanding the co-occurrence of ability loss. In P. M. Langdon, P. J. Clarkson, & P. Robinson (Eds.), *Designing inclusive interactions* (pp. 35–45). London: Springer. ISBN 9-781849-961653.
48. Waller, S. D., Williams, E. Y., Langdon, P. M., & Clarkson, P. J. (2010). Quantifying exclusion for tasks related to product interaction. In P. M. Langdon, P. J. Clarkson, & P. Robinson (Eds.), *Designing inclusive interactions* (pp. 57–69). London: Springer. ISBN 9-781849-961653.

Chapter 4
Designing TV Interaction for the Elderly – A Case Study of the Design for All Approach

José Coelho, Tiago Guerreiro, and Carlos Duarte

Abstract Television based applications are different from traditional desktop applications, even if both can be Web applications. The distinct context surrounding both types of applications influences interaction and is the main driver for treating them differently. As such, not all Desktop design guidelines can be applied to the TV context. Additionally, when focusing on older adults it is mandatory to consider different interaction contexts. Multimodal interfaces can help by offering an interaction more flexible and robust, and by compensating for specific age-related impairments. If modern TV interaction is developed having concerns for motor, sensorial and cognitive impairments (design for all), and considering elderly users in the design process by taking a User Centred Design approach, the results can benefit everyone, social exclusion barriers can be dropped at the same time as usability gains. With all these concerns in mind, this chapter builds on the knowledge gained from designing, prototyping and evaluating different TV applications, supported by multimodal interaction, and aimed at the elderly population, to offer guidelines specific for designing TV interaction.

4.1 Introduction: The Elderly and the TV

The rapid increase of new TV-based systems and applications prevents users with certain impairments or different levels of technology awareness and expertise from accessing the same information as others. By 2050, elderly people will represent 26 % of the developed countries' population. Living in this constantly evolving world is getting harder, leaving them no time to adapt to modern technology from which, sooner or later, their well being and social inclusion will dramatically depend.

J. Coelho (✉) • T. Guerreiro
Faculty of Sciences, University of Lisbon, Lisboa, Portugal
e-mail: jcoelho@di.fc.ul.pt; tjvg@di.fc.ul.pt

C. Duarte
Department of Informatics, University of Lisbon, Lisboa, Portugal
e-mail: cad@di.fc.ul.pt

P. Biswas et al. (eds.), *A Multimodal End-2-End Approach to Accessible Computing*, Human–Computer Interaction Series, DOI 10.1007/978-1-4471-6708-2_4

Crystallized Intelligence refers to the knowledge and life experience of a person. It develops until old age and can be well trained [1]. However, Fluid Intelligence, which refers to reasoning and concentration, decreases with old age [1]. With the decrease of Fluid Intelligence, the ability to cope with new and complex situations decreases too. Additionally, not only cognitive performance, but also motor and sensorial capabilities differ from individual to individual and change with aging processes [2, 3]. The use of technical systems, like the TV, requires both Crystallized and Fluid Intelligences. For that reason, inclusive systems should be designed and developed centred on the end-users and their needs to assure the product fits their psychomotor level and achieves high motivation for use [4].

In the last years, research concentrated on the difficulties of older adults when using new technologies [5–7] and more specifically in age-related decline in vision and hearing, compensational strategies [8] and product guidelines [9]. This is even more relevant when considering the important role modern television has in the daily living of elderly people, especially in preventing social exclusion or guaranteeing they stay adequately informed about the world.

According to a recent study, older people are – contrary to what the stereotypes say – willing to use new technologies [7]. Their level of acceptance even increases if they receive the adequate training and if the benefits of the system are clearly understood [5]. A positive attitude towards technology [10] or self-efficacy beliefs about their capabilities [11] also contributes to increase the use of new technologies.

Historically, there always have been strong assumptions that users could adapt to whatever is built. Systems have always relied on instructions and training in order to influence users to interact in a manner that matches the system's processing capabilities. As systems evolved, complexity rose, causing more interaction difficulties. This is especially true for older people because of age related changes in functional abilities such as psychomotor, perceptive and cognitive skills [6]. Multimodal interfaces, however, are composed of recognition-based technologies capable of interpreting human interaction patterns like speech, gaze, touch and movement patterns. Their main ways of interaction demand from the user what are already highly automatized natural skills. As a result, for the user, requirements are simplified and the system is easier to understand and interact with, even if many of these natural modalities are not under full conscious control [12, 13] and may vary with individual differences [14]. In fact, application of multimodal mechanisms in the development of user interfaces has a strong impact in their expressiveness [15], usability [16, 17], flexibility [15, 18], and robustness [19–21]. For all these reasons, users have a preference for interacting multimodally across a wide variety of different application domains, being most pronounced in visual-spatial domains [16, 18]. When considering that different modes of communication are used differently by different people [22, 23], multimodal interfaces allow the user to exercise selection and control over how users interact with the interface [20]. Even if only interacting multimodally for 20 % of the time [24], users manage to adapt naturally to each context by alternating between several modalities at their disposal [25, 26].

When compared to past graphical user interfaces, multimodal interfaces have the potential to accommodate a broader range of different ages, skill levels, languages, cognitive styles, and any temporary or permanent handicaps. For this reason, multimodal interfaces are especially important for elderly users, and should be considered, together with a user centred design approach, in the development of modern TV applications.

The GUIDE (Gentle User Interfaces for Elderly People) [26] project aims to achieve the necessary balance between developing multimodal adaptive applications for elderly users, while preserving TV and Set-Top Box (STB) developers and manufacturers' development efforts. Focusing always on elderly users, the project's main goal is to provide guidelines for new ways of interacting and designing TV applications, enabling multimodal interaction and supporting the use of different devices and different combinations of input and output techniques. By adapting the interaction to each user's characteristics, GUIDE tries to bring modern TV applications closer to elderly users. At the same time, by including tutorial applications it brings the elderly closer to technology.

In this chapter, the multimodal features of GUIDE will be introduced in the next section, along with the user centred design approach, which focuses on and includes users from the early stages of requirements gathering, through the design of applications and the evaluation phase. The following section presents and discusses results of user trials performed to elicit several user centred design issues, multimodal interaction aspects, developer issues and specific details on the evaluation of the multimodal adaptive framework. Based on the results of these trials, a list of concrete guidelines for the development of multimodal TV-based applications for the elderly is provided as this chapter most valuable contribution. The last section presents an overview of how these guidelines will influence the future of TV, and what could be expected as main innovations in multimodal TV, especially concerning elderly people.

4.2 The GUIDE Approach

4.2.1 Multimodal Interaction

Input modalities supported in GUIDE are based on natural ways of communicating: speech and pointing (and gestures). Complementary to these modalities, and given the TV based environment, the framework supports the usage of remote controls and haptic devices capable of providing input and output. As a result, GUIDE incorporates four main types of UI components: visual sensing and gesture interpretation (VHS); speech recognition (ASR); remote control (RC); and a tablet to be used for input as well as a second screen. Concerning output modalities, it integrates video rendering equipment (TV); audio rendering equipment (Speakers); and tablet supported video and audio rendering. The tablet is used to clone or complement information on the TV screen but essentially as a secondary display. The system is able to generate various configurable visual elements such as text, buttons for navigation purpose, images and video. Additionally, a 3D virtual character (VC) is expected to play a major role for elderly acceptance and adoption of the system, being able to complement speech output with non-verbal expressions to mimic human like communication abilities. These graphical elements allow the system to communicate with its users by illustrating, suggesting, or supporting them during the course of interaction. Both input and output modalities can be used in a combined manner to enrich interaction and reach a wide variety of users.

Without going into too much detail on the architecture of the project's multimodal adaptive framework, following the underlying processes of an interaction cycle helps to understand the multimodal interaction support in GUIDE. A user provides input through multiple devices and modalities. Interpreter modules process the signals from recognition-based modalities (e.g., a series of points from the motion sensor go through a gesture recognition engine in order to detect gestures). The signals from pointing modalities go through input adaptation modules (e.g., in order to smooth tremors from the user's hand). Then, the multimodal fusion module receives, analyses and combines these multiple streams into a single interpretation of the user command based on the user and context and in the abstract representation of the application's UI (generated by the framework in runtime with assistance from the application developer defined semantic annotations). This interpretation is sent to the dialogue manager who decides which will be the application's response. This decision is based on knowledge about the current application state and the possible actions that can be performed on the application in that state. The dialogue manager decision is fed to the multimodal fission module, which is responsible for rendering a presentation in accordance to which output to present (based on application state), the user abilities (accessed through the user model) and the interaction context (made available through the context model). The fission module takes all this information and prepares the content to render, selects the appropriate output channels and handles the synchronization, both in time and space, between channels when rendering. This rendering is then perceived by the user, which reacts to it, and starts a new cycle by providing some new input.

4.2.2 User Centred Design Process

Age related impairments are associated with a variety of causes and conditions and vary in intensity both within and between individuals. This leads to great variability and a demanding design environment that requires close attention to conflicting user requirements and a better understanding of user capabilities. User participation in design process is a fundamental premise to develop products that are suitable for people of all ages (design for all) [27]. Ideally, user involvement, and therefore evaluation of usability, should start as soon as possible in product development to avoid technical disadvantages [28, 29]. Therefore, User-Centred Design (UCD), albeit being a time-consuming approach for establishing the requirements of end users, is a precondition for user acceptance [30].

In GUIDE, end user requirements for ageing and impaired people have been collected using a mixed methods approach based on the advantages of triangulation of data sources [31, 32]. Data is collected from multiple approaches like literature studies, quantitative data analysis of data from user trials, user surveys and focus groups, qualitative analysis of observational data from user interviews, video from user trials and usage ethnography. A triangulated approach then seeks to establish the predominant weight of evidence on the basis of agreement or disagreement between sources, knowing the strengths and limitations of the methods and methodologies [33]. The studies conducted, contributed to the empirical triangulated approach, employing a range of methods that are capable of independent results. This allowed findings to be crosschecked against each other, helping to balance the advantages and disadvantages of the individual methods, and obtaining a spectrum of views at different levels of objectivity [31, 32]. The framing of the project as a design problem constrains the triangulation and assists it by directing the focus of comparison to the design of the final interactions between user, system, technology and usage context. Therefore, the particular methods were based on finding relevant results in literature studies and UI accessibility standards, performing interviews and surveys with both developers and elderly users and performing user trials with older people. From these, technical and interaction requirements have been drawn, laying the basis for the design of multimodal interfaces for elderly. The combination of multiple sources permits triangulation and thus increased validity and reliability of qualitative findings [33].

Departing from the defined basis, a working plan for design was developed with the main aim of requirements identification from users as well as application and framework developers. GUIDE human-centred design process, concerning elderly users was divided into seven main stages (Fig. 4.1):

- The first stage is the early Requirements Stage, where data from literature about models of mild to moderate impaired users and elderly users, technical specifications and standards of accessibility is collected from several sources and compiled into requirements and use cases;
- The second and third stage are the Pilot Stage and the Stakeholders Research (stage) where a guided pilot trial concerning technology and interaction, as well as two user surveys were conducted to infer primary data about the population and technical specifications relating to the use and development of multimodal interfaces;
- The fourth stage is the Initial User Study (stage), where multimodal interaction aspects and UI preferences were tested with a large number of elderly users;
- The fifth stage is the Intermediate User Study (stage), where multimodal interaction aspects were refined now in the context of the GUIDE multimodal framework, together with adaptation aspects;
- The sixth stage is the Framework Development (stage) which runs parallel to the initial and intermediate studies, and is fed by the results related with multimodality and adaptation obtained on those stages;

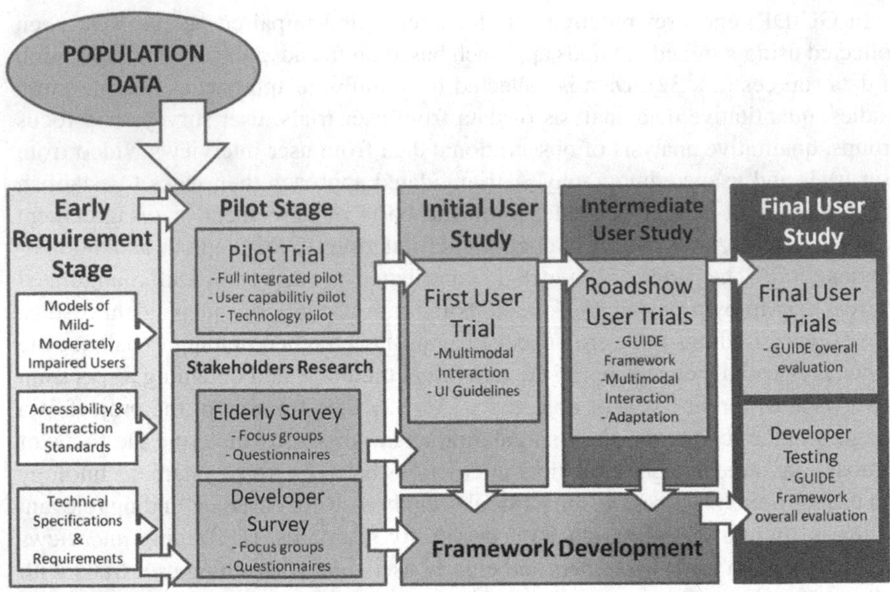

Fig. 4.1 User centered design approach for elderly users in GUIDE

- The seventh stage is the Final User Study (stage), where an overall GUIDE evaluation is performed both with elderly users to cover all multimodal and interaction aspects and with developers to test the framework development features. This last stage differs from the others as it is less focused on guaranteeing a suitable design, being a confirmatory step where all parts of the system are validated.

In the following sub-sections we describe in detail the planning of each of those stages, while in the next section we present all the guidelines extracted from each stage.

Early Requirement Stage The early requirement analysis had three main sources of information as a starting point.

1. Technical interface specifications for the reference applications in GUIDE, considering both technology and interaction contexts.
2. Requirement sources from adopted models of mild-moderately impaired and elderly users from user models, standards and literature.
3. Information related to accessibility guidelines in TV and Web based applications.

This initial stage used as input the basic interactions, usage cases and scenarios of the reference applications and technology contexts. These were combined with the chosen variables of importance from the various models of impaired users adopted in the anticipated contexts of use.

These output requirements were used as input to the next stage of pilot studies. New requirements resulting from the remaining stages of the approach were iteratively added. In the first instance, reference applications consisted of a set of applications (video conferencing, media access, tele-learning and home-automation) with a simplified set of essential basic interactions and constraints. This stage defined the use cases and interaction scenarios for these applications based on the expected usage context.

Finally this stage also specified, for each reference application, I/O devices, modes that could be used and how they can be combined. This information was fed into the pilot and user studies stages and, subsequently, the information generated during trials was documented as the basis of requirements and guidelines.

Pilot Stage The idea behind the pilot stage was to define a small design space with simplified interactions for proof-of-concept tests that comprised the usage requirements of the reference applications. A set of physical measurements and psychologically usable tasks were generated taking in account the general variables and measurements of theoretical interest resulting from the early requirement analysis phase. On the basis of this operationalized set, pilot studies were carried out in order to specify the final set of measurements to be collected in the subsequent user studies. With a small number of representative users (about 15), a fully integrated pilot study was conducted combining user capabilities measurements, tests with various GUIDE technologies, multimodal preferences, typical TV-based interactions and screening tests for the later studies. Therefore, tasks contemplated tests for visual and hearing perception, cognitive memory, speed and executive function (e.g. short term games, task speed, and learning capabilities), as well as standard physical tasks like picking up a controller and pressing OK, pointing at something, moving the arm in front or to one side, or locomotion ones like walking straight and sitting down. The results were categorized in high, medium, reduced or no impairments levels.

An important part of the pilot trials was the provision of continuous feedback allowing modification of technology, and providing valuable data for the requirements regarding capabilities, context and scenario information, allowing optimization of practical design, screening of the sample and reduction of management risk (failure to obtain a useful or complete user model for the next stages of the GUIDE project). As it was already referred, this stage has also allowed initial insights on the viability of the user interfaces for accommodating particular impairments by way of early prototypes and initial user studies.

Stakeholders Research The Stakeholders Research stage is divided in two distinct surveys with the two distinct groups of users: the elderly and the developers of TV-based applications.

Regarding the survey with elderly users, around 50 participants were chosen on the basis of the full integrated pilot and using the operational variables and measurements from the requirements analysis. The aim of the survey was to obtain data related with age-related impairments to help develop the user model component in the GUIDE framework. Qualitative information on socio-demographics, attitudes towards technology, coping styles with new technologies, daily living activities, and vision, hearing, mobility, cognitive and personality traits was collected in this initial user survey. Several tasks, some similar to the ones already performed in the pilot stage, concerning sensorial capabilities were performed. Psychologists administered a set of questions concerning the different topics, where users would typically have to rate their capabilities or feelings in face-to-face interviews.

The large numbers of variables contained in the data set were submitted to a two-stage process of analysis where correlations were made and a k-means cluster analysis [26] was performed, reducing the results to only significant data. With the results, several user profiles capable of discriminating differences between users were created. The profiles were formed by combining and grouping all modalities simultaneously such that a specific grouping represents the capabilities of users perceptual, cognitive and motor capability ranges.

Concerning the survey with developers, the general goal was to explore and understand the common practice among developers working on STBs and TV-based applications. Thus the first objective was to obtain data about current tools and APIs used in Set top box/connected TV platforms and to investigate how accessibility is perceived and applied in the industry. Secondly, we explored developer knowledge in order to identify which tools would developers need, to efficiently integrate accessibility features into their applications. Additionally, we aimed to stimulate new ideas through discussions and to identify new relationships between objects embodying GUIDE concepts and objects embodying common practice. Two focus group sessions were carried out with TV-based applications experts in a natural and interactive focus group setting. Two moderators conducted the sessions. Each session had between six and eight participants and lasted around 120 min. Sessions were initiated with presentations of scripts containing development and use cases that cover different aspects of the GUIDE project and its concepts, including requirements and proposed guidelines from the previous stages. Interactive brainstorming and discussions followed. Additionally, a questionnaire was also designed to investigate how accessibility is currently perceived and applied in the industry. The survey allowed respondents to vote on the most important features of the envisaged discussion. In total, 81 participants from 16 countries, and 30 companies all over the world, participated.

The developer focus groups along with the pilot stage assisted in the specification of the interfaces, architecture and core processes for the GUIDE usable multimodal framework.

Initial User Study The initial user study was a primary source of user requirements engineering, with the aim of observing elderly users in a lab situation interacting with a prototype of a system application, gathering quantitative and qualitative data. It allowed the identification of viable usage methods of novel and traditional UI paradigms for the different impairments in the target groups.

A technological prototype was built for these trials, which were carried out at the end of the first year of the project. The methodology followed in this study was very similar to the one in the pilot study with the difference of having a better technological setup and also some improvements in the assessment protocol.

Seventeen people (4 male and 13 female) between the ages of 55 and 84 years old (average age 65.8) participated. All of them were recruited in Spain and presented different levels of expertise in technology, as well as different levels of physical and cognitive abilities. At the beginning of each user-trial every user was presented with all possibilities of interaction and asked to perform a series of tasks related with TV interaction. The tasks were divided into several scripts concerning different types of interaction or different UI elements:

- Visual: The TV screen presented buttons on different locations. Participants were encouraged to say which location, size and inter-button spacing would suit their preferences. Afterwards, they were asked to select their colour preferences relative to button and background. Subsequently, they were requested to read some texts with different font sizes and comment on which one they would prefer. For each task they were required to point at a concrete button on the screen using their preferred modality.
- Audio: Participants heard different messages at different volumes. They were asked to repeat what they heard and finally to select the most appropriate volume for them. This was asked also while watching TV (with the sound on). Additionally, female and male voices were compared, and participants reported their preference.
- Motor: Participants had to select different buttons on the screen using either a conventional remote control or their fingers. They reported which one suited them better taking into account the button placement on the screen: bottom or top, right or left. They were also asked to interact with Tablet PC applications, entering numbers in a visual keyboard and controlling virtual maps. At last, they performed pointing selections interacting with a gravity-well filter and without any filter to understand if there were big differences.
- Cognitive: Cognitive tests in the form of "games" were performed to evaluate participants' visual memory and attention capacity. Images were showed on the screen, and participants were requested to memorize them. The images then disappeared and participants were asked to select the location where a specific image was. Time of selection was measured.
- Virtual Character: The same message was presented to participants, either by a VC or by an audio voice. Participants then reported their preference. A comparison was also done with the VC a text messages displayed on screen. Finally users were asked to choose one of three types of virtual characters (face avatar, half-body avatar and full-body avatar).
- Multiple Modalities: Participants were asked to perform several selections using only one modality or several modalities at the same time. This was asked also while simulating different contexts of interaction. Participants were also asked which way of presenting information they preferred, combining presentation in one modality and in several modalities at the same time.

The number of errors and the time to complete tasks was measured. The observation of participant's actions and behaviours was also considered. Every user-trial lasted around 60 min and during the trials, participants had to sit down in front of the screen ensuring that the distance was the same for every user. Every assessment was recorded with two cameras, one of them focused on the user and the other on the TV screen. Analysis of the user-trials was made from the analysis of these videos (a detailed explanation can be found in Coelho [26]).

Intermediate User Study The main goal of the Intermediate User Study was to validate the framework, in particular to what concerns adaptation and multimodal mechanisms. That was achieved by assessing the benefits of multimodal adaptation in the interaction of older users with a user interface they are used to, a TV-based Electronic Program Guide (EPG) application. In detail, our objectives included validating the User Initialisation Application (UIA) – an application that resulted from the developer focus groups and initial user trials requirements (and which is described more ahead in this chapter) – and its acceptance by the end-users. More relevantly, we wanted to assess if the users understood the role of the UIA and if they would perform it to benefit from the adaptations it may provide. Also, pertaining adaptation, we wanted to assess if the users were able to perceive it and, most of all, acknowledge the suitability of the adaptations to their needs. Ultimately, we wanted to verify the objective benefits of the usage of the adapted EPG over its non-adapted counterpart. Therefore, in this stage was performed a validation of all the requirements (possible guidelines) identified in the previous stages of this UCD approach, related with adaptation and new ways of providing multimodal interaction to elderly users in modern TV contexts. Knowledge gained in the initial study and in the stakeholders research phase, was also used to develop an Electronic Program Guide (EPG) application focusing on the engagement between users and a realistic TV interaction scenario. This was also another way of validating previously developed notions about elderly users' interaction and application development targeting this group. All verified requirements are presented as guidelines in the following section of this chapter.

For these trials, 52 people (33 female and 19 male) with different disabilities, most of them age-related, were recruited in three countries: 21 participants from Spain, 19 from the UK, and 12 from Germany. The average age was 74.2 years old. The evaluation session, for each user, comprised: (1) running the UIA; (2) performing tasks with the adapted EPG version; and, (3) performing tasks with the Non-Adapted EPG version. For each user, the framework generated a user profile based on the info collected by the UIA and the runtime user model rules. Adapted versions of the EPG were the result of the framework adaption for each user taking the info collected by the UIA application. Output and input modalities were made available and recommended by the runtime user model.

Users were briefed about the framework, its goals and the tasks to perform. Given the specific character of the participants (mainly older adults), traditional usability unaided tasks were sometimes unfeasible. All help requests and interventions were logged and taken in consideration in the analysis.

Quantitative data was retrieved from the UIA (user profile and interface preferences). A satisfaction questionnaire was performed to assess the participants' understanding and acceptance of the UIA. Further, similar subjective procedures were deployed to assess the perceived benefits of adaptation and overall acceptance of the framework. Given the specificity of the population and the semi-supervised methodology, as it is usual in the first contact of older users with novel technologies, objective comparisons were not performed (e.g. task times). However, to enable a more concrete and objective analysis of user performance with and without adaptations, we performed a detailed video analysis to 15 randomly selected users (6 from Spain, 6 from the UK and 3 from Germany). These videos were coded according to pre-defined variables and categories within. Examples of such variables, for each task, were: task understanding, task completion, number of help requests, and number of errors.

Framework Development Concurrently with both the Initial and Intermediate user studies, development evolved in the GUIDE framework components. Starting in the Stakeholders research phase and based on requirements collected, the framework development proceeded and evolved with the continuous input from trial results, especially on how the internals of several components (e.g. multimodal fusion and fission, user model, etc.) should be implemented and how the dialog between components should be performed. Resulting from the Initial User Trials, information related especially with multimodal behaviour and adaptation contexts was considered. In the Intermediate User Studies, information related with multimodal fission and fusion behaviour for adaptation was considered. The development of the framework will end before the final user study phase, where it will be evaluated as a whole.

4.3 Guidelines for the Design of Multimodal TV for Elderly

Specific guidelines applied in the design of the GUIDE system are now highlighted in this chapter, focusing only on the ones derived directly from the analysis processes of each different stage of the employed UCD approach. Several of these guidelines were identified in more than one stage of methodology. We only present those guidelines once, in the stage where it was first identified. Guidelines are also divided into different categories: modalities, adaptation, modern TV (behaviour), and application (design).

4.3.1 Early Requirement Stage

1. **Modalities – RC simplification**. The device has to be simplified so that elderly users can understand it better. Interaction must be more based on directional (arrows) and "OK" keys.
2. **Modalities – provide modality help**. Help and explanation for using any device must be available at any time in the application/system.

3. **Modalities – use any modality for any task**. Every task must be possible to achieve using any modality of interaction available.
4. **Modalities – consider user and interact context in speech**. ASR must consider the user and interaction context to improve recognition.
5. **Modalities – avoid unknown terms in speech**. UIs should avoid presenting unknown terms to the user as it can result in recognition errors, due to misspelling.
6. **Modalities – ASR error recovery**. Multimodal systems must support the user in the prevention and recovering from ASR errors by presenting recognized commands or giving multi-modal feedback.
7. **Modalities – consider speech characteristics of elderly**. ASR must consider language-related aspects of elderly speech (e.g. pauses in word finding, phrases).
8. **Modalities – provide feedback when pointing**. The VHS should provide appropriate means of feedback to the user (e.g. if a button has been pressed).
9. **Modalities – avoid inadvertent activation when pointing**. The VHS should minimize the risk of inadvertent activation of application functionality, by unintended gestures.
10. **Modalities – provide training steps**. Multimodal systems should provide training steps for the user, for each modality of interaction.
11. **Modalities – consistency of user experience in Tablet**. A consistent user experience across application modalities must be provided, especially on the tablet where output should be adapted to user needs and re-enact the main screen.
12. **Modalities – accurate and relevant information in Tablet**. All information displayed on the tablet must be consistent with the information on the main screen and the respective audio information. Delays between rendering devices should not become relevant for distraction from the ICT application.
13. **Modalities – provide one-touch features on Tablet.** Tablet UI should provide API to implement single-touch selections to access the major functionality of the application it controls.
14. **Modalities – VC must be helpful, friendly and realistic**. VC should display a helpful behaviour anytime and also contribute for the general familiarity and user's willingness to use the system. VC should be able to communicate verbally with most accurate lip synchronization possible. Also, VC must support the ability to express facial expressions usually perceptible during human-human conversation, and be able to exemplify how certain commands are employed. To achieve this, it should be possible to display the VC as a visual representation of the whole body, of an upper body or head-only. VC should have expressivity, in order to transmit certain states of the system interaction (e.g. a surprised expression if a command is not recognized by the system). VC should be realistic in terms of facial appearance, movements, and perceptible voice, even if by means of an anthropomorphic representation. VC must be clear and distinct for male or female representation. The aforementioned

characteristics, along with possible others, should be easily parameterized and adapted to each setting and/or user.

15. **Modalities – audio output**. Audio output has to be clear and easy to understand. Audio output should exist for male and female voice representation. Different volumes must be supported to satisfy different user preferences or impairments.
16. **Applications – simple GUIs for elderly**. A simple layout and limited functionality for any graphical user interface should be provided when designing for elderly users. Instructions should be "easy to understand", and icons should be perceived "intuitive".
17. **Applications – should avoid loneliness and foster social inclusion**. When appropriate, applications should support the elderly user in communicating with friends and relatives and share experiences.

Other, more specific, application guidelines were collected at this stage. However, these are not of interest to this chapter as they are relative to specific cases and contexts of the distinct applications and cannot be appointed as general guidelines. Additionally, we collected information that did not constitute a guideline at this stage, but that contributed to derive one at a later stage of the UCD process. Accordingly, this will be presented in the guideline defining stage (typical examples of these are indications related with user profiling and modern TV interaction). This is also true for all other stages described in this chapter. In a general manner, the results obtained in this initial stage are an indication that, when designing for the elderly, special care must be given to personalization as it is indispensable to adapt applications to their wide range of characteristics. It also makes a clear statement related with the fact that new types of applications and interaction should be introduced to new users before being used.

4.3.2 *Pilot and Stakeholders Research Guidelines*

18. **Adaptation – system should be personalized by each user**. When the user is using the system for the first time, the application should automatically personalize the different parameters (mode of interaction, colours, font size, button size, audio messages volume, etc.) based on the initial configurations performed by the user. After this process, the parameters should be reconfigurable by the user at any time.
19. **Adaptation – define preferred modality to prevent contradictions.** When the user accidentally gives contradictory commands between modalities to the system, only one of them should be recognized (e.g. say "Channel 1" and pointing at the same time at "Channel 2" by mistake). Therefore, the system must pre-establish with the user, a preferred modality that will prevail over any other in case of contradiction.

20. **Adaptation – perform re-configuration of system when user characteristics change.** When the user's capabilities experience a change, a re-configuration of the system must be performed to re-establish the adequate parameters according to his or her capabilities. The system should also detect the failures and mistakes made by the user when interacting with the system as a possible indication of a loss of capabilities.
21. **Adaptation – support automatic recognition.** When the user is in front of the TV an automatic recognition of him or her should be made in order to adapt the system to their specific needs (e.g. VHS recognizes facial characteristics of user).
22. **Adaptation – support adaptation to different user contexts**. In different situations the application should be controlled by different methods according to the needs of the elderly. For instance, if the user usually controls the application by voice but for a couple of days he has a cold and he has a loss of voice, the system should be able to adapt the interaction to this situation (e.g. choosing the second preferred modality as the default one).
23. **Adaptation – support adaptation to different ICT skills**. When the user is using the system for the first time the application should evaluate his previous ICT experience, skills and preferences to achieve a better adaptation of the system (e.g. people with better ICT skills might prefer complex menus which offer more information while people with less ICT skills will probably prefer simple menus with less information but easier to control).
24. **Applications – multi-user interaction**. The concept of multi-user is well perceived and identified by the elderly and should be extendable to every application.
25. **Applications – simplification of novel features**. When the user is using an application and wants to do something he or she is not familiar with (e.g. using the application for the first time), steps required should be as few as possible, and the help of the VC (or audio output) is highly recommended.
26. **Adaptation – adapt menus to user impairments**. In modern TV systems for elderly users, adaptation to user characteristics should be provided (e.g. people with visual problems prefer bigger buttons on the screen, while people with hearing problems prefer to have information provided in both visual and audio forms).
27. **Modalities – VC should focus the attention on the message**. The VC must not to be a source of distraction; important is the message given by the VC, not the VC itself.
28. **Modalities – VC help in blocking situations**. If a user is stuck or issues a not recognizable command, VC should automatically appear to help the user. If the application is the responsible for detecting if the user needs help or not, then it must call the VC UI component to present all the necessary information to proceed with the interaction. The user himself may also be able to make the VC component appear by asking for help.
29. **Adaptation – consider most distinctive user characteristics**. The main differences noticed between elderly users are the following: capability to read

perfectly from close and distant vision; capability of seeing at night, and colour perception; capability to hear sounds of different frequencies and to distinguish conversations in a noisy background; cognitive impairments; and mobility diagnosis like muscular weakness and tremors. Therefore, when designing for elderly, user profiles should be created focusing on these differences.

30. **Applications – clear definitions of service requirements**. Before developing a service/application for TV, the requirements of targeted users have to be known and understood.
31. **Modern TV – keep well-known concepts.** Elderly people have problems to adopt new paradigms in interaction, so concepts like remote control and traditional TV application paradigms should be kept.
32. **Modern TV – consistency of user experiences across platforms.** When the user is switching from one platform to another, while consuming the same service, he should be able to use the system/service in the same manner, with the same interaction paradigms.
33. **Modern TV – ease of use is more important than branding.** More importance should be given to interaction design than to interface appearance. This is especially relevant for elderly users.
34. **Applications – clear, simple, uncluttered screens.** Elderly users prefer simple UI designs, with less distractive elements (flashes, animations, etc.).
35. **Applications – provide feedback on user input.** Most of the time, elderly users ask for additional feedback to their input (e.g. a beep, a graphical highlight, a vibration, etc.). This should be supported by any application/interaction.
36. **Adaptation – maintain user profiles across channels.** When a user is using several applications, the same means of personalization should be applied, considering his or hers specific profile.
37. **Applications – one-touch features.** The most important functionality of applications/services should be accessible via simple interaction schemes, like "one-click"/"one-touch".
38. **Adaptation – UI mark-up language as first-step for adaptation**. If UI markup language is used as interface between application and automatic adaptation, developers will be allowed to keep tools and development environments and without too much additional effort, take a first step towards accessible design.
39. **Adaptation – limited screen layout adaptation**. Support for the adaptation of screen layout (UI elements) should be offered in modern TV systems for elderly. However, they should be applied only when related with user impairments or as a result of direct user requests.
40. **Adaptation – adapt to user behaviour/habits**. In modern TV systems for elderly, adaptation to user behaviour/user habits should be provided (e.g. adaptation to user's (daily) schedule, or adaptation to user interaction habits).
41. **Adaptation – maintain user profiles across channels**. A user profile should be maintained across multiple applications. Adaptation of UIs should work in all UI situations and applications, considering the individual impairments of the user.

42. **Adaptation – User Initialization Application (UIA).** In order to adapt to user characteristics, provide tutorials on new ways of interaction and create user profiles (guidelines 11, 27, 28, 29, 32). A user initialization application should be presented the first time a user interacts with the system. The UIA should be as entertaining and short as possible. The user must be able to cancel the initialization process at any time.
43. **Adaptation – user privacy should be maintained**. Applications should maintain a high level of privacy and user data security, and should explicitly tell the user what data is collected and with which goal.
44. **Applications – simplified, but not senior**. Modern TV UIs must support elderly people, but should not appear to be designed only for seniors and be heavily simplified as a consequence. UIs should be maintained clear and simple, without giving the impression that they have been designed for someone with impairments.

The results obtained in these two stages enforce the need of knowing the users before making use of any adaptation features, and also support the UCD approach when designing systems for all (or centred on elderly population).

4.3.3 Initial User Studies

45. **Modalities – always ask for message confirmation**. Whenever a message is given by the system a confirmation action of its reception should be given by the user. The system must also be capable of recognizing if the user has received the message, and, when the message was not received, repeat the process.
46. **Modalities – reduced time for selection when pointing**. Whenever the user needs to select something by pointing at it, the system should require the selection to be maintained for a given amount of seconds, in order to prevent the user from making unwanted selections. However, the system should also reduce the need for unnecessary physical demands in pointing or the user will get quickly tired. One possible solution is to make it dependent on (and configurable by) each user.
47. **Modalities – position the icons on the dominant side when pointing**. When users are required to select something they tend to use their dominant hand independently where the icons are placed. This should be taken into account for placing icons on the screen to increase icon selection efficiency.
48. **Modalities – provide feedback of the selection of the buttons**. When the user selects something by pointing at it, the system should offer ways of providing additional feedback about the selected button (e.g. if change of button colour is not enough, it must be accompanied by voice feedback).
49. **Modalities – increase selection area when pointing**. When mobility impaired user selects something through pointing, the area of selection should be bigger (e.g. surrounding area of the button can be clickable as well).

50. **Modalities – output should always depend on context**. When the user is watching TV, the messages given by the system should be different than the ones rendered when the user is looking at pictures. Also, the speech volume should depend on what is being watched on TV. Each user should also be able to select in which context they want messages rendered by which modality.
51. **Applications – colours**. Avoid the use of bright colours. Avoid the use of too dark colours in backgrounds. Ultimately, users should be able to specify their own background and foreground colour profile preferences.
52. **Modalities – messages should catch the visual attention.** When the system shows visual messages on the screen, these must catch the user's attention. The elderly should clearly differentiate these messages from the ones that usually appear on the TV.
53. **Modalities – customizable VC**. The VC's voice speed (not very slow and not very quick) and accent (not sounding like a fake voice) should be personalized.
54. **Modalities – support automatic adaptation of cursor area when pointing**: VHS should be capable of assigning a cursor area to each tracked user. This area is aligned relative to the body and allows the user to "draw" in the air. All movement in this area is mapped to the cursor movement on the screen. The cursor area should be automatically adjusted and fit to the user's location and body configuration.
55. **Modalities – support automatic recognition of body posture when pointing.** The user should be able to easily perform gestures or cursor movements when sitting on a chair. The system should detect and track the hand without interference with other body parts.
56. **Applications – simplified button configuration.** Applications should present a short number of interactive elements for each screen, focusing on big and well-spaced buttons. Button size should also be configurable by the user.
57. **Applications – configurable text and audio.** Applications should make sure both text size and audio volume are configurable by the user at the beginning as well as during interaction.
58. **Modalities – configurable gestures.** The existence of specific gestures to perform specific tasks should be a reality, but all gesture interaction should be introduced to the user.
59. **Modalities – support pointing adaptation.** Selection of items/buttons should be aided by target approximation or making use of interaction filters. This is especially relevant for motor impaired users.
60. **Modalities – use of activation procedures**. For preventing errors during interaction context changes, specific modalities should be activated by specific procedures (e.g. speech recognition should be activated by specific keywords or gesture interaction should be activated by a specific gesture).
61. **Modalities – support recognition of universal speech terms.** When interacting with an application using speech, words like "Select", "This", "Yes", "No" and "Confirm", should be included in a speech recognition dictionary, and used in helping selecting the option the user is pointing to when the command is issued. "One", "Two", "Three", "First", "Second", "Third", etc.,

should represent keywords, supporting redundancy when a user is pointing and speaking, or when using speech only.

The results obtained in these trials reinforce the need of a multimodal system and also the need for adaptation, as detailed in Coelho [26].

4.3.4 Intermediate User Studies

As mentioned previously, this stage of the GUIDE UCD approach did not aim at eliciting further requirements. Instead, it aimed at validating as guidelines the ones identified in the previous stages. However, focusing on the most relevant guidelines from the UIA evaluation, we concluded that users were positive towards the concept but it was also clear that for it to work there must be a special concern about motivation and helping mechanisms. Additionally, adaptation guidelines were also validated by the results obtained denoting less errors, less requests for help, less blocking situations, and higher rates in the perception and execution of tasks without help in the adapted version of the EPG. From this we can make the general conclusion that adaptation improves the overall interaction relation between the participants and the interface. Additionally, UCD proved to be the correct approach for designing new TV applications considering the elderly population, as even the non-adapted EPG version was already more adapted to their needs than the typical TV systems they have at home.

Lastly, two additional guidelines were validated by preferences stated in every single stage of this UCD process:

62. **Applications – Interaction paradigms should be maintained in all tasks**: Confirming basic notions of Web application design, it is especially relevant for modern TV-based applications to keep the same paradigm for every task to be performed by the user. Typical "select and confirm" tasks normally result in blocking situations; "one-touch" tasks are encouraged for every action.
63. **Modern TV – Speech recognition as the main alternative to remote control.** If users do not have specific impairments that make it harder to use speech, it should be considered as the main alternative to RC interaction.

4.4 The Future of Multimodal TV

The GUIDE project focuses on a specific target population: elderly people. In an aging society, addressing the limitations of such users gains wider relevance as the tendency is to have everyday more people dealing with age-related impairments. Along, several people in this situation will have a past of technologic experience, which does not represent the current stereotypical older adult. Given the increasing number of target users and their openness to novel technologies that help them surpassing their limitations, the opportunities for GUIDE are increasing.

In the preceding sections we have outlined a set of guidelines to improve usability for older people in the particular setting of Digital TV and applications therein. The scenario of the older adult using a TV is limited due to the person's age-inherent limitations, which by turn limits the possibilities for having drastic changes in how a TV is used and interacted with. This automatically makes the aforementioned guidelines valid for longer timespans than what is normally seen in technological settings.

The scope of these guidelines, and the overall development of accessible TV and applications, goes way beyond the usage by older people. If we go back in time, interacting with a TV has been quite steady since its appearance and, albeit its relative longevity, the hardware specifications have been evolving, but the user interaction itself has been evolving quite slowly. The standard remote control yields as the main interface between the user and the TV. Recently, with the emergence of digital TV new sets of applications have been offered to the user but the interface remains equally available to all, disabled or not, and the interaction is still similar to the one available in analog TV. The current panorama shows a user interaction setting that has not evolved to meet the user's needs even though the technology is already available to do so. Although the GUIDE project has presented new adaptation, application and multimodal possibilities particularly for older people, most of the guidelines presented would be an improvement to a more general population. As it has already happen in the past, this is a case where developments in the accessibility field have paved way to improving usability for the population as a whole.

Meanwhile, digital TV is starting to appear in different scenarios like public interactive settings and mobile devices. These settings are once again examples where the general population is likely to benefit from guidelines created within an accessibility context. Every once in a while, everyone is situationally impaired experiencing difficulties that they would not feel in a living room setting. With the appearance of digital TV in more demanding settings, benefiting from adapting contents and interaction along with being able to have a multitude of choices for interacting with the system is likely to improve the user experience and effectiveness.

References

1. Oppenauer, C., Preschl, B., Kalteis, K., & Kryspin-Exner, I. (2007). Technology in old age from a psychological point of view. In A. Holzinger (Ed.), *Proceedings of the 3rd human-computer interaction and usability engineering of the Austrian computer society conference on HCI and usability for medicine and health care (USAB'07)* (pp. 133–142). Berlin/Heidelberg: Springer.
2. Kryspin-Exner, I., & Oppenauer, C. (2006). Gerontotechnik: Ein innovatives Gebiet fur die Psychologie? *Psychologie in Osterreich, 26*(3), 161–169.
3. Lehr, R. (2003). *Psychologie des Alters*. Wiebelsheim: Quelle & Meyer.

4. Holzinger, A., Searle, G., & Nischelwitzer, A. (2007). On some aspects of improving mobile applications for the elderly. In C. Stephanidis (Ed.), *Coping with diversity in universal access, research and development methods in universal access, LNCS* (Vol. 4554, pp. 923–932). Heidelberg: Springer.
5. Mollenkopf, H. (1994). Technical aids in old age – Between acceptance and rejection. In C. Wild & A. Kirschner (Eds.), *Safety-alarm systems, technical aids and smart homes* (pp. 81–100). Knegsel: Akontes.
6. Rogers, W. A., & Fisk, A. D. (2003). Technology design, usability and aging: Human factors techniques and considerations. In N. Charness & K. W. Schaie (Eds.), *Impact of technology on successful aging* (pp. 1–4). New York: Springer.
7. Rogers, W. A., Mayhorn, C. B., & Fisk, A. D. (2004). Technology in everyday life for older adults. In D. C. Burdick & S. Kwon (Eds.), *Gerontechnology. Research and practice in technology and aging* (pp. 3–18). New York: Springer.
8. Fozard, J. L. (2003). Using technology to lower the perceptual and cognitive hurdles of aging. In N. Charness & K. W. Schaie (Eds.), *Impact of technology on successful aging* (pp. 100–112). Heidelberg: Springer.
9. Schieber, F. (2003). Human factors and aging: Identifying and compensating for age-related deficits in sensory and cognitive function. In N. Charness & K. W. Schaie (Eds.), *Impact of technology on successful aging* (pp. 42–84). New York: Springer.
10. Unemuro, H. (2004). Computer attitudes, cognitive abilities, and technology usage among older japanese adults. *Gerontechnology, 3*(2), 64–76.
11. Beier, G. (2001). Kontrolluberzeugungen im Ungang mit Technik. Ein Personlichkeitsmerkmal mit Relevanz gur die Gestaltung technischer Systeme, dissertation.de – Verlag im Internet Gmbh, Berlin.
12. Rayner, K. (1998). Eye movements in reading and information processing: Twenty years of research. *Psychological Bulletin, 124*(3), 372–422.
13. Jacob, R. J. K. (1991). The use of eye movements in human-computer interaction techniques: What you look at is what you get. *ACM Transactions on Information Systems, 9*, 152–169.
14. Oviatt, S. L., Coulston, R., Shriver, S., Xiao, B., Wesson, R., Lunsford, R., & Carmichael, L. (2003). *Toward a theory of organized multimodal integration patterns during human-computer interaction*. Presented at the international conference on Multimodal Interfaces, Vancouver, BC, Canada.
15. Cohen, P., Dalrymple, M., Moran, D., & Pereira, F. (1989). Synergistic use of direct manipulation and natural language. In *Proceedings of the SIGCHI conference on human factors in computing systems* (pp. 227–233). New York: ACM.
16. Hauptmann, A. G. (1989). Speech and gestures for graphic image manipulation. In *Proceedings of the conference on Human Factors Computing Systems (CHI'89)*, 241–245.
17. Leatherby, J. H., & Pausch, R. (1992). Voice input as a replacement for keyboard accelerators in a mouse-based graphical editor: An empirical study. *Journal of the American Voice Input/Output Society, 11*(2), 69–76.
18. Oviatt, S. L. (1997). Multimodal interactive maps: Designing for human performance. *Human Computer Interaction, 12*(1–2), 93–129.
19. Oviatt, S. L., & Olsen, E. (1994). Integration themes in multimodal human computer interaction. In *Proceedings of the ICSLP* (Vol. 2, pp. 551–554).
20. Wickens, C. D., Sandry, D. L., & Vidulich, M. (1983). Compatibility and resource competition between modalities of input, central processing, and output. *Human Factors, 25*, 227–248.
21. Oviatt, S. L. (1999). Mutual disambiguation of recognition errors in a multimodal architecture. In *Proceedings of the conference on Human Factors Computing Systems (CHI'99)*, 576–583.
22. Kricos, P. B. (1996). Differences in visual intelligibility across talkers. In D. G. Stork & M. E. Hennecke (Eds.), *Speechreading by humans and machines: Models, systems and applications* (pp. 43–53). New York: Springer.
23. Argyle, M. (1972). Nonverbal communication in human social interaction. In R. Hinde (Ed.), *Nonverbal communication* (pp. 243–267). Cambridge: Cambridge University Press.

24. Oviatt, S. L., DeAngeli, A., & Kuhn, K. (1997). Integration and synchronization of inputmodes during multimodal human-computer interaction. In *Proceedings of the conference on human factors computing systems (CHI' 97)* (pp. 415–422). New York: ACM.
25. Oviatt, S. L., Bernard, J., & Levow, G. (1999). Linguistic adaptations during spoken and multimodal error resolution. *Language and Speech, 41*(3–4), 415–438.
26. Coelho, J., Duarte, C., Biswas, P., & Langdon, P. (2011). Developing accessible TV applications. In *Proceedings of ASSETS2011*. New York: ACM.
27. Fozard, J. L., Rietsema, J., Bouma, H., & Graafmans, J. A. M. (2000). Gerotechnology: Creating enabling environments for the challenges and opportunities of aging. *Educational Gerontology, 26*(4), 331–344.
28. Eisma, R., Dickinsons, A., Goodmann, J., Syme, A., Tiwari, L., & Newell, A. F. (2004). Early user involvement in the development of information technology-related products for older people. *Universal Access in the Information Society, 3*(2), 131–140.
29. Seale, J., McCreadie, C., Turner-Smith, A., & Tinker, A. (2002). Older people as partners in assistive technology research: The use of focus groups in the design process. *Technology and Disability, 14*, 21–29.
30. Holzinger, A., Sammer, P., & Hofmann-Wellenhof, R. (2007). Mobile computing in medicine: Designing mobile questionnaires for elderly and partially sighted people. In K. Miesenberger, J. Klaus, W. Zagler, A. I. Karshmer (Eds.), *ICCHP 2006. LNCS* (Vol. 4061, pp. 923–932). Heidelberg: Springer.
31. Langdon, P., Aurisicchio, M., Clarkson, P. J., & Wallace, K. (2003). An integrated ethnographic and empirical methodology in a study of knowledge searches in aerospace design. In *Proceedings of the 14th international conference on engineering design* (10 pages). Stockholm: The Design Society.
32. Flick, U. (2006). *An introduction to qualitative research*. London: Sage.
33. Miles, M. B., & Huberman, A. M. (1994). *Qualitative data analysis*. London: Sage.

Chapter 5
Inclusive User Modeling and Simulation

Pradipta Biswas and Patrick Langdon

Abstract This chapter presents a concept of user modeling including users with different range of abilities. The chapter starts with a brief summary of existing approaches of user modeling and points out the uniqueness of our work. The user model is implemented through a simulator and a set of web services. The simulator is intended to be used as a tool for improving interface designs while the web services provide runtime adaptation. We have presented brief detail of both the simulator and the web service, their applications and conclude by discussing implications and limitations of user modeling. Later, Chap. 10 presents a concept of extending the idea of user modeling across different types of projects and standardizing it.

5.1 Introduction

A huge part of social communication now takes place through electronic media though lot of it remains inaccessible to the growing elderly population. Many existing user interfaces often work for 'average' user and does not cater the need of the growing population of elderly users. For example, we may consider a modern smartphone and may find that it is **difficult** for an elderly person accoustomed with traditional telephones, to make a call using the smartphone. Similar case studies are quite prevalent with interfaces of modern digital televisions, computers and other electronic control systems. However these issues often need slight tweaking of the design like changing colour contrast, increasing fontsize, changing layouts of buttons and can make them far more usable as well as increase the market coverage of the products. This chapter presents a user modeling system to help designers in developing accessible systems and to personalize interfaces for end users. The user modeling system has two main parts.

- A Simulator
- A Runtime User Model

P. Biswas (✉) • P. Langdon
Department of Engineering, University of Cambridge, Trumpington Street, Cambridge, Cambridgeshire CB2 1PZ, UK
e-mail: pb400@hermes.cam.ac.uk; pml24@eng.cam.ac.uk

P. Biswas et al. (eds.), *A Multimodal End-2-End Approach to Accessible Computing*, Human–Computer Interaction Series, DOI 10.1007/978-1-4471-6708-2_5

The simulator embodies both the internal state of a computer application and also the perceptual, cognitive and motor processes of its user and helps designers to understand, visualize and measure effect of age and impairment on design using graphical user interfaces. The runtime user model customizes interface parameters across a wide range of devices based on the range of ability of user, collected through an easy to use user initialization application. The user modeling system is relevant for developing a standard on user modeling and simulation as part of the EU VUMS cluster [13]. Initial user trials have proved that our modeling system can enhance the interaction experience of elderly users.

The chapter is organized as follows. Section 5.2 presents a brief literature survey on user modeling followed by descriptions of the simulator and runtime user model at Sects. 5.3, 5.4. Section 5.5 discusses the implication and limitation of user modeling followed by conclusion in Sect. 5.6.

5.2 User Models

A model can be defined as "a simplified representation of a system or phenomenon with any hypotheses required to describe the system or explain the phenomenon, often mathematically". The concept of modeling is widely used in different disciplines of science and engineering ranging from models of neurons or different brain regions in neurology to construction model in architecture or model of universe in theoretical physics. Modeling human or human systems is widely used in different branches of physiology, psychology and ergonomics. A few of these models are termed as user models when their purpose is to design better consumer products. By definition a user model is a representation of the knowledge and preferences of users that the system believes the user posses [3]. Research on simulating user behaviour to predict machine performance was originally started during the Second World War. Researchers tried to simulate operators' performance to explore their limitations while operating different military hardware. During the same time, computational psychologists were trying to model the mind by considering it as an ensemble of processes or programs. McCulloch and Pitts' [21] model of the neuron and subsequent models of neural networks, and Marr's model [20] of vision are two influential works in this discipline. Boden [9] presents a detailed discussion of such computational mental models. In the late 1970s, as interactive computer systems became cheaper and accessible to more people, modeling human computer interaction (HCI) also gained much attention. However, existing psychological models like Hick's Law [15] or Fitts' Law [14] which predict visual search time and movement time respectively were individually not enough to simulate a whole interaction. There was a plethora of systems developed during the last three decades in computer science that are claimed to be user models. Many of them modelled users for certain applications – most notably for online recommendation and e learning systems. These models have a generic structure as shown in Fig. 5.1.

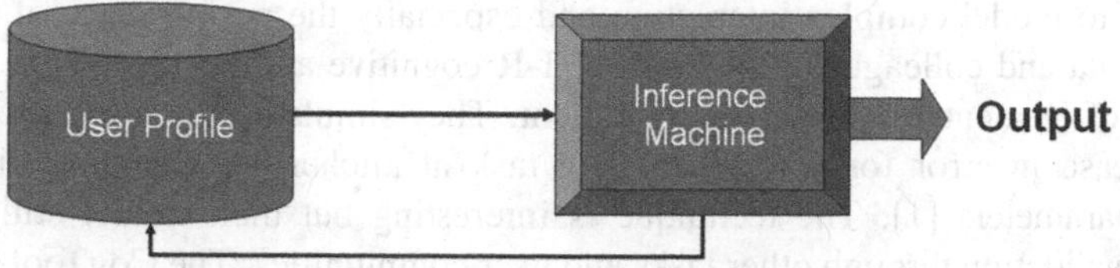

Fig. 5.1 General structure of most user models

The user profile section stores detail about user relevant for a particular application and inference machine use this information to personalize the system. A plethora of examples of such models can be found at the User Modeling and User-Adapted Interaction journal and proceedings of User Modeling, Adaptation and Personalization conference. On a different dimension, ergonomics and computer animation follow a different view of user model. Instead of modeling human behaviour in detail, they aim to simulate human anatomy or face which can be used to predict posture, facial expression and so on. Duffy [12] has presented examples of many such models.

Finally, there is a bunch of models which merges psychology and artificial intelligence to model human behaviour in detail. In theory they are capable of modeling any behaviour of users while interacting with environment or a system. This type of models has also been used to simulate human machine interaction to both explain and predict interaction behaviour. This type of models is termed as cognitive architectures and a few examples are SOAR, ACT-R, EPIC and CORE and so on. A simplified view of these cognitive architectures is known as the GOMS model [17] and still now is most widely used in human computer interaction.

There is not much reported work on systematic modeling of assistive interfaces. McMillan [22] felt the need to use HCI models to unify different research streams in assistive technology, but his work aimed to model the system rather than the user. The AVANTI project [27] modelled an assistive interface for a web browser based on static and dynamic characteristics of users. The interface is initialized according to static characteristics (such as age, expertise, type of disability and so on) of the user. During interaction, the interface records users' interaction and adapts itself based on dynamic characteristics (such as idle time, error rate and so on) of the user. This model works based on a rule based system and does not address the basic perceptual, cognitive and motor behaviour of users and so it is hard to generalize to other applications. A few researchers also worked on basic perceptual, cognitive and motor aspects. The EASE tool [19] simulates effects of interaction for a few visual and mobility impairments. However the model is demonstrated for a sample application of using a word prediction software but not yet validated for basic pointing or visual search tasks performed by people with disabilities. Keates and colleagues [18] measured the difference between able-bodied and motor impaired users with respect to the Model Human Processor (MHP) [11] and motor impaired users were found to have a greater motor action time than their able-bodied counterparts. The finding is obviously important, but the KLM model itself is too primitive to model complex interaction and especially the performance of novice users. Serna and colleagues [26] used ACT-R cognitive architecture [1] to model progress of Dementia in Alzheimer's patient. They simulated the loss of memory and increase in error for a representative task at kitchen by changing different ACT-R parameters [1]. The technique is interesting but their model still needs rigorous validation through other tasks and user communities. The CogTool system combines GOMS models and ACT-R system for providing quantitative prediction on interaction. The system simulates expert performance through GOMS modeling, while the ACT-R system helps to simulate exploratory behaviour of novice users. The system also provides GUIs to quickly prototype interfaces and to evaluate different design alternatives based on quantitative prediction [16]. However it does not yet seem to be used for users with disability or assistive interaction techniques.

5.3 The Simulator

Based on the previous discussion, Fig. 5.2 plots the existing general purpose HCI models in a space defined by the skill and physical ability of users. To cover most of the blank spaces in the diagram, we need models that can:

- Simulate HCI of both able-bodied and disabled users.
- Work for users with different levels of skill.
- Be easy to use and comprehend for an interface designer.

To address the limitations of existing user modeling systems, we have developed the simulator [8] as shown in Fig. 5.3. It consists of the following three components:

The Environment model contains a representation of an application and context of use. It consists of:

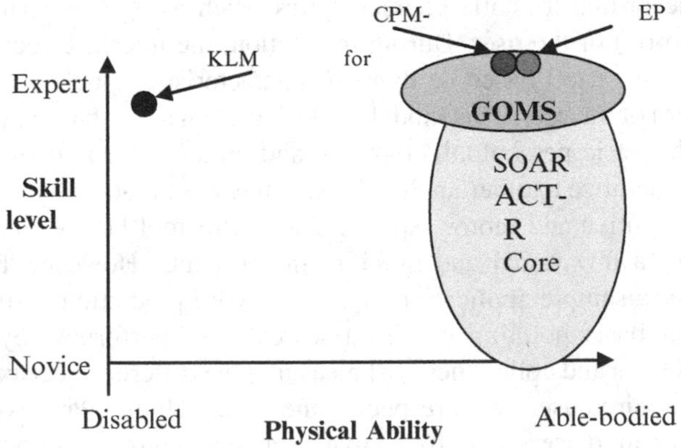

Fig. 5.2 Existing HCI models w.r.t. skill and physical ability of users

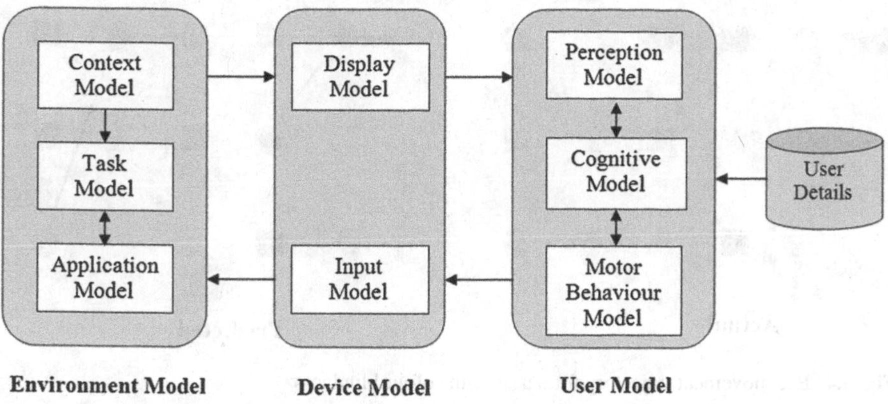

Fig. 5.3 Architecture of the simulator

- **The Application model** containing a representation of interface layout and application states.
- **The Task model** representing the current task undertaken by a user that will be simulated by breaking it up into a set of simple atomic tasks following the KLM model.
- **The Context model** representing the context of use like background noise, illumination and so on.

The Device model decides the type of input and output devices to be used by a particular user and sets parameters for an interface.

The User model simulates the interaction patterns of users for undertaking a task analysed by the task model under the configuration set by the interface model. It uses the sequence of phases defined by Model Human Processor [11].

- The perception model simulates the visual and auditory perception of interface objects. It is based on the theories of visual attention and speech perception.
- The cognitive model determines an action to accomplish the current task. It is more detailed than the GOMS model [17] but not as complex as other cognitive architectures.
- The motor behaviour model predicts the completion time and possible interaction patterns for performing that action. It is based on statistical analysis of screen navigation paths of disabled users.

The details about users are store in xml format in the user profile following the EU VUMS cluster described in detail in a later chapter of this book. The user profile stores demographic detail of users like age and sex and divide the functional abilities in perception, cognition and motor action. The perception, cognitive and motor behaviour models takes input from the respective functional abilities of users.

The perception model [6] simulates the phenomenon of visual perception (like focussing and shifting attention). We have investigated eye gaze patterns (using

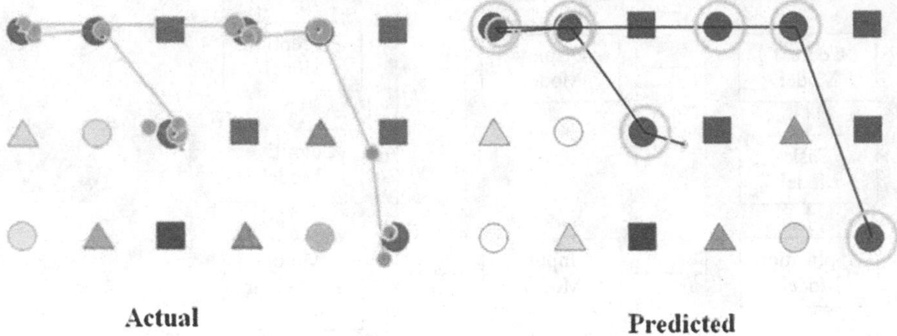

Fig. 5.4 Eye movement trajectory for a user with colour blindness

a Tobii X120 eye tracker) of people with and without visual impairment. The model uses a back propagation neural network to predict eye gaze fixation points and can also simulate the effects of different visual impairments (like Maccular Degeneration, colour blindness, Diabetic Retinopathy and so on) using image processing algorithms. Figure 5.4 shows the actual and predicted eye movement paths (green line for actual, black line for predicted) and points of eye gaze fixations (overlapping green circles) during a visual search task. The figure shows the prediction for a protanope (a type of colour blindness) participant and so the right hand figure is different from the left hand one as the effect of protanopia was simulated on the input image.

The auditory perception model is under development. It will simulate effect of both conductive (outer ear problem) and sensorineural (inner ear problem) hearing impairment. The models will be developed using frequency smearing algorithm [23] and will be calibrated through audiogram tests.

The cognitive model [5] breaks up a high level task specification into a set of atomic tasks to be performed on the application in question. The operation of it is illustrated in Fig. 5.5. At any stage, users have a fixed policy based on the current task in hand. The policy produces an action, which in turn is converted into a device operation (e.g. clicking on a button, selecting a menu item and so on). After application of the operation, the device moves to a new state. Users have to map this state to one of the state in the user space. Then they again decide a new action until the goal state is achieved.

Besides performance simulation, the model also has the ability to learn new techniques for interactions. Learning can occur either offline or online. The offline learning takes place when the user of the model (such as an interface designer) adds new states or operations to the user space. The model can also learn new states and operations itself. During execution, whenever the model cannot map the intended action of the user into an operation permissible by the device, it tries to learn a new operation. To do so, it first asks for instructions from outside. The interface designer is provided with the information about previous, current and future states

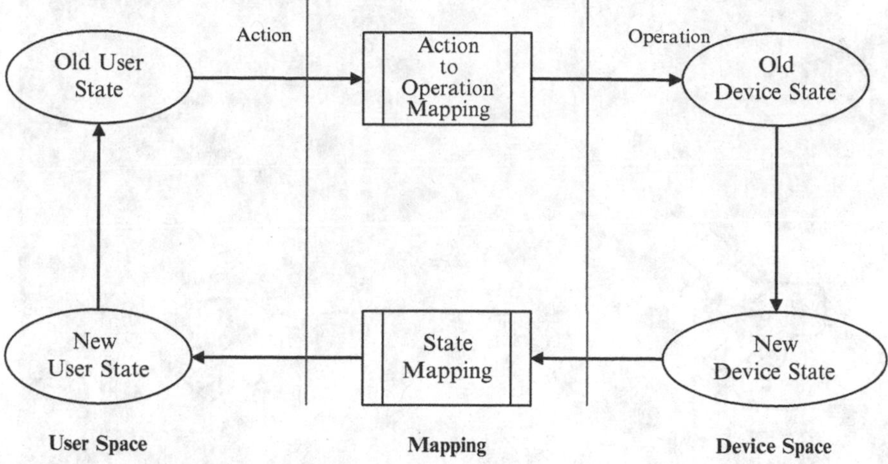

Fig. 5.5 Sequence of events in an interaction

and he can choose an operation on behalf of the model. If the model does not get any external instructions then it searches the state transition matrix of the device space and selects an operation according to the label matching principle [25]. If the label matching principle cannot return a prospective operation, it randomly selects an operation that can change the device state in a favourable way. It then adds this new operation to the user space and updates the state transition matrix of the user space accordingly. In the same way, the model can also learn a new device state. Whenever it arrives in a device state unknown to the user space, it adds this new state to the user space. It then selects or learns an operation that can bring the device into a state desirable to the user. If it cannot reach a desirable state, it simply selects or learns an operation that can bring the device into a state known to the user.

The model can also simulate the practice effect of users. Initially the mapping between the user space and the device space remains uncertain. It means that the probabilities for each pair of state/action in the user space and state/operation in the device space are less than one. After each successful completion of a task the model increases the probabilities of those mappings that lead to the successful completion of the task and after sufficient practice the probability values of certain mappings reach one. At this stage the user can map his space unambiguously to the device space and thus behave optimally.

The motor behaviour model [7] is developed by statistical analysis of cursor traces from motor impaired users. We have evaluated hand strength (using a Baseline 7-pc Hand Evaluation Kit) of able-bodied and motor impaired people and investigated how hand strength affects human computer interaction. Based on the analysis, we have developed a regression model to predict pointing time. Figure 5.6 shows an example of the output from the model. The thin purple (grey) line shows a sample trajectory of mouse movement of a motor impaired user. It can be seen that the trajectory contains random movements near the source and the target. The thick

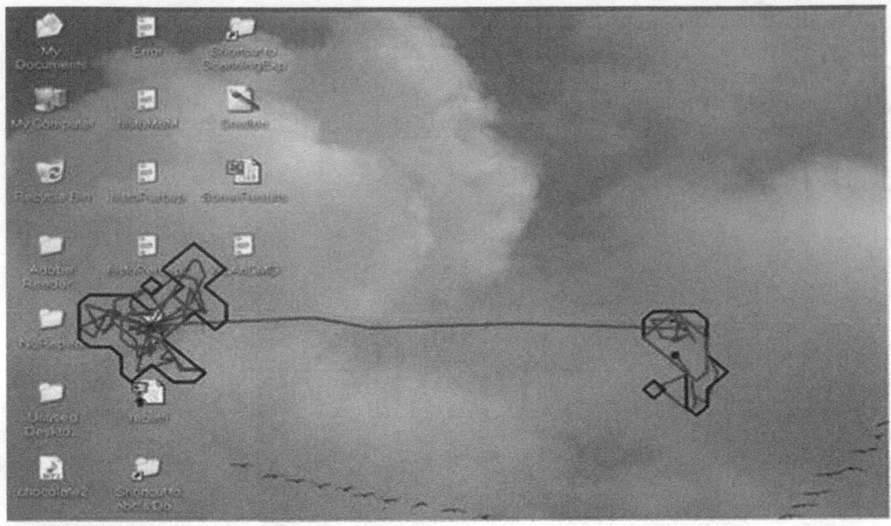

Fig. 5.6 Mouse movement trajectory for a user with cerebral palsy

red and black lines encircle the contour of these random movements. The area under the contour has a high probability of missed clicks as the movement is random there and thus lacks control.

These models do not need detailed knowledge of psychology or programming to operate. They have graphical user interfaces to provide input parameters and showing output of simulation. Figure 5.7 shows a few interfaces of the simulator.

At present it supports a few types of visual and mobility impairments. For both visual and mobility impairment, we have developed the user interfaces in three different levels:

- In the first level (Fig. 5.7a) the system simulates different diseases.
- In the next level (Fig. 5.7b) the system simulates the effect of change in different visual functions (like Visual acuity, Contrast sensitivity, Visual field loss and so on.) hand strength metrics (like Grip Strength, Range of Motion of forearm, wrist and so on) and auditory parameters (like audiogram, loudness and so on).
- In the third level (Fig. 5.7c), the system allows different image processing and digital filtering algorithms to be run (such as high/low/band pass filtering, blurring etc.) on input images and to set demographic detail of users.

The simulator can show the effects of a particular disease on visual functions and hand strength metrics and in turn their effect on interaction. For example, it can demonstrate how the progress of dry macular degeneration increases the number and sizes of scotoma (dark spots in eyes) and converts a slight peripheral visual field loss into total central vision loss. Similarly it can show the perception of an elderly colourblind user, or in other words the combined effect of visual acuity loss and colour blindness. We have modelled the effects of age and gender

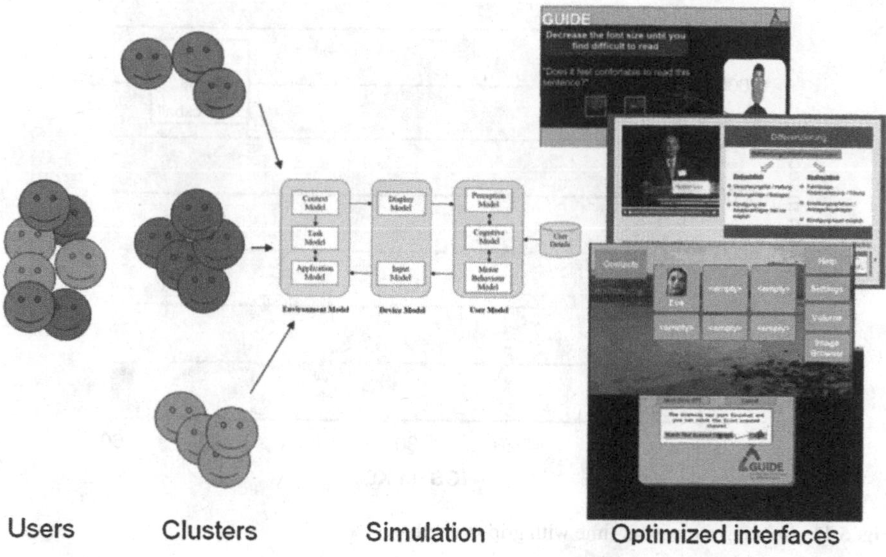

Fig. 5.9 The design optimization process

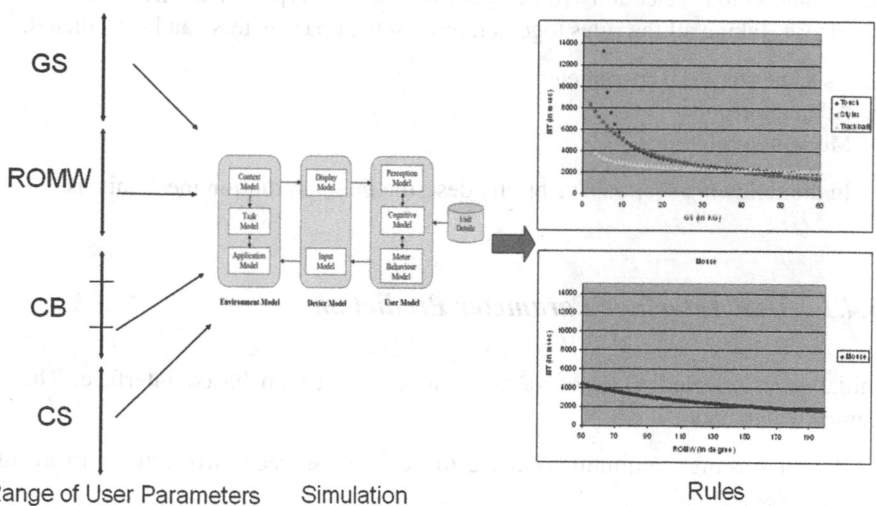

Fig. 5.10 Developing runtime user model. *GS* grip strength, *ROMW* active range of motion of wrist, *CB* type of colour blindness, *CS* contrast sensitivity

the following graph (Fig. 5.11) plots the grip strength in kilograms (kg) with movement time averaged over a range of standard target width and distances in an electronic screen. The curve clearly shows an increase in movement time while grip strength falls below 10 kg and the movement time turns independent of grip strength while it is more than 25 kg.

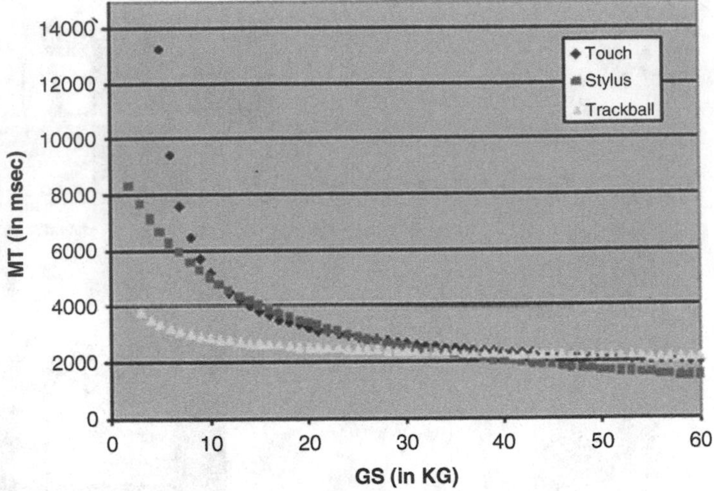

Fig. 5.11 Relating movement time with grip strength

Similar analyses have been done on fontsize selection with respect to visual acuity and colour selection with respect to different types of dichromatic colour blindness. Taking all the rules together, three sets of parameters can be predicted:

1. User Interface (UI) parameters
2. Adaptation code
3. Modality preference

In the following sections we briefly describe these prediction mechanisms.

5.4.1 User Interface Parameter Prediction

Initially we selected a set of variables to define a web based interface. These parameters include:

- Button spacing: minimum distance to be kept between two buttons to avoid missed selection
- Button Colour: The foreground and background colour of a button
- Button Size: The size of a button
- Text Size: Font size for any text rendered in the interface

The user model predicts minimum button spacing required from the users' motor capabilities and screen size. The simulation predicts that users having less than 10 kg of grip strength or 80° of Active Range of motion of wrist or significant tremor in hand produce a lot of random movement while they try to stop pointer movement and making a selection in an interface. The area of this random movement is also calculated from the simulator. Based on this result, we calculated the radius of the region of the random movement and the minimum button spacing is predicted in such a way so that this random movement does not produce a wrong target selection. The exact formula is as follows:

```
If users have Tremor, less than 10 kg of Grip
strength or 80° of ROM in wrist
  Minimum button spacing = 0.2 *distance of
  target from centre of screen
If users have less than 25 kg of Grip strength
  Minimum button spacing = 0.15 *distance of
  target from centre of screen
else
  Minimum button spacing = 0.05 * length of
  diagonal of the screen
```

If a user has colour blindness it recommends foreground and background colour blindness as follows:

```
If the colour blindness is Protanopia or
Deuteranopia (Red-Green) it recommends
    White foreground colour in Blue background
For any other type of colour blindness it
recommends
    White foreground in Black background or vice
    versa
```

The system stores the minimum visual angle based on the device type, screen size and distance of user from the screen and use it to predict minimum font size for different devices in pixel or point.

5.4.2 Adaptation Code Prediction

The adaptation code presently has only two values. It aims to help users while they use a pointer to interact with the screen like visual human sensing or gyroscopic remote. The prediction works in the following way.

```
If a user has tremor in hand or less than 10 Kg
Grip Strength
  The predicted adaptation will be Gravity Well
  and Exponential Average
Else
  The predicted adaptation will be Damping and
  Exponential Average
```

In the first case, the adaptation will remove jitters in movement through exponential average and then attract the pointer towards a target when it is near by using the gravity well mechanism. Details about the gravity well algorithm can be found in a different paper [4]. If the user does not have any mobility impairment, the adaptation will only work to remove minor jitters in movement.

5.4.3 Modality Prediction

The modality prediction system predicts the best modality of interaction for users. The algorithm works in the following way:

```
If User has Maccular Degeneration or User is Blind
BestIP = "Voice"
If DeviceType = TV"
BestOP = "AudioCaption"
Else
BestOP = "ScreenReader"
End If
ElseIf GRIP STRENGTH < 10Kg Or STATIC TREMOR > 499 Then
'Severe Motor Impairment with vision
Select Case DeviceType
Case 'Mobile'
BestIP = "BigButton"
Case 'Laptop'
BestIP = "TrackBall or Scanning"
Case 'Tablet'
BestIP = "Stylus"
Case 'PC'
BestIP = "TrackBall or Scanning"
Case 'TV'
BestIP = "SecondScreenBigButton"
End Select
BestOP = "Screen"
ElseIf GRIP STRENGTH < 20Kg Or STATIC TREMOR > 299 Then
'Moderate Motor Impairment with vision
Select Case DeviceType
Case 'Mobile'
BestIP = "BigButton"
Case 'Laptop'
BestIP = "TrackBall or Mouse"
Case 'Tablet'
BestIP = "Stylus"
Case 'PC'
```

```
BestIP = "TrackBall or Mouse"
Case 'TV'
BestIP = "SecondScreenBigButton"
End Select
BestOP = "Screen"
ElseIf ACTIVE RANGE OF MOTION OF WRIST < 100° Then
Select Case DeviceType
Case 'Mobile'
BestIP = "Stylus or BigButton"
Case 'Laptop'
BestIP = "Trackball or Mouse"
Case 'Tablet'
BestIP = "Stylus"
Case 'PC'
BestIP = "Trackball or Mouse"
Case 'TV'
BestIP = "BasicRemote"
End Select
BestOP = "Screen"
Else 'User without visual or motor impairment
BestIP = "DirectManipulation"
BestOP = "Screen"
End If
```

A demonstration version of this run time user model can be found at the following links.

User Sign Up: This application creates a user profile, http://www-edc.eng.cam.ac.uk/~pb400/CambUM/UMSignUp.htm.

In this application, we calculate the grip strength and range of wrist of motion of users from their age, gender and height using Ergonomics literature [2].

User Log In: This application predicts interface parameters and modality preference based on the user profile, http://www-edc.eng.cam.ac.uk/~pb400/CambUM/UMLogIn.htm.

Table 5.1 shows representative output for different clusters of users.

Figure 5.12a, b show the interfaces before and after application of the model. Since this interface is intended to be used on a rural kiosk with touchscreen, the user model has increased the inter-button spacing to reduce chances of wrong selection. Similarly the user model can change font size or colour contrast of an interface based on the user profile. Figure 5.13 shows an example of that for a mobile phone application of the same e-Agri system.

Table 5.1 User model prediction

GS (in kg)	Tremor	ROMW (in degree)	FontSize (in pixel)	Colour blindness	Adaptation	Modality	Colour contrast	Button spacing
16	YES	71	21	Protanopia	Gravity well	Pointing/Screen	Blue White	20*
25	NO	52	21	Protanopia	Damping	Pointing/Gesture/Screen	Blue White	20
59	NO	66	19	Deuteranopia	Damping	Pointing/Gesture/Screen	Blue White	20
59	NO	66	0	N/A	Damping	Speech/Audio	N/A	20
25	YES	52	21	None	Gravity well	Pointing/Screen	Any	20
59	NO	120	21	Tritanopia	Damping	Pointing/Gesture/Screen	White Black	5*

*20 means: 0.2 *distance of target from centre of screen
5 means: 0.05 * length of diagonal of the screen

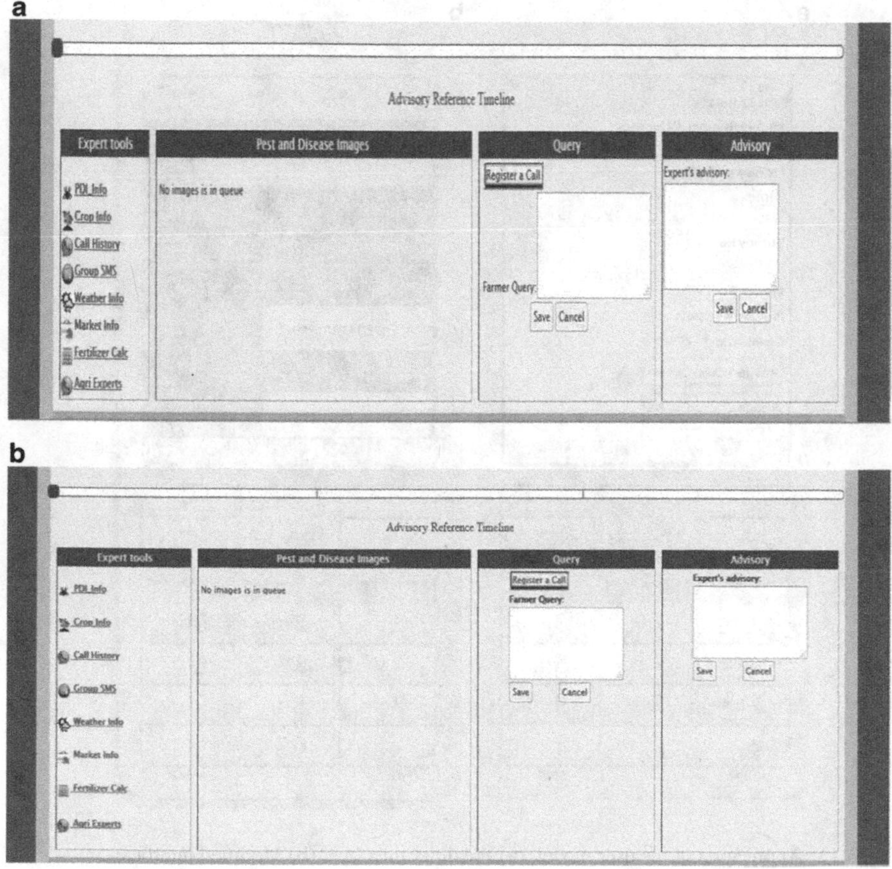

Fig. 5.12 Application of the user model. (**a**) Previous inter-button spacing and hyperlink spacing. (**b**) Modified inter-button spacing and hyperlink spacing

5.5 Implications and Limitations of User Modeling

User trials are always expensive in terms of both time and cost. A design evolves through an iteration of prototypes and if each prototype is to be evaluated by a user trial, the whole design process will be slowed down. Buxton [10] has also noted that "*While we believe strongly in user testing and iterative design. However, each iteration of a design is expensive. The effective use of such models means that we get the most out of each iteration that we do implement*". Additionally, user trials are not representative in certain cases, especially for designing inclusive interfaces for people with special needs. A good simulation with a principled theoretical foundation can be more useful than a user trial in such cases. Exploratory use of modeling can also help designers to understand the problems and requirements

Fig. 5.13 Application of the user model. (**a**) Previous interface. (**b**) Modified interface

of users, which may not always easily be found through user trials or controlled experiments.

This work show that it is possible to develop engineering models to simulate human computer interaction of people with a wide range of abilities and that the prediction is useful in designing and evaluating interfaces. According to Allen Newell's time scale of human action [24], our model works in the cognitive band and predicts activity in millisecond to second range. It cannot model activities outside the cognitive band like micro-saccadic eye gaze movements, response characteristics of different brain regions (in biological band [24]), affective state, social interaction, consciousness (in rational and social band [24]) and so on. Simulations of each individual band have their own implications and limitations. However the cognitive band is particularly important since models working in this band are technically feasible, experimentally verifiable and practically usable. Research in computational psychology and more recently in cognitive architectures supports this claim. We have added a new dimension in cognitive modeling by including users with special needs.

5.6 Conclusion

This chapter presents a new concept of developing inclusive interfaces by simulating interaction patterns of users with disabilities. The user models have been implemented through a simulator that can help to visualize the problem faced by elderly and disabled users. The use of the simulator has been demonstrated through a couple of case studies. The chapter also presents the role of simulation in design optimization and providing runtime adaptation. It concludes through discussing implication and limitation of user modeling and simulation. Later Chap. 9 extends the concept of user profiling and modeling to an international standard.

References

1. Anderson, J. R., & Lebiere, C. (1998). *The atomic components of thought*. Hillsdale: Lawrence Erlbaum Associates.
2. Angst, F., et al. (2010). Prediction of grip and key pinch strength in 978 healthy subjects. *BMC Musculoskeletal Disorders, 11*, 94.
3. Benyon, D., & Murray, D. (1993). Applying user modeling to human computer interaction design. *Artificial Intelligence Review, 7*(3–4), 199–225.
4. Biswas, P., & Langdon, P. (2011). Investigating the gravity well algorithm to help in pointing in electronic interfaces by motor-impaired users. *Journal of Assistive Technologies, 5*(3), ISSN: 1754-9450.
5. Biswas, P., & Robinson, P. (2008). Automatic evaluation of assistive interfaces. In *ACM international conference on Intelligent User Interfaces (IUI)* (pp. 247–256). USA: ACM.
6. Biswas, P., & Robinson, P. (2009). Modeling perception using image processing algorithms. In *23rd British computer society conference on Human-Computer Interaction (HCI 09)*. UK: BCS.
7. Biswas, P., & Langdon, P. (2012). Developing multimodal adaptation algorithm for mobility impaired users by evaluating their hand strength. *International Journal of Human Computer Interaction, 28*(9), 576–596, Taylor & Francis, Print ISSN: 1044-7318.
8. Biswas, P., Langdon, P., & Robinson, P. (2012). Designing inclusive interfaces through user modeling and simulation. *International Journal of Human Computer Interaction, 28*(1), 1–33, Taylor & Francis, Print ISSN: 1044-7318.
9. Boden, M. A. (1985). *Computer models of mind: Computational approaches in theoretical psychology*. Cambridge: Cambridge University Press.
10. Buxton, W. (2009). *Human input to computer systems: Theories, techniques and technology*. Available at: http://www.billbuxton.com/inputManuscript.html. Accessed on 27 Oct 2009.
11. Card, S., Moran, T., & Newell, A. (1983). *The psychology of human-computer interaction*. Hillsdale: Lawrence Erlbaum Associates.
12. Duffy, V. G. (2008). *Handbook of digital human modeling: Research for applied ergonomics and human factors engineering*. Boca Raton: CRC Press.
13. EU VUMS white paper (2012). Availabe at: http://www.myui.eu/deliverables/MyUI-D6-5_VUMS-FinalStandardisationReport.pdf. Accessed on 12 Dec 2012.
14. Fitts, P. M. (1954). The information capacity of the human motor system in controlling the amplitude of movement. *Journal of Experimental Psychology, 47*, 381–391.
15. Hick, W. E. (1952). On the rate of gain of information. *Journal of Experimental Psychology, 4*, 11–26.

16. John, B. E. (2010). Reducing the variability between novice modelers: Results of a tool for human performance modeling produced through human-centered design. In *Behavior representation in modeling and simulation (BRIMS), 2010*, USA.
17. John, B. E., & Kieras, D. (1996). The GOMS family of user interface analysis techniques: Comparison and contrast. *ACM Transactions on Computer Human Interaction, 3*, 320–351.
18. Keates, S., Clarkson, J., & Robinson, P. (2000). Investigating the applicability of user models for motion impaired users. In *ACM/SIGACCESS conference on computers and accessibility, 2000* (pp. 129–136). USA: ACM.
19. Mankoff, J., Fait, H., & Juang, R. (2005). Evaluating accessibility through simulating the experiences of users with vision or motor impairments. *IBM Systems Journal, 44*(3), 505–518.
20. Marr, D. C. (1980). Visual information processing: The structure and creation of visual representations. *Philosophical Transactions of the Royal Society of London, 290*(1038), 199–218.
21. McCulloch, W., & Pitts, W. (1943). A logical calculus of the ideas immanent in nervous activity. *Bulletin of Mathematical Biophysics, 7*, 115–133.
22. Mcmillan, W. W. (1992). Computing for users with special needs and models of computer-human interaction. In *ACM/SIGCHI conference on human factors in computing systems, 1992* (pp. 143–148). USA: ACM.
23. Nejime, Y., & Moore, B. C. J. (1997). Simulation of the effect of threshold elevation and loudness recruitment combined with reduced frequency selectivity on the intelligibility of speech in noise. *Journal of the Acoustical Society of America, 102*, 603–615.
24. Newell, A. (1990). *Unified theories of cognition*. Cambridge, MA: Harvard University Press.
25. Rieman, J., & Young, R. M. (1996). A dual-space model of iteratively deepening exploratory learning. *International Journal of Human Computer Interaction, 44*, 743–775.
26. Serna, A., Pigot, H., & Rialle, V. (2007). Modeling the progression of Alzheimer's disease for cognitive assistance in smart homes. *User Modeling and User-Adapted Interaction, 17*, 415–438.
27. Stephanidis, C., Paramythis, A., Sfyrakis, M., Stergiou, A., Maou, N., Leventis, A., Paparoulis, G., & Karagiannidis, C. (1998). Adaptable and adaptive user interfaces for disabled users in the AVANTwe project. In *Intelligence in services and networks* (LNCS-1430, pp. 153–166). New York: Springer.

Part II
Development

Chapter 6
Intelligent Interaction in Accessible Applications

Sina Bahram, Arpan Chakraborty, Srinath Ravindran, and Robert St. Amant

Abstract Advances in artificial intelligence over the past decade, combined with increasingly affordable computing power, have made new approaches to accessibility possible. In this chapter we describe three ongoing projects in the Department of Computer Science at North Carolina State University. CAVIAR, a Computer-vision Assisted Vibrotactile Interface for Accessible Reaching, is a wearable system that aids people with vision impairment (PWVI) in locating, identifying, and acquiring objects within reach; a mobile phone worn on the chest processes video input and guides the user's hand to objects via a wristband with vibrating actuators. TIKISI (Touch It, Key It, Speak It), running on a tablet, gives PWVI the ability to explore maps and other forms of graphical information. AccessGrade combines crowdsourcing with machine learning techniques to predict the accessibility of Web pages.

6.1 Introduction

Using technology is an ever-growing and seemingly unavoidable aspect of modern life. We communicate with each other using phones that have few if any physical buttons, instead relying upon the rapidly growing ubiquitous touchscreen. We surf the web on a variety of devices from watches to phones to computers of so many shapes and sizes that even the most savvy of technology consumers will be hard pressed to enumerate all the available options. When we wish to consume content such as text, music, video, or other multimedia, we have available to us a wide array of options from our phones, tablets, eyeglasses or contact lenses with built-in screens, projectors, and if any of these options are not to our tastes or do not cater to a specific want or need, we have to only wait months for the next flashy new product.

S. Bahram (✉) • R.St. Amant
Department of Computer Science, North Carolina State University, Raleigh, NC, USA
e-mail: sbahram@ncsu.edu; stamant@ncsu.edu

A. Chakraborty
Udacity
e-mail: arpan@udacity.com

S. Ravindran
Yahoo
e-mail: rsrinath@yahoo-inc.com

P. Biswas et al. (eds.), *A Multimodal End-2-End Approach to Accessible Computing*, Human–Computer Interaction Series, DOI 10.1007/978-1-4471-6708-2_6

With such a myriad of choices, it might seem that there's something for everyone; however, most of these technologies share a fundamental assumption that all their users share the same intellectual, perceptual and mechanical abilities. If one can not see, using a touchscreen presents a unique set of challenges. If one has an intellectual disability, the consumption of a lot of information packed into one small screen is hardly optimal. If dexterity is a challenge for a user, then small onscreen keyboards that require nimbleness and agility, present a significant hurdle to being able to communicate.

Before we quickly dismiss such concerns as applying only to persons with disabilities, it is important to remember that we are all growing older. As we age, our eyesight begins to fail, our dexterity is not what it once was, and our minds may not be as sharp as in decades past. Yet, our desire and need to use technology does not drop off as we age; if anything it grows and becomes stronger. Technology allows us to stay in touch with our circle of friends and loved ones, vicariously enjoy the vacations of children and grandchildren, consume news about the financial markets, politics, and sports in our local and national communities.

The principle of universal design addresses this significant advantage of designing for multiple user groups and functional needs. Such a practice yields the beneficial consequence not only of helping users whose needs might not have been initially known but also of improving the user experience for users without a clear functional limitation. Therefore, it is useful, perhaps even imperative, that we researchers address the functional limitations that we all might experience in one way or another. Whether a disability is permanent, incurable vision loss, for example, or temporary, such as being unable to look at a screen while driving, research into accessibility, eyes-free interfaces, and the use of universal design principles allows us to improve everyone's usability experience.

Users' varying functional needs, whether they be brought on by permanent or temporary limitations, should be at the forefront of any effort to develop user-facing technology. Retroactively adapting technology, designs, or user workflow is not only expensive but often leads to an inferior experience for all users. This principle is not new to those with a background in user experience/interfaces. Doing it right the first time is a better strategy all around and not limited to projects focused on technology. In fact, this insight that retrofitting is more expensive can be easily observed in the construction and architecture of buildings or the design of machinery.

As technologists, researchers, and scientists, we have the opportunity to observe situations in which the existing state of the art is not sufficient to address a given user's functional requirements. Fascinating research opportunities present themselves in these situations. When observing a blind student struggling to understand geography, the thought of making maps accessible to the vision impaired seems all but obvious. When one sees that low vision students have a real and immediate need to consume flowcharts, bar charts, and other graphs and infographics in their science, technology, engineering, and math (STEM) classes, one can not help but think of computer vision, artificial intelligence, and human computer interaction (HCI) research coming together to address this real world need. When one surveys the landscape of web accessibility, the assessment therein, and the solutions available for improving the state of accessible web browsing for all users, it becomes quite clear that there is room for advancement by involving insights from other disciplines such as machine learning or artificial intelligence. Furthermore, such observations are not limited to the virtual world. Thinking about finding physical objects on a cluttered desktop, navigating a crowded unfamiliar room without the use of vision, or receiving information via non-audio means can lead to the examination of haptic feedback systems that communicate with the user through vibration or other forms of tactile feedback.

Solutions based on universal design principles help everyone, not just disabled users. The improvements for users from the implementation of multiple modalities is well explored in the multimodal literature. Integration of speech into a highly visual interface cannot only facilitate access for low vision or blind users but can also accommodate different learning styles, various usage patterns (for example while driving), and can have other beneficial emergent effects. Here again, examples are not limited to the virtual world. In the United States, sloped curbs called curb cuts provide better wheelchair accessibility in compliance with the Americans with Disabilities Act (ADA). One only has to observe a sidewalk with a curb cut at a busy mall, airport, or other populated place to notice the number of parents with strollers, persons with luggage, and elderly individuals who make use of and appreciate these curb cuts. Therefore, even though facilitating access for individuals in wheelchairs might have been the primary goal, the advent of such a practice has led to the improvement for many more individuals than simply those who use wheelchairs.

In our lab at North Carolina State University, we have focused on exploring the research implications of eyes-free physical navigation, eyes-free exploration of highly graphical information, and categorization of the accessibility of Websites to vision impaired users via a user model centered machine learning approach. In this chapter, we offer further information about these three projects: CAVIAR for physical navigation, TIKISI for eyes-free exploration of highly graphical information, and AccessGrade for the categorization of Web page accessibility. After discussing these three projects, we then conclude with some final thoughts on the future direction of research into accessibility with an eye on predicting the nature of such research by the year 2020.

6.2 Research

One of our first forays into accessibility research was a system called Computer-vision Assisted Vibrotactile Interface for Accessible Reaching (CAVIAR). This project studied how blind individuals reach for objects in their peripersonal space and whether we could improve things by using a mobile phone to scan the visual scene and then actuate a vibrating wristband on users' wrist to indicate what direction and how fast they should move their hand to reach the target.

Next, in a project called AccessGrade (hosted at www.AccessGrade.com), we studied the web browsing experience of blind users by implementing a system that assigns a score to webpages representing the level of accessibility. Users are asked to offer their own scores for various pages. The system learns from the user input about various webpages and retrains often to improve the prediction accuracy.

Most recently, our lab has been exploring and developing solutions to facilitate eyes-free exploration of highly graphical information such as maps, flowcharts, bar-charts, and graphs through using touchscreen interfaces to perform this exploration, as well as speech and keyboard modalities. The Touch it, Key it, Speak it (TIKISI) framework was a result of this research. Two projects, with others on the way, have been based on the TIKISI framework. They are TIKISI for Maps and TIKISI for Flowcharts.

6.2.1 CAVIAR

The past few decades have seen increasing interest in automated systems with real-world perception capabilities. Robotic systems are one of the most appealing application areas for applied computer vision, but we find many other examples, such as surveillance systems, assembly-line inspectors, and military applications. Motion tracking for gaming is now commonplace, and self-driving cars are now passing the driving test. Object recognition and text identification on mobile devices have also become popular. These capabilities indicate that state-of-the-art computer vision is capable of providing information for localization and precise manipulation of objects—by automated systems or by users with visual impairment.

6.2.1.1 Related Work

Reaching and manipulating without visual feedback have been studied in psychology and neuroscience, but reaching with tactile feedback has not been studied. One area of HCI research is on tactile directional guidance for navigation, mainly for sighted users. GentleGuide [8], the best-known example, includes vibrating actuators on each wrist to convey signals for indoor navigation.

Another area expands the scope of such work, applying vibrotactile feedback to the learning of new motor skills, with the user wearing a body suit. Spelmezan et al. [34] describe a system of actuators sewn into sports clothing to improve snowboarding and sports that involve similar movements. MusicJacket [36] is a vibrotactile feedback system that guides novice violin players as they learn to manipulate the bow. TIKL (Tactile Interaction for Kinesthetic Learning) [26] is a wearable robotic system that provides feedback for a variety of motor skills, such as carrying out specific arm motions.

6.2.1.2 Overview

One important use of visual perception is to locate and manipulate physical objects—specifically, objects within one's peripersonal space, the immediate surrounding that is within reach of one's limbs. We have developed a way to aid visually impaired people in this process with a system called "Computer-vision Assisted Vibrotactile Interface for Accessible Reaching," or CAVIAR [3].

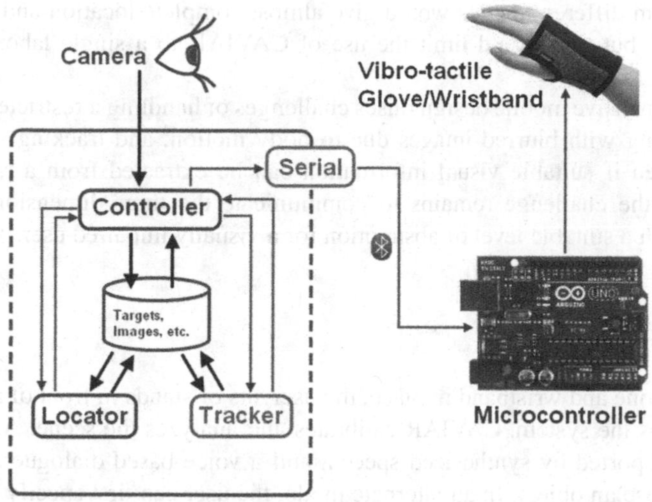

Fig. 6.1 Overview of the CAVIAR system

The CAVIAR project deals with tabletop environments, although our work should apply to other situations in which people interact with nearby physical objects. Helping a user reach nearby objects requires information about the location and identity of objects. Computer vision algorithms are used to extract relevant information from a stream of camera images. The process of locating a desired object may include some interaction with the user to filter and disambiguate among items present in the immediate scene—this disambiguation is established mainly through voice-based interaction. These two steps are performed on a camera-equipped smartphone positioned on the user's chest. Guidance is given by vibrotactile signals to the user's hand using a custom-designed wristband. The wristband communicates with the phone using wireless technology, thus avoiding usability problems that could result from a tether (Fig. 6.1).

6.2.1.3 Challenges

Visual information is rich and high-dimensional, placing heavy demands on computer vision algorithms. Real-time input from cameras is usually treated as a sequence or stream of still images, or *frames*, which means algorithms with high time-complexity reduce the rate at which frames can be processed. When this rate of processing falls below a certain threshold, the algorithm may no longer be usable.

The placement of the smartphone on the user's chest gives the system a good view of objects in the frontal peripersonal space of the user, as well as of the user's hand. The vibrotactile wristband has a visual marker to simplify tracking of the hand. This design is a compromise between the requirements for image processing and the usability of the system. For example, a set of three cameras aimed at a tabletop from different angles would give almost complete location and structural information, but this would limit the use of CAVIAR to a single laboratory-like setting.

The inexpensive mobile design raises challenges of handling a restricted viewing angle, dealing with blurred images due to body motion, and tracking swift hand motion. Even if suitable visual information can be extracted from a raw stream of images, the challenge remains to communicate the three-dimensional spatial location with a suitable level of abstraction for a visually impaired user.

6.2.1.4 Operation

With the phone and wristband in place, the user sits or stands in front of a table top and activates the system. CAVIAR calibrates and analyzes the scene. Any objects found are reported by synthesized speech, and a voice-based dialogue allows the user to choose an object. In an alternate mode, the user can first specify properties of an object, such as color or size, which the system can use as filters for detection. Once a target object has been selected, the system locates the user's hand using a marker on the wristband. Both the locations of the target object and the hand are tracked using particle filters.

These locations are converted from the two-dimensional image space to three-dimensional real-world coordinates relative to the camera position. The assumption that the user's hand and all the objects on the hypothetical tabletop lie in a roughly common plane simplifies calculations in this conversion process, which would otherwise be impossible without stereo vision or other equipment for measuring depth.

The relative difference between the positions of the hand and the target object on the plane is used to select a guidance direction and signal intensity. These parameters are continuously recomputed as new camera frames are processed, and transmitted to the wristband over a Bluetooth link. The wristband has four vibrators that can be activated independently or in combination to signal all four rectilinear (cardinal) directions and four diagonal (super-cardinal) directions, with different levels of intensity. The vibrations indicate which direction the user should move the hand; when the target is reached, the vibrations stop.

6.2.1.5 Computer Vision Results

We tested the computer vision component of CAVIAR by comparing estimated locations against the actual measured locations of 18 objects, treated singly. Three cases resulted in failure due to image segmentation. Figure 6.2 shows the estimated locations of the 15 objects, with arrows pointing to actual locations, from a birds-eye perspective.

The mean error in Euclidean distance for successful cases is 6.1 cm, or 8.1 cm in Manhattan distance, which clearly leaves room for improvement. Estimation errors

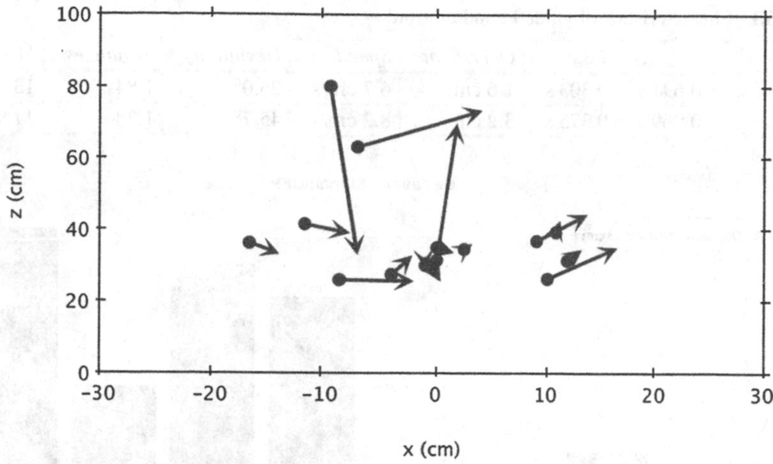

Fig. 6.2 Object location estimates

are due to two main sources. In some cases, only the upper part of an object was captured. In other cases, shadows and other lighting effects influenced estimation. These problems are well-understood, if not completely resolved, in the computer vision literature, and we expect these results to improve with further work.

6.2.1.6 Vibrotactile Interaction Results

We compared different signaling schemes in a sequence of informal studies, with the first author of this chapter acting as the user. Throughout our testing, one vibrating actuator on the wristband would mean movement in a specific rectilinear (cardinal) direction; two simultaneously vibrating actuators would mean movement in a diagonal (super-cardinal) direction. We discovered that guidance using rectilinear directions alone was better than when diagonal directions were also used. Diagonal signals were difficult to interpret due to limited tactile sensitivity on the wrist, resulting in the need for exploratory movement to detect the correct direction. In contrast, rectilinear direction signals were easier to understand and movement could be more deliberate.

We also discovered that directing movement over a period of time posed challenges even for rectilinear paths. When the desired direction was largely diagonal, it would be decomposed into a stair-stepping pattern of rectilinear signals. Frequent switching of directions occurred, and the user experience was degraded. As a solution, we adopted an iterative reduction approach where switching directions would require a certain threshold difference in the distance to be traveled. This prevented direction changes after short durations, and made the guidance signals much easier to follow.

Table 6.1 Characteristics of guided hand motion

	T_{change}	T_{end}	*Overshoot*	$Speed_i$	$Deviation_a$	*#Changes*	*Misses*
Rectilinear	0.691 s	0.303 s	1.6 cm	6.7 cm/s	26.0°	1.84	13 %
Diagonal	0.969 s	0.375 s	3.2 cm	8.2 cm/s	45.7°	1.38	11 %

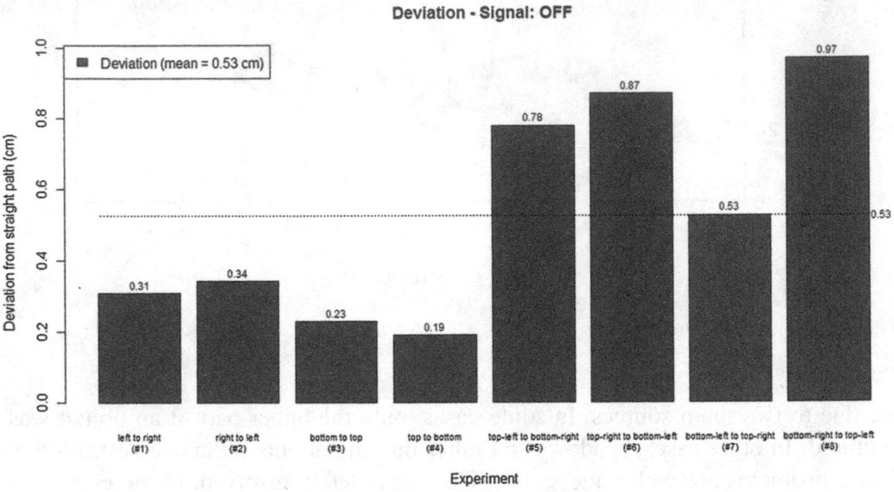

Fig. 6.3 Comparing *Rectilinear* and *Diagonal* blocks

A formative evaluation was carried out to study the efficacy of our guidance mechanism. In a *Rectilinear* block, with only cardinal directions signaled, 100 trials were performed; 50 trials in the *Diagonal* block, where super-cardinal signals were also included. Distances ranged from 27 to 103 cm, with a mean of 52 cm. Trial duration ranged from 516 ms to 41 s, with a mean of 12 s.

As shown in Table 6.1, we found that response to a change in signaled direction (T_{change}) and to a stopping indication once the target was reached (T_{end}) were faster for the Rectilinear trials. Overshooting the target (*Overshoot*) involved a shorter distance for the Rectilinear trials as well. The Diagonal trials involved a higher instantaneous speed ($Speed_i$) along the path followed by the hand, though deviation from a straight-line path ($Deviation_a$) was also higher (comparison shown in Fig. 6.3). The Rectilinear cases required a larger number of changes in direction (*#Changes*) and a slightly higher number of signals that the user did not respond to (*Misses*). Active vibrotactile guidance of this kind has not been studied to a great extent in the past; our work establishes useful metrics for measuring the accuracy and performance of systems that employ such guidance.

Figure 6.4 shows the dynamic aspects of vibrotactile guidance, for a representative path in a Rectilinear trial. The blue dot shows the start of movement, the pink dot the point at which a stopping signal was issued, and the red dot is where the user's hand finally stopped (illustrating the overshoot mentioned earlier).

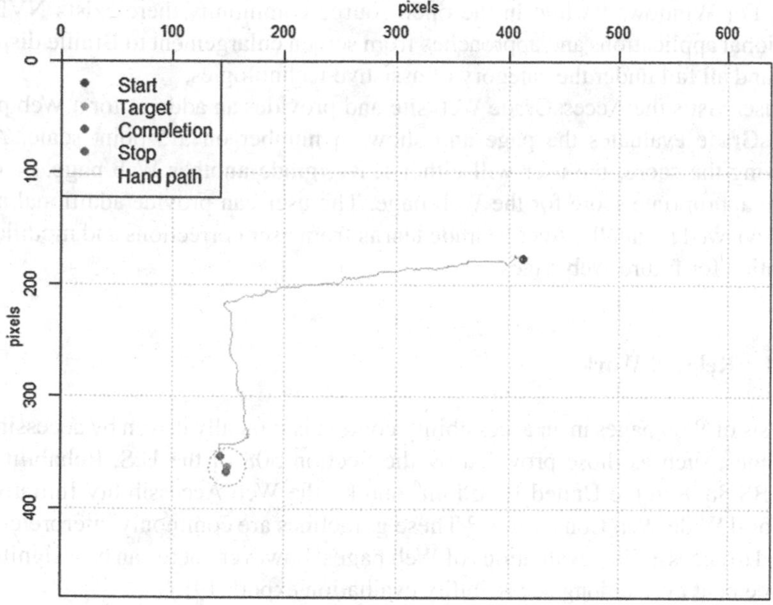

Fig. 6.4 Sample path traversal, iterative reduction guidance

6.2.1.7 Discussion

Our work suggests that movement with vibrotactile guidance is feasible. Speed of movement is variable, even for a single user, with single sessions under different conditions varying between 6 and 18 cm/s. Response times are also variable, but higher for changes of direction than for stopping.

These numbers change with practice, and we expect that individual differences will appear in more extensive experiments, but the results give us preliminary guidelines for the use of CAVIAR. Narrow corridors of movement are impractical and movement along rectilinear paths appears to be more reliable than movement along diagonals. If CAVIAR is to support movement to targets while avoiding obstacles, its signals must be predictive, given the speed of movement and delays in response to signal changes. Prediction of movement at least 300 ms into the future seems to be a reasonable requirement for the system.

6.2.2 Access Grade

A blind user has several ways to access a Web page. The one we will discuss in the context of the AccessGrade project [4] is the use of a screen reader, a program to read out what is on a Web page. The best-known commercial screen reader is

JAWS For Windows,[1] while in the open source community there exists NVDA.[2] Additional applications and approaches from screen enlargement to Braille displays exist, and all fall under the category of assistive technologies.

A user visits the AccessGrade Web site and provides an address for a Web page. AccessGrade evaluates the page and shows a number on a 5-point scale. After reviewing the score, the user will either leave, grade another Web page, or offer a more appropriate score for the Web page. The user can provide additional notes to be reviewed manually. AccessGrade learns from user corrections and modifies its evaluation for future Web pages.

6.2.2.1 Related Work

Analysis of Web pages in an accessibility context is typically driven by accessibility guidelines, such as those provided by the Section 508 of the U.S. Rehabilitation Act,[3] BS 8878 in the United Kingdom[4] and by the Web Accessibility Initiative of the World Wide Web Consortium.[5] These guidelines are commonly interpreted and applied to accessibility evaluations of Web pages; however, there can be a significant disagreement even among accessibility evaluation experts [9].

As Takagi et al. [35] observe, a focus on adherence to guidelines is not enough to ensure that Web pages are actually usable. Metrics have been developed to assess Web page accessibility in quantitative terms, many associated with automated procedures for evaluation [15].

A number of projects have addressed Web accessibility concerns by applying machine learning and data mining techniques. These techniques can provide guidance for identifying the relevant characteristics of usable Web pages, aside from the presence of accessibility-relevant mark-up. Machine learning has been suggested as a promising approach for improving accessibility [5, 27], and some systems have shown significant success.

For example, Kottapally et al. [23] use inductive logic programming and hidden Markov models to infer information about HTML tables and frames. TrailBlazer [6] relies on a naive Bayes classifier to rank suggestions made to users about how to carry out tasks on the Web, using scripts from CoScripter [25]. The HearSay browser [32] uses support vector machines to identify relevant content on successive pages visited by a user, in service of context-directed browsing. HeadingHunter [11] uses a decision tree classifier to identify Web page elements as headings, based on visual

[1] www.freedomscientific.com/jaws-hq.asp

[2] www.nvda-project.org

[3] www.section508.gov

[4] www.access8878.co.uk

[5] www.w3.org/WAI/guid-tech.html

and relational features. HeadingHunter is further notable in providing a practical way of converting such classifiers into JavaScript code appropriate for transcoding.

Considerable research has been devoted to content extraction, especially to identifying the structural and textual features of Web page content. Many approaches rely on DOM (Document Object Model) tree mining. Yi et al. [38] describe entropy-based measures for separating and identifying main content blocks on a page, distinguishing them from navigation links, advertising, and so forth. Part of the functionality of OntoMiner [13] is to identify main content, navigation panels, and advertising on a page, using hierarchical clustering techniques. Webstemmer [39] extracts the main text from Web news articles using inter-page clustering by layout. Such work has reached commercial software as well, as in Readability,[6] which strips out superfluous elements from some types of Web pages to leave only primary content.

A third related area is work on quantitative metrics for Web accessibility, though this is typically applied at a much more detailed level of semantic analysis than that carried out in AccessGrade. Freire et al. [15] give a good survey of recent progress in the area. Most such metrics are based on the concepts of points of failure and potential barriers. As an example, Freire et al. offer the common case of an image with alternative text: this is an accessibility barrier, and all images are thus potential points of failure. The work of Bühler et al. [12] is particularly important in its validation of a specific metric through experimentation with users.

AccessGrade attempts to solve an extremely important problem with the inconsistency of accessibility evaluation. Brajnik et al. [9] show that even among experts of accessibility evaluation, there is a significant amount of disagreement. They report that experts produced 26 % incorrect ratings of Web pages in addition to providing 20 % false positives. Such results help motivate the need for an automated way of performing accessibility evaluations. By using machine learning approaches to capture the complex relationships that are involved in accessibility evaluations, AccessGrade is a step in this direction.

6.2.2.2 Machine Learning for Web Accessibility

A variety of machine learning approaches [28] have been developed over the years to perform prediction tasks. In machine learning, classification refers to an algorithmic procedure for assigning an instance piece of input data one of a given number of categories or classes. A *Classifier* is an algorithmic procedure that performs this classification. For predicting the accessibility of Web pages, each example belongs to one of the five classes in our 5-point scale where 1 represents least accessible and 5 represents most accessible.

Before using a classifier to classify or predict the category of a new instance, it must learn the differences between the categories. This is done using data from a dataset known as a training set. The training set consists of a set of example Web

[6] http://lab.arc90.com/2009/03/02/readability

Table 6.2 Confusion matrix

	Predicted to be accessible	Predicted to be inaccessible
Accessible web page	True positive	False negative
Inaccessible web page	False positive	True negative

pages, each tagged with its category, or class. The classifier learns the differences between the classes by observing the features of the corresponding examples in the training set. After a classifier has been trained, it can be used to predict the accessibility of other Web pages.

The features that we provided our multi-class classifiers for AccessGrade are currently focused upon the structural markup (HTML) used to construct the Web pages. We will be migrating the AccessGrade system to a tree-based representation for all features in the future. This tree-based representation is explained later in this section.

For datasets that only have two classes, a binary classifier can be used. There are two typical ways to evaluate performance, accuracy and false positive rate. False positives and false negatives reduce accuracy in classification. Table 6.2 shows the different possible classifications for a given Web page, in a confusion matrix.

In predicting accessibility, the goal is to produce as few false positives and false negatives as possible. Users and Web developers inform us, however, that the number of false positives is more important than the number of false negatives. The stated reason is based on a violation of expectations. That is, an "Inaccessible" Web page being ranked as "Accessible" is worse than the other way around, at least for users, although content developers, authors, and corporations might have a different opinion. This means that it is relatively worse to predict an inaccessible Web page as being accessible than the reverse. Thus, even though two classifiers may obtain the same prediction accuracy, the one with fewer false positives can be considered better. The same principle has been extended to our multiclass classifier e.g. we prefer classifiers whose performance yields fewer false positives, which is to say fewer scores that are incorrectly high.

6.2.2.3 Features for Predicting Accessibility

Web page accessibility depends on multiple factors, most of which correspond to the DOM (Document Object Model) structure of the HTML file for the page. HTML elements determine the layout and overall presentation of the Web page. Features for classification are obtained by walking the DOM structure. For each HTML element, the number of occurrences of the element in the Web page under consideration is recorded. A small number of features are calculated instead of being direct reports of the number of instances. One example of such a computed feature is the percentage of images with `alt` tags. Another example is the maximum of the `td` elements with the headers attribute and the number of th elements.

The set of features takes into account the presence or absence of HTML elements. While this captures the elements in the structure, it does not capture the structure itself. For example, a Web page with one `h1` followed by `h2` and `p` tags makes more sense than a Web page with an `h2` tag followed by a `p` and an `h1` tag. This is true in terms of readability for both sighted and blind users. Such ordering is not captured in this feature list. The alternative is to treat the entire DOM structure itself as a tree, where each element is a node in the tree. That way, a subtree can be treated as a feature because a subtree preserves the order of elements, and is a better representation of the HTML structure. This tree representation is what the AccessGrade system will be moving towards.

We believe that Web accessibility can be expressed as a function whose parameters are the user's assistive technology, browser, and disability/functional need, coupled with a proper representation of the content. This means that to accurately predict accessibility, we will need to know the user's functional need (e.g. the user is blind and uses a screen reader). We will need to know which screen reader for a reasons having to do with compatibility, standards compliance, accessibility API support, etc. We will need to know the browser being used for virtually the same reasons as the version of the assistive technology. Finally, we will need a model of the Web page that can be broken down into features which can be associated with the proper class by our classifier. Such a model is made possible by the tree-based representation discussed previously.

6.2.2.4 Obtaining Training Data via Crowdsourcing

Crowdsourcing is a process where a given task is "outsourced" to an undefined and distributed group of individuals. The problem to be solved is advertised and broadcast in the form of an open call for participation and interested contributors can submit their solutions to the problem. The contributors are typically compensated for their work, either monetarily or through other intangible benefits; for example, improving an existing service's accuracy. Crowdsourcing has gather speed in the last 5–10 years for accomplishing various tasks primarily because one can obtain a large number of solutions for a given problem at a lower cost compared to directly employing several individuals to complete the same tasks.

While the primary purpose of AccessGrade is to rate Web page accessibility, we gather user feedback on the ratings to improve the prediction algorithm in the backend. Using the information submitted by the users of AccessGrade.com has several advantages. This provides us a dataset with a variety of Web pages. We have seen Web pages originating from various countries with different languages and content. This variety is essential to developing a good predictive system. When the user submits a Web page, the user's rating for that Web page is also recorded. In this case, we trust the user to have navigated the Web page at least once in an attempt to read its contents.

Despite these advantages, there are several issues that we encounter in crowdsourcing. For instance, for a given Web page, a rating of 4 on a five-point scale might mean two different things for two different raters. In order to minimize variations among users, we give AccessGrade the first chance to grade the page submitted by a user. A user who believes the rating is correct enough does not submit a new rating. If AccessGrade makes a mistake, the user can give a better rating. However, we've observed that user's ratings do not show significant disagreement if one accepts that the linear distance between 4 and 5 can be insignificant e.g. 4 and 5 can be treated as an agreement about the score of the Web page. Similarly, 1 and 2 are virtually equivalent as well.

This problem with variance is addressed by our plans to move to a model-based system whereby more metadata is associated with each user submission. This additional information allows the algorithm to draw much stronger conclusions when retraining the machine learning model.

6.2.2.5 Preliminary Results

The current AccessGrade system has an accuracy rate of 84.375 %. This number comes from the implementation of the system sans the tree-based representation or user model-based grading mechanism. It's a measure of accuracy of the AccessGrade system generalized to giving a score applicable to all visiting users. We believe that this number will increase sharply when we tailor the system to each system and begin using the tree-based representation of Web pages.

6.2.3 TIKISI

Graphical information is ubiquitous in the modern world. We use maps to find the locations of businesses in our cities, and we refer to floor plans when entering an unfamiliar building. In newspaper articles and Web sites we find bar charts and line plots that summarize patterns in data. Computer scientists use finite state machines to represent discrete processes and flow charts to represent programs, and scientists of all kinds rely on trees and graphs to represent relationships between the entities they study.

People with vision impairment face enormous hurdles in gaining access to everyday graphical information that sighted people take for granted. Consider a sighted student in a geography class faced with the question, "What countries are to the west of Germany?" The answer is obvious with a glance at a map. Blind students have no such recourse; when they bring up Google maps on a mobile phone, they hear "Google Maps, blank." Or consider a student taking introductory statistics: "Which year, shown on this bar chart, is associated with the highest Presidential election turnout? " Or a computer science student: "From state q_1, which state is reached by a transition for symbol a? "

Examples such as these led us to create the TIKISI framework. TIKISI is a multimodal framework that allows a user to explore graphical information in an eyes-free way. The various input modalities supported include touch (via touching anywhere or issuing gestures), keyboard (via issuing various command sequences, using directional keys to navigate, etc.), and speech (via issuing specific speech commands, domain specific queries, etc.). The output modalities supported at this time are voice output, sonification (non-speech audio), and visual output (via graphical user interface components or more commonly, graphical overlays). Braille output is also forthcoming, given its recent adoption by mobile platforms such as Android and IOS. Currently, we have implemented TIKISI For Maps and TIKISI For Flowcharts. An example use case will illustrate how the system works.

> Jane is a blind middle school student. She is excited about a road trip that she and her family are taking from their home in Florida. Her parents want to use the trip as an educational experience, so they don't tell Jane where they are going. They do give her the hint that it's between Florida and the nation's capital. Jane grabs a tablet and loads TIKISI For Maps, as her parents watch. She says, "Take me to Washington, D.C.," and then zooms in by saying, "Make that larger." Jane places her finger on the tablet and begins exploring, moving out from the center where Washington DC has been placed, tracing over the states around the area. TIKISI reads out map information as she crosses grid boundaries. Jane's finger moves into Virginia after she moves it west from the water she encountered, and then she remembers that she has an aunt in Arlington. Her parents ask her to tell them about all the states they will drive through to get to Arlington. Jane traces her finger down to Florida, and she follows the east coast of the United States up to Virginia, passing through the states: Georgia, South Carolina, North Carolina, and finally Virginia.

6.2.3.1 Related Work

A few systems have been developed to make specific types of graphical information accessible. Those most closely related to maps and flowcharts are discussed.

iGraph-Lite [14] supports exploration of statistical graphs, such as line graphs and bar charts, offering a range of keyboard commands for exploration, such as "Go to the highest point in the graph," and "Read title and axes." Gravvitas [17] uses a multitouch display combined with a wearable haptic feedback device to convey information about diagrams containing circles and polygons. It allows a blind user to ask, "How many objects are there in the graphic?" and "What kind of geometric shape is each object?" for exploration of line charts, floor plans, and other diagrams.

Making touch screens accessible to blind users is an active area of research. Tactile overlays are one popular approach to facilitating access to touch screen interfaces. Systems such as Touch 'n Talk [18], Slate Talker [2], and Talking Tactile Tablet [24] are examples of this approach. Systems also have been designed and implemented that do not force a tangible overlay to be present such as SlideRule [21] and Talking Fingertip [37]. Talking Fingertip and SlideRule serve as the inspiration for the touch and speak functionality used in TIKISI. SlideRule's insistence that no hardware button be necessary, such as in the case of Talking Fingertip, is taken to heart in the design of TIKISI as well; thus, while hardware keys can be used, they aren't necessary for the system's operation. Because TIKISI runs on mobile devices such as smart phones and tablets, onscreen keyboards can be used by a blind user; however, the built-in screen reading functionality natively handles this. For example, TalkBack on Android is available if such a feature is desired.

Exploration of graphical information by blind users is a significantly unexplored area of research, aside from sonification and tactile embossed graphics. To our knowledge, no systems comparable to TIKISI exist that facilitate touch access to graphical information. Systems do exist that allow for tangible or physical overlays, as discussed above, with predefined areas mapping to speech output; however, SlideRule is the only system that facilitates touch access to dynamic and rich information. Even in the case of SlideRule, a user interface is made accessible to the blind users, not graphical information such as a map.

As a further example, Brock et al. present a system, that at first glance, is similar to TIKISI For Maps. They present a prototype of a multitouch enabled multimodal map for the blind. Their system does not appear to achieve many of the goals they lay out [10]. Furthermore, Brock et al. also rely upon a tangible overlay being placed on top of the multitouch screen. Their system can not effectively differentiate reading actions and selection actions, and is also confused by multiple finger touch gestures. Jacobson reviewed augmented tactile maps [19] and found that the addition of audio to a tactile map experience is a definite improvement; however, due to the lack of prevalence of multitouch technology in 2004, Jacobson turns to monotouch tangible overlays as a means of achieving this addition of audio to the tactile map experience. Jacobson also points out the difficulty in adding Braille labels to tactile maps, as well as presents results from a pilot study involving a multimodal map for the blind, though it is monotouch and involving a tangible overlay as discussed previously. For additional overviews of tactile maps, augmented or otherwise, the reader is referred to Siekierska et al. [33] and Perkins and Gardiner [30].

One system that partially allows for the exploration of graphical information via the keyboard is IVEO [16]; however, this system is optimized to be used with an additional piece of hardware technology called the IVEO Touchpad. This touchpad sends the appropriate requests to the IVEO software so that the software knows where the user is touching, and then these regions can be read out loud. Furthermore, keyboard exploration of many of the examples provided with IVEO proved to convey almost no information, as items in the various SVG diagrams were read out as oval, line, ellipse, and so on, with no conveyance of any additional information except for the infrequent text label such as "the sun". IVEO, in addition to some of the systems referenced above, also depends upon an embossed physical overlay to be placed on top of the touchpad as its primary interface for the user.

As a multimodal system, TIKISI currently supports touch, keyboard, and speech inputs along with visual and speech outputs. Braille and haptic feedback are very much of interest and are only omitted on accounts of implementation time, but such features have already been explored and are forthcoming. Oviatt's work on multimodal interactive maps [29] showed that a speech-only interface to interactive maps has a high degree of performance difficulties, spontaneous disfluencies, and long task completion times [29]. However, all of these metrics improved once a multimodal interface was introduced. In addition to better performance, Oviatt reports the users preferring a multimodal interface over a unimodal one. The TIKISI framework is differentiated from Oviatt's interactive maps work in that TIKISI concentrates on blind users, a user group that is completely unaddressed in the interactive maps work. TIKISI facilitates the presentation of graphical information independent of the problem domain, so it might be more appropriate to compare TIKISI For Maps to Oviatt's interactive maps. However, even within this comparative context, TIKISI For Maps facilitates a different set of interactions because of the functional limitation of the user. One area in which Oviatt's work is applicable to TIKISI is in the quintessential example of "place X here" where X is some arbitrary argument. Richard Bolt first established this specific interaction when introducing multimodal interfaces [7], and so it is not a coincidence that all three multimodal interfaces discussed here share this commonality. Such an interaction allows the user to convey information through multiple channels and, in the case of TIKISI, receive that information back through multiple channels as well.

Research on digitization of flowcharts goes back to the 1980s, with the work of Abe et al. [1] on identifying symbols, lines, and characters in flow charts. Yu et al. [40] describe a system for understanding engineering drawings, which include logic circuits, electrical circuits, chemical plant flow diagrams, and program logic flow charts. Their system takes a knowledge-based approach, maintaining separate libraries of pattern matchers for different domains. Their system was tested on 24 drawings, with text manually removed. A later system [41] analyzed 14 flow charts scanned from textbooks, containing 226 symbols in total, and recognized 13 without errors at 300dpi and 12 without errors at 150dpi.

In more recent work, the TeDUB (Technical Drawings Understanding for the Blind) project [31] was aimed at translating raster graphics drawings into textual descriptions. The image processing module had three components: pre-processing, to enhance an image, e.g. through noise reduction; segmentation, to divide an image into regions; and recognition, for matching and combining features of a drawing to a domain-specific ontology. Image analysis in this domain proved "very difficult to accomplish," however [22]. King's work on making circuit diagrams accessible [22] also encountered difficulties in applying image processing techniques to diagrams; results, as with Yu et al., were without text labels. Zapirain et al. [42] describe a system for the same purpose, based on traditional components for segmentation and template-driven recognition. Optical character recognition is used to handle text. Performance of the system was evaluated by a survey of PWVI users, with satisfaction being high.

In 2011, Kane et al. presented access overlays [20] as a set of interaction techniques for user to explore data, user interfaces and spatial data, on large touchscreens. The access overlay named "Neighborhood Browsing" is the closest analog to our TIKISI system.

6.2.3.2 Discretization Grid

The discretization grid represents one of TIKISI's key insights: a separation between the input resolution and the output resolution of an interactive display. Because a blind user does not depend on vision for targeted input actions, the output resolution of the display, whether high or low, is not significant. This allows a user of TIKISI to

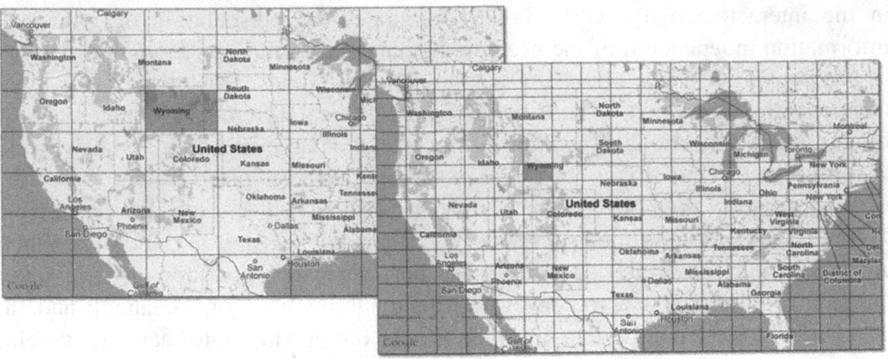

Fig. 6.5 Map of the United States at two different discretization levels

explore graphical information at different resolution levels, dynamically changing the level to match her exploration goals. An arbitrarily high-resolution presentation becomes manageable in this way. For example, if Jane is a blind user of a large touch interface, she can initially set the resolution to a comfortable level, such as a 10 × 10 grid, to gain an overview, and then either zoom in *or* change the grid resolution for more detail.

The discretization grid shares its motivation with Kane et al.'s Voronoi tessellation approach; both address the need to reduce the number of targets on the screen while still maintaining the relative spatial layout of the underlying information. Figure 6.5 shows a map with the discretization grid at two different levels.

6.2.3.3 Domain-Specific Features

TIKISI is designed to support the integration of domain-specific behavior into any implementation using the framework. For example, in TIKISI For Maps, the user can ask to be taken to a location from the country level down to a specific address, query about nearby land, and so forth. In TIKISI For Flowcharts, the user can ask about whether two nodes share a common parent, request a summary traversal of the flowchart, and more. These behaviors exist at the same level of primitive operations such as changing the resolution of the discretization grid, reading by row/column/cell, etc., and are accessed via the same multimodal interaction techniques. This seamless integration of domain specific functionality facilitates the concept of universal design discussed in the beginning of this chapter; namely, offering subtle but effective overlays and other unobtrusive interfaces for making graphical information accessible instead of forcing the user into a different interface from that used by a sighted user.

6.2.3.4 Formative Evaluation of TIKISI for Maps

A formative study of TIKISI For Maps was carried out with a group of 12 people with vision impairment, ranging from 10 to 18 years old, at the Washington State School for the Blind. The users spent a little over an hour with the application, which ran on a tablet; all users used TIKISI For Maps, with some spending more time than others. They appreciated the novelty of using a touch screen (some being comfortable with the use of one through owning an iPhone). Because the iPhone is essentially an extension of the concepts laid out in Kane et al.'s SlideRule work [21], the learning curve was quite small. Furthermore, the users reported surprise, enjoyment, and interest with the ability of hearing each other work on the tablet. Two users tried using the tablet together, which suggested new design requirements for the system, such as the ability to receive input from multiple modalities simultaneously (e.g. keyboard and touch).

At the time of the formative study, the system did not have the "Take me to" functionality implemented. Without prompting, almost every user requested this feature in one way or another, which we found unsurprising. The lack of "Take me to" functionality even had an advantage from the perspective of requirements elicitation—we could observe the users' behavior when they tried to find a specific location without being able to directly center it on the screen. Most users would first assume that they simply cannot find the given location using the system, but then slowly each user would begin experimenting with other features: dialing up the resolution of the grid, zooming in and out, and dialing the grid back down to center themselves mentally on a particular location before changing the resolution level again.

Other feature requests stemmed from wanting to explore where the device is currently located instead of an arbitrary location on the map. This feature is now implemented in current prototypes of TIKISI For Maps. The users also become frustrated and lost in regions of water or seas/oceans between countries on the map of the world. We implemented a "Nearby" action to address this. Here again, the absence of the "Nearby functionality led to an informative result: the children made a game of finding land, going so far as to shout out instructions: Go North," "No, go East! " This highlights the kind of interaction supported by the system: exploration and navigation, and also collaboration. It suggests a reasonable level of engagement among multiple users even though only one is physically in possession of the tablet.

6.2.3.5 TIKISI for Flowcharts

TIKISI For Flowcharts is designed to facilitate access to printed and digital flowcharts. It has slowly started morphing into TIKISI For Diagrams as it can now understand the diagrammatic components common to more than just flowcharts. A use case can help introduce the concept.

> Lenora sits down in front of a surface, and places the flowchart on it. The surface informs her that the sheet of paper is blank; Lenora flips it over. TIKISI For Flow Charts scans the chart, recognizes the relationships between nodes, orients it, and builds a model of the flow

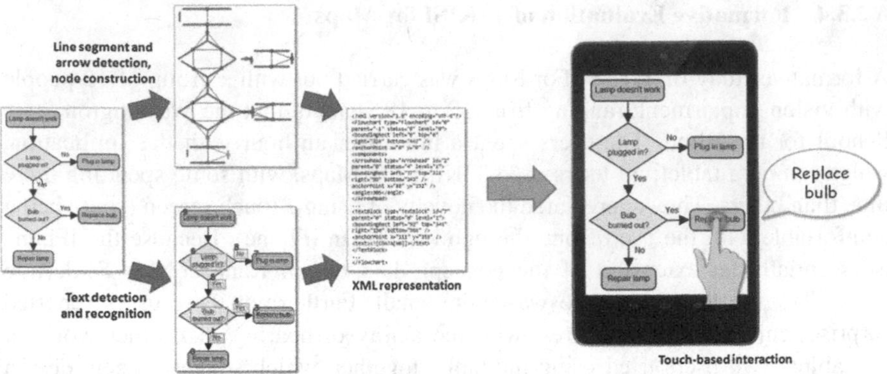

Fig. 6.6 Processing pipeline and sample interaction in TIKISI for FLowcharts

> chart's contents. Lenora asks for an overview. The system checks for a legend (a region of text not within a node) and reads that. It then reads an overview of the nodes, their labels, and relationships to one another, e.g.,"There are five nodes. Start … goes to Accept Data From Sensor … goes to … Transform Sensor Data To Display Data Format … goes to … Send Display Data To Display … goes to … End." She gives a "Silence Speech" command and then resumes an in-order traversal from the node she has reached, using a "Continuous read" command.[7]
>
> Lenora changes gears: She activates "Adventure Mode" (named after the text-based game). The system reads the label of the root node, along with the possible directions or choices from that point: "… The true branch is down and left; the false branch is down and right." Lenora gestures a direction to move to a new node, then another, and then another, as visible in the natural flow of the graphic.

The fact that the flowchart's semantics are understood by the system is important. For example, if the user touches an arrowhead, the arrow and associated label are what's read. Only if no additional semantic or textual information exists, does the arrowhead get read out as it is a lower order diagrammatic component. Composing these lower order components into a high-level view of the semantically important aspects of a diagram is an ongoing area of research. The blending together of computer vision, artificial intelligence to derive what each component means, and human computer interaction is what makes TIKISI For Flowcharts possible. Figure 6.6 illustrates the different steps involved in digesting a flowchart image and presenting the information thus obtained in an eyes-free interface.

[7]The ellipses in the overview Lenora hears indicate prosodic cues. The prosody of speech output affords speech interface users a familiar way of indicating importance in a long stream of speech. The ellipses, which represent pauses, are also exactly the locations where a small audio tone or click can be inserted for further enforcement [21]. The silencing command is similar to that in Gravitas [17] to pause the focus at the given node, and then begin exploring from that point.

6.3 Looking to the Future

The research described in this paper has led to systems that users have found worthwhile and enjoyable in our testing. People of all ages and qualifications from locations throughout the world have written to us about AccessGrade. The children who have experimented with TIKISI were as enthusiastic as children can be—and they are the ones who will eventually design and implement the technologies of the future. Accessibility is one of the most rewarding areas of computing.

To build these systems we have drawn on a wide range of concepts and techniques in computer science: robotics and computer vision, mobile systems, human-computer interaction and intelligent user interfaces, and systems engineering. We believe this breadth is a strength of our research. In universal design, the most effective solutions often arise when designers take a broad perspective on what the design problem is and how it can be addressed; in accessibility, the same breadth of vision is needed.

Ideally, by the year 2020, we will see significant progress towards the integration of accessibility concepts into every area of research and development on interactive systems. If generalizable solutions for interaction and software infrastructure can be improved, then most of today's accessibility concerns will become part of the mainstream. Universal design coupled with powerful customization capabilities will mean that interactive systems can be tailored to individual needs. We can find ourselves no longer building specialized one-off systems to help people with specific accessibility needs to interact with computers; rather, we will ask, "How can the existing capabilities of these systems be combined and adapted, following well-understood procedures, to meet the needs or preferences of *any* individual? " This is a bright future to look forward to and more importantly, help bring about.

References

1. Abe, K., Azumatani, Y., Kukouda, M., & Suzuki, S. (1986). Discrimination of symbols, lines, and characters in flow chart recognition. In *Proceedings 8th ICPR, Paris, France* (pp. 1071–1074).
2. Aratí, A., Juhasz, Z., Blenkhorn, P., Evans, D. G., & Evreinov, G. E. (2004). Java-powered braille slate talker. In J. Klaus, K. Miesenberger, W. L. Zagler, & D. Burger (Eds.), *ICCHP, lecture notes in computer science* (Vol. 3118, pp. 506–513). Springer. URL: http://dblp.uni-trier.de/db/conf/icchp/icchp2004.html#AratoJBEE04
3. Bahram, S., Chakraborty, A., & St. Amant, R. (2012). Caviar: A vibrotactile device for accessible reaching. In *Proceedings of the international conference on Intelligent User Interfaces (IUI)* (pp. 245–248). New York: ACM.
4. Bahram, S., Sen, D., & Amant, R. S. (2011). Prediction of web page accessibility based on structural and textual features. In *Proceedings of the international cross-disciplinary conference on Web Accessibility, W4A '11* (pp. 31:1–31:4). New York: ACM. 10.1145/1969289.1969329. URL: http://doi.acm.org/10.1145/1969289.1969329
5. Bigham, J., Kaminsky, R., Ladner, R., Danielsson, O., & Hempton, G. (2006). WebInSight: Making web images accessible. In *Proceedings of the 8th international ACM SIGACCESS conference on computers and accessibility* (pp. 181–188). New York: ACM.

6. Bigham, J., Lau, T., & Nichols, J. (2009). Trailblazer: Enabling blind users to blaze trails through the web. In *Proceedings of the 13th international conference on intelligent user interfaces* (pp. 177–186). New York: ACM.
7. Bolt, R. A. (1980). "Put-that-there": Voice and gesture at the graphics interface. In *Proceedings of the 7th annual conference on computer graphics and interactive techniques, SIGGRAPH '80* (pp. 262–270). New York: ACM. http://doi.acm.org/10.1145/800250.807503. URL: http://doi.acm.org/10.1145/800250.807503
8. Bosman, S., Groenendaal, B., Findlater, J., Visser, T., Graaf, M., & Markopoulos, P. (2003). Gentleguide: An exploration of haptic output for indoors pedestrian guidance. In L. Chittaro (Ed.), *Human-computer interaction with mobile devices and services* (pp. 358–362). Berlin: Springer.
9. Brajnik, G., Yesilada, Y., & Harper, S. (2010). Testability and validity of wcag 2.0: The expertise effect. In *Proceedings of the 12th international ACM SIGACCESS conference on computers and accessibility, ASSETS '10* (pp. 43–50). New York: ACM. http://doi.acm.org/10.1145/1878803.1878813. URL: http://doi.acm.org/10.1145/1878803.1878813
10. Brock, A., Truillet, P., Oriola, B., & Jouffrais, C. (2010). Usage of multimodal maps for blind people: Why and how. In *ACM international conference on interactive tabletops and surfaces* (pp. 247–248). New York: ACM.
11. Brudvik, J., Bigham, J., Cavender, A., & Ladner, R. (2008). Hunting for headings: Sighted labeling vs. automatic classification of headings. In *Proceedings of the 10th international ACM conference on computers and accessibility* (pp. 201–208). New York: ACM.
12. Bühler, C., Heck, H., Perlick, O., Nietzio, A., & Ulltveit-Moe, N. (2006). Interpreting results from large scale automatic evaluation of web accessibility. In *ICCHP'06* (pp. 184–191). New York: ACM.
13. Davalcu, H., Vadrevu, S., Nagarajan, S., & Ramakrishnan, I. (2005). Ontominer: Bootstrapping and populating ontologies from domain-specific web sites. *IEEE Intelligent Systems, 18*(5), 24–33. New York: ACM.
14. Ferres, L., Lindgaard, G., & Sumegi, L. (2010). Evaluating a tool for improving accessibility to charts and graphs. In *Proceedings of the 12th international ACM SIGACCESS conference on computers and accessibility* (pp. 83–90). New York: ACM.
15. Freire, A. P., Fortes, R. P. M., Turine, M. A. S., & Paiva, D. M. B. (2008). An evaluation of web accessibility metrics based on their attributes. In *Proceedings of the 26th annual ACM international conference on design of communication, SIGDOC '08* (pp. 73–80). New York: ACM. http://doi.acm.org/10.1145/1456536.1456551. URL: http://doi.acm.org/10.1145/1456536.1456551
16. Gardner, J., & Bulatov, V. (2006). Scientific diagrams made easy with IVEO. In *Computers helping people with special needs* (pp. 1243–1250). Berlin: Springer. URL: http://dx.doi.org/10.1007/11788713/s/do5(1)79
17. Goncu, C., & Marriott, K. (2006). Gravvitas: Generic multi-touch presentation of accessible graphics. In *Human-computer interaction–INTERACT 2011* (pp. 30–48). Berlin: Springer.
18. Hill, D. R., & Grieb, C. (1988). Substitution for a restricted visual channel in multimodal computer-human dialogue. *IEEE Transactions on Systems, Man, and Cybernetics, 18*(3), 285–304.
19. Jacobson, R. (1998). Navigating maps with little or no sight: An audio-tactile approach. In *Proceedings of the workshop on Content Visualization and Intermedia Representations (CVIR)* (pp. 95–102).
20. Kane, S., Morris, M., Perkins, A., Wigdor, D., Ladner, R., & Wobbrock, J. (2011). Access overlays: Improving non-visual access to large touch screens for blind users. In *Proceedings of the 24th annual ACM symposium on user interface software and technology* (pp. 273–282). New York: ACM.
21. Kane, S. K., Bigham, J. P., & Wobbrock, J. O. (2008). Slide rule: Making mobile touch screens accessible to blind people using multi-touch interaction techniques. In *Proceedings of the 10th international ACM SIGACCESS conference on computers and accessibility, Assets '08* (pp. 73–80). New York: ACM. http://doi.acm.org/10.1145/1414471.1414487. URL: http://doi.acm.org/10.1145/1414471.1414487

22. King, A. R. (2006). *Re-presenting visual content for blind people*. Ph.D. thesis, University of Manchester.
23. Kottapally, K., Ngo, C., Reddy, R., Pontelli, E., Son, T., & Gillan, D. (2003). Towards the creation of accessibility agents for non-visual navigation of the web. In *Proceedings of the 2003 conference on universal usability* (pp. 134–141). New York: ACM.
24. Landau, S., & Wells, L. (2003). Merging tactile sensory input and audio data by means of the talking tactile tablet. In *EuroHaptics '03, IEEE Computer Society* (pp. 414–418). New York: ACM.
25. Leshed, G., Haber, E., Matthews, T., & Lau, T. (2008). CoScripter: Automating & sharing how-to knowledge in the enterprise. In *Proceeding of the twenty-sixth annual ACM conference on human factors in computing systems* (pp. 1719–1728). New York: ACM.
26. Lieberman, J., & Breazeal, C. (2007). Tikl: Development of a wearable vibrotactile feedback suit for improved human motor learning. *IEEE Transactions on Robotics, 23*(5), 919–926.
27. Mahmud, J., Borodin, Y., Das, D., & Ramakrishnan, I. (2007). Combating information overload in non-visual web access using context. In *Proceedings of the 12th international conference on intelligent user interfaces* (pp. 341–344). New York: ACM.
28. Mitchell, T. M. (1997). *Machine learning*. New York: McGraw-Hill.
29. Oviatt, S. (1996). Multimodal interfaces for dynamic interactive maps. In *Proceedings of the SIGCHI conference on human factors in computing systems: Common ground, CHI '96* (pp. 95–102). New York: ACM. http://doi.acm.org/10.1145/238386.238438. URL: http://doi.acm.org/10.1145/238386.238438
30. Perkins, C., & Gardiner, A. (2003). Real world map reading strategies. *The Cartographic Journal, 40*(3), 265–268.
31. Petrie, H., Schlieder, C., Blenkhorn, P., Evans, G., King, A., O'Neill, A., Ioannidis, G., Gallagher, B., Crombie, D., Mager, R., et al. (2002). Tedub: A system for presenting and exploring technical drawings for blind people. In *Computers helping people with special needs* (pp. 47–67). Berlin: Springer.
32. Ramakrishnan, I., Mahmud, J., Borodin, Y., Islam, M., & Ahmed, F. (2009). Bridging the web accessibility divide. *Electronic Notes in Theoretical Computer Science, 235*, 107–124.
33. Siekierska, E., Labelle, R., Brunet, L., Mccurdy, B., Pulsifer, P., Rieger, M., & O'Neil, L. (2003). Enhancing spatial learning and mobility training of visually impaired people-a technical paper on the internet-based tactile and audio-tactile mapping. *The Canadian Geographer/Le G? ographe canadien, 47*(4), 480–493.
34. Spelmezan, D., Jacobs, M., Hilgers, A., & Borchers, J. (2009). Tactile motion instructions for physical activities. In *Proceedings of the 27th international conference on human factors in computing systems, CHI '09* (pp. 2243–2252). New York: ACM. http://doi.acm.org/10.1145/1518701.1519044
35. Takagi, H., Asakawa, C., Fukuda, K., & Maeda, J. (2004). Accessibility designer: Visualizing usability for the blind. In *Proceedings of the 6th international ACM SIGACCESS conference on computers and accessibility* (pp. 177–184). ACM.
36. Van Der Linden, J., Schoonderwaldt, E., & Bird, J. (2009). Good vibrations: Guiding body movements with vibrotactile feedback. In *Proceedings of 3rd international workshop physicality* (pp. 13–18).
37. Vanderheiden, G. C. (1996). Use of audio-haptic interface techniques to allow nonvisual access to touchscreen appliances. *Human Factors and Ergonomics Society Annual Meeting Proceedings, 40*(24), 1266.
38. Yi, L., Liu, B., & Li, X. (2003). Eliminating noisy information in web pages for data mining. In *Proceedings of the ninth ACM SIGKDD international conference on knowledge discovery and data mining* (pp. 296–305). New York: ACM.
39. Yoshioka, M. (2008). IR interface for contrasting multiple news sites. In *Information retrieval technology* (pp. 508–513). Berlin: Springer.
40. Yu, Y., Samal, A., & Seth, S. (1994). Isolating symbols from connection lines in a class of engineering drawings. *Pattern Recognition, 27*(3), 391–404. 10.1016/0031-3203(94)90116-3. URL: http://www.sciencedirect.com/science/article/pii/0031320394901163

41. Yu, Y., Samal, A., & Seth, S. (1997). A system for recognizing a large class of engineering drawings. *IEEE Transactions on Pattern Analysis and Machine Intelligence, 19*(8), 868–890.
42. Zapirain, B., Zorrilla, A., Oleagordia, I., & Muro, A. (2010). Accessible schematics content descriptors using image processing techniques for blind students learning. In *5th International Symposium on I/V Communications and Mobile Network (ISVC)* (pp. 1–4). New York: IEEE. 10.1109/ISVC.2010.5656270

Chapter 7
Interaction Techniques for Users with Severe Motor-Impairment

Pradipta Biswas, Rohan Joshi, Subhagata Chattopadhyay, U. Rajendra Acharya, and Teik-Cheng Lim

Abstract This chapter presents brief overview of a few new technologies used in interfaces for people with different range of abilities. We discuss about scanning systems that enables one to use a computer or tablet using only one or two switches, eye tracking system that moves a pointer in a screen following eye gaze and finally EEG-based brain computer interfaces. The chapter discusses state of the art on each system, points to a new system by combining more than one modality and finally present existing problems and future vision regarding these technologies.

7.1 Introduction

physically challenged users cannot interact with a computer or tablet through a conventional keyboard, mouse or stylus. For example, spasticity due to Amyotrophic Lateral Sclerosis (ALS) and Cerebral Palsy, which confine movement to a small part of the body. Despite of such disabilities they often need to operate a laptop or

---

P. Biswas (✉)
Department of Engineering, University of Cambridge, Trumpington Street, Cambridge, Cambridgeshire CB2 1PZ, UK
e-mail: pb400@hermes.cam.ac.uk

R. Joshi
Department of Industrial Design, Designed Intelligence Group, Eindhoven University of Technology, KU Leuven, Leuven, Belgium
e-mail: njoshi8@gmail.com

S. Chattopadhyay
Camellia Institute of Engineering, Madhyamgram, India
e-mail: subhagatachatterjee@yahoo.com

U.R. Acharya
Ngee Ann Polytechnic, Singapore, Singapore
e-mail: aru@np.edu.sg

T.-C. Lim
SIM University, Singapore, Singapore
e-mail: tclim@unisim.edu.sg

P. Biswas et al. (eds.), *A Multimodal End-2-End Approach to Accessible Computing*, Human–Computer Interaction Series, DOI 10.1007/978-1-4471-6708-2_7

tablet as an Augmentative and Alternative Communication (AAC) device to interact with others apart from the general use of a computer. These users need special interaction techniques to operate computer or tablets. This chapter introduces three different interaction techniques for users with severe motor impairment. The first section describes a technique called scanning system that enables to use a computer with one or two switches. Section 7.2 presents an eye tracking based system which also leverages the scanning system but works faster than the scanning system. Section 7.3 presents analysis techniques of EEG signals and using them in a Brain Computer Interface (BCI), which might be useful in alleviating the need of body part movements. Section 7.5 highlights present problems with these technologies followed by future scope of improvements in such technologies.

7.2 Scanning System

Scanning is the technique of successively highlighting items on a computer screen and pressing a switch when the desired item is highlighted. The highlighting and pressing goes on until the desired screen item is selected.

Most works on scanning have aimed to enhance the text entry rate of a virtual keyboard. In these systems the mechanism is usually block-row-column-item based scanning [12, 20]. However, navigation to arbitrary locations on a screen has also become important as graphical user interfaces are more widely used. Two types of scanning mechanism are commonly used for general navigation. Cartesian scanning moves the cursor progressively in a direction parallel to the edges of the screen, and polar scanning selects a direction and then moves along a fixed bearing. A particular type of polar scanning that allows movement only in eight directions is commonly used [15, 21] (and in a wheelchair mobility interface [16]). In both Cartesian and polar scanning systems, the interaction rate of users remains very low. Thus, recent scanning systems have tried to combine two or more types of scanning techniques to get better performance.

Examples of some existing systems in the same discipline are the Autonomia System [21], the FastScanner system [15], the Gus Scanning Cursor [11], the ScanBuddy system [23] and the SSMCI system [14]. The Autonomia system [21] replaces the windows and widgets of a typical Windows interface by Frames and Wifsid (Widget for Single-switch input devices) respectively. The system consists of different frames such as Cursor Frame, Virtual Keyboard Frame, Console frame etc. The cursor frame provides eight-directional scanning whereas the frame itself and other frames are scanned using the block-row-item based scanning approach. The FastScanner system [15] starts the scanning process by showing a list of currently open applications and asks the user to choose an application. The scanning procedure then restarts itself to the selected application. The objects of an interface are scanned sequentially based on a predefined order. Screen navigation is done by eight-directional scanning. Additionally, the objects of an interface are divided into four classes (viz. Text entry objects, simple objects, selection objects and container objects) and the user input is interpreted according to the type of the object that has received the input. The Gus Scanning Cursor [11] provides different types of navigation strategies (like Cartesian, Polar, eight-directional) at a single screen and the screen itself is scanned by row-item based scanning. The user has to choose a particular scanning type to navigate through the screen. The ScanBuddy system [23] scans the screen by iteratively dividing it into two equal parts up to 4 times. Finally it scans the smallest part using Cartesian scanning. In the SSMCI (Single Switch Mouse Control Interface) system [14], an intelligent agent operates to guess the target and moves the cursor accordingly. If the guess is incorrect the user has to signal the agent, which then reevaluates the situation and comes up with a new solution. There also exists some scanning application for some specialized tasks like text selection [19] and menu selection process [7].

Most of these scanning systems (except Gus [11] and SSMCI [14]) have a similar structure. They start by dividing the screen into several blocks and then introduce either Cartesian or polar scanning within a block. As a result, users can traverse shorter distances using Cartesian or polar scanning and the time needed to reach a target from long distances is reduced. However, an arbitrary screen layout cannot always be evenly divided into blocks, rows or columns. So different scanning systems define blocks in different ways. The Autonomia system introduces blocks by providing different frames. The FastScanner system defines blocks based on the hierarchy of objects in the Windows operating system. The scan buddy system defines blocks just by dividing the screen in two equal segments.

We have developed the cluster scanning system [2] that works based on iteratively clustering screen objects. Initially it collects all possible targets (e.g. icons, buttons, combo-boxes etc.) by enumerating window processes (currently it operates only for Microsoft Windows operating system). Then it iteratively divides a screen into several clusters of targets based on their locations (Fig. 7.1). We use Fuzzy c-means algorithm [18] to cluster the targets. The user has to select the appropriate cluster that contains the intended target. After reaching a relatively small cluster, the system switches to eight-directional scanning. The user can select the target or can navigate through the screen using eight-directional scanning mechanism.

This particular system does not introduce any new interface element (like a frame or form) in the screen as Autonomia or FastScanner system do. So we can expect users to take less time to learn this system than existing ones. Additionally, the system does not blindly divide the screen in a predefined number of segments (as the ScanBuddy system does). It clusters the target so that the targets are evenly divided into blocks and a block is not drawn in a region that does not contain any target. As a result it can minimize the target selection time. We found that the total task completion time, efficiency, idle time and number of missed clicks are less in the cluster scanning system than traditional block scanning systems. The performance on the scanning system does not also seem to depend on the physical strength of users, or in other words physical impairment does not seem to affect performance for the scanning system. In short, we found that mobility impaired users found the cluster scanning system faster, easier and more accurate than the conventional scanning systems [2].

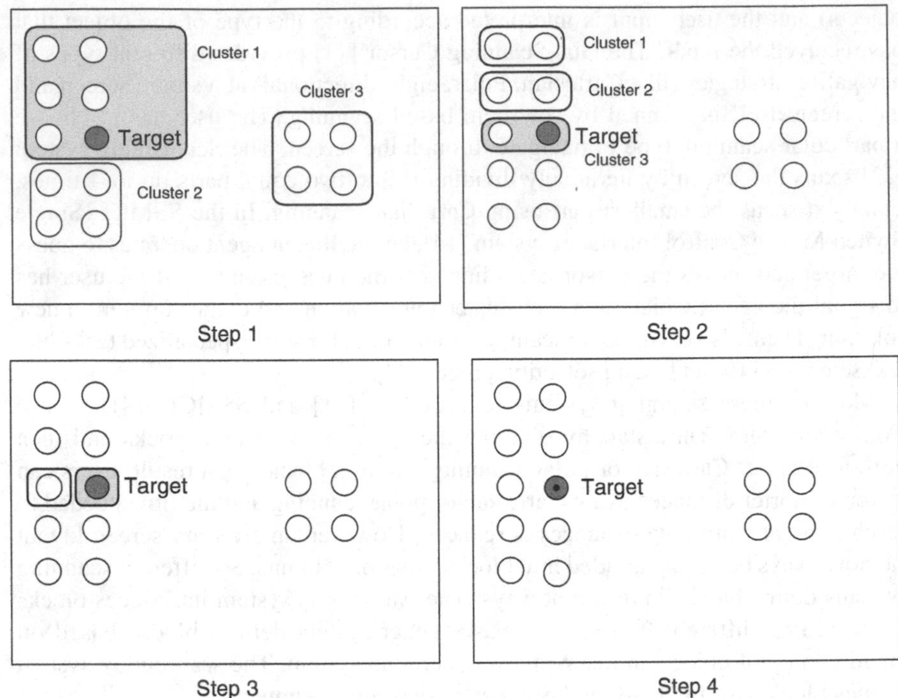

Fig. 7.1 The cluster scanning system

7.3 Eye Tracking System

Eye tracking systems work by detecting eye gaze pattern and then detecting points of eye gaze fixation, saccadic movement of eye gaze and eye blinks (Fig. 7.2). Eye trackers use different technologies to do that – the most common and accurate ones are infrared based. They emit infrared and detect pupil position from the reflected infra red from eyes. Other eye trackers work by analyzing the raw video signal in visible light spectrum. Eye trackers are also different in their size and shape – Tobii X120 or Facelab trackers are non-invasive and sit below or fitted to a screen, while some like the SMI one is fitted to spectacles. There are also a few attempts to develop webcam based eye tracker but with limited success in terms of accuracy.

Most eye tracking based interfaces for people with disabilities use the eye gaze as a binary input like a switch press input through a blink [5, 26]. But the resulting system remain as slow as the scanning system. A better solution may be to use the eye gaze to directly control the pointer position in the screen. Zhai [33] presents a detailed list of advantages and disadvantages of using eye gaze based pointing devices. In short, using the eye gaze for controlling the cursor position pose several challenges as follows.

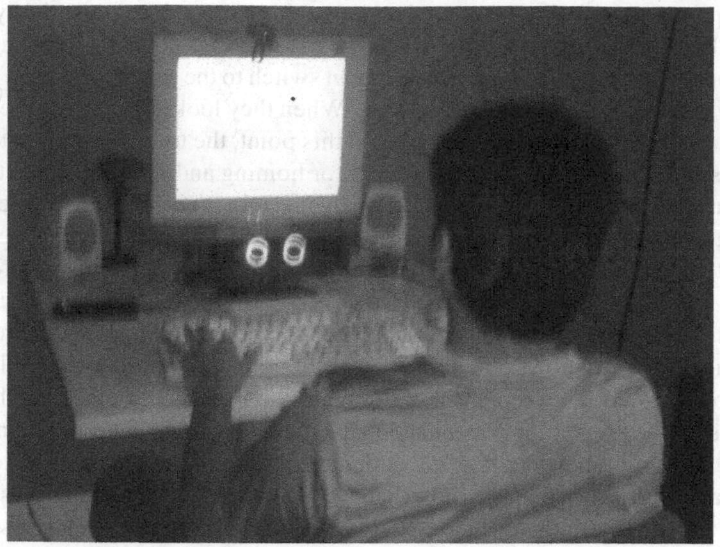

Fig. 7.2 The eye tracking system

Strain It is quite strenuous to control the cursor through eye gaze for long time as the eye muscles soon become fatigue. Fejtova and colleagues [10] reported eye strain in six out of ten able bodied participants in their study.

Accuracy The eye gaze tracker does not always work accurately, even the best eye trackers used to provide accuracy of 0.5° of visual angle. It often makes clicking on small target difficult. So existing systems often change the screen layout and enlarge screen items for AAC systems based on eye gaze. However interface layout of any system can not be always accessed and changed and can not always be enlarged especially for small screen based systems – so surely it is not a scalable solution.

Clicking Clicking or selecting a target using only eye gaze is also a problem. It is generally performed through either dwell time or blinking or both. But either solution increases the chance of false positives or missed clicks.

We tried to solve this problem by combining eye gaze tracking and a scanning system in a unique way. Any pointing movement has two phases [31]

- An initial ballistic phase, which brings one near the target.
- A homing phase, which is one or more precise sub movements to home on the target.

We used the eye gaze tracking for the initial ballistic phase and switch to scanning system for the homing phase and clicking. The approach is similar to the MAGIC system [33] though it replaces the regular pointing device with the scanning system. Our system works in the following way.

Initially, the system [3] moves the pointer across the screen based on the eye gaze of the user. The user sees a small button moving across the screen and the button is placed approximately where they are looking at the screen. We extract the eye gaze position by using the Tobii SDK [24] and we use an average filter that changes the pointer position every 500 msec. The users can switch to the scanning system by giving a key press anytime during eye tracking. When they look at the target, the button (or pointer) appears near or on the target. At this point, the user is supposed to press a key to switch back to the scanning system for homing and clicking on the target.

We have used a particular type of scanning system, known as eight directional scanning [2] to navigate across the screen. In eight-directional scanning technique the pointer icon is changed at regular time intervals to show one of eight directions (Up, Up-Left, Left, Left-Down, Down, Down-Right, Right, Right-Up). The user can choose a direction by pressing the switch when the pointer icon shows the required direction. After getting the direction choice, the pointer starts moving. When the pointer reaches the desired point in the screen, the user has to make another key press to stop the pointer movement and make a click. A state chart diagram of the scanning system is shown in Fig. 7.3. A demonstration of the scanning system can be seen at http://www.youtube.com/watch?v=0eSyyXeBoXQandfeature=user. The user can move back to the eye gaze tracking system from the scanning system by selecting the exit button in the scanning interface (Fig. 7.4). A couple of videos of the system can be found from the following links.

- Screenshot: http://www.youtube.com/watch?v=UnYVO1Ag17U
- Actual usage: http://www.youtube.com/watch?v=2izAZNvj9L0

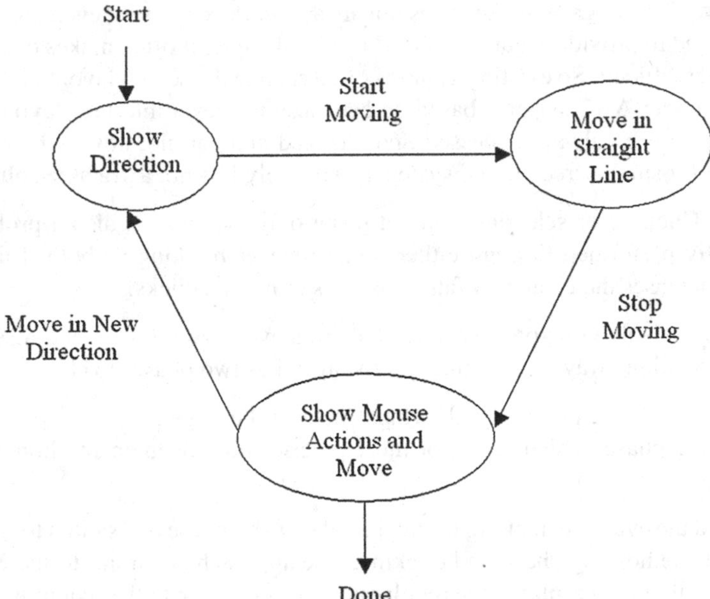

Fig. 7.3 State transition diagram of the eight-directional scanning mechanism with a single switch

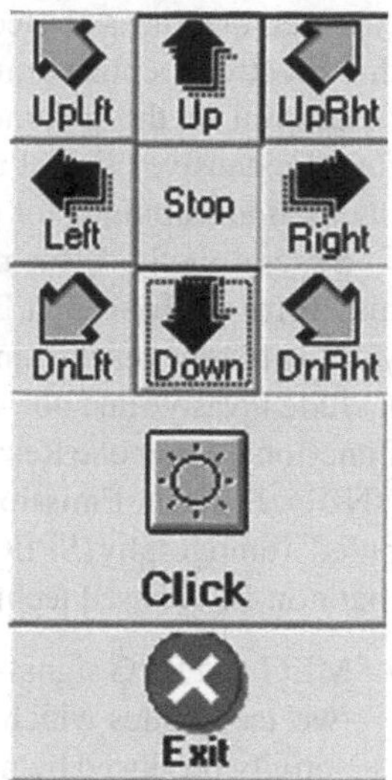

Fig. 7.4 Screenshot of the scanning interface

The technique is faster than only scanning based interface as users can move the pointer through a large distance in screen using their eye gaze quicker than using only single switch scanning interface. For example if the user wants to move the pointer to 300 pixel, it would take msec for the scanning system where d is the unit distance which the pointer cross in every t_l msec and t_l is the scan delay (minimum time needed to change the state of the scanning system).

The technique is less strenuous than the only eye gaze based interfaces because users can switch back and forth between eye gaze tracking and scanning which reduces fatigue to the eye muscles. Additionally, since they need not to home on a target using eye gaze, they are relieved from looking at a target for a long time to home and click on it. Finally, this technique does not depend on the accuracy of the eye tracker as eye tracking is only used to bring the cursor near the target (as opposed to on the target), so it can be used with low cost and low accuracy web cam based eye trackers. Our user trial [3] found that using the scanning system with the eye tracking system did not reduce pointing time significantly compared to only eye gaze based system, rather the system solves a few problems of existing eye gaze tracking based systems by offering more accuracy and comfort to users.

7.4 Brain Computer Interface & EEG

The working physiology of human brain is extremely complex to be completely understood by studying the behavioural patterns. It is the most multitasking organ and therefore highly nonlinear in nature, for example, although all brains are structurally same, yet they act differently. In 1920, a German physician, Hans Berger captured the traces of electrical activities of human brain on the scalp and proposed that Electroencephalogram (EEG) might be the 'window on the mind', which could be helpful in the treatment of psychiatric patients. This technique has not only found extensive clinical applications, but also has the potential to become a main interaction technique for people with severe motor-impairment.

Several methods for monitoring brain activity exist and theoretically all these may form the basis of a Brain Computer Interface (BCI). Different techniques may yield different results since they use different correlates of neural activity. These include invasive and non-invasive EEG recordings, magnetoencephalogram (MEG), Functional Magnetic Resonance Imaging (fMRI), Functional Near-Infrared Imaging (fNIR), Positron Emission Tomography (PET), and Single Photon Emission Computed Tomography (SPECT) [4, 28, 30, 32]. The following discussion makes it clear that non-EEG based techniques are impractical for use in a BCI:

- MEG and EEG signals have the same neurophysiological origin and are the only two techniques which can offer real-time results. MEG measures the magnetic activity produced by neural function and has the advantage of being independent of head geometry and offers better spatial resolution when compared to the EEG [13]. The disadvantages of MEG within the context of BCI research are its bulk, expense and the fact that it cannot be used in real life environments. Another disadvantage is that the association between MEG and motor imagery (imagining movement of the body in its entirety or of body parts) is poorly understood. This poses a potential problem since many BCIs use motor imagery as a control signal.
- fMRI measures the changes in blood flow by measuring the blood oxygen level dissociation (BOLD) and is a safe technique. It is however unsuitable for use in a BCI because of its low sampling rate (and therefore slow feedback), expense, bulk and impracticality in a real life setting.
- fNIR allows noninvasive monitoring of the brain's hemodynamic and metabolic response, and can therefore measure cognitive activity. While fNIR measurements are possible in real life settings, BCIs based on these signals offer low communications speeds (up to 2 min for communicating one bit) and are therefore unsuitable [32].
- PET and SPECT result in exposure to ionizing radiation, require the injection of radioactive substance(s), and have low sampling rates and long preparation times. Hence these are unsuitable for use in a BCI.

Non-invasive EEG based methods which have excellent temporal resolution and robustness in most environments, with the requirement of only simple and inexpensive equipment, have been able to provide the basis for a practical BCI. As far as non-invasive EEG based BCIs are concerned, the three most successful and widely studied BCIs are based on the 'mu rhythm', 'P300 evoked potential' and 'Slow Cortical Potential (SCP)', respectively. While the above mentioned BCIs are mostly capable of only binary control, this control has been used in spelling devices, for environmental control, for answering oral questions etc by developing specific user applications. While greater dimensions of control are possible, they are plagued by accuracy related issues [27].

BCIs based on non-invasive EEG recordings usually have noisy signal quality, long training periods, slow communication speeds, problems with long term recordings like drying of gel, reduction in signal quality and scalp irritation and the requirement of continuous technical attention. This makes invasive EEG based BCIs using microelectrodes implanted subdurally, or in the cortex an attractive option. They offer better SNR, allow detection of high frequency oscillations, and seem to require lower training periods [9, 25]. However, invasive BCIs require neurosurgery and thus have a greater threshold for use. Not surprisingly, very limited studies exist in this field and therefore it is not possible to come to a generalization regarding its potential in real life scenarios. Unless invasive BCIs offer profoundly superior performance, it is unlikely to replace its non-invasive counterpart. Other issues regarding invasive BCIs are its long term stability and safety.

7.4.1 *Typical Signals Used in EEG Based BCIs*

The three commonly used signals in noninvasive EEG based BCIs are the 'mu rhythm', the 'P300' and the 'SCP'. These signals and the features associated with them which allow for their use in BCIs are discussed as follows:

7.4.1.1 Mu Rhythm

When, one is not engaged in processing sensory input or motor output, but in an awake state, the sensorimotor cortex often produces 8–12 Hz EEG activity. This idling activity is called 'mu rhythm' when extracted over the sensorimotor cortex. Electrodes placed in the bipolar montage over 'Cz' and 'C3' (or 'C4') or 3 cm anterior and posterior to 'C3' (or 'C4') according to the 10-20 International System of Electrode Placement (ISEP) can be used to extract the mu rhythm (Fig. 7.5).

Factors suggestive of the potential of 'mu rhythm' for EEG-based communication are [29]:

- Their association with those cortical areas which are most directly connected to the brain's normal motor output channels.
- Movement or preparation for movement is typically accompanied by a decrease in 'mu rhythm', particularly contra lateral to the movement. This decrease is due to desynchronized neuronal firing and is called Event Related Desynchronization (ERD). It's opposite, is a rhythm increase which is known as Event Related Synchronization (ERS) and is a result of synchronized neuronal firing which occurs with relaxation.

'Mu rhythm' is relevant for use as an input to a BCI because ERD and ERS do not require actual movement and occur with motor imagery (i.e. imagined movement) as well.

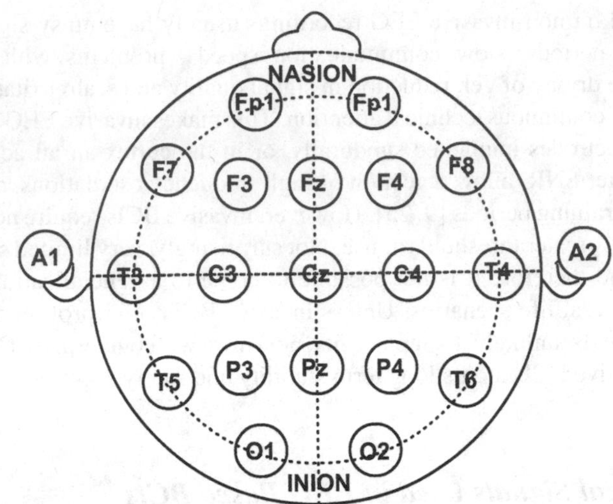

Fig. 7.5 International 10-20 system of electrode placement (*F* frontal, *C* central, *T* temporal, *P* parietal, *O* occipital, *A* auricle, 'z' refers to electrode positions on the mid-line, even and odd numbers refer to electrodes places on the *right* and *left side* respectively) (Reproduced with permission [22])

Several laboratories have shown that people can learn to control 'mu rhythm' amplitudes in the absence of movement or sensation [17, 30]. About 80 % of the users tested on 'mu rhythm' based BCIs had acquired significant control within 2–3 weeks of training and were able to answer yes/no questions with accuracies of up to 95 % in research settings [30]. In initial sessions most employed motor imagery (e.g. imagination of hand movements, whole body activities, relaxation, etc.) to control a cursor. As training proceeded, imagery becomes less important, and users moved the cursor like they performed conventional motor acts [30].

Figure 7.6 shows a mu rhythm waveform. It can be seen that relaxation results in ERS and therefore higher voltage levels in the 8-12 Hz range in comparison to motor imagery where ERD takes place, resulting in a low voltage level. It is important to emphasize that the difference between the voltage levels for relaxation and motor imagery tends to diverge as training proceeds and this helps in improving system performance. A user naïve to the system will be unable to produce any appreciable difference in the 'mu rhythm' power for the states of relaxation and motor imagery.

7.4.1.2 P300

Evoked potentials (EP) are brain potentials that are evoked by the occurrence of a sensory stimulus and these are usually obtained by averaging a number of brief EEG segments, time registered to a stimulus in a simple task [22]. EP can be used to provide control when the BCI application produces the appropriate stimuli. This

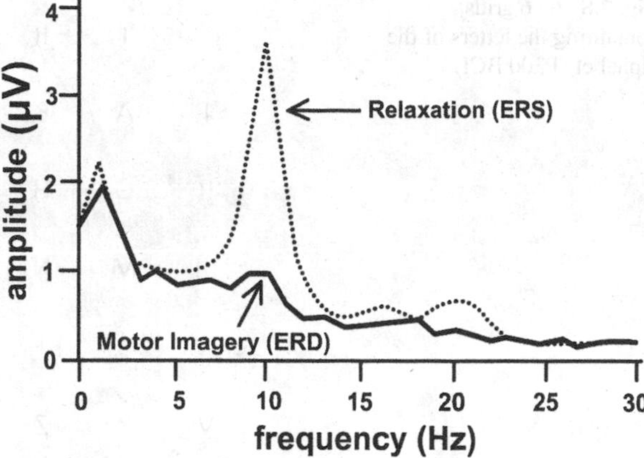

Fig. 7.6 'Mu rhythm' waveform (Reproduced with permission after: Brain-computer interfaces for communication and control, Clinical Neurophysiology, Elsevier[4])

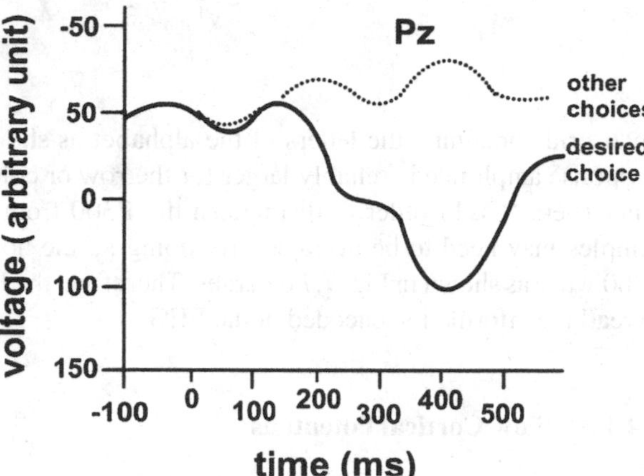

Fig. 7.7 P300 wave (Reproduced with permission [29])

paradigm has the benefit of requiring little or no training at the cost of having to make users wait for appropriate stimuli.

EPs are an inherent response and offer discrete control to almost all users [6]. The P300, a signal used in some BCIs is a positive wave peaking at 300 ms after task-relevant stimuli. It is extracted over the central parietal cortex. Users can change the amplitude of the P300 by paying more attention to a specific event. Figure 7.7 shows a P300 wave. BCIs based on the P300 are cue-based since the user needs to pay attention to stimuli and are therefore considered synchronous.

On the other hand, a BCI based on the 'mu rhythm' requires the user to shift between two different mental states and is totally independent of external stimuli. It is therefore considered asynchronous.

One of the commonly used applications based on the P300 is that of character recognition. Users sequentially focus on the alphabets of the word they want to spell out. This can be done by selecting the letters in a word by counting the number of times the row or column containing the letter flashes. Figure 7.8 shows a typical

Fig. 7.8 6×6 grids containing the letters of the alphabet (P300 BCI)

	I	II	III	IV	V	VI
I	A	B	C	D	E	F
II	G	H	I	J	K	L
III	M	N	O	P	Q	R
IV	S	T	U	V	W	X
V	Y	Z	.	0	1	2
VI	3	4	5	6	7	8

6 × 6 grid containing the letters of the alphabet as shown on a computer monitor. Response amplitude is reliably larger for the row or column containing the desired letter (here 'I'). In order to distinguish the P300 from background noise, several samples may need to be averaged. By doing so the noise tends to cancel and the P300 wave as shown in Fig. 7.7 emerges. Therefore, the P300 is used in BCI systems to read the information encoded in the EEG.

7.4.1.3 Slow Cortical Potentials

Voltage changes occurring in the 0.1 Hz to 2 Hz band are termed as SCP. The origin of SCP is thought to lie in the dendrites of pyramidal neurons in the superficial layers of the cerebral cortex. Interestingly, SCPs originating from posterior parietal and occipital sources are resistant to operant conditioning, while central and frontal SCPs of both hemispheres can be brought under voluntary differential control. The importance of the anterior brain system for acquiring control over SCPs are highlighted in the studies where people with prefrontal dysfunction like those suffering from ADD and schizophrenia have extreme difficulties in acquiring SCP control [28].

Like the 'mu rhythm', control over the SCP is not inherent, and requires training. Since control over the SCP is independent of sensory stimuli, it forms the basis of an asynchronous BCI. Studies have shown that people can be trained to modulate their SCPs reliably [29]. Negative SCPs are typically associated with movement and other functions involving cortical activation, while positive SCPs are usually associated with reduced cortical activation [1]. Figure 7.9 shows a typical SCP waveform.

SCP based BCIs have been tested extensively in people with late stage ALS and have been proved to be able in supplying basic communication capability. However,

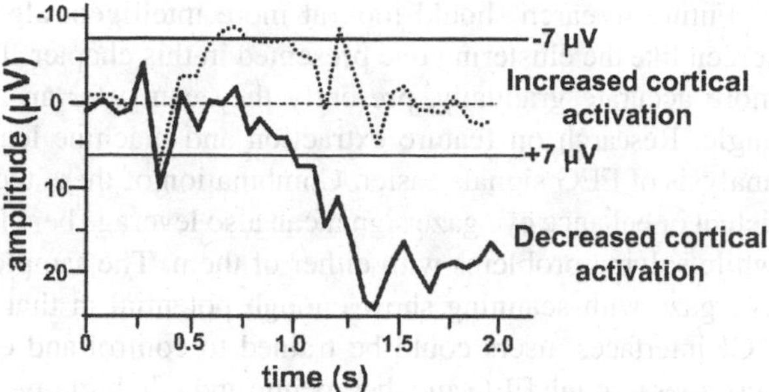

Fig. 7.9 6×6 grids SCP waveform (Reproduced with permission after: Brain-computer interfaces for communication and control, Clinical Neurophysiology, Elsevier[4])

in a study attempting to compare the 'mu rhythm', the 'P300' and the 'SCP'-based BCIs using seven ALS patients who had not yet entered 'Locked-in' state (a state with no motor control whatsoever), the performance of the SCP-based BCI was the poorest. While all seven patients were able to control 'mu rhythm'-based BCIs with more than 70 % accuracy after 20 sessions and four out of the seven could spell with P300 based BCIs, none of the patients achieved acceptable performance rate for the SCP based BCI after 20 sessions. Acceptable performance could be achieved only after much longer training duration [28].

7.5 Issues with Interaction Techniques for People with Severe Disabilities

Present issues with the previously described interaction techniques can be classified into technical and economical issues. Though the technical issues seem to be solved in coming years but the economical issues persist unless change in legislature or regulation.

The technological challenges can be summarized as follows

1. The scanning system even in its best form is very slow compared to other direct manipulation techniques.
2. The eye tracking system is faster than scanning but still slower than conventional interaction techniques. Additionally it may create strain to eye muscles on longer duration of use.
3. The nature of EEG signal makes it difficult to acquire and analyze. There exists a practical problem in acquisition of signal only a few millionths of a volt, embedded in noise that is up to a thousand times greater in amplitude than signal. Users may also be fatigue quickly during using BCI systems.
4. The range of a motor-based vocabulary for a BCI system, given current understanding of imagined movements and technical limitations, is heavily restricted by the challenge of translation into computational input.

Future research should look at more intelligent algorithms to parse targets in screen like the clustering one presented in this chapter. The eye trackers are turning more accurate gradually, presently they can offer an accuracy of 0.4° of visual angle. Research on feature extraction and machine learning are also making the analysis of EEG signals easier. Combination of these techniques like using EEG to detect or enhance eye gaze signal can also leverage benefits of individual techniques while solving problems with either of them. The sample application of combining eye gaze with scanning show enough potential in that direction. For EEG based BCI interfaces, users could be trained to control and even modify their neuronal activities through EEG and therapeutic and rehabilitative measures could be adopted according to the feedback, especially in cases of neuromuscular diseases.

However the economical challenges are more severe than the technical ones. The hardware switches used in scanning are not widely available and often costly. Local manufacturers in developing countries develop these switches but often localized to a certain geographic area. Similarly an accurate eye tracker costs at least £30 k impeding their uses as general interaction devices. Web cam based eye trackers are investigated without resulting much success in terms of accuracy yet compared to infra red based eye trackers. Cheaper eye trackers are [8] often intrusive compared to costlier infrared based one (e.g.: Tobii X120 eye tracker). Similar case studies can be found for BCI devices as well, which confines their uses in research labs only.

In future, we should have legislation or regulation to enforce mainstream commercial vendors of computer peripherals to market assistive devices, perhaps by showing them potential of increasing their market coverage. For example, many recent vendors consider remote control as a computer peripheral and market it with personal computers; it will not cost them a lot to also add a push button switch to be used with a scanning system. Alternatively a scanning software can easily be modified to be used by a switch on the remote. This will not only help severely disabled users but also be helpful for users with age related tremor or spasm in fingers.

7.6 Conclusions

This chapter presents three different interaction techniques for users with severe physical impairment. The interaction techniques can be used to operate a plethora of electronic interfaces like computer, digital TV or tablets and often the only mean of interaction for certain user group. However the hardware and software associated with such interaction techniques are often costly and localized to developed countries only. There is a huge scope to integrate these techniques with mainstream electronic devices which not only help disabled users but also be useful to their able bodied counterpart in situations that impede use of traditional interactive devices.

References

1. Birbaumer, N. (1997). Slow cortical potentials: Their origin, meaning, and clinical use. In *Brain and behavior: Past, present and future* (pp. 25–39). Tilburg: Tilburg University Press.
2. Biswas, P., & Robinson, P. (2012). The cluster scanning system. *Universal Access in the Information Society (UAIS), 12*(3). Special issue on designing inclusive interaction.
3. Biswas, P., & Langdon, P. M. (2011). A new input system for disabled users involving eye gaze tracker and scanning interface. *Journal of Assistive Technologies, 5*(2), 58–66, ISSN: 1754-9450.
4. Dowsett, D. J., Stocker, J. T., & Askinor, F. B. (Eds.). (1998). *The physics of diagnostic imaging* (1st ed.). New York: Chapman and Hall Medical. ISBN 0412401703.
5. Duchowski, A. T. (2007). *Eye tracking methodology*. London: Springer.
6. Elshout, J., & Molina, G. G. (2009). *Review of brain-computer interfaces based on the P300 evoked potential*, Philips Research Europe.
7. Evreinov, G., & Raisamo, R. (2004). Optimizing menu selection process for single-switch manipulation. In *Proceedings of the ICCHP 2004. LNCS 3118* (pp. 836–844). Germany: Springer.
8. FaisalLab Eye Tracker. (2013). Available at http://www.faisallab.com/. Accessed on 3 Jan 2013.
9. Felton, E. A., Wilson, J. A., Williams, J. C., & Garell, P. C. (2007). Electrocorticographically controlled brain–computer interfaces using motor and sensory imagery in patients with temporary subdural electrode implants. *Journal of Neurosurgery, 106*(3), 495–500.
10. Fejtova, M., et al. (2009). Hands-free interaction with a computer and other technologies. *Universal Access in the Information Society, 8*, 277–295.
11. Gus Scanning Cursor. (2007). Available from: www.turningpointtechnology.com/Software/GS/ScanningCursor.htm. Accessed on 21 May 2007.
12. Lesher, G. W., et al. (2002). Acquisition of scanning skills: The use of an adaptive scanning delay algorithm across four scanning displays. In *Proceedings of the annual conference of RESNA, 2002*.
13. Mellinger, J., Schalk, G., Braun, C., Preissl, H., Rosenstiel, W., Birbaumer, N., & Kübler, A. (2007). An MEG-based Brain-Computer Interface (BCI). *NeuroImage, 36*(3), 581–593.
14. Moynahan, A. J., & Mahoney, R. M. (1996). Single switch mouse control interface. In *Proceedings of the annual conference of RESNA, 1996*, USA.
15. Ntoa, S., Savidis, A., & Stephanidis, C. (2004). FastScanner: An accessibility tool for motor impaired users. In *Proceedings of the ICCHP 2004. LNCS 3118* (pp. 796–803). Germany: Springer.
16. O'Neill, P., Roast, C., & Hawley, M. (2002). Evaluation of scanning user interfaces using real time data usage logs. In *Proceedings of the international ACM SIGACCESS conference on computers and accessibility (ASSET 2002)* (pp. 137–141). USA: ACM.
17. Pfurtscheller, G., Neuper, C., Guger, C., Harkam, W., Ramoser, H., Schlögl, A., Obermaier, B., & Pregenzer, M. (2000). Current trends in Graz Brain–Computer Interface (BCI) research. *IEEE Transactions on Rehabilitation Engineering, 8*(2), 216–219.
18. Ross, T. J. (1997). *Fuzzy logic with engineering application* (International Edition). New York: McGraw-Hill Inc.
19. Shein, F. (1997). *Towards task transparency in alternative computer access: Selection of text through switch-based scanning*. PhD thesis, Department of Mechanical and Industrial Engineering, University of Toronto.
20. Simpson, R. C., & Koester, H. H. (1999). Adaptive one-switch row-column scanning. *IEEE Transactions on Rehabilitation Engineering, 7*(4), 464–473.
21. Steriadis, C. E., & Constantnou, P. (2002). Using the scanning technique to make an ordinary operating system accessible to motor-impaired users. The Autonomia system. In *Proceedings of the international ACM SIGACCESS conference on computers and accessibility (ASSET 2002)*. USA: ACM.

22. Teplan, M. (2002). Fundamentals of EEG measurement. *Measurement Science Review, 2*(2), 1–11.
23. The ScanBuddy system. (2007). Available from: www.ahf-net.com/Scanbuddy.htm. Accessed on 21 May 2007.
24. Tobii Eye Tracker. (2008). URL: http://www.imotionsglobal.com/Tobii+X120+Eye-Tracker.344.aspx. Accessed on 12 Dec 2008.
25. Van Gerven, M., Farquhar, J., Schaefer, R., Vlek, R., Geuze, J., Nijholt, A., Ramsey, N., Haselager, P., Vuurpijl, L., Gielen, S., & Desain, P. (2009). The brain–computer interface cycle. *Journal of Neural Engineering, 6*(4), 041001. doi:10.1088/1741-2560/6/4/041001.
26. Ward, D. (2010). *Dasher with an eye-tracker*. URL: http://www.inference.phy.cam.ac.uk/djw30/dasher/eye.html. Accessed on 19 Aug 2010.
27. Wolpaw, J. R., & McFarland, D. J. (1994). Multichannel EEG based brain-computer communication. *Electroencephalography and Clinical Neurophysiology, 78*, 252–259.
28. Wolpaw, J. R., & Birbaumer, N. (2006). Brain–computer interfaces for communication and control. Clinical neurophysiology. In M. E. Selzer, S. Clarke, L. G. Cohen, P. Duncan, & F. H. Gage (Eds), *Textbook of neural repair and rehabilitation; neural repair and plasticity* (pp. 602–614). Cambridge: Cambridge University Press.
29. Wolpaw, J. R., Birbaumer, N., McFarland, D. J., Pfurtscheller, G., & Vaughan, T. M. (2002). Brain–computer interfaces for communication and control. *Clinical Neurophysiology, 113*, 767–791.
30. Wolpaw, J. R., McFarland, D. J., Neat, G. W., & Forneris, C. A. (1991). An EEG-based brain-computer interface for cursor control. *Electroencephalography and Clinical Neurophysiology, 78*, 252–259.
31. Woodworth, R. S. (1899). The accuracy of voluntary movement. *Psychological Review, 3*, 1–119.
32. Wubbels, P., Nishimura, E., Rapoport, E., Darling, B., Proffitt, D., Downs, T., & Downs, J. H. (2007, July 22–27, 23–29). Exploring calibration techniques for Function Near-Infrared Imaging (fNIR) controlled brain–computer interfaces. In *Proceedings of the 3rd international conference on foundation of augmented cognition, China*.
33. Zhai, S., Morimoto, C., & Ihde, S. (1999). Manual and Gaze Input Cascaded (MAGIC) pointing. In *ACM SIGCHI conference on human factors in computing system (CHI)*. USA: ACM.

Chapter 8
Embodied Virtual Agents as a Means to Foster E-Inclusion of Older People

Dominic Noy, Pedro Ribeiro, and Ido A. Iurgel

Abstract How can Embodied Virtual Agents (EVAs, often misleadingly called "avatars") facilitate access to modern information and communication technologies for older people? Several studies and theoretical considerations point out their strong potential benefits, as well as their pitfalls and limitations. This chapter provides a survey of current studies, technologies, and applications, and shall provide guidance as to when and how to employ an EVA for the benefit of older adults. The reviewed studies encompass robotics, EVAs, and specific questions regarding the e-inclusion of the target user group.

8.1 Introduction

Embodied Virtual Agents (EVAs) are autonomous virtual beings that interact with the virtual and real environment through an expressive virtual body, while pursuing particular goals or fulfilling certain tasks. Usually, they are of human or humanoid appearance, even when they represent animals or objects, as for instance a paper-clip. EVAs interact with people or with other EVAs by means of natural verbal and nonverbal channels, e.g. speech and accompanying facial expressions. Nowadays, EVAs can achieve a remarkable level of visual and behavioral realism due to high quality real-time rendering, appealing movements, and integration of results from artificial intelligence and natural language processing technologies.

D. Noy (✉) • P. Ribeiro
Computer Graphics Center (CCG), University of Minho – Campus de Azurém, Guimarães, Portugal
e-mail: dominic.noy@gmail.com; pedro.ribeiro@ccg.pt

I.A. Iurgel
EngageLab, Centro Algoritmi, University of Minho, Guimarães, Portugal
e-mail: Ido.Iurgel@hochschule-rhein-waal.de

P. Biswas et al. (eds.), *A Multimodal End-2-End Approach to Accessible Computing*, Human–Computer Interaction Series, DOI 10.1007/978-1-4471-6708-2_8

As soon as they appeared on stage, EVAs were employed as service assistants on websites, as health advisors, or as social companions, to name only a few functions. Whereas initial research tended to focus on their benefits, as for instance on their capacity to communicate naturally or to enhance trust in a technical system, see e.g. [7, 69, 97], negative aspects could soon not be ignored and some discouraging experiences were made as well.

The following examples may be worth mentioning: In 1995, a Microsoft software package was shipped that included *Microsoft Bob*. This agent was supposed to assist users with low computer literacy skills. In 2000 *Bob* was replaced by *Clippy*, the Microsoft Office Assistant. Albeit *Clippy* was designed to simplify the use of certain programs and to make them more fun, at the end of the day, it actually elicited mostly negative reactions [116].

The *Computers as Social Actors Theory* and the studies of Reeves and Nass achieved some prominence in the area [105, 116], since they postulate that media automatically evoke certain social responses because social-psychological rules that govern interaction between humans also extend to the realm of human-computer interaction. Accordingly, violation of these rules would trigger negative feelings. *Clippy* is an illustration that these rules indeed matter in the field of EVAs – any human service assistant displaying a similar behaviour to *Clippy* would cause user reactance: *Clippy* did not follow social norms, did not learn from earlier interactions, did not develop long-term relationships, and was actually not useful [116] – there was no reason to bear its presence.

Yet, while Microsoft has given up on embodied interface agents as main product feature, other EVAs are more successful in eliciting positive user reactions. In spite of rather limited behavioral capabilities, the continuing use of *Anna*, for years now, points towards a useful design. Anna's functionalities are not very ambitious: it mainly guides users through IKEA's website [66].

Anna and Clippy, respectively, are well-known positive and negative examples of employing and designing EVAs. It is important that today's researchers and developers understand how and when EVAs can be employed usefully for the benefit of older adults and when they are best avoided. This chapter will help making informed decisions on their utilization. The following paragraphs will dwell on aspects that are particularly informative in the context of using EVAs for easing the life of older adults.

The potential of EVAs should be also viewed in the global context of an ageing population and the increase of age related health problems – including mental health, e.g. dementia – and social issues as loneliness. In the next sections, we describe the possible functions of EVAs in the context of old age; we present possible application domains for EVAs; we look at how they should look like and behave; and we dwell on risks and pitfalls.

8.2 Functions of EVAs

8.2.1 Direct Emotional Influence

Often, people unconsciously mimic emotions and behaviour of interaction partners. This plays a role in understanding goals, desires, and intentions of the other person [54]. As part of this mechanism, emotions are carried over so that for example a calm expression of the partner induces similar feelings in the viewer [120]. This *emotional contagion effect* can be found in several scenarios where EVAs are employed, e.g. serious games and fitness or health assistance. It was shown that EVAs displaying empathy, sympathy, compassion, or humour reduce user frustration and interaction times [63, 74, 85, 93, 102]. For example Prendinger et al. frustrated users in a mathematical game and simultaneously presented an EVA that expressed empathy. The presence of the EVA reduced stress and users evaluated the task as easier [102]. Another example is that of an EVA which was designed to accompany physical exercise and thereby leveraged the pressure felt by the user [67].

8.2.2 Non-verbal Communication

Non-verbal communication is more than just an emotional expression which influences the user. Facial expressions and gestures of the body provide information as well [33]. Nonverbal communication influences decision making [41] and can even override verbal messages [2]. Not surprisingly, this effect becomes more prominent the more difficult it is to understand the voice of an interaction partner, due for instance to a noisy environment.

The most common gestures of humans are redundant [49] and only support the spoken message without adding new content to it. In the context of old age, where hearing impairments are prevalent and cognitive capacities often affected, it is plausible that redundant non-verbal information helps in understanding EVAs [13]. Moreover, less effort is needed to follow the conversation [47], partly because important words can be emphasized [46, 76]. Gestures and non-verbal expressions are also important for the control of turn-taking in conversation [36]. A study by Buisine and Martin showed that different gesture-speech combinations influenced in different ways memorization and the perceived quality of a talk and expressiveness of the EVA [31]. For example a study showed that redundant gestures were most effective for recall performance and for several subjective measures like perceived quality of the information [32]. These are then additional aspects to take into consideration when implementing an EVA.

Another potential function of an EVA's non-verbal language is to produce sign language for the hard of hearing, cf. e.g. [4, 110]. In a sign language translation system, a hearing person's spoken or typed words are automatically translated into visual sign language gestures of an EVA. Such a sign language translation

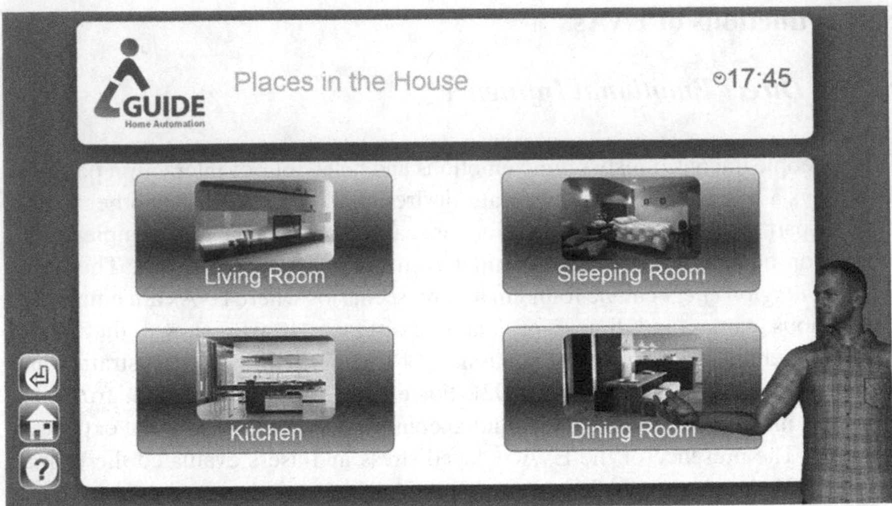

Fig. 8.1 An EVA being developed in the GUIDE project [55] that uses gestures to accompany short verbal presentations

system has been tested in communications between deaf people and office personnel responsible for the renewal of driver's licenses [110]. The communication was mediated by an EVA that translated the hearing person's typed words into sign language for the deaf interaction partner. It should be noted that the EVA was not evaluated very well by the clients who were unsatisfied with the naturalness of the signs and the complexity of the interface. However, these issues do not obviously generalize to the application scenario per se (Fig. 8.1).

8.2.3 Increasing Trust in Computer Systems

Trust in technology can be crucial in areas where privacy is a concern, for instance health [5, 88] or personal hygiene. Since older people tend to be more sceptical when interacting with technology [65], promoting trust into technical systems becomes even more important. There is some research investigating whether trust can be created by giving a face to a technical system, see e.g. [18]. However, an experiment showed that, while social presence effects could be established during net communication, an EVA received surprisingly low trust ratings [14]. Whether EVAs and humans receive different levels of trust was tested in a "trusting game". Behavioural data demonstrated that participants trusted EVAs and humans equally, although underlying cognitive mechanisms may be different, according to brain imaging data [107]. Another study showed that adding an EVA to e-commerce web sites indeed does increase both cognitive and emotional trust [103].

In general, EVAs incite people to personalize technology, and this increases trust [75, 96]. The effect is particularly strong with older users [129]. A system that possesses human features indicates consistent behaviour and thus controllability [119]. These results are complemented by studies showing that EVAs are more trusted if they are expressive [84, 92], show empathy [26], and are of similar ethnicity [91]. These findings suggest that not only the bare presence, but also an EVA's personality, in a broad sense of the word, matters for creating trust into a technical system.

8.2.4 *Increasing Enjoyment of Human-Computer Interaction*

In order to ensure that older people accept and use new technological systems, joy and motivation are crucial factors. Studies of Heerink et al. demonstrated that robots and EVAs can boost the joy of interacting with a system [59, 60], which increases the willingness of older adults to use it. For example *Steffie,* a website interface [114] for delivering information about e.g. the internet, email, or health insurance, added enjoyment to the interaction by creating social presence, which is correlated with the intention to use the system [59]. It was also shown that the robotic pet *Paro* had beneficial effects on older adults, like feeling happier and healthier [113]. Other studies demonstrated that EVAs, used for presenting learning material, increased the enjoyment of the learning process [69, 84]. Behaviour of EVAs that is associated with enjoyment is humour [93], smiling, and expressing believable emotions [6]. Further factors that influence enjoyment and the motivation to use a system are (i) social presence, i.e. the feeling that an interaction partner is actually present; (ii) that the system displays social behaviour [61]; and (iii) that it is able to develop social bounds with the user [90]. Various studies have shown that EVAs can be an effective means for adding these characteristics to technical systems, see e.g. [24, 26, 35, 52, 58, 61, 64, 90, 97, 117].

8.3 Usage Scenarios of EVAs for Older Adults

8.3.1 *EVAs as Interface Agents to Foster E-Inclusion*

With older age, biological, physiological, and cognitive capacities as well as social relationships change [37]. E-Inclusion policies have to take these changes into consideration. E-inclusion means that (a) information technology is made accessible to the entire society and that (b) technology is used to promote inclusion, economic performance, employment opportunities, and the quality of life in general. Although investments are being made to reduce the digital divide, inequalities in terms of access to information technology still exist, particularly with regard to older adults, people with disabilities, and people with low literacy levels [43]. Many technical systems are complex and difficult to use and exclude these groups of people [44].

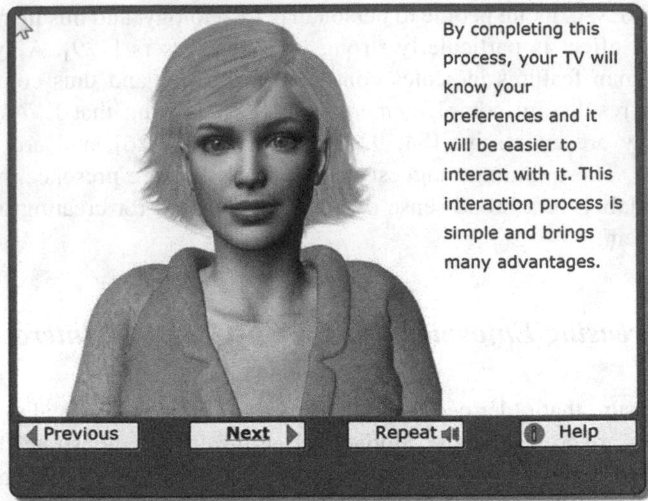

By completing this process, your TV will know your preferences and it will be easier to interact with it. This interaction process is simple and brings many advantages.
Previous
Next
Repeat
Help

Fig. 8.2 Screenshot of the EVA used in the GUIDE project [55]

Accessible systems must be usable, believable, enjoyable, and motivate to use them [45, 61, 90]. There are many approaches to enhance accessibility and usability that rely on an understanding of abstract interfaces. But older users in particular may experience difficulties using abstract interfaces. EVAs can come to rescue here, since they enable a more natural, human like communication and therefore reduce the requirements for the older user to adapt to new systems (this was seen as a paradigm shift by Spierling in [89]). Within the GUIDE project [55], adaptable and interactive EVA's are being developed for assisting and supporting older adults. The EVAs developed in GUIDE assist older adults through the configuration and personalization of user interfaces; they offer explanations and assist the older users during a configuration process that lead to individually adapted user interfaces (cf. Fig. 8.2). Thus, for instance, people with impaired cognitive functions could benefit from EVAs as user interface because these can translate more abstract cognitive tasks like pushing the correct button of a TV command into a natural social interaction move like telling the EVA what to do. Certainly, the success of an EVA as user interface for older adults will depend much on its capacity to understand and express non-verbal, emotional, and communicative signs, because without these, it will not be possible to maintain the naturalness of the interaction.

8.3.2 EVAs as Assistants

In old age, a reduced cognitive flexibility can make it difficult to cope both with daily tasks and with unexpected emergency situations. EVAs and physically embodied agents have been employed to alleviate this problem. Examples are assistive robots for managing and planning daily activities related to safety, health, and hygiene, and robots that serve as reminders or to set alarms [37, 38, 80, 101]. In this context, robots were also built for establishing health related diagnoses by analysing users' reactions to robotic systems [111]. Many of the aforementioned tasks, originally devised for robots, could also be delegated to EVAs.

Higher age is also positively related to motor disabilities as gait and balance disorders, e.g. of post-stroke or Parkinson patients, see e.g. [71] and [109]. Therefore, robots were developed to serve as walking aids to support simple motor skills [57]. EVAs were also envisaged in similar contexts. Examples are a reactive virtual fitness trainer or a virtual physiotherapist: In the first example, the EVA presents exercises that the user is supposed to imitate and provides feedback on the performance [108]. The other example is that of a virtual teacher that also relies on imitation tasks. It could be shown that the system helped to improve the condition of stroke patients with chronic health problems [62].

8.3.3 EVAs for Increasing Compliance and for Motivating Behaviour Change

EVAs have often been employed as coaches and motivators to change negative behaviour and to enhance the compliance with orders or advices. Bickmore et al. could show that EVAs are beneficial for the development of a therapeutic alliance, which is a prerequisite for successful behaviour change, and there are several robots and virtual interfaces that have demonstrated their effectiveness in health behaviour change interventions or medication compliance [19, 21, 23, 24, 26]. For example, a diet promoting system was shown to be more effective if the interface was an embodied robot, rather than a touch screen or a paper diary [73].

Higher age is correlated to physical inactivity [28]. Yet, physical activity plays a key role in maintaining functional abilities, independent living, health, and well-being [28, 39]. Robots and EVAs have already been developed to support people with disabilities and to promote motor activity by enticing, scheduling, fostering compliance, and monitoring, see e.g. [48, 51, 126]. For example, a system designed to increase the level of exercise of older adults with limited computer literacy was better in motivating behaviour change if an EVA was used as interface, rather than a control group [26]. Interestingly, the same effect was present in young adults [20]. Another example is that of a mobile health counselling agent, a portable EVA that was designed to promote physical activity. However, a pilot study that evaluated its influence on motivating to walk showed that a proactive EVA that delivered feed-back based on an accelerometer fostered the building of social bonds between EVA and user, but lead to less walking compared to users who used a passive EVA [25].

8.3.4 EVAs to Facilitate Learning and Cognitive Fitness

From 50 years of age onwards many cognitive functions decline. The prefrontal cortex shrinks, fluid intelligence decreases [37]. But preserving the ability to learn quickly is a requirement for successful aging [98], and ongoing cognitive activity is also important for the regulation of emotions and behaviour [81]. There are several contexts in which EVAs can be expected to contribute to cognitive activity and help maintaining cognitive flexibility, see e.g. [72]. For instance, it was shown that additional visual and auditory cues in a slide show support the memory of people with episodic memory impairment and also reduce caregiver involvement [83]. Moreover, redundant speech accompanying gestures of EVAs increased both recall and likeability, compared to complementary gestures or to no gestures at all [31]. It could also be shown that EVAs enhanced learning transfer [91], memorization [16], and learning experience [9, 77, 121]. Another example that might inspire systems for the older age groups is that of an intelligent tutoring system that used EVAs and direct instructions to support learning of young children with learning disabilities [68]. In sum, several scenarios of the usage of EVAs have already been studied and have proven that EVAs can be beneficial for the cognitively impaired or for learning tasks and specific applications for old age should be easily derived from these experiences.

8.3.5 EVAs as Virtual Companions

Does an "artificial social accompaniment" for the older population make sense? Older people usually have less social relations, but those are perceived as more important, so that the sheer number of relationships does not necessarily have a negative impact on well-being. Nevertheless, there is an elevated risk of loneliness in old age, partly due to higher mortality rates of friends and family [37]. Moreover, rewarding social relationships are related to less stress [70], the maintenance of cognitive capabilities [132], and are predictors of well-being [15] and successful aging [20]. Can EVAs, in this situation, contribute to a happier ageing by acting as some sort of social partners, maybe in the vein of cats and dogs rather than an ersatz family?

In spite of rather limited AI-capabilities of EVAs, some mimicry of human behaviour might be beneficial. There are studies showing that the perception of social support is, under certain circumstances, more important than the actual support itself [127]. Several studies have demonstrated that real or robotic pets, which make use of social cues, can elicit user emotions and thus lead to higher levels of well-being [11, 12, 42, 87, 104, 113, 115, 123, 128]. The utilization of *Paro* the seal robot in an eldercare institution increased the number of social interactions between inhabitants and reduced stress at the same time [124]. Other studies have demonstrated various beneficial social effects of EVAs such as relaxation, reduction of frustration, stress, and loneliness [17, 26, 63, 74, 100, 102]. A longitudinal study of Bickmore has demonstrated that the feeling that the EVA is caring for oneself can last over longer periods of time [22]. Thus, research indicates that the doors of the older population should be wide open for novel kinds of virtual "social companions", albeit the term "companion" might still require replacement by some more appropriate denomination; to call them "companions" easily raises concerns

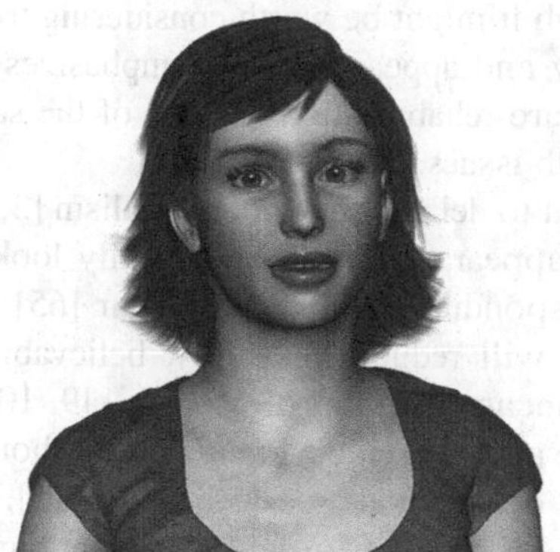

Fig. 8.3 Screenshots of the GUIDE [55] EVA using emotions for enhancing empathy and involvement

that naïve attempts could be going on to "replace" family, friends, and serious care and concern by cheap, insufficient surrogates. It is probably wiser to lower expectations and to initially regard the emerging new kind of "companion" EVAs as some sort of pet, or even only as some sort of technological porcelain doll, or maybe as a new kind of toy. It can only be considered as something that has its ways to contribute to enjoyment and beauty in the life of an old adult, but that certainly will never be able to fully replace human warmth (Fig. 8.3).

8.4 Designing an EVA

8.4.1 Choosing Appearance

What should your EVA look like and how should it behave? In certain cases, this question might be less relevant than expected at first sight. A meta-analysis of Yee et al. revealed that the most important aspect of the use of an EVAs was the fact that it was actually present and running. The visual quality of the representation was only of secondary importance [130]. Yet, the generalization of this result certainly depends on the behavioural capacities of the EVA, as will be described in the next paragraphs.

Concerning their behaviour and appearance, we will first look at properties that are likely to foster the creation of bonds between an older user and its personal EVA, since this is important for long term acceptance, see e.g. [27].

Humans have a strong need to belong [8] and tend to create bonds to things that display human cues as e.g. speech [105]. Visual characteristics that foster the creation of bonds are attractiveness [42, 79], and similarity [8, 65]. In addition, in line with the *Emotional Similarity Hypothesis* of Schachter, see e.g. [56], people tend to get closer to interaction partners that are experiencing similar situations and emotional states. Therefore, often enough it might be worth considering to set an EVA into scene with a background story and appearance that emphasizes the similarity of user and EVA, e.g. when both are rehabilitation patients of the same sex, are of similar age, and have similar health issues.

Some researchers maintain that it is crucial to deliver behavioural realism [3, 27, 94], particularly if the EVA has a realistic appearance. Very realistically looking EVAs give rise to expectations about corresponding life-like behaviour [65] and subsequent violation of these expectations will reduce likeability, believability, competence, and enjoyment (cf. the term "uncanny valley" of Mori in [49, 105]). Thus, the level of realism of their appearance and behaviour should be well thought of and overambitious realism can be quite detrimental, see [50] and [112]. An appropriate way to manage this conflict is to design the EVA with sufficient human characteristics for the user to feel motivated to interact socially, while maintaining sufficient non-realistic characteristics to keep expectations low, concerning the intelligence of EVA's behaviour [49]. Another possibility is to go for cartoon or animal characters, in particular when aiming at long term relationships (cf. remarks above about the role of an EVA as a very limited "companion").

8.4.2 Choosing the Behaviour of an EVA

In order to build effective EVAs, several factors like the situation, the usage scenario, the context, the individuality, and the personality etc. must be considered. The most relevant aspects will be explained in the following sections.

Interpersonal Differences Interpersonal differences have to be taken into account because individuals respond to technological systems in different ways [30]. While some users accepted robots as social actors, others did not [92]. Behavioural realism related e.g. to the expression of emotions should at least match the expectations of the user [105]. Meeting these expectations will foster likeability, enjoyment [6, 75], and believability of the EVA [7].

Another consideration is that female and male behaviour of an EVA should be consistent with gender stereotypes [63] and the user's gender has to be taken into account as well [10]. In contrast to men, women prefer female EVAs and tend to favour more smiling and self-touching behaviours. Another finding of this study was that older people and people with less computer literacy were more nervous during the interaction, and that older people were more attentive if the EVA showed less self-touching behaviour [78]. Moreover, it was shown that personality is a better predictor for subjective feeling and evaluation of the EVA than its concrete behaviour [122], indicating that personality traits of users should be prominent when deciding about design and implementation, cf. e.g. [32]. For example, highly self-conscious people felt more aggression and people with high levels of self-efficacy felt less afraid and less distressed after interacting with an EVA [122]. It was also shown that there are differences concerning the acceptance of an EVA's monitoring behaviour, depending on the personality trait *control orientation*. Users thinking that external factors control their success in life (i.e. *external locus of control*) felt more anxious than people who felt responsible for their success (i.e. *internal locus of control*) [106].

In conclusion, there are many individual differences and dependencies, making it difficult to design a single most adequate EVA that is able to suit all kinds of users. Furthermore, the opinions of users assessed by self-questionnaires do not always correspond to their actual behaviour [99, 106, 130], which hampers the expectation that it is possible to design adequate EVAs only by asking their users. Taking this and the interdependencies between personality and rating of an EVA into account, an ideal system would be highly adaptive to both user's personality traits and interaction history, cf. [29] and [40].

Context Belief and trust are reduced when an EVA's behaviour is inappropriate or unrealistic in a certain context [53]. Therefore, EVAs should display non-verbal behaviour that is consistent with social norms [86] and should for instance smile in appropriate situations [93].

Behaviour can have different meanings, depending on the social or cultural context. Looking into the eyes of the user can be understood as aggression or, on the contrary, be regarded as a lovely gesture [120], depending on the relationship of the user to the EVA and on the cultural background [38].

Function The acceptance of the behaviour of an EVA depends much on its specific role. A study that employed EVAs in a learning context has demonstrated that EVAs displaying emotions were accepted when acting as supportive peers but not when they were tutors [10].

Another important aspect is that non-verbal behaviour like gestures and emotions can affect the perception of the spoken message [2] and induce emotions in the viewer [120]. These emotions can lead to a reduction of effort, in particular when they are positive [34]. There are thus contexts where a less friendly, not always smiling EVA might be more appropriate. For instance, when a user is supposed to follow the prescription to take an essential medicine, an angry or sad EVA might be more effective.

Most importantly, the designer of an EVA has to distinguish between short- and long-term interactions. If he/she is creating an EVA for capturing attention and for achieving short term effects, the task will probably be less demanding, see [105].

But when EVAs shall serve as social companion or as a personal health assistant, the requirements on the behaviour design are likely to become tough, see [49]. Then, more realistic simulation of emotional expressions [6, 75], of interpersonal attitudes, and of personality traits [120] are important. Particularly in the context of building relationships, "physical" approximation to the user (displayed e.g. by forward leaning movements), head nods, lively gestures [120], and behaving as if the EVA liked the user [8], should be effective measures because these behaviours are strongly correlated to a desire for emotional proximity [120]. Moreover, in order to facilitate relationship building, EVAs should certainly provide sufficient support, but they probably should also expect and accept support from the user. This assumption is based on the social-psychological *Equity Theory*, according to which satisfaction is highest if costs and rewards are equal for both interaction partners [1]. A review comprising studies on the utilization of EVAs in psychiatry comes to the conclusion that EVAs should express empathy, involve the user in social dialogue, display humour and happiness, talk about past and future, show appropriate social behaviour, and refer to mutual knowledge in order to build a therapeutic alliance, see [20]. Several studies on the use of EVAs in clinical applications suggest that their behaviour should be variable and dynamic, an EVA should talk about itself (self-disclosure), and should refer to knowledge about prior interactions [20]. Bickmore and Cassel have developed a model of social proximity that summarizes the most relevant factors for building a relationship to an EVA. Mutual familiarity, similarity, and affect are pillars in this model [19].

Arousal Level Older adults usually cope well with a smaller number of stressors that do not last for too long a time period. However, in the presence of many stressors that last longer, older users tend to experience much more stress than younger people, see [37]. Since EVAs can reduce stress (cf. e.g. [102]), there should be certain situations where EVAs can intervene and contribute to stress reduction in a sensitive way whenever higher arousal levels are registered. Certain findings suggest that the presence of other people promotes performance at easy tasks but impairs accomplishment of more difficult tasks. This effect is mediated by the arousal level, i.e. the presence of others increases arousal; this is an advantage when accomplishing familiar activities but detrimental when cognitive effort and focus is required [106, 118, 131]. This *social presence effect* was replicated when the audience was composed of EVAs – and not of humans –, which strongly suggests that task difficulty must be considered when planning the usage of EVAs to reduce stress [106]. These results imply that the most appropriate level of active intrusion and social presence of an EVA depends on the task difficulty of the usage scenario – the more difficult the task, the more cautious and silent the EVA should be.

8.4.3 Pitfalls and Risks of Employing EVAs

In this section, we will expose possible dysfunctional aspects of EVAs and point out why it might be better to abandon the idea of using an EVA under certain circumstances.

Distracting Effects The animations of the EVAs could become sources of stress, cf. [93], and EVAs may require attention resources that are more limited at higher ages; as a consequence, they could cause distraction and decrease performance in tasks like recalling information [75, 95, 125]. But other authors have suggested that the distracting effect of EVAs is likely to disappear after several interactions [95]. There are also other studies that do not report on any negative effects on recall performance, stress, or accuracy of answering a questionnaire, see [64, 102, 125].

Overestimation of the Capabilities of the System EVAs employed as interfaces may raise high expectations about the capabilities of the system, cf. [20]. These exaggerated expectations may lead to disappointment, and may even be dangerous under certain circumstances if the older adult does not recognize its true limitations. As an example, consider EVAs that are used for health monitoring: their user could be at risk of not calling medical support in an emergency situation because he/she relies on the EVA, but it is not able to recognize or emotionally reflect the critical situation. Furthermore, the accuracy of the advice of EVAs about e.g. health issues can be low and there are also the additional risks of misunderstanding their messages [20].

Rejecting the Ludic Aspect It is not clear when an older adult is likely to reject an EVA because he/she finds the idea ridiculous or awkward. Younger users (16–22 years) were shown to develop closer relationships to virtual pets than older adult users [82], an indicator that possibly some older people will not enjoy interaction with an EVA in general.

Dependencies Forming A risk of employing an EVAs as a companion could increase social isolation because the old person might not feel the necessity to participate in real social interactions anymore cf. [20]. Considering that one of the reasons for older adults to have smaller social networks is the desire to avoid conflicts [37], these users could feel compelled to focus on conflict-free interactions with EVAs. Some severely cognitively impaired people may even become confused as to whether an EVA is real or not. Other related ethical issues are related to confidentiality, privacy, monitoring, and provider liability, see [20].

8.5 Conclusion

In many situations, the use of an EVA in a technical system makes sense and older people will benefit from it. With recent technological advances and decrease of prices in IT and hardware, we certainly can expect many innovative, dedicated applications to be developed in the very near future. We have seen that emotional effects, communicative advantages, task simplification, or learning effects can speak for EVAs. Generalization of the aforementioned findings to different applications and usage scenarios is difficult and must be done with care, since many aspects will influence their validity for different contexts. For example, the exact user group, its culture, the possible cognitive disorders or health issues of its members, and the application scenario with its specific goals and interaction logic are aspects that will determine whether to employ an EVA is appropriate or not, and which properties it should eventually possess.

Some sort of user involving design process when developing systems with EVAs for old persons is thus necessarily required, but attention must be paid to the fact that the old users' report may differ considerably from their actual behaviour, and long term effects and usefulness may not be the same as those observed in short terms.

Acknowledgements This work was partially funded by the GUIDE Project of the European Commission's Seventh Framework Programme (FP7/2007–2013) under grant agreement 24889.

References

1. Adams, J. S. (1965). Inequity in social exchange. *Advances in Experimental Social Psychology, 2*, 267–299.
2. Argyle, M., Trower, P., & Kristal, L. (1979). *Person to person: Ways of communicating*. London: Harper & Row.
3. Bailenson, J. N., & Blascovich, J. (2004). Avatars. In *Encyclopedia of human-computer interaction*. Great Barrington: Berkshire Publishing Group.
4. Barberis, D., Garazzino, N., Prinetto, P., & Tiotto, G. (2011). Improving accessibility for deaf people: An editor for computer assisted translation through virtual avatars. In K. F. McCoy & Y. Yesilada (Eds.), ASSETS (pp. 253–254). ACM.
5. Barefoot, J. C., Maynard, K. E., Beckham, J. C., Brummett, B. H., Hooker, K., & Siegler, I. C. (1998). Trust, health, and longevity. *Journal of Behavioral Medicine, 21*(6), 517–526.
6. Bartneck, C. (2003). Interacting with an embodied emotional character. In *Proceedings of the 2003 international conference on designing pleasurable products and interfaces* (pp. 55–60). New York: ACM.
7. Bates, J. (1994). The role of emotion in believable agents. *Communications of the ACM, 37*(7), 122–125.
8. Baumeister, R. F., & Leary, M. R. (1995). The need to belong: Desire for interpersonal attachments as a fundamental human motivation. *Psychological Bulletin, 117*(3), 497.
9. Baylor, A. L., & Ryu, J. (2003). The effects of image and animation in enhancing pedagogical agent persona. *Journal of Educational Computing Research, 28*(4), 373–394.
10. Beale, R., & Creed, C. (2009). Affective interaction: How emotional agents affect users. *International Journal of Human-Computer Studies, 67*(9), 755–776.
11. Beck, A. M., & Meyers, N. M. (1996). Health enhancement and companion animal ownership. *Annual Review of Public Health, 17*(1), 247–257.
12. Beck, A. M., Edwards, N., Friedman, B., & Khan, P. (2003). Robotic pets and the elderly. *Project overview:*http://www.ischool.washington.edu/robotpets/elderly
13. Benoît, C. (1996). On the production and the perception of audio-visual speech by man and machine. In *Multimedia & video coding*. New York: Plenum Press.
14. Bente, G., Rüggenberg, S., Krämer, N. C., & Eschenburg, F. (2008). Avatar-mediated networking: Increasing social presence and interpersonal trust in net-based collaborations. *Human Communication Research, 34*(2), 287–318.
15. Berkman, L. F., & Syme, S. L. (1979). Social networks, host resistance, and mortality: A nine-year follow-up study of Alameda County residents. *American Journal of Epidemiology, 109*(2), 186–204.
16. Beun, R. J., De Vos, E., & Witteman, C. L. M. (2003). *Lecture Notes in Computer Science, 2792*, 315–319.
17. Bickmore, T. W. (2003). *Relational agents: Effecting change through human-computer relationships*. Cambridge, MA: Massachusetts Institute of Technology.
18. Bickmore, T., & Cassell, J. (2001). Relational agents: A model and implementation of building user trust. *Proceedings of the SIGCHI conference on Human factors in computing systems,* 396–403. http://dl.acm.org/citation.cfm?id=365304
19. Bickmore, T., & Cassell, J. (2005). Social dialogue with embodied conversational agents. In *Advances in natural multimodal dialogue systems* (pp. 23–54). Netherlands: Springer.
20. Bickmore, T., & Gruber, A. (2010). Relational agents in clinical psychiatry. *Harvard Review of Psychiatry, 18*(2), 119–130.

21. Bickmore, T. W., Puskar, K., Schlenk, K. A., Pfeifer, L. M., & Sereika, S. M. (2010). Maintaining reality: Relational agents for antipsychotic medication adherence. *Interacting with Computers, 22*(4), 276–288.
22. Bickmore, T. W., & Picard, R. W. (2004). Towards caring machines. *CHI'04 extended abstracts on Human factors in computing systems,* 1489–1492.
23. Bickmore, T. W., & Picard, R. W. (2005). Establishing and maintaining long-term human-computer relationships. *ACM Transactions on Computer-Human Interaction (TOCHI), 12*(2), 293–327.
24. Bickmore, T. W., Caruso, L., & Clough-Gorr, K. (2005). Acceptance and usability of a relational agent interface by urban older adults. In *CHI'05 extended abstracts on Human factors in computing systems* (pp. 1212–1215). New York: Elsevier Science Inc.
25. Bickmore, T. W., Mauer, D., & Brown, T. (2009). Context awareness in a handheld exercise agent. *Pervasive and Mobile Computing, 5*(3), 226–235.
26. Bickmore, T. W., Pfeifer, L. M., & Jack, B. W. (2009a). Taking the time to care: Empowering low health literacy hospital patients with virtual nurse agents. In *Proceedings of the 27th international conference on Human factors in computing systems* (pp. 1265–1274). New York: ACM. http://dl.acm.org/citation.cfm?id=1518891
27. Blascovich, J., Loomis, J., Beall, A. C., Swinth, K. R., Hoyt, C. L., & Bailenson, J. N. (2002). Immersive virtual environment technology as a methodological tool for social psychology. *Psychological Inquiry, 13*(2), 103–124.
28. Booth, M. L., Owen, N., Bauman, A., Clavisi, O., & Leslie, E. (2000). Social-cognitive and perceived environment influences associated with physical activity in older Australians. *Preventive Medicine, 31*(1), 15–22.
29. Bosse, T., Siddiqui, G., & Treur, J. (2010). An intelligent virtual agent to increase involvement in financial services. In *Intelligent virtual agents* (Lecture notes in computer science, Vol. 6356, pp. 378–384). Berlin/Heidelberg: Springer.
30. Brewer, M. B., & Hewstone, M. (2004). *Emotion and motivation.* Hoboken: Wiley-Blackwell.
31. Buisine, S., & Martin, J. C. (2007). The effects of speech-gesture cooperation in animated agents' behavior in multimedia presentations. *Interacting with Computers, 19,* 484–493.
32. Buisine, S., & Martin, J. C. (2010). The influence of user's personality and gender on the processing of virtual agents' multimodal behavior. *Advances in Psychology Research, 65,* 1–14.
33. Burgoon, J. K. (1994). Nonverbal signals. In M. L. Knapp & G. R. Miller (Eds.), *Handbook of interpersonal communication* (2nd ed., pp. 229–285). Thousand Oaks: Sage.
34. Carver, C. S., & Scheier, M. F. (2009). Action, affect, and two-mode models of functioning. In *Oxford handbook of human action* (pp. 298–327). Oxford: Oxford University Press.
35. Cassell, J. (2000). Nudge nudge wink wink: Elements of face-to-face conversation for embodied conversational agents. In *Embodied conversational agents* (pp. 1–27). Cambridge: MIT Press.
36. Cassell, J., & Thorisson, K. R. (1999). The power of a nod and a glance: Envelope vs. emotional feedback in animated conversational agents. *Applied Artificial Intelligence, 13*(4-5), 519–538.
37. Charles, S. T., & Carstensen, L. L. (2010). Social and emotional aging. *Annual Review of Psychology, 61,* 383–409.
38. Cortellessa, G., Scopelliti, M., Tiberio, L., Koch Svedberg, G., Loutfi, A., & Pecora, F. A. (2008). Cross-cultural evaluation of domestic assistive robots. In *Proceedings of AAAI fall symposium on AI in eldercare: New solutions to old problems, November 7–9, Arlington, VA, USA.*
39. Crombie, I. K., Irvine, L., Williams, B., McGinnis, A. R., Slane, P. W., Alder, E. M., & McMurdo, M. E. T. (2004). Why older people do not participate in leisure time physical activity: A survey of activity levels, beliefs and deterrents. *Age and Ageing, 33*(3), 287–292.

40. Dautenhahn, K. (2004). Robots we like to live with?! – A developmental perspective on a personalized, life-long robot companion. *Robot and human interactive communication, 2004. ROMAN 2004. 13th IEEE International Workshop on,* 17–22.
41. de Melo, C., Carnevale, P., & Gratch, J. (2010). The influence of emotions in embodied agents on human decision-making. In *Proceedings of Intelligent Virtual Agents (IVA'10)* (pp. 357–370).
42. DiSalvo, C., Gemperle, F., Forlizzi, J., & Montgomery, E. (2003). The hug: An exploration of robotic form for intimate communication. *Robot and human interactive communication, 2003. Proceedings. ROMAN 2003. The 12th IEEE international workshop on,* 403–408.
43. European Union. (n.a.). *E-Inclusion ... what next? Embracing the future of social innovation 2010–2015.* http://ec.europa.eu. Accessed 30 May 2012.
44. Eizmendi, G., & Craddock, G. M. (2007). *Challenges for assistive technology: AAATE 07* (20th ed.). Amsterdam: IOS Press Inc.
45. Emiliani, P. L., Stephanidis, C., & Vanderheiden, G. (2011). Technology and inclusion–past, present and foreseeable future. *Technology and Disability, 23*(3), 101–114.
46. Fagel, S. (2006). Emotional mcgurk effect. *Proceedings of the international conference on speech prosody* (Ed. 1).
47. Fagel, S., & Madany, K. (2008). *Computeranimierte Sprechbewegungen in realen Anwendungen.* Berlin: Univ.-Verl. der TU, Univ.-Bibliothek.
48. Feil-Seifer, D., & Mataric, M. J. (2005). Defining socially assistive robotics. *9th international conference on rehabilitation robotics, ICORR 2005,* Berlin, 465–468. http://ieeexplore.ieee.org/xpl/login.jsp?tp=&arnumber=1501143&url=http%3A%2F%2Fieeexplore.ieee.org%2Fxpls%2Fabs_all.jsp%3Farnumber%3D1501143
49. Fong, T., Nourbakhsh, I., & Dautenhahn, K. (2003). A survey of socially interactive robots. *Robotics and Autonomous Systems, 42*(3), 143–166.
50. Garau, M., Slater, M., Vinayagamoorthy, V., Brogni, A., Steed, A., & Sasse, M. A. (2003). The impact of avatar realism and eye gaze control on perceived quality of communication in a shared immersive virtual environment. *Proceedings of the SIGCHI conference on Human factors in computing systems,* 529–536. http://lirec.eu/biblio/1497
51. Gockley, R., & Mataric, M. J. (2006). Encouraging physical therapy compliance with a hands-off mobile robot. In *Proceedings of the 1st ACM SIGCHI/SIGART conference on human-robot interaction, Salt Lake City,* March 2–3 (pp. 150–155).
52. Gockley, R., Bruce, A., Forlizzi, J., Michalowski, M., Mundell, A., Rosenthal, S., Sellner, B., et al. (2005). Designing robots for long-term social interaction. *2005 IEEE/RSJ international conference on intelligent robots and systems, 2005 (IROS 2005),* 1338–1343. https://www.ri.cmu.edu/publication_view.html?pub_id=5168
53. Gong, L. (2007). Is happy better than sad even if they are both non-adaptive? Effects of emotional expressions of talking-head interface agents. *International Journal of Human-Computer Studies, 65*(3), 183–191.
54. Gratch, J., Okhmatovskaia, A., Lamothe, F., Marsella, S., Morales, M., van der Werf, R., & Morency, L. P. (2006). Virtual rapport. In *Intelligent virtual agents* (pp. 14–27).
55. Guide. (2007). GUIDE project webpage. http://www.guide-project.eu/. Accessed 3 Jan 2013.
56. Gump, B. B., & Kulik, J. A. (1997). Stress, affiliation, and emotional contagion. *Journal of Personality and Social Psychology, 72*(2), 305.
57. Hans, M., Graf, B., & Schraft, R. D. (2002). Robotic home assistant care-o-bot: Past-present-future. In *Proceedings of 11th IEEE international workshop on robot and human interactive communication, 2002* (pp. 380–385). Berlin: IEEE.
58. Heerink, M., Kröse, B., Wielinga, B., & Evers, V. (2006). Studying the acceptance of a robotic agent by elderly users. *International Journal of Assistive Robotics and Mechatronics, 7*(3), 33–43.
59. Heerink, M., Kröse, B., Evers, V., & Wielinga, B. (2008a). The influence of social presence on enjoyment and intention to use of a robot and screen agent by elderly users. In *Proceedings of the 17th IEEE international symposium on robot and human interactive communication, 2008 (RO-MAN 2008)* (pp. 695–700). Munich: IEEE.

60. Heerink, M., Kröse, B., Wielinga, B., & Evers, V. (2008b). Enjoyment, intention to use and actual use of a conversational robot by elderly people. *3rd ACM/IEEE international conference on human-robot interaction (HRI)* (pp. 113–119). Munich: IEEE.
61. Heerink, M., Kröse, B., Evers, V., & Wielinga, B. (2010). Assessing acceptance of assistive social agent technology by older adults: The almere model. *International Journal of Social Robotics, 2*(4), 361–375.
62. Holden, M. K., & Dyar, T. (2002). Virtual environment training: A new tool for neurorehabilitation. *Journal of Neurologic Physical Therapy, 26*(2), 62.
63. Hone, K. (2006). Empathic agents to reduce user frustration: The effects of varying agent characteristics. *Interacting with Computers, 18*(2), 227–245.
64. Hongpaisanwiwat, C., & Lewis, M. (2003). Attentional effect of animated character. *Proceedings of the human-computer interaction,* 423–430. http://www.isp.pitt.edu/node/1033
65. Hudlicka, E., Becker-Asano, C., Payr, S., Fischer, K., Ventura, R., Leite, I., & von Scheve, C. (2009). Social interaction with robots and agents: Where do we stand, Where do we go? In *3rd international conference on affective computing and intelligent interaction and workshops, 2009 (ACII 2009)* (pp. 1–6). Amsterdam: IEEE.
66. Inter Ikea Systems B. V. (1999–2012). *Ikea, Welcome*. http://idea.com/us/en/. Accessed 12 Dec 2012.
67. Ijsselsteijn, W. A., Kort, Y. A. W., Westerink, J., Jager, M., & Bonants, R. (2006). Virtual fitness: Stimulating exercise behavior through media technology. *Presence Teleoperators and Virtual Environments, 15*(6), 688–698.
68. Jensen, A., Wilson, D.-M., Jordine, K., & Sakpal, R. (2012). Using embodied pedagogical agents and direct instruction to improve learning outcomes for young children with learning disabilities. *Global TIME 2012, 2012*(1), 235–239.
69. Johnson, W. L., Rickel, J. W., & Lester, J. C. (2000). Animated pedagogical agents: Face-to-face interaction in interactive learning environments. *International Journal of Artificial Intelligence in Education, 11*(1), 47–78.
70. Kamarck, T. W., Manuck, S. B., & Jennings, J. R. (1990). Social support reduces cardiovascular reactivity to psychological challenge: A laboratory model. *Psychosomatic Medicine, 52*(1), 42–58.
71. Kaminsky, T. A., Dudgeon, B. J., Billingsley, F. F., Mitchell, P. H., Weghorst, S. J., et al. (2007). Virtual cues and functional mobility of people with Parkinson's disease: A single-subject pilot study. *Journal of Rehabilitation Research and Development, 44*(3), 437.
72. Kanda, T., Hirano, T., Eaton, D., & Ishiguro, H. (2004). Interactive robots as social partners and peer tutors for children: A field trial. *Human Computer Interaction, 19*(1), 61–84.
73. Kidd, C. D. (2007). *Engagement in long-term human-robot interaction*. PhD thesis in Media Arts & Sciences, MIT, Cambridge, MA.
74. Klein, J., Moon, Y., & Picard, R. W. (2002). This computer responds to user frustration: Theory, design, and results. *Interacting with computers, 14*(2), 119–140.
75. Koda, T., & Maes, P. (1996). Agents with faces: The effect of personification. *5th IEEE international workshop on robot and human communication, 1996* (pp. 189–194). Tsukuba: IEEE.
76. Krahmer, E. J., & Swerts, M. (2006). Hearing and seeing beats: The influence of visual beats on the production and perception of prominence. *Proceedings of speech prosody 2006*. http://psycnet.apa.org/psycinfo/2007-13192-004
77. Krämer, N. C., & Bente, G. (2010). Personalizing e-learning. The social effects of pedagogical agents. *Educational Psychology Review, 22*(1), 71–87.
78. Krämer, N., Hoffmann, L., & Kopp, S. (2010). Know your users! Empirical results for tailoring an agent's nonverbal behavior to different user groups. *Intelligent virtual agents* (pp. 468–474). Heidelberg: Springer.
79. Krämer, N. C., Eimler, S., von der Pütten, A., & Payr, S. (2011). Theory of companions: What can theoretical models contribute to applications and understanding of human-robot interaction? *Applied Artificial Intelligence, 25*(6), 474–502.
80. Kriglstein, S., & Wallner, G. (2005). HOMIE: An artificial companion for elderly people. *CHI* (Bd. 5, S. 02–07).

81. Kryla-Lighthall, N., & Mather, M. (2009). *The role of cognitive control in older adults' emotional well-being*. In V. Berngtson, D. Gans, N. Putney, & M. Silverstein (Eds.), *Handbook of theories of aging* (2nd ed., pp. 323–344). Springer.
82. Lawson, S. W., & Chesney, T. (2007). The impact of owner age on companionship with virtual pets. In *Eighth international conference on Information Visualisation* (IV'04) (Vol. 4, pp. 1922–1928).
83. Lee, M. L., & Dey, A. K. (2008). Lifelogging memory appliance for people with episodic memory impairment. *Proceedings of the 10th international conference on Ubiquitous computing*, 44–53.
84. Lester, J. C., Converse, S. A., Kahler, S. E., Barlow, S. T., Stone, B. A., & Bhogal, R. S. (1997). The persona effect: Affective impact of animated pedagogical agents. *Proceedings of the SIGCHI conference on human factors in computing systems* (pp. 359–366). New York: ACM. http://dl.acm.org/citation.cfm?id=258797
85. Looije, R., Cnossen, F., & Neerinex, M. (2006). Incorporating guidelines for health assistance into a socially intelligent robot. *The 15th IEEE international symposium on robot and human interactive communication, 2006, ROMAN 2006* (pp. 515–520). Hatfield: IEEE.
86. Mark, G. (1999). Designing believable interaction by applying social conventions. *Applied Artificial Intelligence, 13*(3), 297–320.
87. McCalley, T., & Mertens, A. (2007). The pet plant: Developing an inanimate emotionally interactive tool for the elderly. *Proceedings of the 2nd international conference on persuasive technology* (pp. 68–79). Berlin/Heidelberg: Springer.
88. Mohseni, M., & Lindstrom, M. (2007). Social capital, trust in the health-care system and self-rated health: The role of access to health care in a population-based study. *Social Science & Medicine, 64*(7), 1373–1383.
89. Morandell, M., Fugger, E., & Prazak, B. (2007). The Alzheimer Avatar-Caregivers' faces used as GUI component. In *Challenges for assistive technology AAATE* (pp. 180–184). IOS Press: Amsterdam.
90. Morandell, M., Hochgatterer, A., Fagel, S., & Wassertheurer, S. (2008). Avatars in assistive homes for the elderly. In *HCI and usability for education and work* (pp. 391–402). Berlin/Heidelberg: Springer. http://link.springer.com/chapter/10.1007%2F978-3-540-89350-9_27
91. Moreno, R., Mayer, R. E., Spires, H. A., & Lester, J. C. (2001). The case for social agency in computer-based teaching: Do students learn more deeply when they interact with animated pedagogical agents? *Cognition and Instruction, 19*(2), 177–213.
92. Nass, C., Isbister, K., & Lee, E. J. (2000). Truth is beauty: Researching embodied conversational agents. In J. Cassell, J. Sullivan, S. Prevost, & E. L. Churchill (Eds.), *Embodied conversational agents* (pp. 374–402). Cambridge: MIT Press.
93. Nijholt, A. (2002). Embodied agents: A new impetus to humor research. In *The April Fools' Day workshop on computational humour* (pp. 101–111), Trento, Italy, 15–16 April.
94. Nowak, K. L., & Biocca, F. (2003). The effect of the agency and anthropomorphism on users' sense of telepresence, copresence, and social presence in virtual environments. *Presence Teleoperators & Virtual Environments, 12*(5), 481–494.
95. Okonkwo, C., & Vassileva, J. (2001). Affective pedagogical agents and user persuasion. In *Universal access in human-computer interaction*. New Orleans, USA.
96. Ortiz, A., del Puy Carretero, M., Oyarzun, D., Yanguas, J., Buiza, C., Gonzalez, M., & Etxeberria, I. (2007). Elderly users in ambient intelligence: Does an avatar improve the interaction? *Universal Access in Ambient Intelligence Environments, 4397*, 99–114. http://link.springer.com/chapter/10.1007%2F978-3-540-71025-7_8
97. Pandzic, I. S., Ostermann, J., & Millen, D. (1999). User evaluation: Synthetic talking faces for interactive services. *The Visual Computer, 15*(7), 330–340.
98. Papalia, D. E., Camp, C. J., & Feldman, R. D. (1996). *Adult development and aging*. New York: McGraw-Hill.
99. Parise, S., Kiesler, S., Sproull, L., & Waters, K. (1999). Cooperating with life-like interface agents. *Computers in Human Behavior, 15*(2), 123–142.

100. Picard, R. W., & Klein, J. (2002). Computers that recognise and respond to user emotion: Theoretical and practical implications. *Interacting with Computers, 14*(2), 141–169.
101. Pollack, M. E., Brown, L., Colbry, D., McCarthy, C. E., Orosz, C., Peintner, B., Ramakrishnan, S., & Tsamardinos, I. (2003). Autominder: An intelligent cognitive orthotic system for people with memory impairment. *Robotics and Autonomous Systems, 44(*(3), 273–282.
102. Prendinger, H., Mori, J., & Ishizuka, M. (2005). Using human physiology to evaluate subtle expressivity of a virtual quizmaster in a mathematical game. *International Journal of Human-Computer Studies, 62*(2), 231–245.
103. Qiu, L., & Benbasat, I. (2005). Online consumer trust and live help interfaces: The effects of text-to-speech voice and three-dimensional avatars. *International Journal of Human Computer Interaction, 19*(1), 75–94.
104. Raina, P., Waltner-Toews, D., Bonnett, B., Woodward, C., & Abernathy, T. (1999). Influence of companion animals on the physical and psychological health of older people: An analysis of a one-year longitudinal study. *Journal of the American Geriatrics Society, 47*(3), 323–329. http://www.ncbi.nlm.nih.gov/pubmed/10078895
105. Reeves, B., & Nass, C. (1996). *How people treat computers, television, and new media like real people and places*. Stanford: CSLI Publications/Cambridge University Press.
106. Rickenberg, R., & Reeves, B. (2000). The effects of animated characters on anxiety, task performance, and evaluations of user interfaces. In *Proceedings of the SIGCHI conference on Human factors in computing systems* (pp. 49–56). New York: ACM. http://dl.acm.org/citation.cfm?id=332406
107. Riedl, R., Mohr, P., Kenning, P., Davis, F., & Heekeren, H. (2011). Trusting humans and avatars: Behavioral and neural evidence. *ICIS 2011 Proceedings* (Paper 7).
108. Ruttkay, Z., Zwiers, J., van Welbergen, H., & Reidsma, D. (2006). Towards a reactive virtual trainer. In *Intelligent virtual agents* (pp. 292–303). Berlin/New York: Springer.
109. Salzman, B. (2010). Gait and balance disorders in older adults. *American Family Physician, 82*(1), 61–68.
110. San-Segundo, R., López, V., Martín, R., Lufti, S., Ferreiros, J., Córdoba, R., & Pardo, J. M. (2010). Advanced speech communication system for deaf people. In *Proceedings of INTERSPEECH 2010, 11th annual conference of the international Speech Communication Association.*
111. Scassellati, B. (2007). How social robots will help us to diagnose, treat, and understand autism. *Robotics Research, 28*, 552–563.
112. Schroeder, R. (2002). *The social life of avatars: Presence and interaction in shared virtual environments*. Berlin: Springer.
113. Shibata, T., Wada, K., & Tanie, K. (2003). Statistical analysis and comparison of questionnaire results of subjective evaluations of seal robot in Japan and UK. *Robotics and Automation, 2003. Proceedings. ICRA'03. IEEE international conference on* (Vol. 3, pp. 3152–3157). Berlin/Heidelberg: Springer.
114. Stichting, S. (2007). www.steffie.nl, zo werkt het. http://steffie.nl. Accessed 3 Jan 2013.
115. Stiehl, W. D., Breazeal, C., Han, K. H., Lieberman, J., Lalla, L., Maymin, A., Salinas, J., et al. (2006). The huggable: A therapeutic robotic companion for relational, affective touch. *ACM SIGGRAPH 2006 Emerging technologies,* 15. In *Proceedings of AAAI fall symposium on caring machines: AI in Eldercare,* 2006, Washington.
116. UbiComp. (2014). *Proceedings of the 2014 ACM international joint conference on pervasive and ubiquitous computing* (pp. 62–74).
117. Takeuchi, A., & Naito, T. (1995). Situated facial displays: Towards social interaction. In I. Katz, R. Mack, L. Marks, M. B. Rosson, & J. Nielsen (Eds.), *Human factors in computing systems: CHI + 95 conference proceedings* (pp. 450–455). New York: ACM Press.
118. Teigen, K. H. (1994). Yerkes-Dodson: A law for all seasons. *Theory & Psychology, 4*(4), 525–547.
119. Tognazzini, B. (1992). *TOG on interface*. Reading: Addison-Wesley.
120. Vinayagamoorthy, V., Gillies, M., Steed, A., Tanguy, E., Pan, X., Loscos, C., Slater, M., et al. (2006). Building expression into virtual characters. In *Eurographics conference state of the art reports,* Vienna, Austria, 4–8 September 2006 [Conference or Workshop Item]

121. Voerman, J. L., & FitzGerald, P. J. (2000). Deictic and emotive communication in animated pedagogical agents. In J. Cassell, J. Sullivan, S. Prevost, & E. L. Churchill (Eds.), *Embodied conversational agents* (p. 123). Cambridge: MIT Press.
122. von der Pütten, A., Krämer, N., & Gratch, J. (2010). How our personality shapes our interactions with virtual characters – Implications for research and development. In *10th International conference on intelligent virtual agents* (pp. 208–221). Berlin/New York: Springer.
123. Vormbrock, J. K., & Grossberg, J. M. (1988). Cardiovascular effects of human-pet dog interactions. *Journal of Behavioral Medicine, 11*(5), 509–517.
124. Wada, K., & Shibata, T. (2007). Living with seal robots—Its sociopsychological and physiological influences on the elderly at a care house. *IEEE Transactions on Robotics, 23*(5), 972–980.
125. Walker, J. H., Sproull, L., & Subramani, R. (1994). Using a human face in an interface. *Proceedings of the SIGCHI conference on Human factors in computing systems: Celebrating interdependence* (pp. 85–91). New York: ACM. http://dl.acm.org/citation.cfm?id=191708
126. Werry, I., & Dautenhahn, K. (1999). Applying mobile robot technology to the rehabilitation of autistic children. In *Proceedings of SIRS99, 7th symposium on intelligent robotic systems*, p. 265.
127. Wethington, E., & Kessler, R. C. (1986). Perceived support, received support, and adjustment to stressful life events. *Journal of Health and Social Behavior, 27*(1), 78–89.
128. Edney, A. T. (1995). Companion animals and human health: An overview. *Journal of the Royal Society of Medicine, 88*(12), 704p–708p.
129. Wu, P., & Miller, C. (2005). Results from a field study: The need for an emotional relationship between the elderly and their assistive technologies. In *1st international conference on augmented cognition, Las Vegas*.
130. Yee, N., Bailenson, J. N., & Rickertsen, K. (2007). A meta-analysis of the impact of the inclusion and realism of human-like faces on user experiences in interfaces. In *Proceedings of the SIGCHI conference on Human factors in computing systems* (pp. 1–10). New York: ACM. http://dl.acm.org/citation.cfm?id=1240626
131. Zajonc, R. B. (1965). Social facilitation. *Science, 149*(3681), 269–274.
132. Zunzunegui, M. V., Alvarado, B. E., Del Ser, T., & Otero, A. (2003). Social networks, social integration, and social engagement determine cognitive decline in community-dwelling Spanish older adults. *The Journals of Gerontology. Series B, Psychological Sciences and Social Sciences, 58*(2), 93–100.

Chapter 9
Building an Adaptive Multimodal Framework for Resource Constrained Systems

Carlos Duarte, Daniel Costa, Pedro Feiteira, and David Costa

Abstract Multimodal adaptive systems have typically been resource consuming systems, due to the requirements of processing recognition based modalities, and computing and applying adaptations based on users and context properties. In this chapter, we describe how we were able to design and implement an adaptive multimodal system, capable of performing in a resource constrained environment such as a Set-top Box. The presented approach endows standard non-adaptive, non-multimodal applications with adaptive multimodal capabilities, with limited extra effort demanded of their developers. Our approach has been deployed for Web applications, although it is applicable to other application environments. This chapter details the application interface interpretation, multimodal fusion and multimodal fission components of our framework.

9.1 Introduction

The current trend shows computational devices moving into the living room. People use tablets and smartphones while they watch TV, for tweeting about what their watching, or to find additional information about the show [1]. Set-top boxes and connected TVs are making this possible even without the additional devices. This trend also means the number of potential users is increasing, and with it the diversity of users' abilities, characteristics and technical knowledge will also increase. Combine this increasingly diverse user population with their lack of knowledge about the use of such applications, and the lack of traditional input devices (i.e. mouse and keyboard) in the living room setting, for which most web applications (that are now being made available in TV sets) have been built, and it is possible to envision a high resistance to their adoption. A solution to such problem requires

C. Duarte (✉)
Department of Informatics, University of Lisbon, Lisboa, Portugal
e-mail: cad@di.fc.ul.pt

D. Costa • P. Feiteira • D. Costa
Faculty of Sciences, University of Lisbon, Campo Grande, 1749-016 Lisboa, Portugal
e-mail: dancosta@di.fc.ul.pt; pfeiteira@di.fc.ul.pt; dcosta@lasige.di.fc.ul.pt

P. Biswas et al. (eds.), *A Multimodal End-2-End Approach to Accessible Computing*, Human–Computer Interaction Series, DOI 10.1007/978-1-4471-6708-2_9

an approach that can support natural interaction modalities, with the capability to interpret inputs from multiple modalities, and the capability to adapt the presentation of current and future web applications to the abilities and skills of the user and to the context of use, characterized by the existing devices and the surrounding environment (which takes particular importance in the living room scenario).

Multimodal input interpretation (involving recognition of speech, gestures, and possibly other modalities), and distribution and adaptation of output rendering over different modalities, are computationally expensive operations. On the other hand, set-top boxes have limited processing power, so some constraint on the multimodal operations has to be exercised. Still, their processing power is increasing, and the differences to other living room devices, like gaming consoles, can be expected to decrease, and even possible merge into one device, which opens new perspectives for the future. However, presently, limitations still have to be built into the adaptation process, as will be presented in the corresponding sections of this chapter. Nevertheless, the features that motivate this development have to be retained, or else the platforms will not be adopted by end-users.

Platform and service providers are not expected to deliver a platform with adaptive multimodal characteristics. The work on these platforms have been conducted almost exclusively in the realm of academia and research institutions, although in the recent years, natural interaction modalities have been making their way into the living room, promoted essentially by gaming consoles. As such, to further their adoption, and to bring the benefits of adaptation and multimodal interaction to all the strata of the population, the solution must be a framework capable of interfacing between the user and a standard application. A service provider, will then benefit from having a framework that can translate multimodal inputs into something that the application can process, and that additionally is capable to adapt the application's interface in a way that best suits the user. The end-user benefits from having the adapted presentation and from being able to interact naturally. This chapter presents that framework, focusing on the mechanisms that enable adaptive multimodal fusion and fission.

The next section will give a brief overview of the framework's architecture. The following section describes how the framework and applications communicate user interface (UI) information between them. The following two sections describe the mechanisms that endow the framework with adaptive multimodal fusion and fission capabilities. The final section concludes this chapter and presents an outlook for future developments.

9.2 Architectural Overview

The GUIDE[1] project has developed a framework, that sits between the interaction devices employed by users and applications deployed by service providers, endowing applications with adaptive multimodal interaction capabilities.

[1] http://www.guide-project.eu/

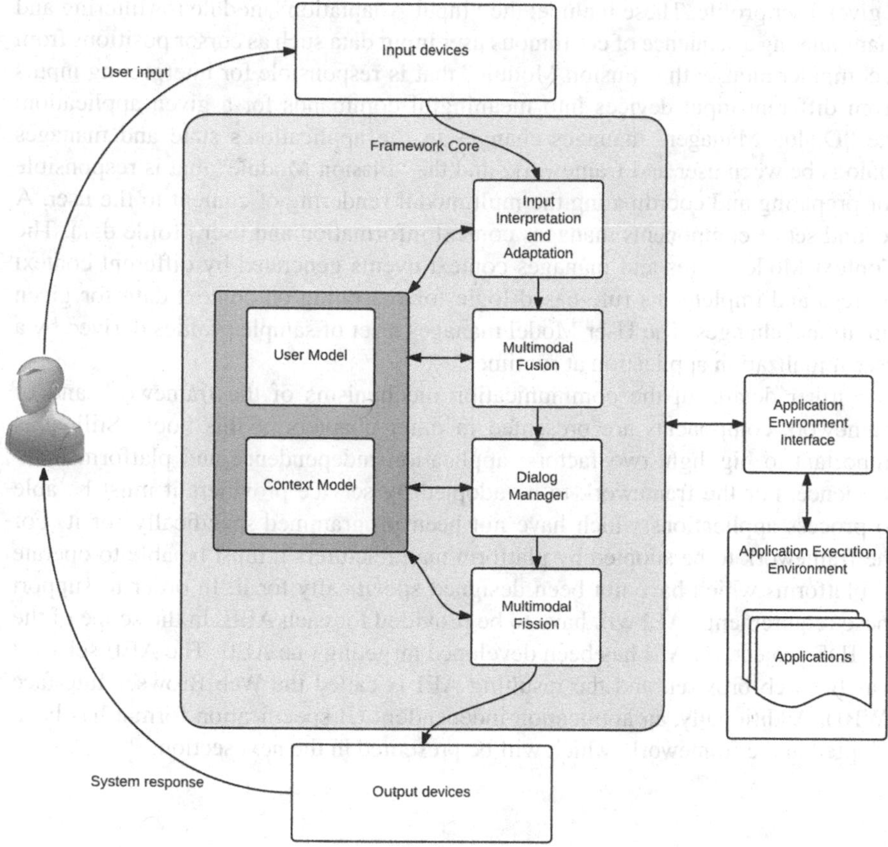

Fig. 9.1 Architectural overview of the GUIDE framework

Figure 9.1 presents an architectural overview of the GUIDE framework and communication system.

Applications are executed in environments (e.g. web applications in browsers, java applications in java runtime environments). The framework abstracts this into the concept of Application Execution Environment (AEE). For each AEE, an Application Environment Interface (AEI) needs to be provided. The AEI is responsible for managing the communication between applications and framework, which includes translating the application's UI into a representation that is understood by the framework and exchanging events between application and framework. Based on the application's abstract representation the framework performs runtime adaptation of the interface elements (such as adjusting text-size, font-size, color, and contrast) and uses different input and output modalities for interaction with the user.

The framework core specification defines two groups of components. The first set of components implements multimodal adaptation algorithms for processing and managing input and output data as well as to adapt parameters across modalities for a given user profile. These include: the "Input Adaptation" module for filtering and manipulating a sequence of continuous user input data such as cursor positions from a computer mouse; the "Fusion Module" that is responsible for interpreting inputs from different input devices into meaningful commands for a given application; the "Dialog Manager" manages changes in the application's state and manages dialogs between user and framework; and the "Fission Module" that is responsible for preparing and coordinating the multimodal rendering of content to the user. A second set of components manages context information and user profile data. The Context Model stores and manages context events generated by different context sources and implements rule-based logic for reasoning on context data for given situational changes. The User Model manages a set of sample profiles derived by a user initialization application at runtime.

Further details of the communication mechanisms of the framework and of framework components are presented in other chapters of this book. Still, it is important to highlight two factors: application independence and platform independence. For the framework to be adopted by service providers it must be able to process applications which have not been programmed specifically for it. For the framework to be adopted by platform manufacturers it must be able to operate in platforms which have not been designed specifically for it. In order to support these requirements, AEI will have to be provided for each AEE. In the scope of the GUIDE project, on AEI has been developed targeting one AEE. The AEE selected was the web browser, and the resulting AEI is called the Web Browser Interface (WBI). Additionally, an application independent UI specification format has been adopted in the framework, which will be presented in the next section.

9.3 Interfacing with Applications

In order for an adaptive system to adapt a user interface or to apply the interpreted commands from combinations of different inputs, it needs to have knowledge about the application's user interface. One the GUIDE framework's goals is to be compatible with any type of application. As it isn't feasible to develop an instance of the core for each application type (and associated development language), we needed a standard UI description language (UIDL) to interface between framework and application.

Further, as has been discussed above, framework requirements specify that application designers and developers should have little effort to make their applications compatible with the framework. At the same time, the extraction of the UI representation should be possible without requiring much processing power due to the constraints imposed by set-top box environment. To meet these requirements each AEI must have a component, named User Interface Extraction Component (UIREC), that is responsible for extracting the application's UI representation.

The following sections describe the alternatives and choices we have faced during the development of this component for the WBI.

9.3.1 User Interface Description Languages

As mentioned before, it is a requirement of the GUIDE framework to analyze, choose and adhere to one of existing abstract UI representation language standards. In order to ensure a complete separation of application logic from its presentation, the GUIDE Framework should support a standard interface vocabulary that abstracts the semantics and intents of an application from its concrete user interface implementation. Thus a design consideration in GUIDE is to evaluate and select from the plethora of existing abstract UI description standards, one that meets its abstract UI description needs but at the same time, also requires minimal effort in implementation and re-use. Table 9.1 shows the considered UIDLs.

XForms cannot cover all the requirements for GUIDE as it is incapable of describing more specific properties or attributes of certain elements (Buttons, Images, etc.) such as position values, size, color or other style properties. Although much more complete than XForms, UsiXML fails in giving the location of objects which is an important property for Fusion and User Model components in the

Table 9.1 User interface description languages considered in the GUIDE project

UIDL name	Description
XForms (http://www.w3.org/MarkUp/Forms/)	XML application that represents the next generation of forms for the web, and has introduced the use of abstractions to address new heterogeneous environments. When comparing XForms with HTML Forms, the main difference, apart from XForms being in XML, is the separation of the data, from the markup of the controls
UsiXML (http://www.usixml.eu/)	Standing for USer Interface eXtensible Markup Language, it is an XML-compliant markup language that describes the UI for multiple contexts of use such as Character User Interfaces (CUIs), Graphical User Interfaces (GUIs), Auditory User Interfaces, and Multimodal User Interfaces
XIML (http://www.ximl.org/)	It is an extensible XML-based specification language for multiple facets of multiple models in a model-based approach, developed by a forum headed by RedWhale software. It was introduced as a solution that enables a framework for the definition and interrelation of interaction data items
UIML (https://www.oasis-open.org/)	The User Interface Markup Language, is an example of a language that has addressed the multi-device interface issue. It is an XML-compliant language that supports a declarative description of a user interface in a device-independent manner. In UIML, a user interface is a set of interface elements with which the user interacts. These elements may be organized differently for the different categories of users and types of appliances

GUIDE Core. Although the tag and property names are a bit sloppy they are indeed complete, but the main drawback connected to XIML is the fact that, differently from the majority of the other User Interface description languages, it is developed within a software company, and therefore its use is protected by copyright. UIML specification does not define property names. This is a powerful concept, because it allows UIML to be extensible: one can define whatever property names are appropriate for a particular element of the UI. For example, *color* might be a useful property for a button, while *text-size* might be appropriate for a label. This flexibility allows us to define all the properties needed for all GUIDE components (Input Adaptation, Fusion, Fission, Dialogue Manager, User Model, etc.). Additionally, they might be used to represent the information developers might provide using WAI-ARIA [2] markup tags. UIML seems to be the most complete and flexible UI representation, therefore it was chosen as the standard language to be used as the interface language between the framework and the applications.

Other adaptive multimodal systems such as EGOKI [3] also use this UIDL. However, our approach is different as the framework is the one generating the UIML automatically based only on the UI elements, discarding the logical specification of the application.

9.3.2 Implementation Alternatives

Before the UIREC was made part of the WBI different approaches on where and when this extraction was to be done were considered.

One of the first approaches was to do it in design time, i.e., when developers finished their application they would use a tool to extract a UIML file describing the entire application. However, this approach was discarded because different developers use different implementation methods. For instance, some developers use separate files for different application states (e.g. one HTML file for each state) and other developers use one single file. Developing a parser for this scenario would be a task of extreme complexity.

The next approach was to integrate this component in the GUIDE core serving as an Application Model that would derive and extract automatically the states and UI representations. However, this suffered from the same limitations and, additionally, this approach would require a change inside the GUIDE core every time a new application execution platform, and thus application language, is integrated.

The final approach is to make this extraction state by state and outside the core. This approach has the advantage of delegating to the AEI the job of delivering the code that belongs to a determined state, and any change in the program language doesn't imply any change in GUIDE's main components. Currently, it was implemented in the WBI, as part of the Javascript API. The advantages of this approach are the full access to the DOM tree and the ability to cope with the dynamically introduced elements as the extraction is made in browser processing time.

The following section details how this extraction is made.

9.3.3 *In Browser User Interface Description Language Creation*

In order for the UIREC to obtain meaningful information for the several components of the GUIDE framework, some conditions have to be verified in terms of the application's implementation: all the elements that are meant to be adapted and recognized by GUIDE, preferably the majority of the elements presented on the interface, must have a unique id and the respective WAI-ARIA tag describing the role of the element.

The process starts after the application loads its resources (e.g. style-sheets and scripts), and proceeds during the *Framework phase*. Then, the HTML and CSS information is sent to the UIREC, where the parsing takes place in two phases: (1) extraction of the structure of the user interface by parsing the HTML and (2) extraction of the style information of each element by parsing both HTML and CSS information.

The parser goes through the DOM in search for the elements correctly marked with an id and the WAI-ARIA role, and starts forming the structure section of the UIML. The structure is formed with a set of <part>tags with the id and class properties. The id's match with the HTML elements and the classes with the WAI-ARIA roles. There are some roles that encompass other roles, which is the case of *menu* that has *menuitems*. In these cases, the parser takes into account the parent and child elements.

The style section on the UIML corresponds to the properties defined on the style-sheets and/or HTML properties. This section is composed of <property>tags, each one having a *part-name* tag, that matches the *part* id on the structure section, the property *name* (e.g. background-color) and the value. The UIREC can understand specific CSS properties as well as properties defined in CSS classes.

Besides CSS properties, the UIREC needs positioning and size information about the elements. As most of these properties have different representations (e.g. relative positions, percentage, pixels), the WBI has the ability to add to each element GUIDE specific properties. These properties contain *x*, *y*, *width* and *height* absolute pixel values divided by the screen size (e.g. $guidePositionX = 0.124$). The UIREC adds these properties to the style section.

When the processing is finished, the UIML document is sent to the GUIDE framework's bus system and collected by the interested components.

The next section describes what is the real effort made by TV application developers to integrate their applications with the Framework.

9.3.4 *Implications for Application Developers*

As discussed above, the TV applications considered so far in GUIDE are based on web-based languages like HTML, CSS and JavaScript because of their wide acceptance among developers and general compliance with STB and HybridTV [4] specifications.

In the end, what is expected from the developers is nothing but the specification and integration of WAI-ARIA tags to define the role of the different UI elements and, possibly, some accessibility considerations such as the compliance with WCAG 2.0 guidelines [5]. The only additional effort is the integration with the GUIDE Javascript API, which is accomplished with a very small number of lines of code.

We believe that this effort represents a very small overhead for application developers. A similar or, more probably, an even larger effort, would have to be made if the application was intended to be accessible, in the first place, following current practices.

9.4 Interpreting Input

One of the most crucial aspects of multi-modal interactive systems is interpreting user input, which can either be a simple or complex task, depending on factors such as the number and type of modalities involved, architectural and implementation choices, or even user and contextual requirements.

As a system grows or branches in terms of interaction mechanisms available, so does the amount and variation of information received by it. For this reason, a way of correctly interpreting all of this data is needed, along with adaptation mechanisms that make the interaction experience the most adequate for each user. In addition, users, the way they interact with applications, and their surroundings, can also evolve over time, which forces a fusion engine to constantly adapt its process of decision-making in order to provide trustworthy results.

The GUIDE framework is an user oriented system, capable of providing distinct modalities and devices for providing input, which includes speech and gestures recognition, remote control, among others. For these reasons, a great focus of the framework development was set on creating an approach capable of processing data from these sources, combine it when needed and provide high-level interpretations that are of use to other components of the system.

9.4.1 Requirements for Input Fusion

The main task of the GUIDE fusion engine is to potentially combine any incoming input from recognizers, reach an interpretation of that data and forward it to a dialog manager that continues the process, ending with a response that is returned to the user. The key to provide the most suitable interpretation for a given situation is to take into account critical information from three main sources: input events, a user model and a context model.

When the user is interacting with GUIDE, input recognizers are constantly capturing and generating events that will be sent to the fusion module, which constitute the base for creating interpretations. These events, which contain temporal (e.g. timestamps) and semantic attributes (e.g. what the user said, which key was pressed) can be considered the most important piece of knowledge, because without it there would not exist a purpose for data fusion. Information about the user, although not essential for understanding input, it is of extreme importance for the fusion process, because it allows to tweak models and algorithms in accordance to each user's necessities and preferences. This type of data is extracted from user models that are constructed a priori by an initialization application, and allow the fusion engine to have access to data such as the level of user proficiency with each modality or device available. Knowing the extent of user capabilities towards the system is an important asset, but it is also quite important to understand how the environment, that surrounds the user, affects the way in which these capabilities are used. The context model is the third component used by the fusion engine to create decisions about what is happening between user and system. The information that must be contained in this model includes, for example, how current environmental conditions are affecting the usage of a certain modality or device (e.g. a noisy room can have a negative impact on speech recognition) or the engagement between user and system (e.g. if the user is passive for a long time, it may need some assistance using an application).

9.4.2 *Previous Works on Multimodal Fusion*

Multimodal interfaces and ways of interacting with them have been subject of study for the past two decades [6]. This is also true for the process of multimodal fusion, for which there have been envisioned different levels, architectures and algorithms. Sharma et al. [7] considers three levels for fusion of incoming data: sensor-level (or data-level) fusion, feature level-fusion and decision level-fusion. Other authors such as Sanderson and Paliwal [8] define terms with similar meanings such as pre-mapping, midst-mapping and post-mapping fusion. The difference between these types of levels, is essentially, at which time, information combination takes place. Pre-mapping data-level fusion, deals with raw data coming from recognizers, representing the richest form of information possible, quantitatively speaking. Because the signal is directly processed, no information loss occurs, although it is very susceptible to noises and failures. Due to the heavy processing involved, sensor-fusion is most suited for situations where multiple streams of a single modality are involved. Pre-mapping feature-level fusion, is a type of fusion oriented for closely-coupled or time synchronized modalities such as, for example, speech and lips movement recognition. In this type of fusion, features are extracted from data collected by several sensors, and if they are commensurate they can be combined. Unlike data-level fusion, it can suffer from data loss, but manages noise interference better. In midst-mapping fusion several information streams are processed concurrently while the mapping sensor-date/feature space to decision/opinion space takes place. This type of fusion, similarly to feature-level fusion, is also oriented for closely coupled modalities such as lips and speech recognition.

One of the most common and widely accepted forms of fusion is decision-level fusion, and that is because it allows multi-modal systems to make effective use of loosely-coupled modalities, such as the case of GUIDE. Because the information received by the fusion engine has already been processed, noise and failure are no longer issues to deal with. This means, that fusion will have to rely on preprocessed information in order to construct semantic meaning from combining partial semantic information coming from each input mode. That preprocessed information constitutes a concrete decision that was produced by one or more recognizers. Opinion-level fusion (also called score-level fusion) is very similar to decision-level because both of them operate after the mapping of data/feature-level space into decision/opinion space. In fact, some literature [9] considered the former as a sub-set of the latter. However, in the case of opinion-level fusion, a group of experts provides opinions instead of hard decisions, and for that reason Sanderson and Paliwal [8] found more adequate to make a distinction between the two types. Opinions combination can be achieved, for example, through weighted summation or weighted product approaches, before using a classification criterion (e.g. MAX operator) in order to reach a final decision. The main advantage of using opinion over feature vectors concatenation or decision fusion is that opinions from each expert can be weighted. Fusion classifiers can be distinguished not only by the type of fusion or architecture they possess, but also by whether they are adaptive or non-adaptive [10]. The basic concept around adaptive, or quality fusion, is to assign different weight values associated with a modality. This allows to imprint adaptive features into a system, by setting the reliability and discrimination of experts through time according to the state of the environment, signal quality, users, or application logic.

As for options to implement these ideas and approaches, Dumas et al. [11] considered the following as typical choices for decision-level architectures: frame-based fusion, using data structures called frames or features for meaning representation of data coming from various sources or modalities, modeling objects as attribute-value pairs; unification-based fusion which is based on recursively merging attribute-value structures to obtain a logical whole meaning representation; symbolic/statistical fusion, an evolution of standard symbolic unification-based approaches, which adds statistical processing techniques to the frame-based and unification-based fusion techniques.

Taking into account the low and mid-levels of fusion described, it is clear that these approaches have severe limitations that make them not suitable for the fusion engine of the GUIDE framework, which has to deal with loosely-coupled modalities and a high flow of data that must be handled quickly and efficiently, while at the same time consuming the minimal amount of system resources, which are heavily demanded by other components. As for high-level types of fusion, decision-level is also not a completely optimal solution to embrace, due to the fact that it is not directly oriented for systems that must deal with unpredictability or uncertainty, something that is quite important for GUIDE.

9.4.3 Adaptive Multimodal Fusion in GUIDE

In a system like GUIDE, which runs in a set-top box environment with limited processing capabilities, it is of extreme importance to minimize the workload of each component in the framework. For this reason, the approach taken in designing the fusion module was centered on a high-level type of fusion, namely opinion-level fusion, which assigns a considerable part of the responsibility of understanding input to the recognizers, that provide opinions that must be interpreted and merged into an interpretation. From an architectural point of view a frame-based strategy [11] was chosen due to its simplicity and also because it could easily be augmented to fulfill other requisites such as imprinting adaptability in the system and consider uncertainty in the provided input. This implementation uses data structures entitled *frames*, which consists of two major sets of data. The first one is a set of slots, which can either contain triggers or sub-frames. Triggers are conditions that are to be met in order for the slot to be activated, while a sub-frame is a regular frame contained inside another frame, allowing the representation of more complex interaction scenarios. A trigger is associated with one and only one modality (such as speech or pointing) and contains data related to an input event, that essentially represent user actions. The second set contained inside a frame consists of results, which are interpretations or commands that have to be forwarded to the next component in charge, when frame activation occurs. This activation can occur in different conditions, because, for example, in some contexts we want all the slots conditions to be triggered while in others only one might suffice. Taking into account temporal constraints is also crucial when dealing with input, and for that reason, this frame structure also keeps track of when conditions are met so that dynamic thresholds can be set, in order to allow slower or faster-paced interactions, which is convenient for users that have different characteristics.

The frame-creation process is something that is expected to occur many times during an application life-cycle. As the context of the applications changes, the fusion module must prepare itself to potentially receive different types of input events and send the appropriate responses. To this, whenever the application context is modified, a message is received from the system's dialog manager, containing the representation of the current UI displayed on the screen, expressed in UIML. When the fusion obtains this knowledge the frames creation process can then begin. For each kind of interactive element, specific frames will have to be considered and created. In the case of buttons, for instance, frames will have to be created so that these elements can be clicked using voice or pointing gestures. It also important to notice that the frames created are not solely related to the UI itself. There are other commands that should be available at all times, and are independent of the application context. Examples of such situations would be the user requesting a list of available speech commands or an explanation of a certain element. Upon this process finalization, all the inputs relevant for the current context and their respective responses are defined. As the user produces input, the fusion module assesses at all times which frames can be activated with the input events received.

As previously mentioned, this approach is based on opinions, and therefore it is expected to received, from most input recognizers, a confidence value along with the semantic data involved with the input event. In this way, whenever an event can trigger a certain slot, this slot is also given a confidence value. However, the slot confidence does not depend only on the input, because the fusion module also has to consider the user capabilities and the surrounding environment. For this reason, the fusion engine is constantly being updated, by other components, regarding changes on the user and context, which are also used to calculate the confidence on each slot. For instance, if the system knows the user has difficulties using the speech modality, it will assign a smaller weight to this modality, which in conjunction with a low confidence speech event may trigger a slot. The purpose of defining confidence values for each slot is to attribute an overall confidence value for the frame, which will serve as a mean to compare activated frames and deciding which one is more likely to represent the actions expressed by the user at that point, in order to return the appropriate interpretations.

9.5 Generating Output

Another crucial component of the framework is the multimodal fission module. Fission is responsible for generating the appropriate UI adaptations and for delivering the output to the user using more modalities if necessary, in order to achieve the best possible user experience.

Using a unimodal system limits information presentation into a single modality, this excluding persons who suffer from an impairment to the sensory channel needed to perceive that information (a blind person cannot see graphical information and a deaf person cannot hear sounds). Additionally, a person might be temporarily precluded from using one sensory channel (e.g. her visual attention might need to be focused elsewhere). For these reasons, it can be very important for an application to be relieved of the limitation to present information in a single modality. The multimodal fission component allows applications to present their information using different modalities.

Modes are the sensorial system of a human with which he perceives the world. A modality is defined by the structure of the information that is perceived by the user (e.g. text, sound, vibration, etc.) and a medium is a channel or the mean used to express the modality, i.e., the peripheral devices such as a monitor or a TV screen, loudspeakers and so on. All these three components are dependent on each other's [12]. By combining the information presentation into an adaptive multimedia output, we can enable a more natural and effective interaction whichever mode or combination of modes are best suited to a given situation, context and according to user's preferences and abilities.

The adaptive multimodal fission component is responsible for dividing or selecting the output channels to distribute the information through the available outputs and according to the user profile and environmental context. We also consider the existence of active and passive outputs, or primary and secondary outputs. For example when using a form of haptic feedback through vibration you can actually hear it too, being vibration the primary output and auditory the secondary output.

9.5.1 Requirements of Multimodal Fission

We defined since the beginning of this project that the developing strategy would be an user centered methodology. This methodology aims to meet the user's requirements, behaviors and specificities by studying and analyzing their interactions with a multimodal system in the most likely end user environment. The target user population considered in the scope of the GUIDE project are elderly people, but many of the findings can be generalized to other population groups.

After conducting user studies and by analyzing the data, we could conclude that applications should always present a short number of interactive elements for each screen, focusing on big buttons. If developers make complex UIs, GUIDE has to be capable of dividing one screen in multiple screens (and provide navigation through them), or present options to the user in alternative modalities. Applications should make sure both text size and audio volume are configurable by the user at the beginning as well as in the middle of an interaction. If the application by itself doesn't offer this option, GUIDE UI adaptation should offer this possibility.

The existence of a strong relation between arm used for pointing and item location on screen, will influence the way developers design the layout of their applications, as it also affects the configuration and parametrization of GUIDE presentation manager, as both have to contemplate the existence of this user-UI relation.

If system feedback and presentation could only be performed in one modality (Avatar, Audio or Visual information), the way to do it would depend on the interaction and application context but also on the user's preferences and capabilities. This is also true for the type of Avatar: head only avatar would be more suitable for talking with the user or giving simple feedback, while half and full-body Avatar would be suitable for instructing the user on how to do certain gestures, or on how to perform certain tasks. However, and independently of which output modality chosen, output should be repeatable every time the user asks for it again, solving problems derived from lack of attention or changes in the context of interaction.

Trials showed that each user has its own characteristics and interaction patterns, but they can be grouped into different clusters. Somehow, information about the user must be collected by the system in order to perform the right adaptation.

To reach the elderly population, characterized by a set of age related disabilities, but traditionally also by some reluctance to adopt new technologies, GUIDE instead of relying on new interaction devices, opted for interaction modalities that are already familiar to the target population. This multimodal interaction scenario might demand a set of skills from its users, not for the interaction itself, but for the setting up and configuration, that certainly should not be imposed on a regular TV viewer, be him or her elderly or not. As such, in order to achieve the best interaction experience and performance possible from the multimodal interaction set-up, GUIDE includes the possibility to automatically adapt its features and their operation parameters. Another benefit from presenting users with natural interaction modalities, is that they do not require long learning periods in order to be used, thus overcoming another factor that drives away users from new interaction technologies.

A fission component needs to have knowledge of the application's UI and that information must be structured and has to contain all elements and their properties in order to be possible to adapt that content to the user. The Application Environment Interface translates the application state (e.g. a Web page) into UIML to represent the application's UI in a language that is understood by the GUIDE core. The multimodal fission processes the UIML representation of the application's state and decides on how to adapt presentation and interaction aspects. The results of this adaptation are then transmitted to the interface who must translate them for the application. As stated before each user has his own characteristics and set of skills and fission will chose the most appropriate modalities based on an user profile (if two or more users are in front of the TV, their profiles will be merged into a single one). These parameters are divided in two types:

- A set of modalities (input/output) with a value representing their likeability to be used and the level of necessity to be adapted by Multimodal Fission;
- A set of more specific parameters for visual or auditory properties. This data represents the minimum recommendations by the User Model (e.g. the smaller font size a given user can read) and are subject to change by the Multimodal Fission's decision evaluation system.

Adaptations do not depend solely on the user who is interacting with the system. Some contextual elements change how the presentation should be rendered. A good example is the ambient noise in the environment where the system is being used. If the room is full of persons actively chatting with each others, the system will gather the noise ratio level and fission will use modalities alternative to auditory modalities (e.g. avoid auditory messages and use text visual messages). Other example is the user distance to the screen which needs to be considered when adapting visual elements of the screen (e.g. when calculating the font-size or buttons' size). The requested environmental data is the responsibility of a Context Model which fission, and other components, will query whenever needed.

9.5.2 Existing Approaches in Multimodal Systems

Systems that combine outputs evolved since the early nineties where text and graphics were combined (e.g. COMET [13]). More recent systems combine speech, haptic, graphics, text, 2D/3D animations or avatars (e.g. SmartKon [14], MIAMM [15]). Although most applications use few output modalities and consequently straightforward fission techniques, dealing with the above-mentioned combination of outputs can make the presentations more complex, difficult to coordinate and ensuring coherence.

According to Oviatt [16], fission engines should follow three tasks:

- Message construction. The presentation content to be included must be selected and structured, i.e., it is necessary to decompose the semantic information issued from the dialogue manager into elementary data to be presented to the user. There are two main approaches for content selection and structuring that can be employed – schema-based [17] or plan-based [18]. However, in GUIDE this task begins before the fission component processing begins, since it is constrained by the application's layout and content design.
- Modality selection. After the message construction, the presentation must be allocated, i.e., each elementary data is allocated to a multimodal presentation adapted to the interaction context. This selection process follows a behavioral model that specifies the components (modes, modalities and medium) to be used. The available modalities should be structured according to the type of information they can handle or the perceptual task they permit, the characteristics of the information to present, the user's profile (abilities, skills, impairments and so on) and the resource limitations. Taking this into consideration is necessary for optimal modality selection. For the completion of this goal there are three approaches: rule based [19], composite based [17] and agent based [20].
- Output coordination. Once the presentation is allocated, it needs to be instantiated, which consists in getting the lexical syntactic content and the attributes of the modalities. First the concrete content of the presentation is chosen and then attributes such as modality attributes, spatial and temporal parameters, etc., are fixed. For a coherent and synchronized result of the presentation, all used output channels should be coordinated with each other.

9.5.3 Adaptive Multimodal Fission in GUIDE

GUIDE's fission component, although based on the aforementioned approaches, follows the What-Which-How-Then (WWHT) approach, a conceptual model of Rousseau et al. [12]. This component must know what information to present, which modalities to choose to present that information, how to present it using those modalities and coordinate the flow of the presentation.

In order to select the most appropriate modalities to use, it is necessary to define how deep the adaptation level will be. Three levels of adaptation of the interaction and presentation interface were envisioned, which were characterized as Augmentation, Adjustment and Replacement. These levels represent an increasing change to the visual presentation defined by the application, from no change to the visual rendering to a, possibly, complete overhaul.

Augmentation is the lightest form of adapting the interface implemented by the developer. The visual rendering is not subjected to any change, as GUIDE only complements it with other modalities. Usually, applications are developed using primarily visual presentation mechanisms. As a consequence, audio modalities will, foreseeably, be the most used in such situations in the form of redundant information (e.g. speech synthesis of content presented on screen).

Adjustment is the level of adaptation where the visual interface rendering is adjusted to the abilities of the user and which can also be combined with augmentation. Once again, considering applications are primarily developed taking into account visual rendering, this corresponds to adjusting several parameters of the visual rendering (e.g. font size and contrast). If other modalities are employed, their parameters can also be target of adaptation (e.g. adjusting audio volume).

Replacement level is the most complex adaptation scheme as it means that, not only presentation changes can be made to the application's interface (i.e. the adjustment level), but it can also result in the replacement of some interactive elements for other (e.g. menus for buttons) or even in the distribution of content over different modalities or different screens in case of visual rendering. This level is extremely useful for users with cognitive impairments, who, while navigating through an application, can become lost due to the tangle of menus and buttons displayed. The content of an application state can be simplified and divided by various screens or rendered through other modalities such as the Avatar or speech synthesis.

Given that GUIDE aims to support legacy applications (with changes as small as possible to their code) we must consider that these applications have been developed without accessibility concerns towards impaired users. Ideally, GUIDE would be able to evaluate if the application's presentation is close to the recommended presentation parameters for the current user and context specifications (e.g. the text sizes are between the values perceived by the user's vision), and based on that analysis select which adaptation level to apply. In practice, this represents a loss of control for application developers and publishers which they do not agree to. As such, the level of adaptation an application might be subjected to, can be limited by the application publisher. If the application developer allows, GUIDE can apply the computed adaptations. Alternatively, GUIDE can forward these adaptations to the applications through the GUIDE API, and the application can choose which adaptations to apply, thus retaining a greater degree of control.

The replacement level has been left out of project developments, given two factors: first, the reluctance shown by application developers in having a *foreign* framework taking over the rendering of their applications, and second, the computational requirements for such a complex decision process, might be too much for the processing power of a set-top box. Still, it is envisioned that in the future new algorithms will be devised to this end, replacing current algorithms since the variables at play are substantially different than the ones for the two first adaptation levels.

After the selection of the adaptation level best suited to the situation, the modalities to render the content are chosen through weights selected in accordance with the availability or resource limitations (context model) and with the user specificities described in the user model. This means that fission uses a rule based system to decide which modalities are the best for a given situation. There are two types of decisions to be made, one is the modalities which will see their content adapted and the other is the modalities that will be used to complement other modalities.

Using the information provided by the user and context models, the fission module is capable of calculating the best values for visual elements within the recommended ones by evaluating the presentation coherency (e.g. assuring that bigger buttons will not overlap each other or reach screen boundaries). Once the presentation is ready to be rendered, the necessary messages to the output devices are sent in a coordinated way. To synchronize the presentation flow, coordination events are sent to the bus in order to start or stop rendering, or to be notified when a render is completed. These rendering instructions are handled by a buffer in the fission module, which sends one instruction for each device at a time. The device will then respond with a notification of completion or failure. By controlling the flow of events sent and notifications received, instructions that do not get a chance to be rendered because a new state needs to be loaded due to user intervention are not even sent to the rendering devices, saving bandwidth and making the whole process more efficient.

9.6 Future Outlook

This chapter presented the GUIDE framework, a solution to endow applications with adaptive multimodal mechanisms, benefiting both end-users, by providing them with natural interaction mechanisms and adapted presentations, and application developers, by empowering their applications with these mechanisms requiring only a small effort.

GUIDE builds on the current trend that is bringing multimodal interaction into the living room. Gaming consoles have started the momentum, but more entertainment appliances with multimodal interaction capabilities have recently entered the market. GUIDE expands on these offerings by integrating more modalities, by complementing multi modality with adaptation capabilities, and by making it easy for platform developers to integrate it into their offerings, be it on the application, platform or interaction device level.

In the coming years, it can be expected that the computing power of set-top boxes and connected TVs will keep increasing, making this solution more viable, powerful and adoptable. The technical restrictions that are still felt will become weaker, and more powerful algorithms will be enabled, thus affording interaction paradigms even more suited to their environments.

Additionally, future users will already be more acquainted with natural interaction modalities, since we are already being more and more exposed to these in current interaction devices, like tablets and smartphones where gesture and speech interaction are becoming common.

Taking all this into consideration, we can expect that this kind of interaction, and its supporting frameworks will enter the marketplace sooner rather than later, and become standard in the living rooms. Furthermore, it is not hard to imagine the next step, where this type of frameworks becomes ubiquitous, supporting personalization and adaptation, not only in the living room, but everywhere where a networked device is available.

References

1. Lochrie, M., & Coulton, P. (2012). Sharing the viewing experience through second screens. In *Proceedings of the 10th European conference on interactive tv and video (EuroiTV '12)* (pp. 199–202). New York: ACM.
2. *Accessible Rich Internet Applications (WAI-ARIA) 1.0*. (2011). From: http://www.w3.org/TR/wai-aria/.
3. Abascal, J., Aizpurua, A., Cearreta, I., Gamecho, B., Garay-Vitoria, N., & Miñón, R. (2011). Automatically generating tailored accessible user interfaces for ubiquitous services. In *The proceedings of the 13th international ACM SIGACCESS conference on computers and accessibility (ASSETS '11)* (pp. 187–194). New York: ACM.
4. *Hybrid Broadcast Broadband TV*. (2012). From: http://www.hbbtv.org/pages/about_hbbtv/introduction.php.
5. Caldwell, B., Cooper, M., Reid, L., & Vanderheiden, G. (2008). Web content accessibility guidelines 2.0 (W3C Note, December 2008). From http://www.w3.org/TR/WCAG20/.
6. Nigay, L., & Coutaz, J. (1993). A design space for multimodal systems: Concurrent processing and data fusion. In *Proceedings of the INTERCHI 93 conference on human factors in computing systems* (pp. 172–178). New York: ACM.
7. Sharma, R., Pavlovic, V. I., & Huang, T. S. (1998). Toward multimodal human-computer interface. *Proceedings of the IEEE, 86*, 853–869.
8. Sanderson, C., & Paliwal, K. K. (2002). *Information fusion and person verification using speech & face information* (Research paper IDIAP-RR 02-33).
9. Hall, D. L., & Llinas, J. (2001). Multisensor data fusion. In D. L. Hall & J. Llinas (Eds.), *Handbook of multisensor data fusion* (pp. 1–10). Boca Raton: CRC Press.
10. Poh, N., Bourlai, T., & Kittler, J. (2010). Multimodal information fusion. In J.-P. Thiran, F. Marqués, & H. Bourlard (Eds.), *Multimodal signal processing theory and applications for human computer interaction* (p. 153). Oxford: Academic Press.
11. Dumas, B., Lalanne, D., & Oviatt, S. (2009). Multimodal interfaces: A survey of principles, models and frameworks. *Human Machine Interaction, 5440*(2), 3–26.
12. Rousseau, C., Bellik, Y., & Vernier, F. (2005). WWHT: un modele conceptuel pour la presentation multimodale d'information. In *IHM* (Volume 264 of ACM international conference proceeding series, pp. 59–66). New York: ACM.
13. Feiner, S. K., & McKeown, K. R. (1993). *Automating the generation of coordinated multimedia explanations* (pp. 117–138). Menlo Park: American Association for Artificial Intelligence.
14. Reithinger, N., Alexandersson, J., Becker, T., Blocher, A., Engel, R., Lockelt, M., Muller, J., Pfieger, N., Poller, P., Streit, M., et al. (2003). SmartKom: Adaptive and flexible multimodal access to multiple applications. In *Proceedings of the 5th international conference on multimodal interfaces (ICMI 2003)* (pp. 101–108). New York: ACM.
15. Reithinger, N., Fedeler, D., Kumar, A., Lauer, C., Pecourt, E., & Romary, L. (2005). Miamm – A multimodal dialogue system using haptics. In J. van Kuppevelt, L. Dybkjaer, & N. O. Bernsen (Eds.), *Advances in natural multimodal dialogue systems*. Dordrecht: Springer.
16. Oviatt, S. (2003). Multimodal interfaces. In A. Sears & J. Jacko (Eds.), *The human-computer interaction handbook: Fundamentals, evolving technologies and emerging application* (pp. 286–304). Hillsdale: L. Erlbaum Associates Inc.

17. Fasciano, M., & Guy, L. (2000). Intentions in the coordinated generation of graphics and text from tabular data. *Knowledge and Information Systems, 2*, 310–339.
18. Duarte, C. (2008). *Design and evaluation of adaptive multimodal systems*. Phd thesis, University of Lisbon.
19. Bateman, J., Kleinz, J., Kamps, T., & Reichenberger, K. (2001). Towards constructive text, diagram, and layout generation for information presentation. *Computational Linguistics, 27*, 409–449.
20. Han, Y., & Zukerman, I. (1997, March). A mechanism for multimodal presentation planning based on agent cooperation and negotiation. *Human-Computer Interaction, 12*, 187–226.

Chapter 10
A New Agriculture Advisory System with Personalised Interfaces

Jayalakshmi Umadikar, Pradipta Biswas, Patrick Langdon, and Ashok Jhunjhunwala

Abstract The 2011–2012 State of Indian Agriculture notes that even while half of the country's population depends on agriculture for its livelihood, the sector contributes only 13.9 % of the Gross Domestic Product, reflecting the dismal productivity in the sector. The focus has rightly shifted from providing generic, block-level advisory to more personalized advisories to farmers, with the aim of improving productivity and profitability. Most agricultural advisory systems in the country today have not succeeded in the objective of providing easily accessible, sustainable, personalized advisories to farmers. Under the Indo-UK Advanced Technology Centre of Excellence in Next Generation Networks, Systems and Services (IUATC), a major technology transfer initiative, supported by the Department of Science and Technology (DST) in India and UK Government under the Digital Economy Theme, there is an attempt to address the challenges in Indian agriculture through Information and Communication Technology (ICT) networks. This chapter presents a functioning Agricultural Advisory System that has been built with the aim of bridging information gaps between farmers and agriculture knowledge workers (such as agricultural scientists and extension workers). The system not only enables personalized advisories, it can also render personalized interfaces that take into account various user impairments, for both the experts and farmers – a truly personalized experience for all the users.

J. Umadikar (✉)
RTBI, IIT Madras, Chennai, TN, India
e-mail: jaya@rtbi.in

P. Biswas • P. Langdon
Department of Engineering, University of Cambridge, Trumpington Street, Cambridge, Cambridgeshire CB2 1PZ, UK
e-mail: pb400@hermes.cam.ac.uk; pml24@eng.cam.ac.uk

A. Jhunjhunwala
Department of Electrical Engineering, IIT Madras, Chennai, TN, India
e-mail: ashok@tenet.res.in

P. Biswas et al. (eds.), *A Multimodal End-2-End Approach to Accessible Computing*, Human–Computer Interaction Series, DOI 10.1007/978-1-4471-6708-2_10

10.1 Introduction

The challenge facing the agriculture sector in India is obvious from the State of Agriculture report [1] which has noted that the contribution of Indian agriculture has fallen from 30 % in 1990–1991 to a mere 13.9 % in 2012. This is even more concerning, considering that a large section of the Indian population – close to 52 % – depends on agriculture for their livelihoods. With urbanization and increasing incomes, there has been an increase in demand; however with productivity not improving, supply from the farmer side in terms of quantity and specific requirements has not been able to match this demand. This has led to increasing food inflation in the recent years. The question is, why have farmers not diversified into crops that are in demand and increased their productivity and profitability. The answer in this information-age may seem hard to believe, but is simply lack of timely access to correct information [2]. Farmers can respond to challenges and take timely action if they are provided the right information at the right time; especially if it is personalized to meet specific farmers' specific needs. As each farmer's land is different from that of others, generic advisory is less meaningful; what is required is advisories customized to each land. The challenge is in understanding how best such personalized advisories can be provided to the 88 million farmers in India, cultivating over 98.5 million holdings [3].

Fortunately, ICT and mobile telephony today provide the required infrastructure for such a service [4]. Farmers seem very comfortable in carrying out voice conversations and this suggests a possible way of enabling personalized interactions with the large and dispersed base of farmers in India.

Leveraging the power of two-way communication over mobile phones, IIT Madras and IITM's RTBI has envisioned bridging the information gaps existing between farmers and experts using a system that provides personalized services to farmers. The mobile based Advisory System for Krishi, hereafter referred to as mASK, has been functioning in its present form, since 2013 [5] to serve a set of farmers by providing them with personalized agricultural advisories. The system leverages adaptable user interfaces which take into account the needs of its users – the farmers and the agricultural-experts.

10.2 Review of Existing Agriculture Advisory Systems and Their Limitations

There have been a number of initiatives which use mobiles to communicate agriculture related information to farmers. Some of them are:

- IFFCO Kisan Sanchar Ltd. (IKSL) in collaboration with Airtel (IFFCO Kisan Sanchar Limited) [6] – Provides very generic, pure voice-based advisories where information is pushed to farmers over voice calls.

- Digital Mandi [7] – Interface with Ministry of Agriculture, NIC, BSNL and State Agriculture Marketing Boards (Punjab and Haryana). Application to access commodity pricing. Facing deployment issues and mobile application limitations.
- Reuters Market Light [8] – Proprietary product that needs to be purchased by a farmer and then customized to his preferences. Messages are then sent through SMS, in local language.
- Nokia Life Tools [9] – Available only on Nokia mobiles through subscription packages. Information about local weather, market prices and input prices are made available.

In addition there have been initiatives that use mobile phones in combination with web services:

- E-Sagu [10] – Depends purely on internet access to deliver information. Aims to provide personalized agro-advisory services to farmers registered for its service. However, coordinators or farmers need access to computers to be able to receive or update information.
- Lifelines [11] – Uses computing technology with mobile phones to deliver advice. However, advisories are very generic in nature.
- aAqua [12] – A purely web-based Question-Answer forum set up to answer questions asked by farmers in the local language.
- mKrishi [13] – Proprietary mobile application that allows personalized advice to be given to farmers in the local language. However, farmers have to use this application for accessing any information or updating their farm-crop data.

There are also web portals that act purely as information repositories – Tamil Nadu Agricultural University (TNAU) Agritech [14], AGMARKNET [15], Agropedia [16], Agriwatch [17], and iKisan [18].

We highlight below, the limitations found in most of these initiatives.

10.2.1 Advisory Systems Are Region Specific

Most agricultural experts agree that today farmers need farm-specific advisory as opposed to generic or block-specific advisories that most agricultural advisory systems tend to deliver. Only then can variances that occur at the individual farm levels be taken into account and productivity of individual farmers increased.

10.2.2 Advisory as a One Way Communication

Rather than a one-way communication system wherein specific questions are answered by an expert, there should be efforts to also capture the farm knowledge of farmers. Only through two-way communication can the advisory knowledge bank be further enriched and thereby personalized advisories be provided to individual farmers. Also, two-way communication implies a discussion between farmers and experts and not just experts providing advisories.

10.2.3 In-Person Communication Does Not Scale

The current challenge facing agricultural extension workers is that they are unable to provide in-person advice to the farmers given the large farming population and their geographical spread. Considering that it is impossible to scale an in-person advisory approach, ICT has to be looked at to bridge distances and bring farmers, extension workers and experts together.

10.2.4 Limited Communication Mode

It has to be appreciated that while the Internet remains a powerful tool, farmers face real challenges in making full use of the same. The issue is not merely access to computers and accompanying infrastructure, but more of the requirement of multi-level literacy. A farmer not only has to be literate, but also somewhat knowledgeable in English and computer/Internet savvy. Each of these adds a level of difficulty and for years to come will remain as obstacles for the majority of the farmers in India. On the other hand, a large majority of farmers today own mobile phones and are comfortable with making and receiving calls, conversation largely being in the local language and local dialect. Text messaging and other modes are not that commonly used or preferred.

RTBI's Agriculture Advisory System mASK, hopes to overcome several of the above limitations by leveraging the power of mobile phones in combination with other cutting edge technologies to provide interactive, personalized farm-plot specific advice to farmers.

10.3 A Personalized Agriculture Advisory System (mASK)

10.3.1 Personalized Dashboard for Every Farmer with Crop and Advisory Timeline

The key component of the mASK system is a personalized dashboard, developed for every farmer who has registered in the system.

The objective of the dashboard is to display the essential information needed by an agricultural expert in order to provide personalized advisory to the farmer raising a query. As soon as the farmer calls into the system, the farmer-specific dashboard would appear on the screen using the Caller-Line Identification (CLI) feature. The dashboard helps the expert quickly understand the farmer's specific

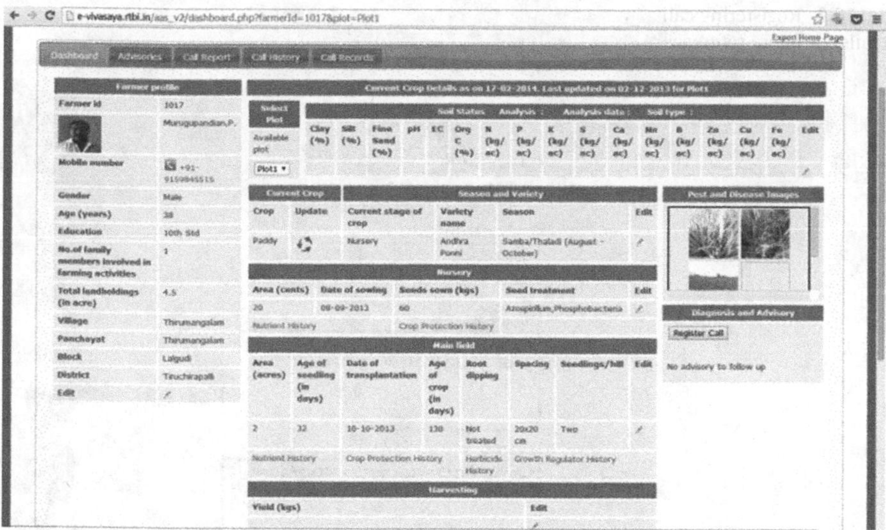

Fig. 10.1 Dashboard showing farmer profile, current crop information and uploaded PDIU image

situation; it helps him/her to provide personalized advice as well as add information on service provided/comments to the dashboard. The dashboard has been designed such that the required information is presented in a single screen to the expert consultant through a user-friendly interface so that the various sections can be easily and efficiently navigated through.

The highlights of the dashboard (see Fig. 10.1) are as follows:

- Contains farmer profile, farm, and current crop details as well as past crops timeline. Current crop details cover the plot/crop soil test report, seed variety, age of crop, spacing, seed treatment, nutrient history, pesticide history and weedicide history. Currently 121 farmers have been registered into our system with all farm activities being regularly updated by the farmers by calling into the call-centre.
- As mentioned earlier, when the farmer calls in to seek advisory the farmer-specific dashboard will pop up enabling the expert to view relevant crop details. Instead of spending valuable time in gathering background/history information from the farmer (all of which is already available on the dashboard), the expert can engage the farmer to understand in greater details the problem faced by him/her and provide a truly personalized advisory. At the same time, any new information that the farmer may share during the interaction, is also recorded.
- While giving advisory to the farmer, the expert records the query raised, diagnosis made and suggested recommendation (see Fig. 10.2). The conversation is also recorded allowing for later reviews on the quality of recommendation and assessing the comfort of the farmer during the conversation. The expert can also indicate a follow-up date when the system will prompt the expert to call the farmer and understand if the suggested recommendation had been followed and if not, understand why.

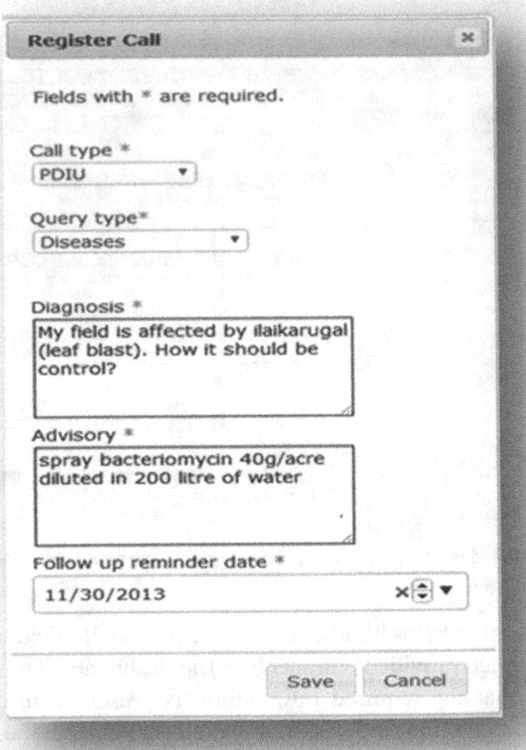

Fig. 10.2 Registering call details for future reference

- The Crop History Timeline allows the expert to track the crops traditionally cultivated by farmers during various seasons. While currently this allows for tracking of cultivation history including yields through subsequent years, it could, in future, enable the expert to make recommendations about growing high-value agricultural crops that the farmer might not be aware of. The advisory reference timeline quickly enables the expert to understand previous pest-disease infestations affecting the crop and make future recommendations.

10.3.2 Pest and Disease Image Upload Application (PDIU)

When the farmer is faced with a pest/disease infestation in the field and they call into the mASK system, it is not easy for them to describe the nature of the problem or mention the name of the pest/disease as they very often do not know the same. If an image of the site of attack is made available to the expert, it will then assist the expert in identifying the cause and provide a solution. A visual tool that could capture the pest/disease infestation and assist the expert in identifying the cause, and provide a

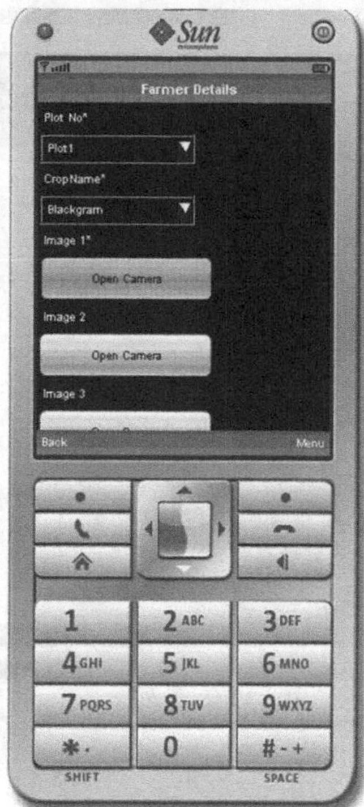

Fig. 10.3 Pest Disease Image Upload (PDIU) application

solution was the need of the day. This led to the development of the Pest and Disease Image Upload (PDIU) application. A Java based mobile application requiring GPRS connectivity, it provides farmers with a simple tool to capture photographs of their pest/disease infested crop and upload it to the mASK system (see Fig. 10.3)

These images would be integrated into the farmer-specific dashboard and just as with a call, the dashboard would immediately come up before the expert (see Fig. 10.1). The images act as an excellent aid for the expert to understand the nature of the pest or disease and provide personalized advisory to the farmer.

10.3.3 Personalized Interfaces for Dashboard and PDIU

The web-based Dashboard system runs on a personal computer and is used by experts to provide agricultural advisory to farmers. Experts can be across all age levels and it is therefore important to design a user interface that is comfortable to navigate as also that takes into account specific preferences for experts given their abilities. For example, the interfaces could be designed based on the visual acuity of the user as also any impairment such as colour blindness, tremors in the hand, etc.

The application has exploited the user modelling and interface personalization framework discussed in Chap. 5.

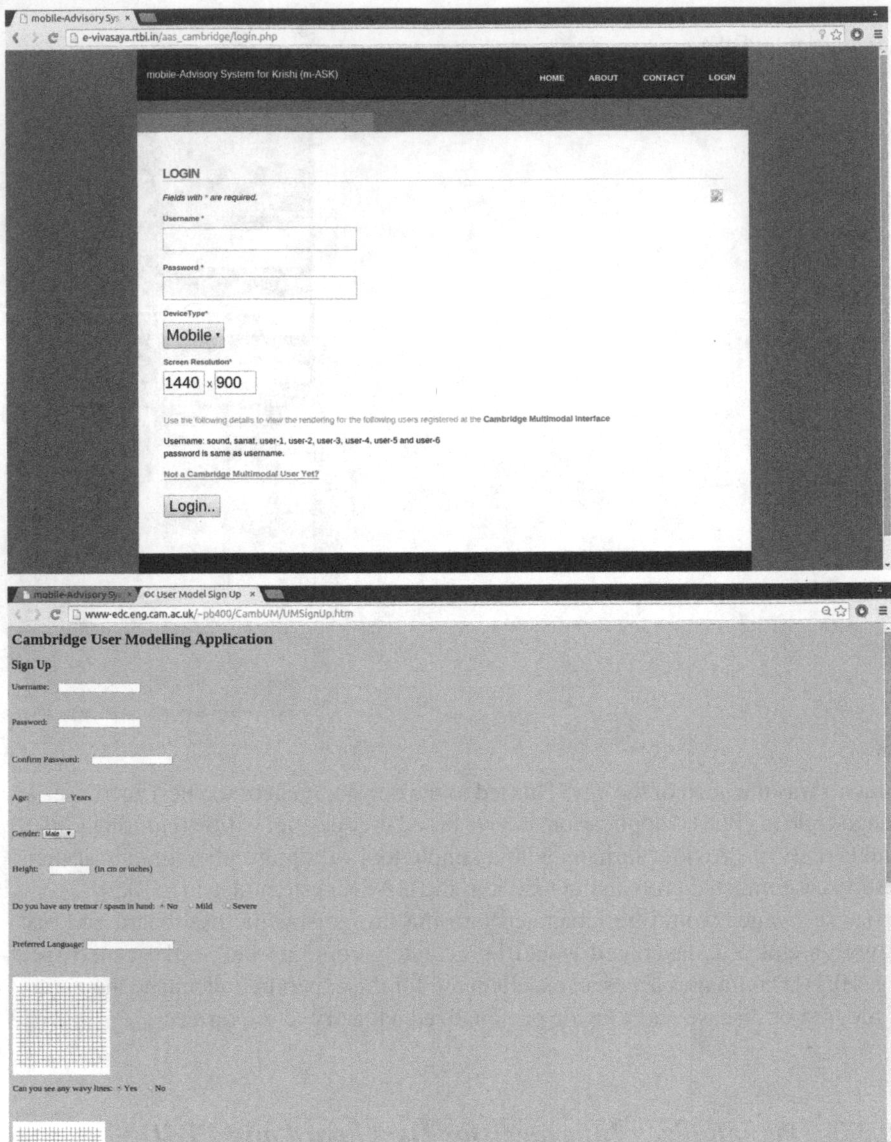

Fig. 10.4 Sign Up Page for experts using the mASK system

An expert registering with the system for the first time would be taken to a sign-up page (Fig. 10.4). With the help of the responses filled in, the framework would be able to generate a user interface that takes into account the different abilities of the individual – the next time the expert signs in, he/she will be presented only with this personalized interface.

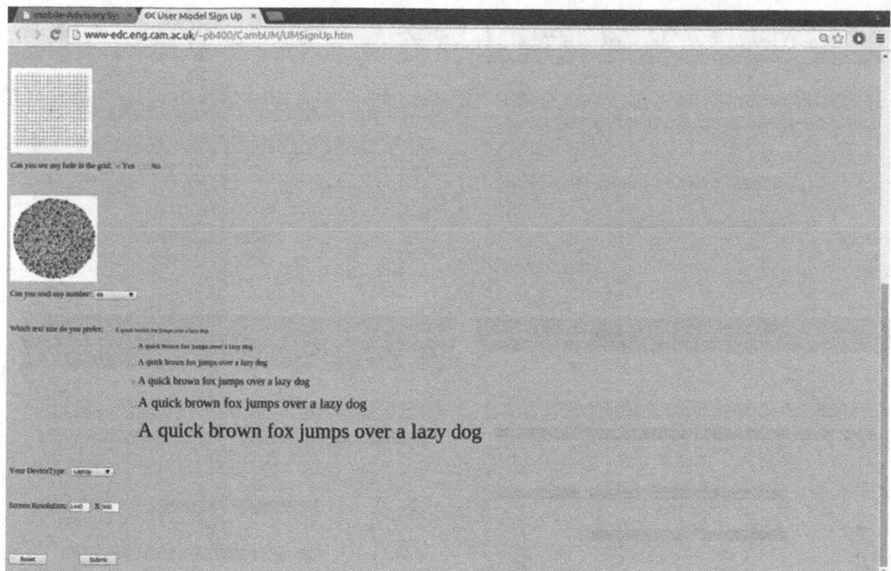

Fig. 10.4 (continued)

Figure 10.5 shows a few variations of the dashboard application. The personalization framework enables a change in font size and colour contrast of the interface, based on the framework's recognition of the abilities of the person, during sign-up, as shown in Fig. 10.5.

On the other hand, the Pest-Disease Image Upload (PDIU) application is used by farmers to upload images of infested crops, while they are in the field. The uploaded images will automatically be sent to remotely located experts, who will advise farmers about remedy. The application runs on low-end mobile phones or smart phones. Providing personalized interfaces not only makes it easy for farmers who have difficulty in operating a keypad but also accommodates those suffering from poor vision or cognitive impairments.

The application is enabled with a sign-in page very similar to the expert interface. For a farmer using the application for the first time, the application redirects to a sign-up page where the abilities of the user are assessed. See Fig. 10.6.

The next time, the farmer uses the application, his/her personalized interface would be displayed. Figure 10.7 shows three different rendering of the PDIU interface with different font sizes and colour contrast to suit users with different range of visual acuity and colour blindness.

The framework to generate adaptable user interfaces has currently been integrated into the mASK system and will soon go under trials with both experts & farmers.

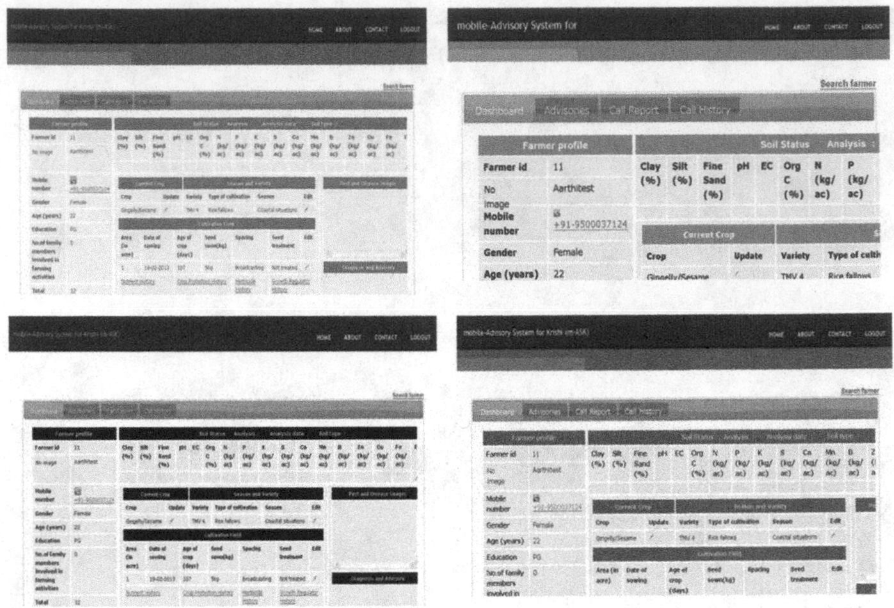

Fig. 10.5 Personalization of dashboard application

10.4 User Trial on PDIU Agriculture Advisory System

The following study aimed to improve the PDIU interfaces by recording interaction patterns and then analysing task completion times and wrong key presses by users. Based on the analysis we recommend a few changes in the interface and application logic to facilitate users' interaction. The study is not a comparison between adaptive and non-adaptive interface, rather it is an overall external validity test of the adaptive PDIU system. This last study is described in the following sub-sections.

10.4.1 Participants

We collected data from five young users (age range 24–40 years) and five elderly users (age range 56–65 years) from Mandi. They were all male, related to farming profession and use low-end mobile phones. Young users were educated above matriculation level. One of the young users needed big font size and one had Protanopia colour blindness. Elderly users' education levels vary from high school to Matriculation. All elderly users preferred biggest text size and two had colour blindness. They can all read English words used in the PDIU interfaces. The study was conducted at Mandi, India.

Fig. 10.6 Sign-up page for farmers on the PDIU application

10.4.2 Material

The study was conducted on a Nokia 301 mobile phone.

10.4.3 Procedure

The task involved taking photographs of three leaves arranged on a desk using the PDIU application. At first they were registered to the application. The system then asked their preferred font size and conducted the Ishihara Colour Blindness Test [5] using the plate number 16. Based on their response, the application adapted itself and users were asked if they found the screen legible. Then they were demonstrated the task of taking photographs and after they understood it, they were requested to do the same. The experimenter recorded a video of the interaction. During the task, users needed to go through the screenshots shown in Fig. 10.8. The sequence of actions were as follows

Fig. 10.7 Personalization of PDIU application

1. Select PDIU from PDIU home screen (Fig. 10.8a)
2. Scroll down to Open Camera under Image 1 (Fig. 10.8b)
3. Select OpenCamera and take a photograph
4. Scroll down to Open Camera under Image 2 (Fig. 10.8b)
5. Select OpenCamera and take a photograph
6. Scroll down to Open Camera under Image 3 (Fig. 10.8c)
7. Select OpenCamera and take a photograph
8. Press Menu (Fig. 10.8c)
9. Scroll Down to Save option (Fig. 10.8c)
10. Select Save (Fig. 10.8c)

After they completed the task, we conducted a general unstructured interview about their farming experience and utility of the system.

10.4.4 Results

The following graphs (Figs. 10.9 and 10.10) plot the task completion times for the operations involving taking three pictures and saving them. In these figures, C1 to C5 stands for young participants while P1 to P5 stands for their elderly counterpart. An one factor ANOVA found a significant effect of type of tasks among all 10

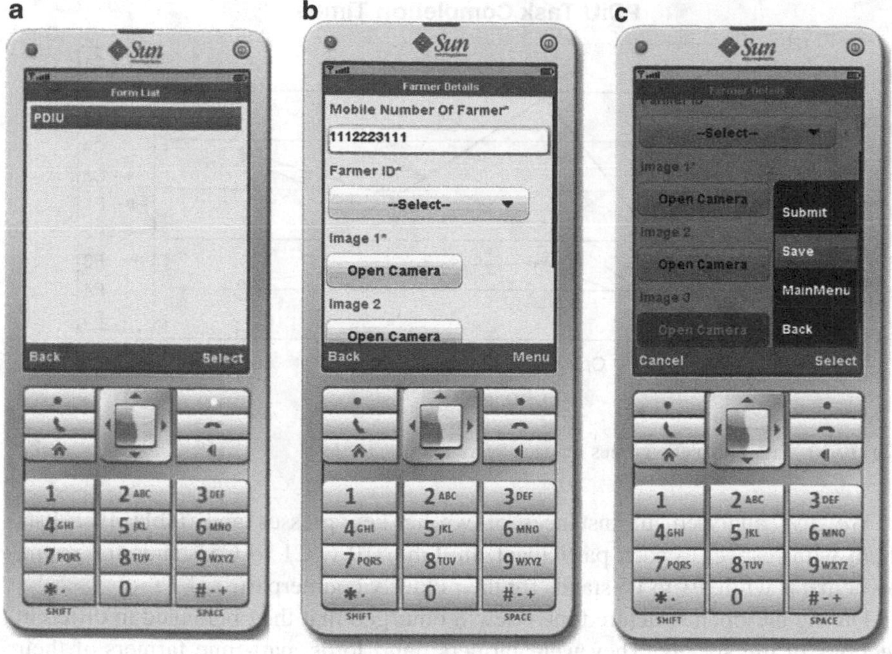

Fig. 10.8 PDIU interfaces used in the study. (**a**) PDIU Home screen. (**b**) Open Camera screen. (**c**) Menu screen

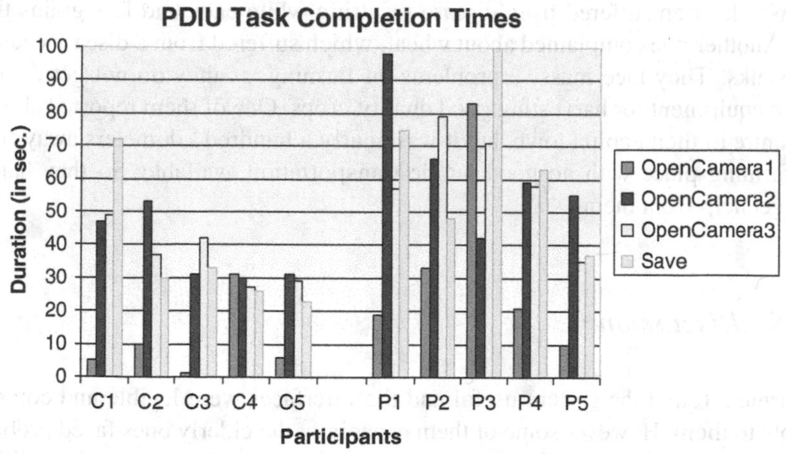

Fig. 10.9 Task completion times for participants

participants [$F(3, 36) = 4.05$, $p < 0.05$]. Users took only 21.9 s on average to record the first image while they took 51.2 s on average to record the second image, 48.4 s on average to record the third image and 50.7 s on average to go to the Menu and press Save button.

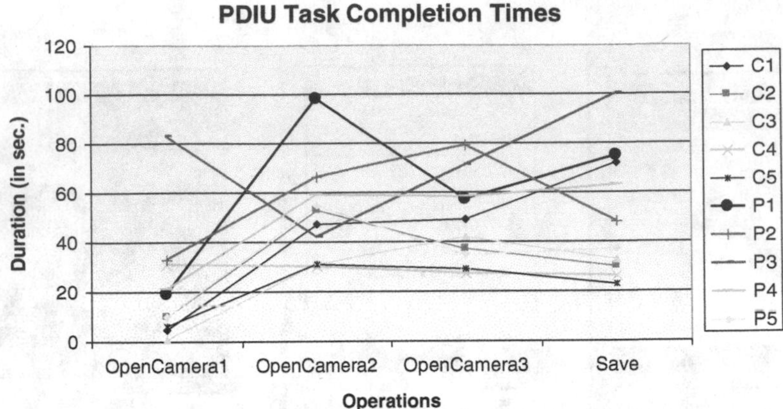

Fig. 10.10 Task completion times for each operation

We also analysed all instances of wrong key presses and Table 10.1 lists them with respect to each participant. In Table 10.1, C1 to C5 stands for young participants while P1 to P5 stands for their elderly counterpart.

During the open structured interview it emerged that they belonged to different sections of the society. They were farmers, land lords, part-time farmers of their ancestral agrarian land pursuing another profession like bus driving. They mostly harvested crops like corn, maize, bajra, wheat and so on. One of their major problems was the quality of grains. One of them reported problem with harvesting corn, which often suffered from disease resulting white ends and less grains than usual. Another one complained about wheat, which suffered from a disease causing dried stalks. They face massive problems on farming, as they do not get enough modern equipment for harvesting good quality crops. One of them reported about a help centre in their capital town, but it was nearly a hundred kilometers away from their farming place with no good public transportation available. So they hardly could get help from them.

10.4.5 Discussion

The farmers found the system useful and the interfaces were legible and comprehensible to them. However some of them especially the elderly ones faced problem in scrolling and recovering from error. It seemed to us a simpler interface will be more useful to the elderly users. Based on the study and list of errors we propose the following recommendations.

(a) **Initial focus on OpenCamera Screen**

This initial focus can alleviate a few scrolling errors as users will understand that they need to scroll down to select the open Camera buttons.

Table 10.1 Lists of wrong selection

Participants	Wrong key presses
C1	Went back from OpenCamera2 to OpenCamera1, scrolled up instead of down, recovered himself
	Cancelled Save option, was confused but then recovered and finished successfully
C2	Pressed middle button to select the PDIU in home screen
	Selected OpenCamera1 second time instead of scrolling to OpenCamera2
C3	No wrong key press
C4	Scrolling up instead of scrolling down before reaching OpenCamera buttons
C5	Pressed Submit instead of selecting Save, had trouble between selection and scroll down buttons
P1	Scrolling up instead of scrolling down before reaching OpenCamera buttons
	Pressed Back button instead of Selecting OpenCamera2
	Pressed Back button again in the PDIU home screen
	Pressed Back button again instead of Selecting OpenCamera2
	Could not scroll down to Save button in Menu items
P2	Pressed middle button of Scroll Button instead of selecting Capture in OpenCamera2
	Pressed Menu instead of going to OpenCamera3
P3	Pressed Back button in PDIU Home screen
	Pressed Back button from the OpenCamera screen
	Pressed Back button again from the OpenCamera screen
	Pressed Left button instead of Middle button in one system message screen
	Pressed OpenCamera1 second time instead of scrolling down to OpenCamera2 button
	Pressed Back button instead of capturing image in OpenCamera3
	Scrolled up to OpenCamera2 from OpenCamera3
	Scrolled down from Save button but then get back to Save button
P4	Pressed middle button instead of Capture button in OpenCamera2
P5	No wrong key press

(b) **Only one OpenCamera button with automatic Save option**

The ANOVA shows that users were significantly slower in taking the second or third photograph and saving them. If there is only one OpenCamera button which automatically saves or submits the picture, a lot of scrolling errors can be avoided and the overall task completion time will also reduce significantly.

(c) **Confirmation of Back action in middle of interaction**

We found users were often confused if they pressed the back button. It may be useful to add a confirmation dialog if they press the back button in the middle of taking a photograph or saving it.

(d) **Overridden buttons while capturing images**

Users pressed the middle button to capture image which is a common feature in most mobile phones with a camera. It will be a good idea to let users do so making the system more intuitive.

10.5 Conclusions

This chapter presents a new agriculture advisory system for providing personalized advisories to farmers. It consists of a farmer dashboard (in the form of a web interface) that enables an agricultural expert to view farmer, farm-specific information and provide advisories. Also, it discusses a mobile phone based application that enables farmers to take photographs of diseased plants and send those to experts while experts will use the web-based system to analyze the pictures and advise farmers. More importantly, the system is also integrated to a user modelling system and offers personalized user interfaces based on users' range of abilities and preference. We also presented a short user trial to investigate the utility and future modifications of the system.

Acknowledgement This work is being carried out under the IU-ATC project funded by the Department of Science and Technology (DST), Government of India and, the UK EPSRC Digital Economy Program. Our special gratitude to the Department of Agriculture, Government of Tamil Nadu who helped us in identifying the locations and also for helping us mobilize field workshops. We would also like to thank Tamil Nadu Agricultural University (TNAU), Coimbatore and National Agriculture Innovation Project (NAIP) for their aid in implementation of the systems. Finally, a special thanks to Suma Prashant, Director – RTBI and the team at RTBI, without whose support this work would not have been possible.

References

1. State of Indian Agriculture, Department of Agriculture and Cooperation, Government of India, 2011–2012.
2. Babu, S., Asenso-Okyere, K., & Glendenning, C. J. (2010). *Review of agricultural extension in India: Are farmers' information needs being met?* Washington, DC: International Food Policy Research Institute.
3. Census Reference Tables – Number of Villages [Online]. Available: http://censusindia.gov.in/Census_Data_2001/Census_data_finder/A_Series/Number_of_Village.htm
4. Telecom Regulatory Authority – Highlights on Telecom Subscription Data [Online]. Available: http://www.trai.gov.in/Content/PressDetails/32246_0.aspx.
5. Jhunjhunwala, A., Umadikar, J., Prashant, S., & Canagarajah, N. (2013). *A new personalized agriculture advisory system*. In European Wireless Conference 2013, Surrey.
6. IFFCO Kisan Sanchar Limited [Online]. Available: http://www.iksl.in/
7. Digital Mandi for Indian Kisan, IIT Kanpur [Online]. Available: http://digitalmandi.iitk.ac.in/new/index.php?l=en&p=about_us
8. Reuters Market Light [Online]. Available: http://www.reutersmarketlight.com/index.html

9. Introducing Nokia Life Tools [Online]. Available: http://www.nokia.com/NOKIA_COM_1/Microsites/Entry_Event/phones/Nokia_Life_Tools_datasheet.pdf
10. eSagu [Online]. Available: http://agriculture.iiit.ac.in/html/esagu2012/overview.php
11. LifeLines Agriculture [Online]. Available: http://lifelines-india.net/agriculture
12. Almost all questions answered [Online]. Available: http://aaqua.persistent.co.in/aaqua/forum/index
13. mKrishi: A Rural Service Delivery Platform [Online]. Available: http://www.tcs.com/offerings/technology-products/mKRISHI/Pages/default.aspx
14. TNAU Agritech Portal [Online]. Available: http://agritech.tnau.ac.in/
15. Agricultural Marketing Information Network [Online]. Available: http://agmarknet.nic.in/
16. Agropedia [Online]. Available: http://agropedia.iitk.ac.in/
17. Agriwatch [Online]. Available: http://www.agriwatch.com/
18. iKisan [Online]. Available: http://www.ikisan.com/

Chapter 11
Audio Games: Investigation of the Potential Through Prototype Development

Jarosław Beksa, Sonia Fizek, and Phil Carter

Abstract This article discusses the potential of audio games based on the evaluation of three projects: a story-driven audio role-playing game (RPG), an interactive audiobook with RPG elements, and a set of casual sound-based games. The potential is understood, both in popularity and playability terms. The first factor is connected to the degree of players' interest, while the second one to the degree of their engagement in sound-based game worlds. Although presented projects are embedded within the landscape of past and contemporary audio games and gaming platforms, the authors reach into the near future, concluding with possible development directions for this non-visual interactive entertainment.

11.1 Introduction

11.1.1 Audio Games

Audio games exist only in the world of sounds. Contrary to popular video games, they do not rely on visuals [5] – the sonic layer becomes the basis for gameplay mechanics and interface design. The game world is created in the player's imagination based on the omnipresent soundscape.

The first attempts to build audio games may be tracked to late 1970s, when Atari designed *Touch Me*, an electronic rhythm game on a handheld device, which became an inspiration for the popular *Simon* (1978). Although sounds played a crucial

---

J. Beksa (✉)
School of Computer and Mathematical Sciences, Auckland University of Technology, Auckland, New Zealand
e-mail: jbeksa@aut.ac.nz; beksa@inkubator.leuphana.de

S. Fizek
Gamification Lab, Centre for Digital Cultures, Leuphana University, Lüneburg, Germany
e-mail: fizek@inkubator.leuphana.de

P. Carter
School of Computer and Mathematical Sciences, Auckland University of Technology, Auckland, New Zealand
e-mail: pcarter@aut.ac.nz

P. Biswas et al. (eds.), *A Multimodal End-2-End Approach to Accessible Computing*, Human–Computer Interaction Series, DOI 10.1007/978-1-4471-6708-2_11

role, the gameplay relied on the visual output from the device. The player had to memorize and reproduce the sequence of four buttons lighting up with particular sounds attached to them. In 1996 another sound-based handheld playful device appeared on the market – *Bop It*. This time the interaction pattern was designed solely with audio in mind. The device featured a button, a lever, and a handle. The player's task was to listen to the commands (Bop it, Twist it, or Pull it) and interact with respective parts of the electronic console. Interestingly, point values were also represented by various tones. These games and toys, however, were not designed with visually impaired players in mind, and more importantly did not develop alongside story-based digital games. One of the reasons may be that text-based adventure games – Multi User Dungeons (MUDs) – developed at the end of 1970s and beginnings of 1980s, were still easily accessible to the visually impaired due to their non-graphical nature. Once adventure and role-playing games became heavily reliant on the graphical layer, the gap between the visual and non-visual players rose exponentially.

One of the first commercial story-driven audio games was *Real Sound – Kaze No Regret* (1999), an audio adventure game created for Sega Dreamcast and Sega Saturn. Unlike several previous electronic and video games, the mechanics of *Real Sound* was entirely dependent on sound. In 2001 GMA Games released *Shades of Doom*, the first Windows-based adventure title fully accessible to the visually impaired. Inspired by the graphical game *Doom* (1993), it adapted the first-person shooter (FPS) genre to the world of sounds. The players oriented themselves in the soundscape by the echo of footsteps, the wind howling through the passages, and the sounds of nearby equipment. The titles designed by the GMA Games in the last 13 years are exclusively tailored to the visually impaired community and known only in relatively small circles.[1]

In the recent years, however, the status of audio games has been gradually changing. An increasing interest has been noticed among sound artists and game developers. Several games based on moving through space have been created, predominantly for tablets and smartphones: *Papa Sangre* (2010), *Sound Swallower* (2011), *The Nightjar* (2011), *Papa Sangre II* (2013), *Audio Defence: Zombie Arena* (2014), and *Blindside* (2012) for PC. An interesting experimental project was developed by a Copenhagen Game Collective, using the existing commercial game controllers. In *Dark Room Sex Game* (2008) two players bring their invisible avatars to orgasm by shaking the Wii motion controls [10].

With the popularization of touchscreen portable devices (smartphones and tablets), the ubiquity of mobile game platforms (e.g. App Store, Google Play, Windows Store), and the proliferation of independent scene ("indie" games), audio games seem to be entering a brighter future and yet to be explored territory. More importantly, they become visible outside the VI community and, as we will demonstrate, have the capacity to attract also visual players.

---

[1]More audio games designed specifically for visually impaired may be found on the official GMA Game's website and on AudioGames.net [1, 8].

11.1.2 Project Goals

Our goal was to verify the potential of audio games. The three projects described in this article have been developed over a span of 7 years, in different market realities, for various platforms, and with diverse game genres in mind. The first one was a small-scale prototype. The second project was completed and tested in the commercial setting. This allowed for the evaluation of the marketability potential of an audio game. The last one is a research work-in-progress at its final stage of completion.

What is crucial in all the three cases are the game interface solutions, which do not rely on any graphical elements. Any implemented visuals play a supportive role and are not necessary to interact with the games. The gesture-based audio interface is what differentiates our two last projects from those already existing in the mobile audio game scene.

The following introductory questions were set at the initial stages of development:

- Is it possible to create immersive and playable computer games based on sound only?
- Can they be played successfully on touch screen devices?
- Will such games be attractive for sighted players?
- And finally, can audio games become a new successful trend in the electronic entertainment?

11.2 Prototypes and User Tests

11.2.1 Adventures of Jolan

The first audio game prototype was developed in 2007 for the PC Windows platform. It was based on the *Last Crusade* – an audio game engine developed at the University of North Carolina by Patrick Dwyer and Peter S. Van Lund [7]. *Adventures of Jolan* is an audio computer role-playing game (RPG) enriched with a non-linear story and a simple character development system. To enhance the player's immersion in the story world, we implemented a range of voice recordings, sound effects and background music. The prototype did not have any graphical interface. The keyboard was used as an input device.

11.2.2 User Tests

Twelve computer game players (both male and female) were invited to participate in the tests. They were divided into three focus groups:

- Sighted high school students
- Sighted college/university students
- Visually impaired of various education levels

Participants were asked to play the game for 20 min and share their general opinions about it. To our surprise, the game was very well received by sighted players. Some of their opinions were as follows [3][2]:

- "Revolution in the gaming system",
- "More relaxing than video games",
- "Improves imagination"
- "There is no need to stare at the screen",
- "Saves sight",
- "Porting to a mobile platform would be a great idea".

Test results assured us that the audio game concept is very promising and gave us further motivation to develop the first large-scale multiplatform audio game. Our initial belief was further strengthened by the research done in the visually impaired player community, which confirmed to have a very limited set of audio games at their disposal.

11.3 Interactive Audiobook

The initial audio adventure project evolved into a large-scale interactive audiobook. For commercial implementation we chose an interactive audio story with RPG elements to give the players a fully playable immersive story world. Having studied past audio RPG projects (by GMA Games for PCs), and with the development experience of the *Adventures of Jolan,* we decided to design a completely new type of sound gaming experience. As most of the available and known titles were designed for stationary computers, we were determined to experiment with mobile technology, and export an interactive audio story to smartphones. The production required the development of the following elements:

- Game story
- Audio game engine
- Audio game editor
- Music
- Sound effects
- Dialog recordings

[2] *Authors' translation.*

11.3.1 Game Story and Game Play

We acquired a non-linear story through a contest announced in December 2008 by the Polish Telecom. From over 130 submitted scripts we selected *1812: Heart of Winter* written by Magdalena Reputakowska and Maciej Reputakowski.

The interactive story is set in the nineteenth century during the times of Napoleon Bonaparte's army invasion on Russia. Is has both, historical and fantasy elements. A non-linear plot allows completing the game in numerous different ways, encouraging gamers to play more than once and enhancing the replayability factor.

The gameplay is based on the elements characteristic for interactive digital fiction and a role-playing game. The core experience includes choosing alternative story paths and exploring the virtual story world, which in this case is represented by means of a soundscape. The player may traverse through the selected locations in the game, which are indicated by the narrator's descriptions as well as background sounds. For instance, once the player reaches fireplace, they hear the sounds of the fire burning, and the buzz of voices of other characters. Additionally, for the visual players, the game world is depicted on the map. More importantly, the players may interact with non-player characters (NPCs) – by engaging in dialogues and battles – and in-game objects. Once collected, the props end up in an inventory, which may be accessed by pressing a dedicated button on the keyboard, performing a gesture or selecting a respective option from the menu.

11.3.1.1 Binaural Dialog Recordings

All the game dialogs were recorded using a binaural technique, which uses a special microphone arrangement and is intended for replay using headphones. The sounds are recorded with microphones embedded in the ear canals of an artificial mannequin head (the so called "dummy head"). When they are then listened to via headphones, there is a realistic perception of three-dimensional auditory space. The player feels as if they were thrown into the middle of the scene. Any set of headphones that provides good stereo channel isolation is sufficient in order for the recording effects to be heard (Fig. 11.1).

In *1812: Heart of Winter*, all the actors were recorded from different angles and distances to create an even more immersive sound effect.

11.3.1.2 Music and Sound Effects

The game's atmosphere was enhanced by dedicated music composed by Marcin Przybyłowicz and a rich variety of sound effects. Each location in the game is defined by a unique set of ambience effects. This further enhances the feeling of immersion and gives the player the possibility to create associative cognitive maps of thc in-game locations, which "are complex mental interpretations of a real or fictional environment, and its components that live in the fictional plane" ([9], 161).

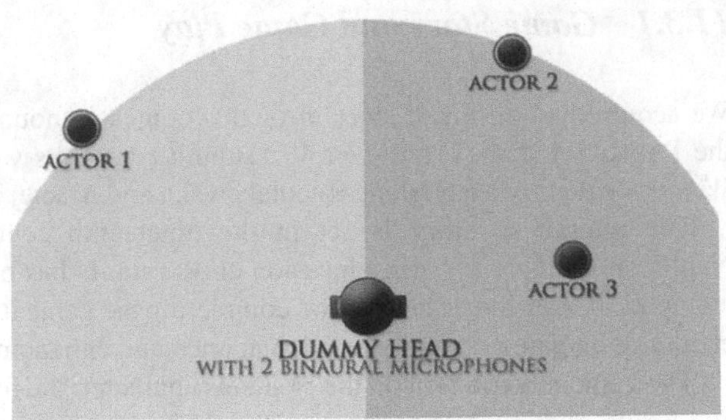

Fig. 11.1 Binaural recording of dialogs scheme

The development of *1812: Heart of Winter* was a large-scale endeavor, which involved 36 voice actors, includes over 60 min of dedicated music, more than 6,000 sound files, and over 10 h of game play. The game was also developed in three languages: Polish (full version), English (demo version), and French (demo version).

11.3.2 Game Engine

The Game Engine is based on the library developed by BL Stream [4]. It is capable of displaying graphics, handling I/O and playing up to 5 ogg streams simultaneously. Currently the engine is available on four platforms: PC Windows, iOS, Android and Symbian S60.

The Game Engine allows running any audio game developed in the Game Editor and is fully accessible to visually impaired players. A minimalistic graphics interface was prepared to increase the attractiveness for visual players. Also, due to the users' suggestions, the text and audio elements were synchronized, turning the game into a combination of an e-book, audiobook and a role-playing game (Fig. 11.2). We were also driven by the feasibility of a similar approach, implemented in an early interactive audiobook prototype by Röber et al. who combined non-linear and linear narratives present in books and radio plays, with interactive elements characteristic of computer games [11].

The Game Engine can be easily customized to any game created with the Game Editor and localized in any language.

11.3.2.1 User Interface

Creating a multiplatform audio game required a complex user interface design. Our goal was to create an engine fully accessible to visually impaired and similar for each platform. Every action performed in the game is represented by a kinesonically syncretic interactive sound, fused not to image, but to action. As Collins explains, "... interactive sound is event-driven, and the sound controlled by an action or

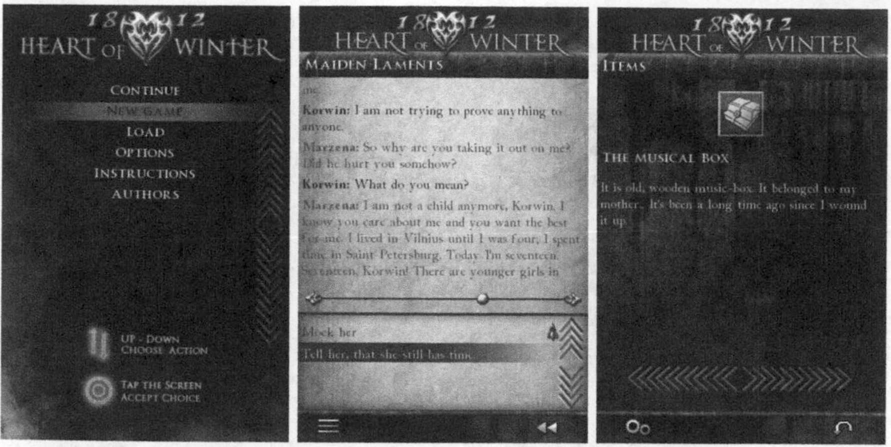

Fig. 11.2 Game Engine screens (from *left*): main menu, dialogues, inventory

occurrence that is initiated by the game or by the player" ([5], 32). We used sounds as feedback to acknowledge the events.

Developing an accessible user interface on keyboard devices (PC, Symbian and Android phones) was relatively easy. Users were able to customize buttons according to their own preferences.

The real challenge was the development for touch screen devices. After many sessions with visually impaired players, we designed a gesture-based interface with corner buttons. This approach was device independent – the interface was consistent for all the devices (Fig. 11.3). This interface design differentiated us from the interactive audiobooks developed in parallel by, for instance, Audiogent in Germany, which have been always heavily reliant on a complex graphical interface necessary to traverse through the audio stories [2].

11.3.3 Game Editor

To accelerate the process of story implementation and to manage multiple story plots, we developed an editor, which allows creating any audio game (from simple interactive audio books to advanced role playing audio games). It is running on the PC platform and uses a graphical user interface (GUI) (Fig. 11.4).

11.4 Market Results

The game *1812: Heart of Winter* was released in November 2011 in Poland. It was published by the Polish Telecom and was neither advertised nor promoted on a large scale. Despite this fact, during the past 3 years it has been downloaded more

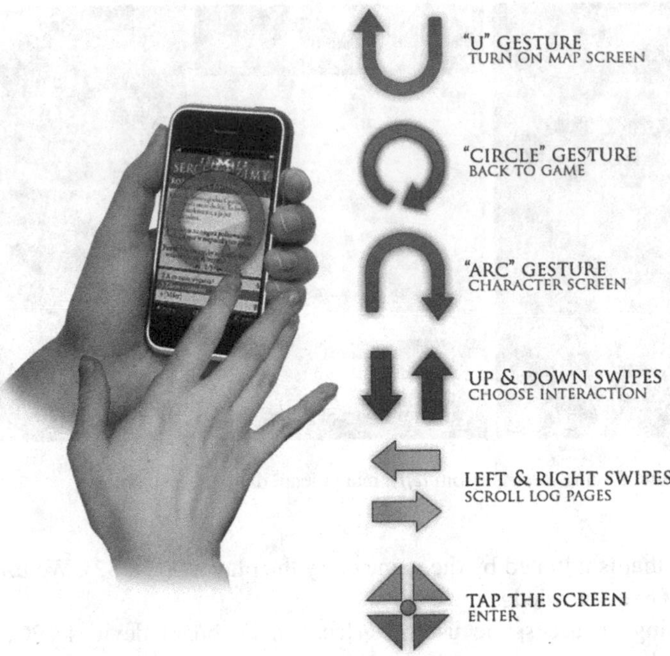

Fig. 11.3 Touchscreen user interface design

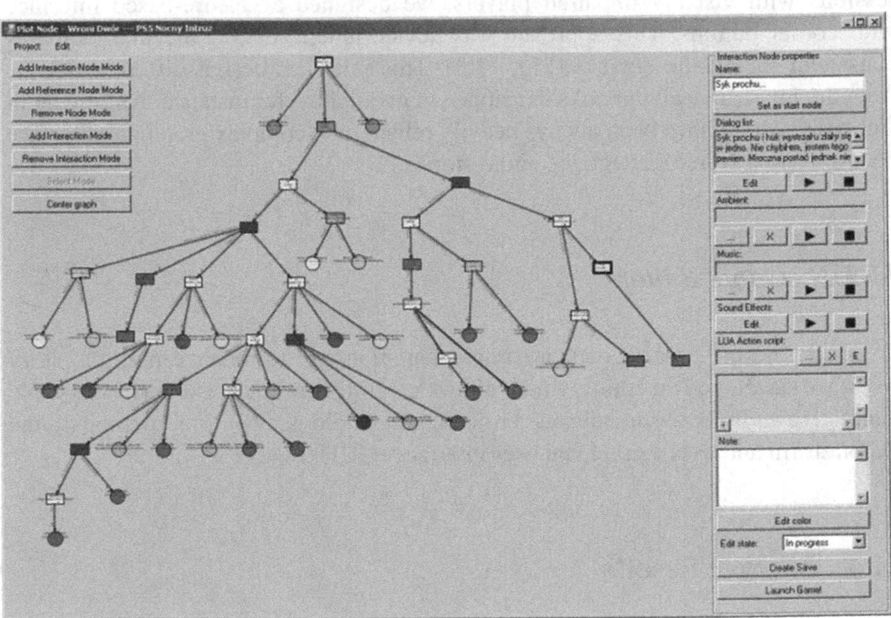

Fig. 11.4 Game editor story view

than 60,000 times in Poland (all platforms) and acquired excellent user reviews. An average rating on Apple's App Store (iOS) was 4,5 stars out of 5. It was available free of charge for four platforms (there was a short period when the game was available at different price levels to test the sales potential).

The most surprising fact was that over 95 % of downloads came from sighted players (survey data from PC version downloads).

Gaming web-portals and communities also valued the interactive audiobook design concept:

> "The first interactive audiobook in the history of Polish literature" (www.masz-wybor.com.pl)
>
> "Heart of winter is one of the best productions of 2011." (www.dubscore.pl)
>
> "A brilliant combination of an audio book with a role-playing game" (www.mackozer.pl)
>
> "Heart of winter is something we've been waiting for." (www.tyflopodcast.net)

11.5 Casual Audio Games

Audio-based games are also naturally adaptable to a genre focused on non-visual space exploration, where binaural audio technology is used to create 3D spatial environments for the player to traverse through.

In our current project we are focusing on adapting multiple genres, belonging to the casual games category, into the audio sphere. A combination of simple arcades and platform games constitutes a perfect playground sample, as it allows for the evaluation of various mechanics and interface solutions in a homogeneous project.

11.5.1 Audio Game Hub

The *Audio Game Hub* (2014) is a practice-led research project and a work-in-progress. It includes a collection of several mini-games, each of which requires a different type of audio gameplay mechanics. The application is developed for mobile platforms (iOS, Android, Windows Phone) and as a desktop version (Windows, OSX). It may be operated with: touchscreen, touchpad, keyboard and mouse. The Audio Game Hub project is being developed at the Gamification Lab, Centre for Digital Cultures (Leuphana University Lüneburg).

11.5.1.1 User Interface

The *Audio Game Hub* interface uses a set of gestures and corner buttons, which allows the player to navigate through the available options and menu elements. A

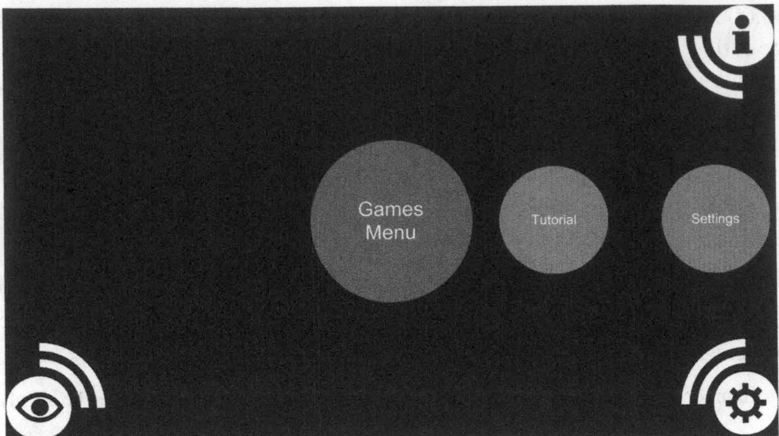

Fig. 11.5 *Audio Game Hub* main menu

minimalistic graphical interface was implemented to reduce the entry barrier for sighted players. It can be disabled and enabled at any time. This feature will be used for further user tests with sighted players (Fig. 11.5).

The main focus was laid on audio interface. Each user action is represented by an interactive sound. Also, every mini game consists of unique sounds and voices. Numerous audio samples were recorded using the binaural method. Each game starts with an audio tutorial explaining the rules and game mechanics. We also implemented an array of background sounds to represent each of the game worlds and enhance the immersion of the player. Selected interactive sounds used in the game's menu and in individual games have been assigned to the same actions and events. This points to another crucial aspect of interactive sounds – their repeatability, which "... establishes an expectation that we will hear the same sound as a reaction to the same action" ([5], 33).

To minimize the problems with "dead" borders of touchscreen devices, we implemented a calibration step, where users can learn the physical size of their active touchscreen area. In all the games subtle audio cues are available, informing about reaching a corner button or the edge of the screen.

11.5.2 The Hunt

The Hunt is a shooting game, where user has to hit moving targets – forest animals. With each level of difficulty the targets move faster. The aiming system in *The Hunt* (see Fig. 11.6) is based on a 2D soundscape represented by stereo panorama (the "x" axis) and pitch (the "y" axis). There are two sound sources placed within the 2D game world and available to the player:

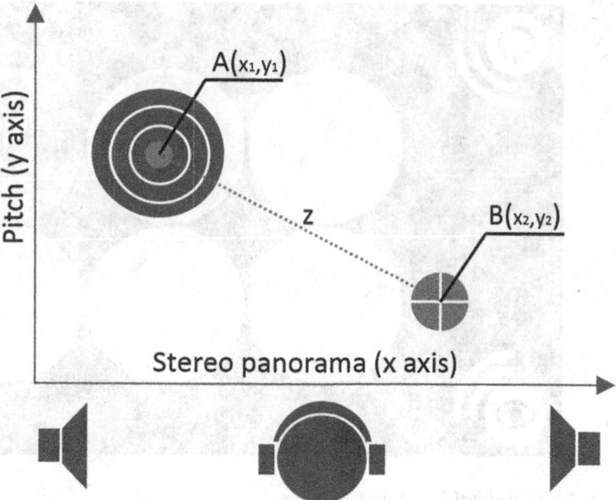

Fig. 11.6 Game mechanics in *The Hunt*

- The target board (A)
- The aiming point (B)

In each round the target sound (A) is placed along the "x" axis (heard to the left or to the right), and along the "y" axis (heard in a higher pitch when placed up, and in a lower pitch when down). The aiming point sound (B) corresponds to the finger position. When the finger moves closer to the target, the corresponding targeting sound is played more frequently (z – distance between the target and the aiming point).

11.5.3 Animal Farm

Animal Farm is an adaptation of a classic memory game. The player's task is to find matching pairs of farm animals stored in boxes. To locate the box, the interactor needs to move a finger on the screen (looking for a wooden box sound). The box is opened by a double tap gesture, which triggers the sound of a selected animal (Fig. 11.7).

11.5.4 Samurai

Samurai is a reflex based game for up to four players. The screen is divided into four equal parts corresponding to the game space occupied by each of the players. The goal of the game is to beat other opponents by touching the screen faster than other players after hearing the trigger time. The game also supports one and two player modes (Fig. 11.8).

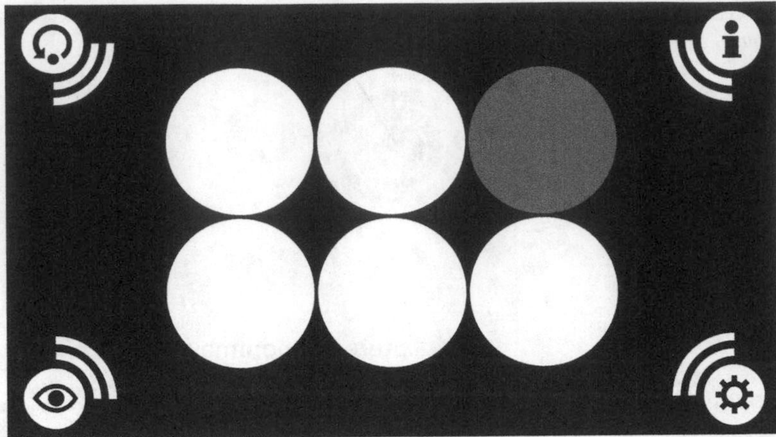

Fig. 11.7 *Animal Farm* game screen

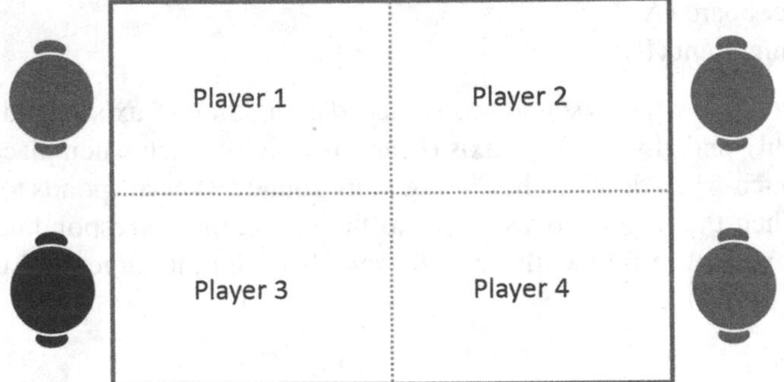

Fig. 11.8 *Samurai* user interface scheme

11.5.5 Labyrinth

Labyrinth is a classic arcade maze. The player's goal is to find the exit by following the "guiding" sound. When getting closer to the exit, the guiding sound becomes louder. The game consists of randomly generated rooms, whose borders are drawn by sounds signifying the player stepping against a wall (Fig. 11.9).

11.5.6 User Tests

During the development process (Agile method) each of the mini games and the main user interface was tested with visually impaired players in three countries: Germany, Poland and New Zealand. Gathered feedback allowed us to improve user

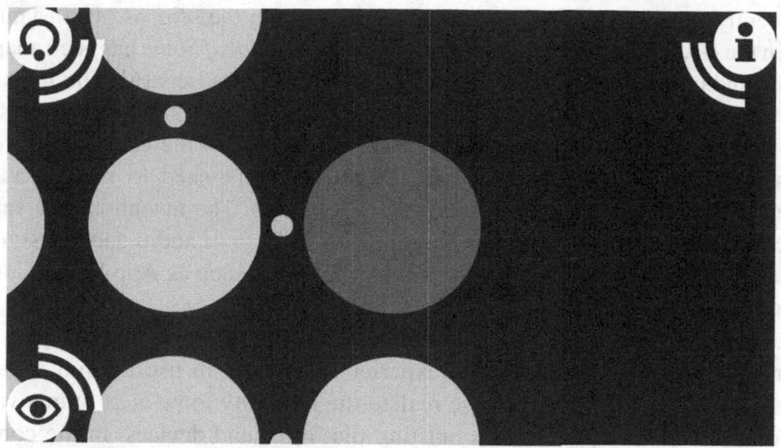

Fig. 11.9 *Labyrinth* game screen

interface and game mechanics so that they can be played by visually impaired who never had contact with touchscreen devices before. We also tested the Audio Game Hub on two groups of sighted casual gamers (12 in each group), and one group of 5 visually impaired users:

- Group one: playing games with visual aids on, then again with visuals off
- Group two: playing games with visual aids off, then again with visuals on
- Group three: playing games without being able to see the screen at all

First prototype test results have shown that immersion is increasing when graphics interface is turned off. Visual aids, on the other hand, lower the entry barrier for sighted players. Since the *Audio Game Hub* is a project-in-progress, the testing data with sighted and visually impaired players are in the process of evaluation.

11.6 Conclusions

Our work has demonstrated a great potential of interactive audiobooks with RPG elements and other genres of audio games. User tests and players' reviews demonstrated that this form of entertainment may be attractive for both, sighted and visually impaired players. Currently, we are experimenting with various types of casual audio games and the most effective sound and gesture interface solutions.

We need to realize, however, that the potential of audio games is not a stable indicator and depends on various factors, surpassing the gameplay design itself. The interactive digital entertainment has matured over the past few decades. An independent scene focused on the development of experimental projects is also contributing to the growing popularity of audio games. Contemporary players are more likely to turn to games initially reserved for the visually impaired community.

Recently, even the film industry seems to be turning the screens off. In January 2015 in the UK an experimental 1962 horror film *Carnival of Souls* has been adapted to a 3D audio-only experience relayed across wireless headsets [6]. The members of the audience included sighted as well as blind and partially sighted members.

The potential of audio gaming is also increasing due to the constant improvements in technology. Since sound-based games do not need to rely on visual elements, mobile devices seem to be perfect solutions. The invention of a smartphone in the late 2000s opened new possibilities in front of audio game designers. The ease of access to mobile digital content platforms, such as App Store, Google Play, and Windows Store should also be acknowledged.

We have been carefully observing other audio game projects, both past and present, and learning from our own experience in order to use the full capacity of the mobile medium. However, we realize the necessity to be alert to innovative solutions while developing for the existing platforms and devices. In the coming years the importance of smart watches, wearable technology, smart clothing, or even such novelties as fiber implants should not be underestimated. Although the latter ones still seem to belong to the science fiction realm of *H+: The Digital Series* (2012).

References

1. AudioGames. (2015). Available at: http://www.audiogames.net/list-games. Accessed 15 Jan 2015.
2. Audiogent. (2015). Available at: http://audiogent.com. Accessed 15 Jan 2015.
3. Beksa, J., & Szewczyk-Biedrzycka, A. (2008). Audio game test report. Consumer Research Centre, Polish Telecom R&D.
4. BL STREAM. (2015). Available at: http://www.blstream.com. Accessed 15 Jan 2015.
5. Collins, K. (2013). *Playing with sound: A theory of interacting with sound and music in video games*. Cambridge, MA: The MIT Press.
6. Cornerhouse.org. (2015). Carnival of souls. Available at: http://www.cornerhouse.org/film/film-events/carnival-of-souls. Accessed 27 Jan 2015.
7. Dwyer, P., & VanLund, P. S. (2015). RPG game engine and map maker. University of North Carolina. Available at: http://www.cs.unc.edu/Research/assist/et/projects/RPG/index.html. Accessed 15 Jan 2015.
8. GMA Games. (2015). Available at: http://www.gmagames.com/ourgames.shtml. Accessed 27 Jan 2015.
9. Nitsche, M. (2008). *Video game spaces: Image, play, and structure in 3D worlds*. Cambridge, MA: The MIT Press.
10. Oldenburg, A. (2013). Sonic mechanics: Audio as gameplay. In Game Studies.org 13(1). Available at: http://gamestudies.org/1301/articles/oldenburg_sonic_mechanics. Accessed 15 Jan 2015.
11. Röber, N., Huber, C., Hartmann, K., Feustel, M., & Masuch, M. (2006). Interactive audiobooks: Combining narratives with game elements. In S. Göbel, R. Malkewitz, & I. Iurgel (Eds.), *Technologies for interactive digital storytelling and entertainment* (Lecture notes in computer science, Vol. 4326, pp. 358–369). Berlin: Springer.

Part III
Maintenance

Chapter 12
R&D for Accessible Broadcasting in Japan

Takayuki Ito

Abstract Broadcasting is one of the most important infrastructures of the society. It plays a key role in information exchange to ensure safety and security of population in natural and man-made disasters. Broadcasting is also playing an important role as one of the most familiar and easy-to-use media that can provide information to anyone. It is expected, therefore, the broadcasting keeps these roles and its services should be provided anytime, anywhere, and to anyone with sufficient accessibility. In this chapter, various technologies which improve accessibility of broadcasting will be discussed through introducing research and development in Japan and the vision of accessible broadcasting in the future will be presented.

12.1 Introduction

Broadcasting is one of the most important infrastructures of the society. It gives basic everyday information and pleasure to the life of people by providing news of various fields and entertainment programs. Moreover, it plays a key role during natural and man-made disasters in terms of information exchange in the society to ensure safety and security of population.

The East Japan Great Earthquake on March 11, 2011 clearly proved that the broadcasting plays a deterministically important role in such a catastrophic disaster. Broadcasting, as the social information infrastructure, kept providing important information on the disaster to all the people with or without impairments including elderly, visually- or hearing-impaired people, and people from foreign countries [1].

The incident also proved, however, that current social functions in Japan including broadcasting are not as sufficient for disabled people to save their lives from disasters as for people without disabilities. A survey of mortality rate of officially registered persons with disabilities during the East Japan Earthquake and the following tsunami shows that the mortality of persons with disabilities including the visual and/or auditory impaired was twice as high as for persons without

T. Ito, Ph.D. (✉)
NHK Engineering System Inc., 1-10-11, Kinuta, Setagaya-ku, Tokyo 157-8540, Japan
e-mail: itou.takayuki@nes.or.jp

P. Biswas et al. (eds.), *A Multimodal End-2-End Approach to Accessible Computing*, Human–Computer Interaction Series, DOI 10.1007/978-1-4471-6708-2_12

disabilities [2]. This fact suggests that it is vitally important in such a disastrous situation that people with disabilities can definitely access important information from its early stage although the accessibility may not be only the cause.

Broadcasting also plays another important role in many aging countries such as Japan and some other countries in Asia and Europe [3]. It is one of the most familiar and easy-to-use electronic media that anyone can share and enjoy information from it. Broadcasting is expected, therefore, to bond the society members including elderly people who are apt to be isolated.

Visual and auditory sensory functions or cognitive functions of elderly people generally get degraded with increasing age. Such degradation decreases capability of information acquisition and communication and thus causes information barrier and resulting isolation from the society.

Communication and broadcasting are now digitized and devices such as telephones and television receivers have many functions with complex user-interface. People cannot utilize such devices, which causes another information barrier, "digital divide". Elderly people who cannot follow new technologies tend to become victims of the digital divide.

To ensure the broadcasting keep playing above mentioned social roles, broadcasting services should be provided anytime, anywhere, and to anyone, or in other words, broadcasting services should be provided with sufficient accessibility. Research for new technologies is, therefore, required to improve accessibility of broadcasting services and of receiving equipment for broadcasting.

This chapter describes development of such new technologies for the accessibility of broadcasting currently conducted mainly in NHK (Japan Broadcasting Corporation), which is the only public broadcasting organization in Japan.

In the following sections, various research and development to improve accessibility of broadcasting are described.

12.2 Activities to Make Television Accessible in Japan

12.2.1 Closed Caption and Audio Description: Overview

Closed captioning (CC) or subtitles and audio description (AD) broadcast were launched in analog broadcasting era in Japan. CC was started in 1984 by a technology called teletext which is to send additional text information to viewers. AD broadcast started in a drama program in 1992 by using audio multiplex broadcasting.

In the case of analog broadcasting system, both services had issues to be solved. For CC, the function of receiving teletext was not a mandatory of television receivers. Users needed to purchase a set-top-box to receive teletext separately from a TV set. It therefore prevented both growth of CC service and penetration of the set-top-boxes.

Table 12.1 Target quotas of CC and AD percentage for broadcasters

	Quota for CC (set in 1997)	Quotas for CC and AD (set in 2007)
Target year	2007	2017
Scope	Recorded programs	All programs from 7 A.M. to 12 P.M.
CC	100 %	100 %
AD	–	10 % (15 % for NHK 2 (Ed.))

Whereas, as to AD, the audio channels for multiplex broadcasting was shared among AD, stereophonic broadcast, and dual-language broadcast, and therefore AD service was not possible to programs of stereo sound such as dramas nor of dual-language programs such as dubbed foreign movies. This also prevented increasing AD service.

In digital broadcasting, reception functions of CC and AD were set mandatory for TV receivers. In addition, the number of audio slots for a TV channel was also designed to be enough for AD to be attached even to a program with stereophonic audio. Thus the issues on the hardware at receiving end are mostly solved now.[1]

In order to increase programs of CC and AD services, however, facilities and personnel for CC and AD also need prepared. Former Ministry of Posts and Telecommunications and Ministry of Internal Affairs and Communications established goals of 10 years later for quotas of CC programs and AD programs in 1997 and 2007, respectively as shown in Table 12.1. It also requests for broadcasters to submit a plan of quotas every year toward the goal, which encourages broadcasters to expand the services step by step.

It should be noted that there is a barrier of language in CC in some countries. Japanese has many character sets such as 50 of hiragana set, 50 of katakana set, and some thousands of Kanji character set. These sets of characters produces vast variety of expression in text and many homonyms, which make it very difficult to make speech into captions accurately by selecting exact combination of characters in real-time. It is quite contrasted with the case of countries using alphabet, where stenotype machines have been used since eighteenth century.

The first quota of closed caption set in 1997 was targeted only for recorded programs because of the above language barrier. The second quota of closed caption which was established in 2007 includes live broadcast as well as recorded one because innovations in speech recognition technology and stenographic keyboard technique for Japanese were thought to enable live captioning to most of TV programs in near future.

At this moment, a quota of audio description was also set for the first time because of stronger request from visually impaired group.

[1]Digital TV broadcasting enables 5.1 surround audio. Recently the number of programs with 5.1 surround audio is increasing, which causes similar issue that programs with 5.1 surround audio cannot provide audio description because of lack of audio slots. This is not a standardization issue but an issue of facility equipping of each broadcasting station.

12.2.2 *Technology for Closed Caption*

As mentioned in the previous section, Japanese language has difficulty in typing speech into captions in real-time. Now it has become possible thanks to technological and operational innovations. In NHK, the following five systems are adopted as means to produce closed caption to live broadcasts.

1. Two or more operators input the speech contents using a conventional keyboard. This system is used in programs with few speech portions such as music programs.
2. Stenographic keyboard system called "Stenoword," which was invented by Speed-WP, Inc., is used in major national news programs. With the system six professional operators of special skill work together in three groups and each group sequentially types out phrase by phrase in round-robin.
3. The re-speak system is applied to some of sports programs and cultural programs. Speech recognition is applied to voice of a "respeaker," who listens sound track of the program and rephrases in a quiet booth.
4. Direct speech recognition is applied in special programs such as Major League Baseball. It is possible because an announcer and a commentator talk in a studio in Japan while watching the video with ambient sound sent from the U.S.A.
5. A hybrid system which combines direct speech recognition and re-speak method is applied for short news programs on-aired every hour and local news programs. The system combines direct speech recognition and re-speak method as shown in Fig. 12.1. Direct speech recognition is applied to voices of announcers and news reporters because their recognition accuracy is higher than 95 %, which is high enough for error correction. In interviews to non-professional speakers, re-speak method is applied to avoid low recognition accuracy caused by noisy sound source and lower vocal quality of utterance. The system thus covers a whole news program by the speech recognition technology.

The hybrid speech recognition system is the latest one developed in NHK. It was test-operated during the East Japan Great Earthquake in 2011 and was introduced

Fig. 12.1 Hybrid closed captioning system

in regular operation from April 2012 mainly for closed captioning of short news programs every hour in national service. It is also set ready to use in emergency news programs.

The hybrid captioning system began used in several major local stations of NHK too. It has a feature that less operational cost is required compared to the stenographic keyboard system. It is, therefore, easy for small scale local broadcasters to introduce. It also matches needs of viewers with auditory impairment who request CC to local news programs and local emergency news programs. The system will hopefully be introduced in local stations nation-wide in a few years.

In order to expand the number of programs applicable to speech recognition, various functions of speech recognition need to be improved. For example, raising the recognition accuracy to spontaneous speech is effective for scenes in which commentators and reporters talk each other. In the re-speak recognition system, an effective training method of the language model of recognition system (a kind of linguistic dictionary in a speech recognition system) is definitely important for efficient adaptation of the recognition system to a new topic of a program. A new technology is also investigated which enables topic sensitive selection of language models while speech recognition is in operation.

12.2.3 Technology for Audio Description

Audio description is sometimes mentioned as “another radio drama”. The workflow of producing audio description is shown in Fig. 12.2. In the flow, the scriptwriter of audio description plays a key role, who determines scripts and their positions according to the video of a finished program, fitting its length so that it may not overlap with the sound of the original program. In the case of a drama program,

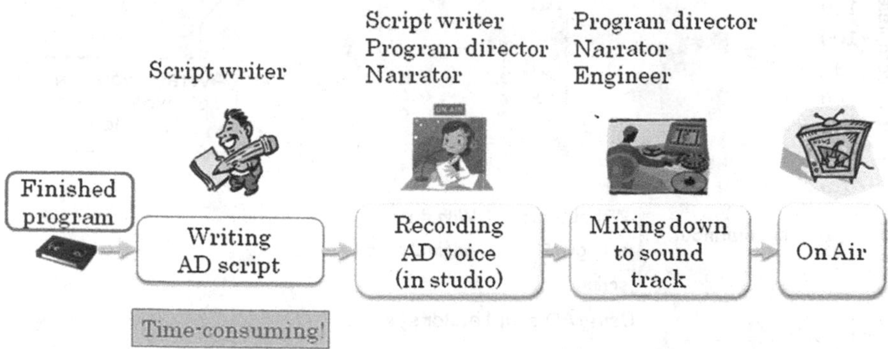

Fig. 12.2 Workflow of producing audio description program

scripts sometimes accompany notes on how to utter the scripts so that atmosphere of the scene may not be broken. Writing description script is the most time-consuming process in the workflow.

Since the work of producing audio description is based on the professional skills and know-how written above, it is very difficult to automatize the production by computer. A system which supports writing a description script, instead, may help producing audio description efficiently.

Such a script editor system may have following functions.

1. When the video of a program is to read, the sound track of the video program is analyzed and sections of voice, non-voice, and music will be automatically distinguished.
2. Maximal number of characters or words to be inserted is automatically calculated on each non-voice section. It warns the script writer when inserted characters or words of the portion exceed the maximal number.
3. When the electronic script of a program is available, stage directions are extracted and a corresponding video portion is automatically identified. Candidates of a description script will be shown using the stage direction.

A prototype system which includes above functions was developed and evaluated. A simple evaluation experiment was conducted by persons without experience of AD writing but only with that of typing by PC. The result showed that total work time to finish a AD script for a 15-min TV program was shortened into two thirds in time, comparable length of professional script writers as shown in Fig. 12.3.

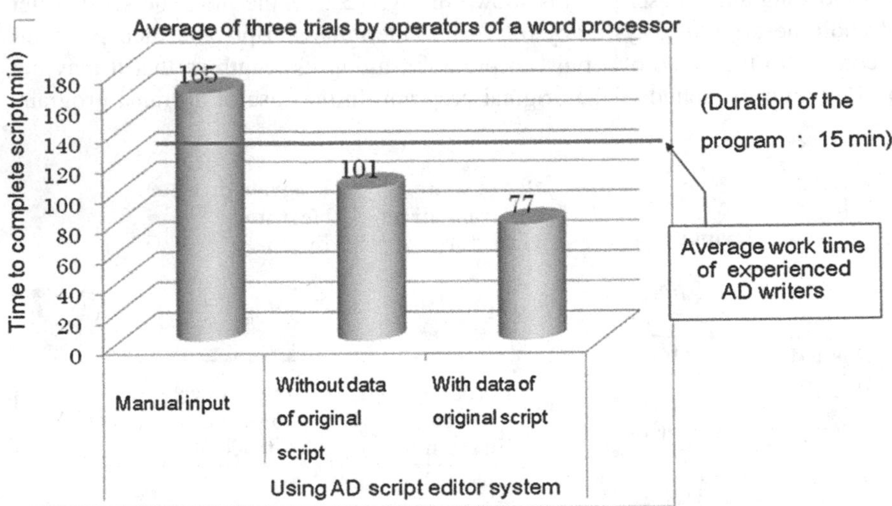

Fig. 12.3 Effect of using a script editor system

The result suggests that this kind of assistive system has potential to promote participation to less experienced writers into production of AD programs and to accelerate the increase of AD programs.

12.3 Further Improvement in Accessibility of Broadcast

In the previous section, two major access services, closed caption and audio description are discussed mainly in terms of technologies. In this section, various topics of accessibility other than above two are discussed.

12.3.1 Sign Language Interpretation

Sign language is the first language for deaf people, or persons who lost hearing from birth or in their small childhood. For them, the spoken language is the second language mastered later. This is the reason why they request to broadcast not with closed caption but with sign language interpretation.

Sign language interpretation services to TV programs have not readily increased in these 10 years of digital TV broadcasting. This is mainly because of following two reasons; one is that video of sign language interpreter has to be mixed at broadcaster side because of bandwidth limitation of digital TV channel and therefore it cannot be switched on/off at the receiver side; the other is limited number of sign language interpreters who can translate complex news stories in simple and easy-to-understand sign language expression.

The first, bandwidth limitation issue can be solved by combining two transmission pathways such as two broadcasting channels or broadcasting and broadband, one for main program channel and the other for supplementary signer's video. "Medekiku-TV" or "Listen with your eyes TV" in Japan provides through a satellite channel a supplementary sign language interpretation video stream for TV programs of other broadcasters [4]. A special set-top-box for the service synthesizes two video streams into one display screen.

The same idea is going to be applied in a new broadcasting scheme combining broadcasting channel and broadband network. In some countries or regions in the world, varieties of this kind of scheme have been researched and tested, including HbbTV [5] in EBU and Hybridcast [6] in Japan. In the scheme, TV programs will be provided through broadcasting channel as usual while supplementary data or video will be provided through internet or broadband synchronously with the broadcasting video. The two streams will be synthesized in a specialized receiving terminal according to the viewer's request. One of the typical usages of this scheme is a sign language interpretation service [6].

In order to overcome the lack of sign language interpreters suited for broadcasting, one of technical solutions may be automatic translation from text to computer

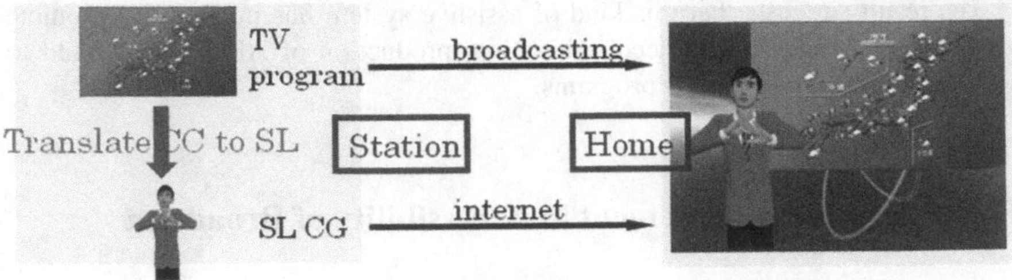

Fig. 12.4 Scheme of closed sign language service of weather news

graphics (CG) of sign language interpreter. NHK has been conducting research on automatic sign language translation technology in the domain of meteorological news [7, 8]. This technology is especially useful for emergency news such as an earthquake or a typhoon, which may happen even in the midnight.

Figure 12.4 shows a schematic illustration of the service using the Hybridcast. Closed caption or news script of weather news is translated into sign language CG video. The translated video stream of the CG is transmitted to receivers through internet while the original TV program is broadcasted as usual. This transmission scheme enables "closed signing", in which individual user can switch on/off the signer's video according to his/her need.

Similar projects on sign language interpretation are conducted in various countries such as ATLAS Project organized by RAI and Politecnico di Torino [9] and a project on Thai Sign Language [10].

12.3.2 Digital Receivers for Visually Impaired People

Television is not a media only for visually non-impaired people. Recent survey in Japan shows that TV is the most frequently used media to enjoy information for visually impaired people [11]. Accessibility of television receiver for visually impaired people is therefore as important as for visually non-impaired people.

12.3.2.1 Accessible Digital TV Receiver

As most of digital information and communication devices, digital TV receivers usually have functions based on visual expressions. Pop-up menus appear when selecting a function of the TV receiver and a full-screen table of program guide can be used to select a program. These visual expressions are used in order to show a viewer the complex and diverse functions in a well-organized style and actually quite useful for visually non-impaired people. These visually dependent functions

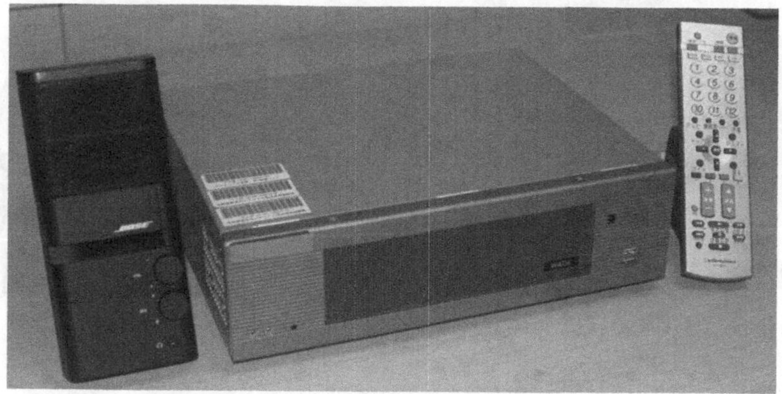

Fig. 12.5 A prototype set-top-box for visually impaired people

of TV set are, however, big barriers for visually impaired people to access television programs.

Accessible digital TV receivers for visually impaired people are developed utilizing text-to-speech (TTS) technology [12] by several TV set manufacturers. Requirements of TTS functionality for television were also standardized in IEC recently. It specifies TTS functionality for a broadcast receiver with text-to-speech system.

NHK is conducting a research and development to improve accessibility of digital broadcasting for visually impaired people, partially sighted people, and deaf and blind people [13]. It includes

1. In addition to the text-to-speech of EPG and channel information, it has a function of text-to-speech of data broadcasting which contains graphics and images as well as text information.
2. It has an interface for a Braille terminal, which visually impaired people or visually and auditorily impaired people can access news text in data broadcasting or closed caption by finger-reading.
3. It can enlarge a part of screen and change contrast or color of text for partially sighted people or amblyopia.

A prototype of such a set-top-box is shown in Fig. 12.5.

12.3.2.2 Two Dimensional Interactive Tactile Display

A two dimensional tactile display is a candidate of accessible user-interface of information terminals for visually impaired people. This is a pin display which presents figures or Braille text by binary up/down positions of pins in an array.

NHK developed an interactive tactile display shown in Fig. 12.6, which has a function to detect the touching position of a finger and finger gestures such as

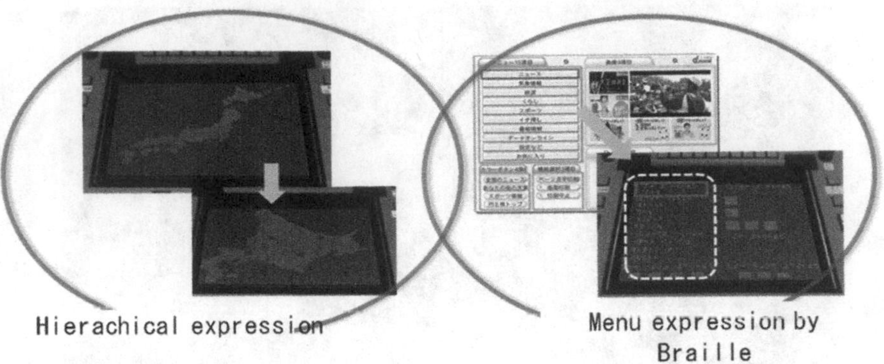

Fig. 12.6 Interactive tactile display

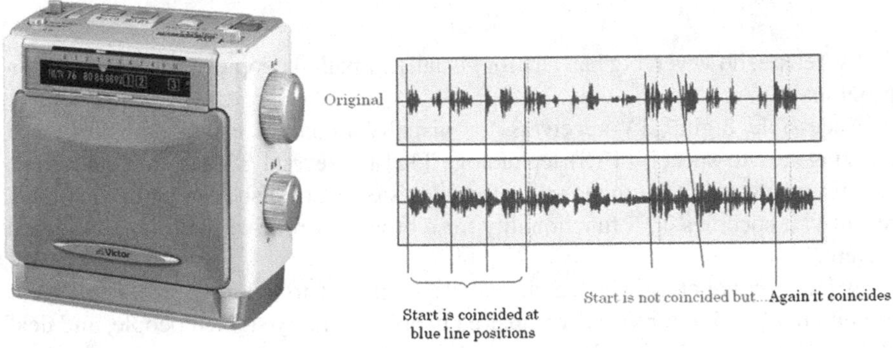

Fig. 12.7 A radio set with speech speed control (*left*) and its principle (*right*)

tapping on a two-dimensional pin display [14]. Thus this device is applicable as a GUI device for a visually impaired person just as a LCD display screen with touch sensor or a mouse for visually non-impaired people.

12.3.3 Speech Signal Processing for Elderly People

12.3.3.1 Speech Rate Conversion for Elderly People

Elderly people tend to have degradation of perceptual and cognitive ability. As to auditory functions, perceptual degradation typically appears in difficulty to hear higher frequency sound and cognitive degradation appears difficulties in catching speech buried in background sound or speech spoken rapidly.

NHK has invented a technology which can change speech speed slower or faster without changing vocal quality. It was in practical use in the market since 2000 such as radio receivers and television sets with the function of "slow speech" embedded as shown in Fig. 12.7 left.

This technology can change speech speed slower or sometimes faster without changing total time length of the vocal signal. To realize this, portions of a speech signal such as the start of a sentence and portions with higher voice energy or with higher pitch frequency are made slower, which are considered to be more important. Instead the rest of the signal is made faster in speed, especially silent portion of breathing being shortened. Thus the audio signal length is kept unchanged as the whole as shown in right of Fig. 12.7, so it is applicable to the television broadcasting accompanied by video.

In more general, this technology can change speech speed with total length of the signal longer or shorter than the original while important portions kept slower than others.

This technology is utilized in various fields:

1. Radio news is provided as an internet service with slow speed version and fast speed version as well as normal one.
2. An application software of speech rate conversion for a smart phone has been developed for foreign language learning. It can convert speech speed slower so that the user can catch up speech easily and effectively train listening ability.
3. Visually impaired people listen to reading-out of text such as audio books and Web pages sometimes in faster speed than normal for information search or skimming. The speech rate conversion technology is applicable for this purpose because it can make total length of vocal signal shorter but with important portions in slower speed. For this purpose, plug-in for a video player software and a special version of the DAISY player has been developed.

12.3.3.2 Clear Audio

Elderly people sometimes feel background sound of a broadcast program too loud and find it difficult to catch the talk of an announcer or an actor.

Using separate audio channels for main voice and for background sound and mixing them at receiving side is one of the solutions. This consumes, however, another audio channel and it has no compatibility with the current TV receivers based on the current broadcasting system.

Another candidate of the solutions is to broadcast two versions of the audio track; one is normally mixed sound track for younger generations and the other is mixed with lower level of background sound for elderly people. This may satisfy the compatibility issue but it changes workflow of program production into cost- and time-consuming one. Moreover, the effect of this method is limited because appropriate balance between main voice and background sound is different in each listener.

A new technology to solve this issue has been conducted in NHK. This technology recognizes and divides the program sound into voice segments and non-voice segments, and for the voice segments, a component with high correlation between left and right stereo signals is extracted as "voice component" and that with lower correlation as "non-voice component". The system then can change the mixing level between voice and non-voice components and can emphasize voice component to compensate hearing loss of a listener.

An experimental system of this technology is developed recently. It automatically extracts "voice component" and "non-voice component" from voice segments and performs the mixing balance alteration and the enhancement in real-time [15].

12.3.4 News Service Using Simplified Japanese

East Japan Great Earthquake in 2011 clearly revealed the importance for life-saving information to be transmitted to everybody such as people with or without impairments and those speaking different languages. People from abroad who live in Japan are yearly increasing; for example, in 2009 registered foreign residents form 1.7 % of total population of Japan and the national origin amounts to 190 nations.

News in simplified Japanese which is understandable for most of them is helpful since limited number of multilingual services cannot cover all foreigners. It is also expected to contribute to transmit information to people with intellectual disabilities.

Research of converting regular news scripts into those in simplified Japanese has been conducted and a web service of simplified Japanese news "NEWS WEB EASY" has launched in April 2012 [16]. One of the major research topics is an assistive tool for converting news scripts into simplified Japanese. It can manage versions of article and can compare intractability of Japanese in each version calculated from levels of words used and average length of sentences.

12.4 Discussion – Aiming at the More Accessible Society

In this chapter current situation of accessible services for broadcasting in Japan and related new technologies have been introduced. These include services and technologies for visually or hearing impaired people and elderly people as well as those with difficulty in information acquisition because of the intellectual disability and language difference. In this section, commercialization of these new technologies and services will be discussed.

Access services always encounter cost issue. This is true for any services but in the case of access services the number of users is limited to elderly people and/or visually or hearing impaired people. Therefore the cost issue sometimes becomes a barrier for implementation of access services compared to other services of general purpose.

In implementing access services, following four points should be considered.

1. Reducing the cost

Even a useful service may not be implemented if it entails too much of operational cost. Innovation to reduce the cost is inevitable.

For example the hybrid closed captioning system mentioned in Sect. 12.2.2 requires at most two operators while the conventional system using stenographic keyboard needs six operators. The new hybrid captioning system drastically reduces operational cost. This reduction contributes for smaller broadcasters to introduce closed caption service.

Another example is the script editor system for audio description mentioned in Sect. 12.2.3. This system assists script writing aiming that even a non-proficient script writer can efficiently produce an audio description script of a TV program and is expected to reduce the production cost.

2. Expanding needs

Closed caption text is generally produced for hearing impaired people. It is becoming more widely usable, however, because it is expected to be used as annotation data of TV programs. As viewers usually search their favorite video with keywords when viewing video through the internet, closed caption text or its abstracted text may be used as the search object. If new needs like this are opened up, data for the access service becomes much valuable and cost for producing the access service can be reduced.

Another example is the speech rate conversion technology mentioned in Sect. 12.3.3. It was developed to compensate degraded cognitive ability of speech for elderly people but it is also shown to be able to use in various purposes such as training of listening a foreign language or audio skimming. Total cost of R&D can be reduced by realizing the variety of the use.

3. Increasing social awareness

Unfortunately necessity of access services is not widely recognized in the society although people concerned have paid a lot of effort. Nevertheless it is very important to widely appeal what are obstacles for impaired people and what they need, and to evaluate organizations and corporations which sincerely exert an effort to meet their needs.

For example, if sponsors of a TV program with closed caption get good reputation from the society, it would be a incentive for sponsors to support programs with closed caption. Another example is advertisements with closed caption. In Japan some companies started providing TV advertisements with closed caption responding to the request from hearing impaired people. If social evaluation of such a company increases and products of them sell better, it will be a great incentive for other companies to start TV advertisements with closed caption.

4. Legislation and support

As described in Sect. 12.2.1, targets are sometimes set for broadcasters to have some percentages of programs with closed caption or with audio description, and etc. Broadcasters are also sometimes encouraged to make yearly action plans how the targets will be attained in a limited period. These measures are usually very effective to increase the number of programs with certainty. It also effective to provide budget support for such services.

It may be also necessary to financially back up R&D to implement access services and innovations to reduce operational cost. For example, machine translation from caption text to animation of sign language requires not only R&D of translation technology but also developing a large scale corpus which contains caption text data and corresponding sign language video with their word-by-word relations. Developing such a large scale database is a time- and money-consuming work.

References

1. Sakai, T. (2012, May 28). *How was disaster information distributed through broadcasting in the Great East Japan earthquake?* ITU workshop on "making television accessible – From idea to reality" hosted and supported by NHK. http://www.itu.int/dms_pub/itu-t/oth/06/5B/T065B00001B0001PDFE.pdf
2. Fujii, K. (2012). *The Great East Japan earthquake and disabled persons –Background to their high mortality rate*. Disability Information Resources. http://www.dinf.ne.jp/doc/english/twg/escap_121031/fujii.html
3. Cabinet Office of Japan. (2010). *The aging society: Current situation and implementation measures*. Annual report on the Aging Society: 2010 (Summary). http://www8.cao.go.jp/kourei/english/annualreport/2010/2010pdf_e.html
4. Medekiku TV. http://www.medekiku.jp/ (in Japanese).
5. HbbTV. http://www.hbbtv.org/
6. Ohmata, H., Takechi, M., Mitsuya, S., Otsuki, K., Baba, A., Matsumura, K., Majima, K., & Sunasaki, S. (2012, April). Hybridcast: A new media experience by integration of broadcasting and broadband. In *Proceedings of the ITU Kaleidoscope Academic conference 2013*, S5.1, Geneve, Switzerland.
7. Report ITU-R BT.2207-1. (2011). *Accessibility to broadcasting services for persons with disabilities*, Geneve, Switzerland.
8. Kaneko, H., Hamaguchi, N., Doke, M., & Inoue, S. (2010, December). Sign language animation using TVML. In *Proceedings of the 9th ACM SIGGRAPH international conference on virtual-reality continuum and its applications in industry (VRCAI 2010)* (pp. 289–292). New York, USA.
9. Lombardo, V., Battaglino, C., Damiano, R., & Nunnari, F. (2011, June). An avatar-based interface for the Italian sign language. In *International conference of complex, intelligent and software intensive systems (CISIS)* (pp. 589–594). Seoul, South Korea.
10. Chauksuvanit, T., Chalidabhongse, T., & Aramvith, S. (2012, March). Progress-electronics for Thai sign language. In *Annual international technology & persons with disabilities conference, (CSUN2012), DHH-018*. Northridge, CA, USA.
11. Iwai, K. (2012, May). *Hopes for media accessibility from the blind and low-vision*. ITU workshop on "making television accessible – From idea to reality", Tokyo. http://www.itu.int/dms_pub/itu-t/oth/06/5B/T065B00001B0012PDFE.pdf
12. Sonoe, H. (2012, May). *Television receiver accessibility and international standardization activities at IEC*. ITU workshop on "making television accessible – from idea to reality", Tokyo.
13. Sakai, T., Handa, T., Matsunuma, K., Kanatsugu, Y., Hiruma, N., & Itoh, T. (2007). Information barrier-free presentation system for visually impaired users. In *Northridge's Center on Disabilities 22nd annual international technology and persons with disabilities conference (CSUN 2007), BLV-3141*, California State University, Northridge, CA, USA.

14. Shibata, M. (2012, May 28). *Research on universal broadcasting at NHK STRL*. ITU workshop on "making television accessible – From idea to reality" hosted and supported by NHK. http://www.itu.int/dms_pub/itu-t/oth/06/5B/T065B00001B0031PDFE.pdf
15. NHK STRL. (2013, May). *Adjustment system of sound levels in TV programs for elderly listeners*. Open House 2013: Exhibition, No. 19. http://www.nhk.or.jp/strl/open2013/tenji/pdf/19_e.pdf
16. NHK NEWS WEB EASY. http://www3.nhk.or.jp/news/easy/

Chapter 13
Evaluating the Accessibility of Adaptive TV Based Web Applications

Nádia Fernandes, Daniel Costa, Carlos Duarte, and Luís Carriço

Abstract The accessibility evaluation of Web applications has been gaining momentum in previous years. Several guidelines and systems are now available to assess the accessibility of a Web page. However, these guidelines have been show to be inadequate when assessing dynamic Web applications. Furthermore, when considering adaptive Web applications, another layer of dynamism is introduced, further complication the problem. This chapter presents a framework for accessibility evaluation of adaptive Web applications, expanding on previous work for evaluating dynamic Web applications. The framework will be described in the context of an evaluation of TV based Web applications, and the results will assist in the characterization of the accessibility of this particular field of Web applications.

13.1 Introduction

The Web is becoming more and more dynamic. User actions and automatically triggered events can alter a Web page's content. The presented content can be substantially different from the initially received by the browser. With the introduction of new technologies, Web sites/pages are becoming complex Web applications [7].

Being TV widely accepted and used on all homes over the world it is common sense to make this device accessible to most of its users. In the past recent years, started the Digital TV switchover around the world. In Europe this transition is planned to end in the year 2015. The substitution of the analogue signal to the digital enables besides of better image and sound quality, additional features such as interactivity, audio description and subtitling for people with visual and audio impairments. The Connected TV and the delivery of multimedia content to the home user via the Internet are also becoming increasingly common (although only

---

N. Fernandes (✉) • D. Costa • L. Carriço
Department of Informatics, LaSIGE/University of Lisbon, Campo Grande, Edificio C6, 1749-016 Lisboa, Portugal
e-mail: nadiaf@di.fc.ul.pt; dancosta@di.fc.ul.pt; lmc@di.fc.ul.pt

C. Duarte
Department of Informatics, University of Lisbon, Lisboa, Portugal
e-mail: cad@di.fc.ul.pt

P. Biswas et al. (eds.), *A Multimodal End-2-End Approach to Accessible Computing*, Human–Computer Interaction Series, DOI 10.1007/978-1-4471-6708-2_13

20–30 % of connected TVs in Europe are actually online), with major brands such as Apple, Google and Samsung investing in this field.

Hybrid Broadcast Broadband TV (HbbTV) [21] is both an industry standard and promotional initiative for hybrid digital TV to harmonise the broadcast, IPTV, and broadband delivery of entertainment to the end consumer through connected TVs and set-top boxes. The HbbTV consortium, grouping digital broadcasting and Internet industry companies, established a standard for the delivery of broadcast TV and broadband TV to the home, through a single user interface, creating an open platform as an alternative to proprietary technologies. This standard provides the features and functionality required to deliver feature rich broadcast and internet services. Utilizing standard Internet technologies such as HTML and Javascript it enables rapid application development. This means that much of the accessibility problems found on traditional Web pages are carried also to the TV field.

Currently, there are several projects regarding accessibility in TV platforms, such as GUIDE [22]. These projects focus on adapting the user interface considering the skills of elderly or disabled users [13]. However, the resulting adapted user interfaces are not guaranteed to be accessible. First, because the original applications may lack fundamental content, alternative modalities, or simply be built in a way that the adaptation engines are not able to correct. Secondly, because the resulting user interfaces should be validated during the refinement and development of those engines and supporting models. Either way, it is fundamental to find ways to evaluate the TV web applications, and give developers of TV applications and platforms a report of accessibility errors and warnings.

This chapter proposes a new type of accessibility evaluation of Web applications (or Web TV application). First it considers the evaluation of the Web application nearer to what the users actually may perceive, i.e., after browser processing. Then it further addresses the dynamics and complexity of Web and Web TV applications by expanding the initial Web pages to the full state-graph of the application. It also merges Web and selected adequate guidelines for the TV applications world. Finally, it copes with the possible adaptation process by selecting and applying the requested adaptation profiles and evaluating the result considering only the techniques for that profile. The contribution of this work is thus a framework, methodology and tools, for the evaluation of Web TV adaptive applications, considering dynamic, complexity and user adaptation profiles.

A preliminary experimental evaluation was performed that emphasises the differences between our approach and the classical Web evaluation ones. Furthermore, the adequacy and applicability of our evaluation strategy was demonstrated by its application to a couple of profile adapted applications validated by expert evaluations.

13.2 Requirements and Related Work

Evaluating Web accessibility involves three main aspects: the set of guidelines to be applied on the evaluation, the adaptation of the content to the target users and contexts that will be evaluated, and the process by which those guidelines are applied.

13.2.1 Guidelines and TV

The Web Content Accessibility Guidelines (WCAG) 2.0 [9] are the standards to Web accessibility, covering a wide range of recommendations for a large number of disabilities. However, considering Web TV applications, some may be misleading, since it can be different to experience Web application content in a TV instead of a regular computer screen. For instance, TV screens have higher contrast and saturation levels, so developers must be conscious of these characteristics. The possible outcomes considered by the WCAG 2.0 techniques are: fail, pass or warning [11]. A failure occurs in the cases where the evaluator can automatically and unambiguously detect if a given HTML element has an accessibility problem, whereas the passing represents its opposite. Warnings are raised when the evaluator can partially detect accessibility problems, but which might require additional inspection (often by experts).

There are also Universal Design guidelines for Digital TV services [26], which establish some specific accessibility guidelines for Digital TV. The Global Visual Language, from BBC [6] also proposes a set of design guidelines specific for TV. Google, recently investing in this field, also provides some design considerations which can be helpful to use as well [18]. To maintain the accessibility of TV applications it is important to consider all these types of guidelines. However, a balanced revision and integration should be endeavoured, considering not only the overlapping, the specificity of TV but also the developments and trends in Web technologies.

13.2.2 Target Users and Adaptive User Interfaces

An Adaptive User Interface is an interface able to adapt its elements to a given context, taking into account the knowledge stored (implicitly or explicitly) on different kinds of models. The User model is considered the main drive of the adaptation process.

By monitoring the user's actions and obtaining information on data models representing the environment and user's abilities, these systems can adapt automatically in order to improve the interaction. These adaptive capabilities are important when dealing with users with different physical and cognitive characteristics.

Usually, the component responsible to adapt the outputs is the Output Modalities Fission [14] also known as Presentation Manager, which can find the knowledge it requires to perform the adaptations, on the several models these systems may have (e.g. User Model, Context Model).

Examples of such systems are ELOQUENCE [24] or EGOKI [1], a system that automatically generates an accessible user interface for ubiquitous services.

Considering the trend of some TV frameworks [13, 22] to support adaptive UIs [12], it is a requirement to evaluate the adequacy of the performed adaptations. In this case the application of guidelines should not be straightforward. In fact, if the framework transforms the application UI to a specific user profile (say, colour-blind) or Context, it makes no sense to evaluate the result considering guidelines targeting another disability (e.g. motor impaired).

ACCESSIBLE [10] already provides a harmonized methodology enabling the selection of WCAG guidelines based on disability. Its articulation with the profile selection of the adaptation engines and the merging of specific TV guidelines could provide the necessary means for an adequate accessibility evaluation of the adaptive UIs.

13.2.3 Dynamics and the Evaluation Process

Web Accessibility Evaluation is an assessment procedure to analyse how well the Web can be used by people with different levels of disabilities [20]. Conformance checking [3] with the aid of automated Web accessibility evaluation tools is an important step for the accessibility evaluation. Most of these use WCAG guidelines [2].

However, traditionally, evaluators assess the original Web code as provided by the server. Although, in the past, the predominant technologies in the Web were HTML and CSS, which resulted in *static* Web pages. Today, on top of these technologies, newer technologies have appeared (e.g. Javascript). The Web is becoming more and more dynamic. User actions and/or automatically triggered events can alter a Web page's content. Because of that, the presented content can be substantially different from the initially provided by the server.

Fernandes et al. [15] already performed a study that shows that there are real differences between the accessibility evaluations performed before and after the browser processing. This happens, because a lot of transformations take place during the browser's processing, which significantly alter the HTML document.

The importance of performing evaluation after the Web browser processing of the page is starting to be considered and is already used in a few tools:

- *Foxability* [25] an accessibility analysing extension for Firefox that uses WCAG 1.0;
- *Mozilla/Firefox Accessibility Extension* [17] an extension of Firefox that uses WCAG 1.0 and performs report generation;
- *WAVE Firefox toolbar* [27] is a Web Accessibility Evaluation Tool that provides a mechanism for running WAVE reports directly within Firefox, using WCAG 1.0, but it does not perform reporting;
- *Hera-FXX Firefox extension* [17] semi-automatic tool to perform accessibility evaluation, using WCAG 1.0.

These tools focus only on the use of WCAG 1.0, which has been obsolete by its latest 2.0 incarnation. Also they are embedded specific browser extensions, becoming more limited in terms of their application, because they cannot be used outside the Web browser. Analysing large amounts of data or using different browser is, to say the least, a difficult task.

Still, the analysis of complex Web applications holds more than just the dynamic assessment of pages after browser processing. These applications include a complex network of states that must be accessed in order to be fully evaluated. Usually, these states are only triggered by user interaction with the Web page. Therefore, a major part that composes the Web page is not properly evaluated.

Besides, another level of possible evaluation flaws rises when we add the Adaptive aspect to this equation as potentially the majority of the interface properties can be modified.

13.2.4 Subsuming the Challenges

Web TV applications, and particularly those that are handed to and result from an adaptation process, impose different challenges: (1) as rich Web applications, the evaluation should cope with the dynamically introduced code, i.e. code introduced after browser processing; (2) the applications are composed by several states which are only identified by simulation; (3) evaluate the outcome of the adaptation of the interface, taking into account the adequacy and coverage of existing guidelines; (4) as specific TV components, this reassessment should further be refined to cope with TV idiosyncrasies; (5) as inputs of an adaptation process, the evaluation should deal with the assurance of the adaptability of the original TV applications, applying only those guidelines that cannot be automatically solved by the adaptation; and (6) as outputs of that process, the evaluation should consider the specific target users, selecting only those guidelines that apply to the users' profile.

13.3 The Framework for Accessibility Evaluation of Web TV

This section describes the approach and architecture of a framework that performs automated accessibility evaluation of Web applications.

The proposed solution is based on the QualWeb evaluator [15]. The evaluator assesses accessibility after browsing processing, thus focussing on the DOM as presented to the user and considering all the different scenarios or stages that the rich internet applications may have.

13.3.1 Architecture

The architecture (depicted in Fig. 13.1) is composed of four major components: Interaction Simulator, QualWeb Evaluator 3.0, Techniques and Formatters. The Interaction Simulator component was added to the previous version of the evaluator [15], and replaces the Environments module.

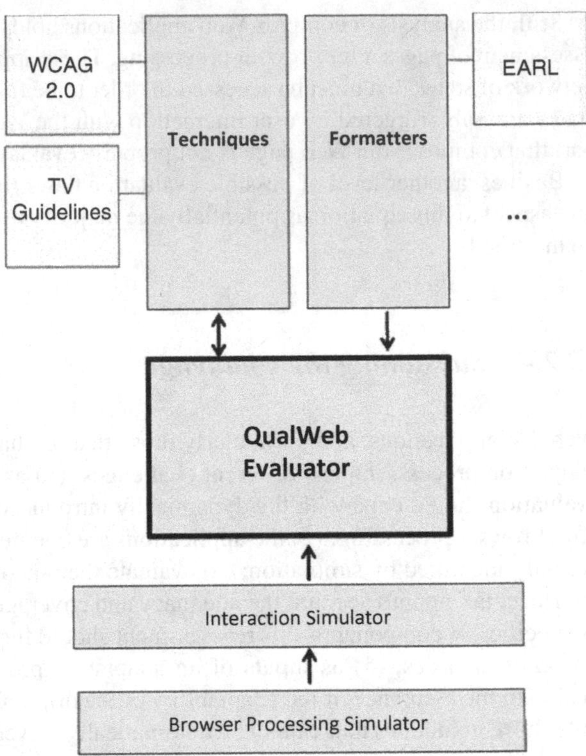

Fig. 13.1 Architecture of the framework

13.3.1.1 Browser Processing Simulator

This module simulates the processing of the Web browser using *CasperJs*.[1] *Casper.js* is a navigation scripting & testing utility for PhantomJS, written in Javascript. *PhantomJS*[2] is a command-line tool that uses WebKit (e.g. WebKit is the rendering engine used in web browsers to render pages [28]), it works like a WebKit-based web browser, with no need to display everything on the screen. Besides, it could be controlled using Javascript, being consistent with our implementation. This way, we can run a lot of evaluations sequentially. Besides, we can obtain the HTML document after the "Web browser processing" – *onLoadFinished* – simulated by the *Phantom.js*. Thus, we achieve the content as normally perceived by the users and overcome the challenge 1.

Next, the Interaction Simulator performs its functionality over the processed content of the page obtained by the Browser Processing Simulator.

---

[1] http://casperjs.org/

[2] http://phamtomjs.org/

13.3.1.2 Interaction Simulator

To cope with the challenges of the dynamic Web applications, we have integrated an Interaction Simulator. This component is responsible for simulating user actions and triggering the interactive elements of the interface. As a result we have access to all the different states (in DOM format) of the Web application [16]. This addresses challenge 2.

To perform the simulation of the several stages of a Web page, we used *Crawlers* (similarly to *Mesbah and van Deursen* [23]) which are attached to each element that is *clickable* and has an *onclick* function assigned. These *Crawlers* periodically perform the click action on these interactive elements. Every time a new version of the same Web page is detected (i.e. a new *state*), a scan is performed in order to find eventual new interactive elements.

Simultaneously, we have an *Observer* which has the responsibility to detect changes in the DOM tree. In case that happens, we consider it as a new state and the DOM is sent to the evaluation module.

It is important to refer that the Interaction Simulator keeps navigating the Web application until all the interactive elements have been activated. For that, it keeps a list of the found elements and which of those have been already activated. Besides, to avoid sending duplicated DOM threes to evaluation, a list of already evaluated documents (i.e. states) is also kept.

13.3.1.3 QualWeb 3.0

It is at the Interaction Simulator level that the new QualWeb will produce the states by simply executing the original Web application or by requesting first an adaptation to a specific user profile. This lays the grounds to fulfil either challenge 3 or 4. The DOMs are then fed to the QualWeb evaluator 3.0 that cumulatively assesses the quality of the application.

To perform the evaluation *QualWeb* uses the features provided by the *Techniques* component. It uses the *Formatters* component to tailor the results into specific serialisation formats, such as EARL reporting [4], since EARL is a standard format for accessibility reporting. This way, it can be interpreted by any tool that understands this format, and even allow comparing the results with other tools.

QualWeb currently implements 27 HTML and 19 CSS WCAG 2.0 techniques (i.e., the basic practices of creation of accessible content as basis of testable success criteria). From those we selected 25 HTML and 14 CSS that are suited for the TV platform specificities. From the Universal Design guidelines for Digital TV services [26], six extra guidelines are implemented. Thus, a total of 52 accessibility guidelines were used for the evaluation. The integration of these new techniques was easily supported by the modular approach of QualWeb.

Concerning the adaptation nature of the envisioned TV platforms, the QualWeb evaluator 3.0 was modified to cope with the selective application of techniques. Basically, in this new version it is possible to select a subset of the techniques that will be applied. Predefined subsets were established according to the adaptation profiles. Challenges 3 and 4 are then addressed by this selection in conjunction with the Interaction Simulator option of requesting the previous adaptation of the DOM. Overall, the modifications to the evaluator addressed all the requirements raised in the previous section.

The next subsection details which WCAG 2.0 will be applied into the evaluation after the adaptation, depending on the type of disability.

13.3.2 Chosen Techniques

The guidelines selected to a project can have major implications in its results, as well as on the process of adaptation to the users. It is important to understand that different techniques applicable for each disability type, meaning that the guidelines that can be applied and verified can be really different depending on the user profile that we are using in the adaptation. When each user can have different type of disabilities or impairments.

This way, to identify the WCAG techniques that are relevant in the evaluation framework, we performed the correlation of the type of disability or impairment with the guidelines that can be applied in that case. We used as basis: (1) user categories and possible barriers of the Barrier Walkthrough [8], (2) the disabilities/impairments consider on GUIDE project [19], and (3) the correlation between guidelines and disabilities of ACCESSIBLE project [5]. Therefore, we could cross all that information and obtain a more complete correlation between the guidelines (WCAG 2.0 success criteria' and techniques') and the disability types, which can be seen in Tables 13.1–13.4. Besides, to the visual disabilities there are considered three types of important sub-disabilities that are correlated with the guidelines in Table 13.4.

We have a coverage of 47 % of the WCAG 2.0 HTML rules and 80 % of the WCAG 2.0 CSS rules (consult Tables 13.5 and 13.6). The HTML rules not implemented yet are dependent of the complex media processing, which were are working on. Considering the CSS rules not implemented, they are not objective enough to be evaluated without the human innervation, because they are dependent of the human observation or of the devices where the content is observed.

Besides, we also considered the Universal Design guidelines for Digital TV services [26] where we have a coverage of 60 %, some of these guidelines overlap with the CSS guidelines. Those that do not overlap consider: colours and contrast, ensure that text and graphics appear within the area of the screen, that can be clearly seen, avoid scrolling, font family.

Table 13.1 Correlation between the guidelines and the cognitive impairments

Disability type	WCAG 2.0 success criteria
Cognitive impairments	1.1.1
	1.2.1, 1.2.3, 1.2.5, 1.2.6, 1.2.7, 1.2.9
	1.3.1, 1.3.3
	1.4.5, 1.4.8, 1.4.9
	2.2.1, 2.2.2, 2.2.3, 2.2.4, 2.2.5
	2.3.2
	2.4.1, 2.4.2, 2.4.4, 2.4.5, 2.4.6, 2.4.7, 2.4.8, 2.4.9,
	2.4.10
	3.1.1, 3.1.2, 3.1.3, 3.1.4, 3.1.5, 3.1.6
	3.2.1, 3.2.2, 3.2.3, 3.2.4, 3.2.5
	3.3.1, 3.3.2, 3.3.3, 3.3.4, 3.3.5, 3.3.6
	4.1.1, 4.1.2

Table 13.2 Correlation between the guidelines and the hearing impairments

Disability type	WCAG 2.0 success criteria
Hearing impairments	1.1.1
	1.2.1, 1.2.2, 1.2.4, 1.2.6, 1.2.8, 1.2.9
	1.3.1, 1.3.2
	1.4.2, 1.4.7
	2.2.3
	3.3.4, 3.3.5, 3.3.6
	4.1.1, 4.1.2

Table 13.3 Correlation between the guidelines and the upper limb impairments

Disability type	WCAG 2.0 success criteria
Upper limb impairments	1.1.1
	1.2.1, 1.2.3, 1.2.5
	1.3.1
	2.1.1, 2.1.2, 2.1.3
	2.2.1, 2.2.3, 2.2.4, 2.2.5
	2.4.1, 2.4.2, 2.4.3, 2.4.4, 2.4.6, 2.4.7, 2.4.9, 2.4.10
	3.2.1
	3.3.2, 3.3.3, 3.3.4, 3.3.5, 3.3.6
	4.1.1, 4.1.2

13.4 Validating the Approach

To validate the approach we devised an experimental study first on an Electronic Programme Guide (EPG), and then on two other TV applications. One common characteristic about these three applications is that they are implement on only one

Table 13.4 Correlation between the guidelines and the visual sub-disabilities

Visual sub-disabilities	WCAG 2.0 success criteria
Blind	1.1.1
	1.2.1, 1.2.3, 1.2.5, 1.2.7, 1.2.8
	1.3.1, 1.3.2
	1.4.4, 1.4.5, 1.4.9
	2.1.1, 2.1.2, 2.1.3
	2.2.2
	2.4.1, 2.4.2, 2.4.3, 2.4.4, 2.4.7, 2.4.9, 2.4.10
	3.1.1,3.1.2
	3.2.1, 3.2.5
	3.3.1, 3.3.2, 3.3.3
	4.1.1, 4.1.2
Low-vision	1.1.1
	1.3.1, 1.3.2
	1.4.1, 1.4.3, 1.4.6
	2.1.1, 2.1.3
	2.2.2, 2.2.4
	2.4.1, 2.4.10
	3.1.1, 3.1.2
	3.2.1, 3.2.5
	3.3.3
	4.1.1
Colour-blind	1.4.1, 1.4.3, 1.4.6

HTML file, in which each state is triggered by user actions, i.e. new content is presented according to which button a user presses.

We have assessed the applications using the proposed platform at three phases of delivery: (a) before browser processing, as it would be done by traditional evaluators; (b) after browser processing and before the adaptation, considering the whole set of states of the application, to assess the intrinsic quality of the application; and (c) after the adaptation, considering two user profiles. The resulting evaluation, in EARL format, was subsequently analysed. Also the application, as perceived by users before and after the adaptation, was inspected by experts.

13.4.1 Results

13.4.1.1 Before Browser Processing

As a baseline for our experiment, we conducted a pre browser processing evaluation of the accessibility of three TV applications: the EPG, Home Automation (HA) Fig. 13.2 and Video Conferencing (VC), Fig. 13.3. In terms of the number of

Table 13.5 Mapping between the WCAG success criteria (SC) and the WCAG techniques

WCAG 2.0 SC	Techniques
1.1.1	H44, H65, h67, c9, H36, H2, H37, H35, H53, H24, H86, H30, H45, h46, C18
1.2.3	H53
1.2.8	H55, H46
1.2.9	
1.3.1	H51, H39, H63, H43, H44, H65, H71, H85, H48, H42, C22
1.3.2	H34, H56, C6, c8,c27
1.4.1	H92, c15
1.4.4	C28, c12, C13, C14, C17, C20, C22
1.4.5	C22, C30, C12, C13, c14, C8, C6
1.4.8	C23, C25, H87, C20, C19, C21, C26
1.4.9	C22, C30, C12, C13, C14, C8, C6
2.2.1	H91
2.4.1	H69, H50, H70, C6
2.4.2	H25
2.4.3	H4, c27
2.4.4	H30, H24, H33, C7, H77, H78, H79, H80, H81, H2
2.4.5	H59
2.4.7	H15
2.4.8	H59
2.4.9	H30, H24, C7, H2, H33
3.1.1	H57
3.1.2	H58
3.1.3	H40, H60, H54
3.1.4	H28, H60, H28
3.1.6	H62
3.2.2	H32, H84
3.2.3	H76, H87
3.2.5	H76, H87
3.3.1	
3.3.2	H90, H44, H71, H65
3.3.5	H89
4.1.1	H88, H74, H75
4.1.2	H91, H44, H64, H65, H88

elements found, the analysis shows that in average the applications have 54 elements. As can be seen on Fig. 13.4, the applications have few Pass results (3 each), some Fails (15 for the EPG, 1 for HA and 3 for VC), and high Warning numbers, with an average of 17. The next step was performing the evaluation on the same three applications, but this time performing it after browser processing and considering all the application states. The following section presents the results.

Table 13.6 Implemented techniques

WCAG 2.0 HTML techniques	WCAG 2.0 CSS techniques
h2, h24, h25, h27, h30, h32, h33, h35, h36, h37, h39, h43, h44, h46, h53, h57, h63, h64, h65, h67, h71, h73, h76, h81, h83, h89, h93	c6, c7, c8, c9, c12, c13, c14, c15, c17, c18, c19, c20, c21, c22, c23, c24, c25, c26, c28

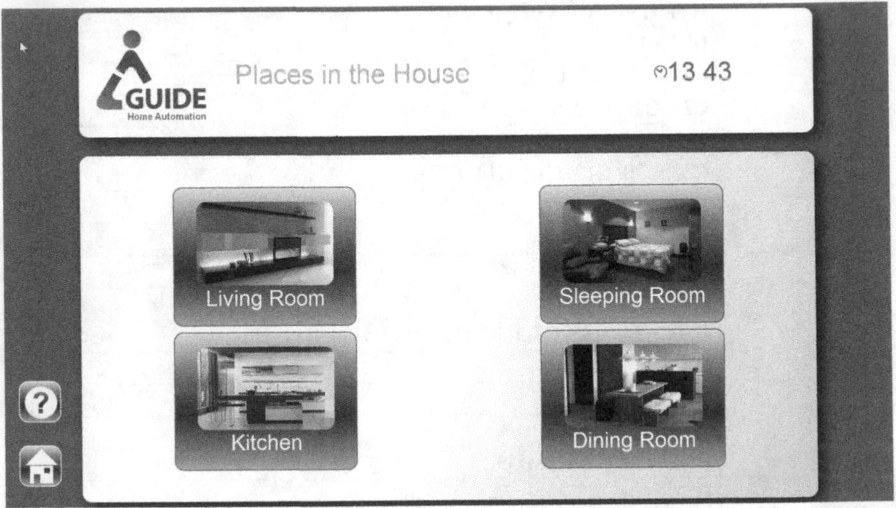

Fig. 13.2 Home automation application screen

13.4.1.2 The Dynamical Application Evaluation

In this case we recorded an average increase of the number of elements of about 455 %, meaning an average of 300 elements. This is explained by two arguments: (1) after processing, the scripts are loaded and new elements are injected; and (2) the Interaction Simulator detects a large number of new states as it triggers Javascript functions attached to the many interactive elements of the applications. In [16] is stated that the framework can find an average of 5 different states per application.

Regarding the results presented on Fig. 13.5, we can now see a big difference in the numbers when comparing with the previous evaluation.

The Pass results have increased much more relatively to Fails and Warnings in this evaluation, confirming that a post processing evaluation is more adequate when evaluating the accessibility of a Web based application.

13.4.1.3 Evaluation of the Adapted Applications

Finally, we performed the evaluation taking in account the user profile of the adaptation. Thus the Interaction Simulator has requested a profile to the adaptation engine and only a subset of the accessibility techniques was used on the evaluation process.

Fig. 13.3 Video conference application screen

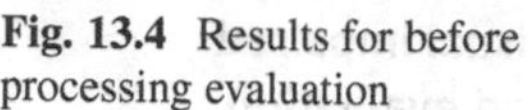

Fig. 13.4 Results for before processing evaluation

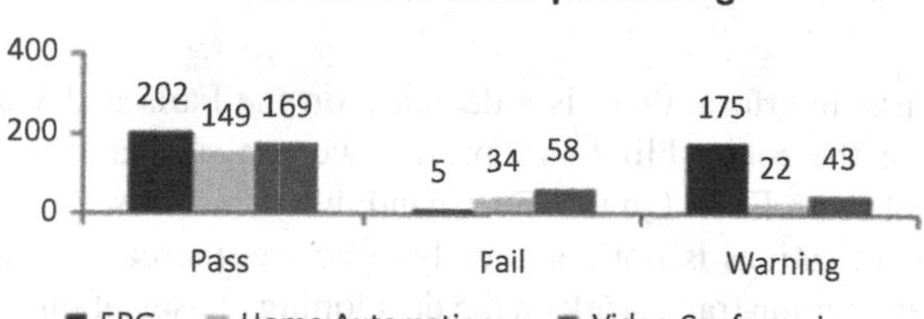

Fig. 13.5 Results of the evaluation after browser processing

Two different user profiles were used, based on real data gathered on user trials conducted by the GUIDE project. The first case accounts a user that has Tritanopia, a specific type of colour blindness. In this case the adaptation engine of GUIDE will render the application taking into account the user's problem, adapting the colour scheme (see Fig. 13.6). The second User Model represents a user that has some visual acuity problems, meaning some adjustments on font size are needed.

The results, depicted on Fig. 13.7, clearly show that when we choose the appropriate techniques for a specific user profile and the corresponding adapted

Fig. 13.6 EPG adapted for a user with visual impairments

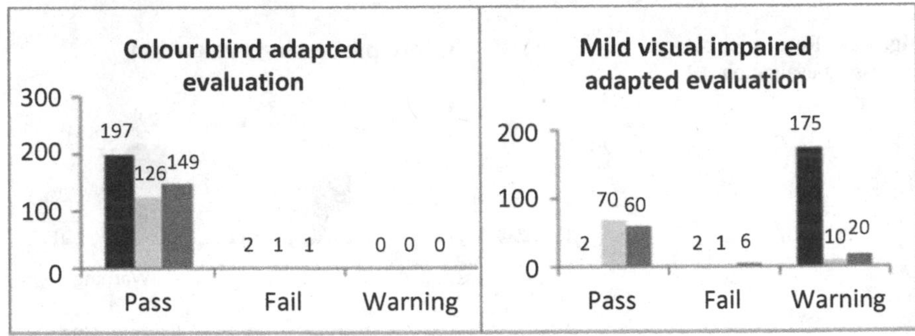

Fig. 13.7 Evaluation results of the adapted versions

user interface, there is a decrease on the Fails and Warnings scores. For instance, for the colour blind user profile, we can state a 100 % decrease on Warnings and 44 % on Fails. On the other hand, we can also see that the adaptation made on the applications is not completely effective, increasing the potential of this proposed evaluation framework on the developing phases of this kind of adaptive frameworks, aiding on perfecting the adaptation engines.

13.4.1.4 The Expert Analysis

As mentioned before, we made an expert analysis on the three TV based applications. For each application three versions were inspected: the standard version, a version with the interface adapted for color blind persons and a version adapted for users with moderate visual impairments. The expert analysis reported that the structure of the applications was consistent, with clear separation between page sections and consistent location of scene objects. The layout supports enlargement of screen fonts. The version adapted for colour blind users provides a high contrast alternative, although the initial version was already suitable for most types of colour blindness. The version adapted to visual impaired users offers bigger font size. However, not all the text was increased (only the actionable items), which means moderately impaired users might still have to resort to increasing the font size themselves.

Finally, a comparison between the expert analysis and the results obtained via automated evaluation points out that in general the reports are similar regarding the failures, passes, and warnings.

13.4.1.5 Discussion

The results demonstrated the differences between the three phases of delivery. It was possible to confirm the inadequacy of pre browser processing evaluation and to notice the differences between the pre and post adaptation versions. The analysis of the EARL and inspection of the applications showed the correctness, yet incompleteness, of the automatic evaluation process and confirmed the need to select the adequate techniques to be applied before and after the adaptation. The experiment also raised a couple of interesting issues on the adaptation itself. In particular it showed some caveats on the adaptation models, by detecting issues on the adapted versions of the UI that should be handled by the engine. That led to the refinement of those models and the engine parameters.

13.4.2 Limitations

Our experiment has faced some limitations on the type of results that can be extrapolated, including:

- *Techniques coverage:* we used the 27 HTML and 19 CSS WCAG 2.0 implemented techniques on QualWeb, as well as 6 from Digital TV Guidelines not considered on the CSS techniques;
- *Automated evaluation:* since this experiment is centred on automated evaluation of Web accessibility quality, it shares all of the inherent pitfalls.

13.5 Conclusion and Future Work

This work provides a solution for automatic evaluation of Web TV applications. It considers the dynamic aspects of these applications and is able to cope with reformulations and refinements of standard accessibility guidelines, as well as the integration of new ones. Besides, it offers the flexibility of filtering the guidelines to be applied thus coping with the adaptation process proposed by some accessibility TV platforms. The experiment provided an initial evaluation of the approach and highlighted the need for the rationalization of techniques on different rendering contexts of the adaptation process. Besides the tool itself, and the approach it underlies, this paper's contribution is the proposed conceptual framework for the evaluation of Web TV applications that are delivered through and adaptive accessible framework.

Ongoing work is being conducted in the following directions: (1) implementation of more techniques; (2) testing with more applications.

Acknowledgements This work was funded by Fundação para a Ciência e Tecnologia (FCT) through the QualWeb national research project PTDC/EIA-EIA/105079/2008, the Multiannual Funding Programme, and POSC/EU; and by GUIDE Project – the European Union's Seventh Framework Programme (FP7/2007-2013) under grant agreement no 24889.

References

1. Abascal, J., Aizpurua, A., Cearreta, I., Gamecho, B., Garay-Vitoria, N., & Miñón, R. (2011). Automatically generating tailored accessible user interfaces for ubiquitous services. In *The proceedings of the 13th international ACM SIGACCESS conference on computers and accessibility (ASSETS '11)* (pp. 187–194). New York: ACM.
2. Abou-Zahra, S. (2006, March). *Complete list of web accessibility evaluation tools*. From: http://www.w3.org/WAI/ER/tools/complete.
3. Abou-Zahra, S. (2010). *WAI: Strategies, guidelines, resources to make the web accessibly to people with disabilities – Conformance evaluation of web sites for accessibility*. From: http://www.w3.org/WAI/eval/conformance.html.
4. Abou-Zahra, S., & Squillace, M. (2009). *Evaluation and report language (EARL) 1.0 Schema (W3C)*. From: http://www.w3.org/TR/2009/WD-EARL10-Schema-20091029/.
5. *ACCESSIBLE – Applications design and development*. (2010). From: http://www.accessible-eu.org/.
6. BBC. *BBC – Future media standards and guidelines – Global visual language v2.0*. From: http://www.bbc.co.uk/guidelines/futuremedia/desed/visual_language.shtml.
7. Bhattacharya, P., & Neamtiu I. (2010). Dynamic updates for web and cloud applications. In *Proceedings of the 2010 workshop on APLWACA*, Toronto.
8. Brajnik, G. (2009, March). *Barrier walkthrough*. From: http://sole.dimi.uniud.it/~giorgio.brajnik/projects/bw/bw.html.
9. Caldwell, B., Cooper, M., Reid, L., Vanderheiden, G. (2008). *Web content accessibility guidelines 2.0* (W3C Note, December 2008). From http://www.w3.org/TR/WCAG20/.
10. Chalkia, E., et al. (2009, September). *HAM accessible harmonized methodology* (Technical report, ACCESSIBLE, Grant Agreement No 224145).
11. Cooper, M., Loretta Guarino Reid, G., Vanderheiden, G., & Caldwell, B. (2010, October). *Techniques for WCAG 2.0 – Techniques and failures for web content accessibility guidelines 2.0* (W3C Note, October 2010), From: http://www.w3.org/TR/WCAG-TECHS/.
12. Costa, D., & Duarte, C. (2012). Adapting TV based applications? User interface. In *IADIS international conference interfaces and human computer interaction 2012*, Lisbon.
13. Duarte, C., Coelho, J., Feiteira, P., Costa, D., & Costa, D. F. (2011). Eliciting interaction requirements for adaptive multimodal TV based applications. In *Proceedings of the 14th HCII*, Orlando.

14. Dumas, B., Lalanne, D., & Oviatt, S. (2009). *Multimodal interfaces: A survey of principles, models and frameworks*. In D. Lalanne & J. Kohlas (Eds.), *Human machine interaction* (pp. 3–26). Berlin/Heidelberg: Springer.
15. Fernandes, N., Lopes, R., & Carriço, L. (2011). On web accessibility evaluation environments. In *Proceedings of the W4A 2011*. New York: ACM.
16. Fernandes, N., Costa, D., Duarte, C., & Carriço, L. (2012, April). Evaluating the accessibility of rich internet applications. In *Proceedings of the W4A 2012*, Lyon. New York: ACM.
17. Fuertes, J., González, R., Gutiérrez, E., & Martínez, L. (2009). Hera-FFX: A firefox add-on for semi-automatic web accessibility evaluation. In *Proceedings of the W4A 2009*, Madrid. New York: ACM. From: http://foxability.sourceforge.net/.
18. Google. (2011). *Google designing for TV*. https://developers.google.com/tv/web/docs/design_for_tv.
19. *GUIDE Project*. (2012). From: http://www.guide-project.eu/.
20. Harper, S., & Yesilada, Y. (2008). *Web accessibility*. London: Springer.
21. *Hybrid Broadcast Broadband TV*. (2012). From: http://www.hbbtv.org/pages/about_hbbtv/introduction.php.
22. Jung, C., & Hahn, V. (2011). GUIDE – Adaptive user interfaces for accessible hybrid TV applications. In *Second W3C Workshop Web & TV*, Berlin.
23. Mesbah, A., & van Deursen, A. (2009). Invariant-based automatic testing of ajax user interfaces. In *Proceedings of the ICSE 2009*. Washington, DC: IEEE Computer Society. From: doi:http://dx.doi.org/10.1109/ICSE.2009.5070522.
24. Rousseau, C., Bellik, Y., Vernier, F., & Bazalgette, D. (2006). A framework for the intelligent multimodal presentation of information. *Signal Processing, 86*(12), 3696–3713. Special section: Multimodal human-computer interfaces.
25. Seppä, J., Friman, T., Koljonen, J., Ruokoja, K., & Nupponen, S. (2008). *Foxability – Accessibility analyzing extension for firefox*. From: http://foxability.sourceforge.net/.
26. *Universal Design Guidelines for Digital Television Equipment and Services Draft for Public Consultation, Centre for Excellence in Universal Design*. (2011, November). From: http://www.universaldesign.ie/digitaltv.
27. WebAIM. (2009). *WAVE – Web accessibility evaluation tool*. From: http://wave.webaim.org/toolbar/.
28. Webkit. (2011). *The webkit open source project*. From: http://www.webkit.org/.

Chapter 14
Television Accessibility in China

Dongxiao Li and Peter Olaf Looms

Abstract This chapter addresses the strategic options for making television accessible in China. As a national case, it highlights the need to understand the social, cultural, market and political contexts in which such changes happen.

In terms of audience size, China is the largest television market in the world. For much of the rural population, TV is still the most widely-used medium, although the expansion of mobile and broadband Internet in urban areas in eastern China is changing the way television content is delivered and used.

The first section outlines the main changes in the provision of television content in China. The underlying business models for content provision are being transformed by the ascendance of mobile and Internet distribution. There is a need for policies to focus on content provision on multiple distribution platforms rather than focusing narrowly on broadcasting.

The second section addresses the case for providing accessible television content in China. It summarises recent research into the prevalence of various disabilities in China.

The third section discusses the strategic options available to China in the medium to long term to ensure that television is truly accessible to the whole population.

14.1 Introduction

Television is an integral part of the lives of most people on our planet. In China, it appeared on a regular basis in 1958. For the second half of the twentieth century, the main challenge was to make TV universally 'available'. This has now been joined by the challenge of making it 'accessible' or 'inclusive' – the nature of the accessibility challenge and the options available in China to make this a reality.

D. Li (✉)
College of Media and International Culture, Zhejiang University, Hangzhou, China
e-mail: 80295230@qq.com

P.O. Looms
ECOM-ICOM Programme, University of Hong Kong, Hong Kong SAR, China
e-mail: polooms@gmail.com

P. Biswas et al. (eds.), *A Multimodal End-2-End Approach to Accessible Computing*, Human–Computer Interaction Series, DOI 10.1007/978-1-4471-6708-2_14

But before discussing television accessibility, it is necessary to scope the term 'television' – which connotations of the term do we need to address?

Television is often associated with technologies for distributing programmes and channels. Frieden [1] argues that television is evolving from 'a channel based, medium specific process to a platform capable of accessing all kinds of content stored somewhere within the Internet cloud'. In this chapter, we choose to include both traditional broadcast platforms for distributing television programmes and platform using Internet and mobile networks. Our focus is on the content.

Television is, however, more than just a platform. Television in the sense of content provision requires an understanding of context. Lathan [2] makes some useful suggestions: 'In thinking about television as a feature of contemporary popular culture, it is important to consider television not simply as a collection of channels and programs but as ... a range of things that people do and talk about. /.../ We have to consider not just what is watched but how it is watched and by whom.' Yong et al. [3] and Hanging [4] are two sources that address television from a number of user perspectives including the demographics of television audiences. We feel that an understanding of television use and television users is within the scope of this chapter.

Television can be viewed from a market perspective. Reports by Istituto nazionale per il Commercio Estero [5], Twiddle [6], Zhu and Berry [7] and the introduction of a master's thesis by Hanging [4 op. cit.] all provide insights on how the provision of television content is changing in China. As the authors of the Italian study point out: "... conducting market research in China is different and significantly more challenging than it is in developed countries because of (1) the size and diversity of the country; (2) [the] lack of fully reliable centralized/official information databases; (3) change is constant and extremely rapid ...". Given the relatively recent emergence of independent television audience research in China discussed in detail in page 176 of Zhu and Berry [7 op. cit] we use an eclectic approach, drawing on multiple sources to make inferences on key trends in the television market, including the business models for television content provision.

Brahima [8] provides the societal and political context for the shift in focus from merely providing television to making it accessible: "Television is important for enhancing national identity, providing an outlet for domestic media content and informing the public about news and information, which is especially critical in times of emergencies. Television programmes are also a principal source of news and information for illiterate segments of the population, many of whom are persons with disabilities. In addition, broadcasting can serve important educational purposes, by transmitting courses and other instructional material.

While the availability of broadcasting in terms of coverage is nearly complete, with practically the whole planet covered by a signal, and with televisions in over 1.4 billion households around the world, representing 98 % of households in developed countries and nearly 73 % of households in developing countries, the question now is how to make this widely available ICT accessible for persons with disabilities."

As the Peoples Republic of China is a signatory of the UN Convention on the Rights of Persons with Disabilities (CRPD), there is a good case to look at the progress being made in China in relation to Article 9 of CRPD, This deals specifically with the accessibility of information and communications technologies (ICTs).

A prerequisite for television accessibility is a shared understanding of some of the core concepts and processes. In everyday language we talk about 'access to television', being 'inclusive' and 'barrier-free media' (无障碍传播), but the connotations of these terms vary from one person to the next. In part two of this chapter, we aim to clarify the scope of the key concepts by addressing four key questions:

- What is meant by 'disability' – and how does it relate to TV accessibility?
- What is the conceptual relationship between TV availability, usability, and accessibility – and where does digital literacy fit in?
- To what extent do existing approaches deliver results when it comes to accessible TV?
- Which key components are missing in order to make TV accessible in China?

In the final part of this chapter the aim is to outline the strategic options available to China in the medium to long term to enhance the accessibility of television content.

14.2 Television in China

Many westerners may be unfamiliar with television in China. Coonan [9] graphically makes the point that China is the world's largest television market measured by audience size: "Some 814 million tuned in to the China's Lunar New Year TV extravaganza this year [2014], with 704 million welcoming the Year of the Horse on TV and 110 million tuning in online, according to data from state broadcaster China Central Television (CCTV). The 2014 Super Bowl, by comparison, became the most watched program in U.S. TV history on Sunday, with 111.5 million viewers". Fifty two percent of the Chinese population saw this CCTV gala show on a TV set while 8 % saw it on their smartphone, tablet or computer. The figures support our contention to look at multiple platforms for delivering television content rather than focusing exclusively on broadcast television. New distribution channels for television content such as Internet Protocol Television (IPTV) and streaming services on mobiles and computers continue to erode the positions held by digital terrestrial television broadcasting, cable and satellite TV.

Television began in China in September, 1958. Initially there was one channel provided by China Central Television (CCTV), the state-run national television broadcaster. Since then, there have been considerable changes in the supply of television content:

- CCTV has increased its output to domestic audiences – both the number of channels and programmes.

- CCTV is no longer the only broadcaster. Within 2 years of its launch, CCTV was joined by regional broadcasters and there are now some 700 television stations offering more than 3,000 TV channels in China.
- Television has evolved from national television in Mandarin to broadcasters operating at national, regional, local and city level and offering programming in a number of regional languages as well as Mandarin.
- The availability of television receivers has grown from 1958 onwards and stabilized about 10 years ago, rural China lagging behind the more affluent urban areas in the east of the country. In rural China television viewing was initially a communal activity. As rural household ownership of TV sets began to converge with urban ownership, viewing patterns increasingly resemble those in cities and the coastal part of the country in the east.
- The shift to a market-oriented model for television in China has been accompanied by a shift from state funding to a mixture of advertising and government funding.
- Conventional distribution (broadcasting via terrestrial, cable or satellite networks) now has to coexist with IPTV, Integrated Broadcast Broadband (IBB) supported by Chinese organisations involved in standardization [10], or streaming services on mobiles and computers. The use of Video On Demand (VOD) services such as YouKu, Tudou, PPTV or Sohu that are funded by advertising is accelerating. In China. The 450 million VOD users are predominantly young adults living in first- and second-tier cities in the eastern part of the country according to The Economist [11] and Ericsson [12]. Young adults are more likely to access 'must-see' content on a laptop or tablet. In some cases, this is television-like content available online only. Examples include 女神办公室 ['The Goddess Office'] that launched on the online video service PPTV in China in 2013 and the Netflix remake of BBC's 'House of Cards'. Ma [13] describes the impact this series is having in China and notes the regulatory overlaps when screening non-Chinese content delivered via the Internet.
- 'Second-screen' viewing is on the increase in China. Dayasena-Lowe, M [14] reports on 'Connected Life', a study of over 55,000 Internet users worldwide. In the study, the audience research company TNS found that almost half of people (48 %) who watch TV in the evening simultaneously engage in other digital activities. These 'second-screen' activities are not necessarily related to viewing on the main screen. TNS noted that one quarter (25 %) of those surveyed worldwide watch content on a PC, laptop, tablet or mobile daily. This proportion is one third (33 %) in mainland China. The TNS survey found that viewers own about four digital devices each. The demand for live and on-the-go content increased during the FIFA World Cup in 2014. Viewers worldwide were accessing this international sporting event via multiple devices at home and on the move, while also engaging in conversations about specific matches on social media platforms.
- The use of multiple screens to view and discuss television-like content has required changes in the way in which quantitative audience research is conducted to meet the interests and needs of advertisers, broadcasters and platform

operators. Nielsen [15] discusses some of these challenges in its annual report for media in Asia. In July 2013, the culture media data consulting service Zemedia released "Chinese TV ratings and rankings for all television platforms (January–June 2013)" [16], collating ratings from network audience metering, TV show searches on Baidu, Google and VOD data Youku, Todou, Sohu, Tencent video and other video sites. Around the same time, Nielsen [17] launched a three-screen audience research pilot. The pilot project uses a people meter developed by the Chinese joint venture CR-Nielsen. Homes for the study are primarily recruited from the Shanghai TAM database.

- The transition from analogue to digital broadcasting has already begun. Analogue switch-off for cable systems is foreseen in 2015–2018.

The key points to carry forward to television accessibility strategy are

- Multiple distribution platforms for television content (not just broadcast networks but also broadband and mobile Internet to TV sets, computers, tablets and mobile phones).
- The differences in household income in rural and urban China
- The differences in the availability of broadcast, broadband and mobile Internet networks in rural and urban areas; and
- The importance of reliable audience measurement systems that can underpin revenue streams from advertising to those producing and delivering content.

14.3 The Case for Providing Accessible Television Content in China

In the section on television, we touched obliquely on accessibility. In this section, the aim is to address three questions:

(A) What is the scope of television accessibility?
(B) What are the options for making television accessible in China?
(C) What are the arguments for making television accessible?

(A) *What is the scope of television accessibility?*

Li and Looms [18] contains a detailed review of the history of the central terms associated with media accessibility. In the paper we noted that "Choosing the right words is often crucial. The United Nations Convention on the Rights of Persons with Disabilities (UN CRPD) uses the term 'disability', although NGOs representing such individuals prefer not to use terms such as 'handicap' or 'disability'. Different stakeholders in this field have very different, sometimes conflicting views on the subject. If we are to make progress on media accessibility, some clarification of terms and their connotations is needed".

Li [19] reports official statistics that quantify disabilities in China: there are 13 million visually-impaired persons in China (0.1 % of total population) and

27.8 million persons (2.1 %) with serious hearing impairments. Expressed as a percentage of the population, the numbers are somewhat lower than in many western countries. Mellors [20] in a paper on disability statistics suggests that variations from one country to another are often due to different criteria as to what constitutes a recognised disability. The UN note that "due to differences in the concepts and methods used to identify persons with disabilities, prevalence rates should not be compared across countries." UN [21].

The key take-away here is caution when deciding on target groups for television accessibility. The nature and size of the accessibility challenge will depend on the definitions used to define which users we are talking about. In China, removing the barriers facing persons who are deaf and blind clearly have a high priority. What needs to be resolved are the priorities for other groups of persons with disabilities – which groups should be addressed and in what order?

(B) *What are the options for making television accessible in China?*

Watching TV consists of a number of 'tasks' or activities. These tasks typically include the following five:

- *Getting started* – setting-up the TV receiver
- *Discovering content* and the related access services – what is on offer, finding something to watch
- *Selecting content* – choosing something to watch
- *Using content* – watching a programme, spot, trailer and the programme guide.
- *Fulfilment* – enjoying, talking about or learning from the content (and achieving some of the explicit or implicit aims the viewer has, such as participation, keeping up to date or just killing time).

The capabilities of the TV viewer influence the use of the television service and the tasks that each viewer can carry out. Viewing fulfilment – whether the experience is satisfying – depends on the interplay of user capabilities (for example the nature of the viewer's disablements), the content and access services available, and the demands made of the viewer when carrying out tasks to do with watching TV. Environmental factors (for example the availability of electricity and network coverage) also influence all three.

Accessibility is a general term used to describe the degree to which a product, device, service, or environment is available to as many people as possible. Accessibility can be viewed as the "ability to access" and benefit from some system or entity, discussed in more detail in the terminology section of Looms [22].

According to the ISO 9241 family of standards, usability is "extent to which a product can be used by specified users to achieve specified goals effectively, efficiently and with satisfaction in a specified context of use". Bevan [23] offers a critical overview of ISO 9241. In addition to 'quality in use' (to usability as product use in specified contexts) he covers 'product quality' (interface and interaction), 'process quality' (used-centred development processes) and 'organizational capability' (addressing usability issues throughout the lifecycle processes of the product) (Fig. 14.1).

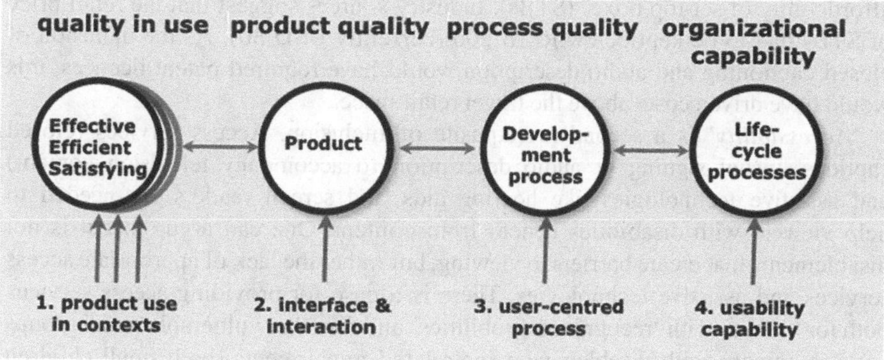

Fig. 14.1 Usability (Based on Bevan [23])

Fig. 14.2 The inclusion pyramid for television

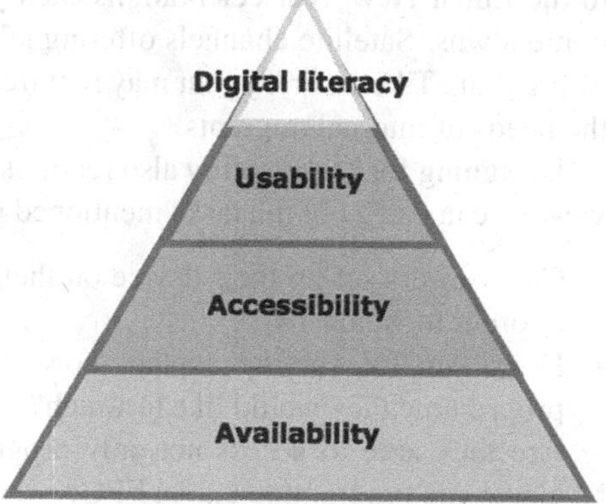

If we combine perspectives from the literature, keeping in mind the aim of inclusion, the accessibility and usability can be organized hierarchically as is shown in Fig. 14.2:

How are these four concepts related?

'*Availability*' is the foundation of the inclusion pyramid. It covers prerequisites for accessing media – economic and technological. In the case of China, there are significant differences in the availability and affordability of media such as TV and the Internet in first-tier cities in the east of the country and in the west of China which is still predominantly rural. The lack of electricity and network coverage are two instances of availability barriers.

Household income – 'affordability' – is a prerequisite of availability. There are still significant differences in the household ownership of television sets in rural and urban China. Household incomes have increased steadily over the last two decades, but mean incomes are often three times higher in the east than in the west of the country. One of the reasons for not including the capability to offer closed captions or audio description in China's digital television standard, China Multimedia Mobile Broadcasting (CMMB) 10 years ago was a concern about the affordability of set-top boxes (STBs). Industry sources suggest that the retail price of STBs had to be kept below RMB 200 (currently USD 30). As the inclusion of closed captioning and audio description would have required patent licences, this would have driven costs above the target retail price.

'*Accessibility*' is a second prerequisite of inclusion. Access services (closed captions, visual signing or audio description to accompany television content) and assistive technologies like hearing aids and screen readers are needed to help viewers with disabilities benefit from content. One can argue that it is not disablements that create barriers to viewing, but rather the lack of appropriate access services and assistive technologies. There is a case for providing access services both for viewers with 'recognized disabilities' and for other vulnerable social groups such as persons with disablements: age-related impairments (both small children and older viewers), migrants, immigrants and refugees. Internal migration within China is thought to exceed 10 % of the population, as can be seen in the run-up to the Lunar New Year celebrations each year when many Chinese return to their home towns. Satellite channels offering television channels in Cantonese, Kazakh, Mongolian, Tibetan or Uyghur may require subtitles in Mandarin in order to address the needs of internal migrants.

Designing for accessibility also requires awareness of viewer capability, whether viewers can carry out the tasks mentioned previously:

- Can viewers set-up their device on their own or through some help mechanism in order to watch TV?
- Does the TV service explain how they can find the access service for a programme they would like to watch?
- Are they able to access not only programmes, but also spots, trailers and the electronic programme guide, EPG?

For viewers with hearing disabilities, clear, intelligible sound may not only be the consequence of the way in which audio is handled during production and distribution but also of the environment in which viewing takes place (which includes the layout and acoustics of the room). Vlaming [24] notes that hearing disabilities frequently lead to a reduced ability to discriminate speech from background noise and competing speech sources. The use of wireless connections to hearing aids allows the direct transmission of audio information (speech, music, alarms, etc.) from the source to the ear, rather than using the built-in microphone of a hearing aid. This reduces the level of disturbing background noise and competing sources, thus improving the capability to understand speech for users with hearing disablements.

'*Usability*' in the context of television is often associated with *the attributes of the content itself*: the intelligibility of the audio and the legibility of titles, on-screen text and subtitles. Broadcasters such as the BBC encourage internal and external production teams to think about these issues and provide guidelines and examples of good practice introduced by Cohen [25].

If we apply Bevin's ontology mentioned earlier when discussing the ISO definition, usability also applies to the television *interface* – how theviewer carries out the various TV viewing tasks effectively, efficiently and to his or her satisfaction. In terms of the efficiency and effectiveness of viewer action we can paraphrase the earlier questions to assess the interface itself:

- How easily and quickly can the viewer set-up the device on his own or with the aid of somebody else in order to watch TV?
- Can the viewer easily and quickly find the access service for a programme he or she would like to watch?
- How easily and quickly can the viewer select and watch programmes, but also spots, trailers and the electronic programme guide, EPG?

'*Digital literacy*' is at the top of the inclusion pyramid. Literacy and numeracy were the central competencies in the nineteenth and twentieth centuries, joined in the twenty-first century by digital literacy (also termed 'information and media literacy' by UNESCO). "Knowledge about how to do things, how to communicate, and how to work with other people has therefore been regarded, since ancient times, as the most precious 'wealth' that humans possess," according to Moeller et al. [26]. Literacy levels in China are high and increasing, but digital literacy is less well-developed among certain demographic groups, particularly the elder part of the population.

The key take-aways here are that accessible, or barrier-free television can be interpreted in a formal sense or more broadly in line with the spirit of the UN CRPD. Using the accessibility pyramid can help clarify the accessibility options and their economic implications.

As a minimum, there should be the provision of captioning, subtitles for programmes for languages other than Mandarin and some experimentation with audio description, building on experience gained in Taiwan and Hong Kong.

(C) *What are the arguments for making television accessible?*

Putting together a compelling case for action is often the first step to make television accessible.

A recent case was the introduction in 2012 of spoken subtitles in Denmark, an access service that allows the viewer to hear subtitles for TV programmes in a foreign language read aloud in their own language. One of the first steps was to prepare estimates of the likely impact of this service would have. About 10–12 % of the adult population cannot read the Danish language subtitles and do not benefit fully from viewing such programmes in foreign languages. Those excluded are persons who:

- Are blind or have serious visual impairments (1.4 %)
- Have cognitive impairments including dyslexia (0.12 %)
- Have moderate visual impairments including myopia (5.5 %)
- Are weak readers (5.5 %)
- Are immigrants or refugees and are thus not native speakers of Danish (9.6 %)

This case highlights the implications of pivoting, looking at the impact that the service will have rather than starting with the problems of audiences with specific disabilities. Changing the focus from disability to accessibility alters the perspective. Decision-makers are required to think about how to help multiple target groups with the same initiative. Addressing the needs of multiple target groups often strengthens the case for action, as the total number of potential beneficiaries increases, in the case of spoken subtitles from 1.4 % to somewhere nearer 10–12 %.

The case for accessible television is rarely based on commercial imperatives. Discussions with decision-makers in television since 2011 indicate that the main drivers are *regulatory pressure* (the threat of sanctions for not complying with national legislation or regulations on TV accessibility) and *improved image* (the corporate social responsibility of the broadcaster or content provider offering accessible content).

The example of spoken subtitles in Denmark shows that offering access services has the potential of improving the viewing experience. Our current hypothesis is that offering access services improves viewer satisfaction ratings. For content providers, increased satisfaction can lead to improved loyalty and lower churn figures.

When presenting the case for accessible television, it will be necessary to look at the costs and benefits. Broadcasters and VOD companies often have concerns about the capital and operational costs of providing access services. For national broadcasters, offering closed captioning and audio description along with sign language of selected programmes will rarely increase production costs by more than 1 %.

Making the case for accessible television can be summed up under three headings: establishing a clear consensus on television accessibility as a frame of mind, assessing the options for making television accessible and presenting a compelling and honest case for making television accessible. If the case is presented well, it will usually be possible to get the necessary buy-in from the key stakeholders in television.

14.4 The Strategic Options for Television Accessibility in China

Li [19 op. cit.] provides a wealth of detail on the current situation on television accessibility in China. Persons with hearing impairments are quite well served at national level with open captions/subtitles with the exception of live content such as news. Sign language interpretation is available to a more limited extent, mainly at local and regional level. Audio description is not as widespread as it is in Taiwan and Hong Kong.

When digital television was introduced in China almost a decade ago, there were legitimate concerns about both availability and affordability, especially for those living in rural China. To keep the cost of a digital set-top box (STB) as low as possible, the technical capabilities required to offer closed captioning/subtitles and audio description were removed from the specification.

In the meantime, the cost of television receivers, computers and tablets has come down fast. Today it would be feasible to make a STB with access service provisions that could retail for as little as RMB 200. The challenge is the considerable installed base of devices built to the original specification that cannot handle things like closed captioning/subtitles and audio description. Updating the specification is possible and China has all the necessary technical expertise to do this and to build digital TV receivers that can handle access services, as Chinese manufacturers already produce comparable devices for various export markets.

The Chinese media industry itself is undergoing rapid transformation. Yong et al. [3 op. cit] noted that "as of December 2011, there were 513 million internet users, 155 million broadband subscribers, and over 1 billion mobile phone users in China. At the same time, the Internet is still beyond the reach of 800 million Chinese who rely almost exclusively on television for their information and entertainment, in particular the mammoth state broadcaster China Central Television (CCTV). But a sign of the profound changes taking place is that this year (2012) the time people spend on the internet is set to overtake that which they spend watching television."

In first-tier cities, the availability of broadband Internet means that young adults in particular choose to watch TV and video on their laptops, tablets and phones rather than using broadcast. In second and third-tier cities and rural China, good quality broadband is less common. iResearch [27] reports that watching video accounts for about one-third of effective Internet consumption and this share is increasing. Laptops are the dominant devices but their share of total online video consumption is being eroded by smartphones and computer tablets.

Broadcast media and the business models that sustain them are under pressure from the convenience and choice of Internet distribution. Content choice is also a driver. SARFT, the film and broadcasting regulator in China, currently makes more use of self-regulation for online video while focusing its attention on broadcast media. One of the results is that the content available online is more in tune with the interests of young viewers than the heavily regulated content available on broadcast television. As online video continues to grow, the regulation of Internet content may well change.

Given these developments in content and its regulation, there seem to be three main strategic options for enhancing audio-visual media accessibility in China:

(A) Increasing the provision of access services such as closed captioning/subtitles, audio description and sign language interpretation on TV programmes both at national and regional level.
(B) Increasing the provision of open captioning/subtitles, audio description and sign language interpretation for online video on the Internet in China.
(C) Delivering access services via the Internet to homes that have both a broadcast and an Internet connection and a TV receiver that can handle both.

These three options are not mutually exclusive. If China plans to maintain its progress on media accessibility and comply with the requirements of the UN CRPD, a realistic scenario could be as follows:

Short Term (2015–2018)

- Set up a media industry forum to enhance digital broadcast standards in China to allow for the delivery of closed captioning/subtitles and audio description (A)
- Agree metrics and objectives for a national awareness campaign to promote the use of access services (A, B, C)
- Introduce requirements for open captioning/subtitles for online video and television to make content accessible in areas with good broadband services (B)
- Set up a media industry forum in China to agree standards for integrated broadcast/broadband (IBB) delivery of audio-visual content and access services similar to the HBBTV forum in Europe and the HybridCast forum in Japan (C).

Medium to Long Term (2018–2025)

- Conduct a regional pilot project on digital terrestrial television using the enhanced broadcast standards to introduce closed captioning/subtitles and audio description for Chinese viewers in areas where Internet delivery is not realistic (A)
- Use the results of the regional pilot project to make digital terrestrial television accessible in the whole of China, increasing the access service targets to their final levels over a period of 5–10 years (A)
- In first-tier cities roll out closed captioning, audio description and closed sign language interpretation on the hybrid, IBB platform over a 5–10 year period to allow broadcasters and online video companies time to make the necessary investments in technical infrastructure and human resources (C)

"Where there is a will, there is a way". Over the last three decades China has made outstanding achievements in fighting poverty and investing in infrastructure projects that benefit the whole nation. Consolidating this work to create a truly harmonious society through barrier-free media is one of the next challenges.

References

1. Frieden, R. (2014). Next generation television and the migration from channels to platforms. In Y.-l. Liu & R. Picard (Eds.), *The digital media and new media platforms: Policy and marketing strategies*. New York: Routledge Press.
2. Lathan, K. (2007). *Pop culture China!: Media, arts and lifestyle* (p. 71). Santa Barbara: ABC-Clio.
3. Yong, Hu, et al. (2012). *Mapping digital media: China*. Open Society Foundations. http://www.opensocietyfoundations.org/reports/mapping-digital-media-china
4. Hanging, D. (2011). *Chinese audiences' preference for, dependence on, and gratifications derived from CCTV 1, Dragon TV and Hunan TV News Programs*. Graduate theses and dissertations, Paper 10072, Iowa State University, USA.
5. Istituto nazionale per il Commercio Estero [Italian Trade Commission, Shanghai Office]. (2011, June 3). *China television industry market report*. Shanghai: Italian Trade Commission.
6. Twiddle, N. (2011). *CCTV, 1.2 billion viewers strong*. INA, France. http://www.inaglobal.fr/en/television/article/cctv-12-billion-viewers-strong

7. Zhu, Y., & Berry, C. (2009). *TV China: A reader on new media*. Bloomington: Indiana University Press.
8. Brahima, S. (2011). Making TV accessible for persons with disabilities is everyone's business. In P. O. Looms (Ed.), *Making television accessible*. Geneva: G3ict-ITU, ITU.
9. Coonan, C. (2014, February 4). *China crushes Puny US Super Bowl Audience: 704 Million Watch New Year Gala*. Hollywood Reporter, USA. http://www.hollywoodreporter.com/news/china-crushes-puny-us-super-676907
10. ITU-T. (2014). *Technical report of the focus group on smart cable television* (Focus Group Technical Report (12/2013)). Geneva: ITU.
11. The Economist (2013, November 9). *Online video in China: The Chinese stream*. The Economist Print Edition.
12. Ericsson. (2011). *ConsumerLab releases report on mobile broadband usage in China*. http://www.ericsson.com/news/111219_consumerlab_report_on_mobile_broadband_usage_in_china_244188808_c
13. Ma, W. (2014, February 18). 'House of Cards' breaks barriers in China. *The Wall Street Journal*, New York.
14. Dayasena-Lowe, M. (2014, July 21). Digital devices drive new viewing habits. *TVBEurope*. http://www.tvbeurope.com/digital-devices-drive-new-viewing-habits/
15. Nielsen. (2012). Turning digital: The Asian media landscape. *Media and Entertainment*. 03-09-2012. http://www.nielsen.com/us/en/insights/reports/2012/turning-digital--the-asian-media-landscape.html
16. Zemedia. (2014). 《视听界》:全媒体收视率的统计意义 [The media industry: Statistically significant cross-media ratings]. http://www.zemedia.com.cn/html/baodao/meitibaodao_2014/2014/0709/130.html
17. Nielsen. (2013). *Pilot Project – China 3-Screen Measurement*. http://www.agbnielsen.net/whereweare/dynPage.asp?lang=nglish&country=china&id=420
18. Li, D., & Looms, P. O. (2014, April). *Media accessibility: Conception, model and designing* (China Media Report, Vol. 50, No. 2). Hangzhou: Zhejiang University Press.
19. Li, D. (2013). *Hear & see: Audio-visual media for all*. Hangzhou: Zhejiang University Press.
20. Mellors, W. J. (2006). *WGHI – Working Group on Hearing Impairment Statistics on age and disability and in relation to telecommunications – A significant market*.http://www.tiresias.org/wghi/stats.htm
21. United Nations Statistics Division – Demographic and Social Statistics. http://unstats.un.org/unsd/demographic/sconcerns/disability/disab2.asp
22. Looms, P. O. (2011). *Making television accessible*. Terminology and definitions Page 79. Geneva: G3ict-ITU, ITU. There is a link to download the report here: http://www.itu.int/en/ITU-T/focusgroups/ava/Pages/default.aspx
23. Bevan, N. (2006). *International standards for HCI: Encyclopedia of human computer interaction*. Hershey: IGI Global.
24. Vlaming, M. (2012). *Wireless connections to hearing aids: European Hearing Instrument Manufacturers Association (EHIMA)*. Page 1. Working document AVA-I-30. Geneva: ITU-T Focus Group on Audiovisual Media Accessibility (FG AVA).
25. Cohen, D. (2012). *Sound matters: Why we need a best practice guide to clear sound*. BBC – College of Production. http://www.bbc.co.uk/academy/collegeofproduction/articles/tv/sound_matters_cohen
26. Moeller, S., Joseph, A., Lau, J., & Carbo T. (2011). *Towards media and information literacy indicators*. Background document of the expert meeting, 4–6 November 2010, Bangkok, Thailand. Paris: UNESCO. Retrieved July 7, 2012, from http://www.ucm.es/BUCM/boletin/doc17043.pdf
27. iResearch. (2013). *2012–2013 China Online Video Report* (Brief Edition). November 26, 2013, 3:00 PM http://www.iresearchchina.com/samplereports/5288.html

Chapter 15
An Interoperable and Inclusive User Modeling Concept for Simulation and Adaptation

Pradipta Biswas, N. Kaklanis, Y. Mohamad, M. Peissner, Patrick Langdon, D. Tzovaras, and Christophe Jung

Abstract User models can be considered as explicit representations of the properties of an individual user including user's needs, preferences as well as physical, cognitive and behavioral characteristics. Due to the wide range of applications, it is often difficult to have a common format or even definition of user models. The lack of a common definition also makes different user models – even if developed for the same purpose -incompatible to each other. It does not only reduce the portability of user models but also restricts new models to leverage benefit from earlier research on similar field. This chapter presents a brief literature survey on user models and concept of an interoperable user model that takes a more inclusive approach than previous research. It is an initiative of the EU VUMS cluster of projects which aims to simulate user interaction and adapt interfaces across a wide variety of digital and non-digital platforms for both able bodied and disabled users. We have already been successful to define an application and platform-independent user model exchange format and the importing of any user profile across all projects.

P. Biswas (✉) • P. Langdon
Department of Engineering, University of Cambridge, Trumpington Street, Cambridge, Cambridgeshire CB2 1PZ, UK
e-mail: pb400@hermes.cam.ac.uk; pml24@eng.cam.ac.uk

N. Kaklanis • D. Tzovaras
Information Technologies Institute, Centre for Research and Technology Hellas, Thessaloniki, Greece
e-mail: nkak@iti.gr; Dimitrios.Tzovaras@iti.gr

Y. Mohamad
Fraunhofer FIT, 53754 Sankt Augustin, Germany
e-mail: yehya.mohamad@fit.fraunhofer.de

M. Peissner
Fraunhofer-Institut für Arbeitswirtschaft und Organisation IAO, Leiter Competence Center Human-Computer Interaction, Nobelstr. 12, 70569 Stuttgart, Germany
e-mail: Matthias.Peissner@iao.fraunhofer.de

C. Jung
Fraunhofer IGD, Darmstadt, Germany
e-mail: christoph.jung@igd.fraunhofer.de

P. Biswas et al. (eds.), *A Multimodal End-2-End Approach to Accessible Computing*, Human–Computer Interaction Series, DOI 10.1007/978-1-4471-6708-2_15

15.1 Introduction

Chapter 2 presents an inclusive user model and demonstrates its application in simulation and adaptation. This chapter takes the user model further beyond a single research group and presents a concept of an interoperable user model and a set of prototype applications to demonstrate its interoperability between the different projects in the EU VUMS cluster. VUMS stands for "Virtual User Modeling and Simulation". The cluster is formed by four projects (GUIDE [4], MyUI [18], VERITAS [19] and VICON [24]) funded by the European Commission and is partially based on the results of the VAALID [18] project. The User Modeling concept takes care of users with a wide range of abilities for different applications and platforms.

The next section of this chapter presents a detailed literature review on user modeling in different disciplines followed by the VUMS approach in Sects. 15.3 and 15.4. The VUMS approach describes a set of terms and their definitions. It also defines a common syntax and ethics format to exchange between different applications. Section 15.5 presents the structure of VUMS user model. In Sect. 15.6, we demonstrate the interoperability principle by considering a single user profile in VUMS exchange format and showing effects of simulation and adaptation on automobile, digital TV, tablet and mobile phone interfaces for this profile. Finally we concluded in Sect. 15.7.

15.2 Literature Survey

In our everyday life we use a plenty of gadgets, especially electronic devices offering a variety of services. We cannot imagine a single day without a mobile phone, TV or a computer. These devices have huge potential to help people engage with society and surroundings; however the enormous number of features often turns overwhelming for older users or users with disabilities, and may make devices unusable. At present there is no way of choosing appropriate accessibility options for different users and media, except a case by case analysis, which is not a scalable approach. User Modeling provides a way of choosing an appropriate feature or service based on the user and context of use.

User models can be considered explicit representations of the properties of an individual user including needs, preferences as well as physical, cognitive and behavioural characteristics. Due to the wide range of applications, it is often difficult to have a common format or even definition of user models. The lack of a common definition also makes different user models – even if being developed for same purpose – incompatible to each other. It does not only reduce portability of user models but also restricts new models to leverage benefit from earlier research in a similar field. The concept of user modeling has been explored in many different fields like ergonomics, psychology, pedagogy and computer science. However, it still lacks a holistic approach. Psychological models often need a lot of parameter tuning reducing their use by non-experts [1] while ergonomic models often lack appropriate cognition modeling. Carmagnola et al. [6] presented an excellent literature survey on web-based user models but completely missed out user models in human computer interaction. Additionally, user modeling is not explored well for users with age related or physical impairment except a few specific applications.

Simulation of virtual humans can be a powerful approach to support engineers in the product development process. Virtual human modeling reduces the need for the production of real prototypes and can even make it obsolete [5]. During the past years, research interest in using digital human modeling for ergonomics purposes increased significantly [22]. Lamkull et al. (2009) [23] performed a comparative analysis on digital human modeling simulation results and their outcomes in the real world. The results of the study show that ergonomic digital human modeling tools are useful for providing designs of standing and unconstrained working postures. The use of virtual humans and simulation in the automotive industry showed also great potential. Porter et al. (1993) [34] presented a summary of applications of digital human models in vehicle ergonomics during the early years of personal computers.

Researchers worked on modeling various body parts, including face [9, 17], neck [25], torso [10], hand [39], and leg [20]. In particular, many researchers [7, 13, 15, 21, 33] concentrated on the biomechanical analysis of the human upper limb. Hingtgen et al. (2003) [14] constructed an upper extremity (UE) model for application in stroke rehabilitation to accurately track the three-dimensional orientation of the trunk, shoulder, elbow, and wrist during task performance. Research has also focused on the lower human body. For example Apkarian (1989) [2] dealt with the modeling of the human lower limbs, and Eng and Winter (1995) [11] presented a three-dimensional mechanical model of the human body, in order to analyse kinetic features such as joint torques. Dealing with human gait analysis from a biomechanical perspective, many researchers [27–29, 31, 32] proposed models that considered the postural stability and balance control of young and older humans.

Biomechanical models recently also focussed on modeling users with disability. Rao et al. (1996) [36] used a three-dimensional biomechanical model to determine upper extremity kinematics of 16 male subjects with low-level paraplegia while performing wheelchair propulsion. Sapin et al. (2008) [37] reported a comparison of the gait patterns of trans-femoral amputees using a single-axis prosthetic knee that coordinates ankle and knee flexions (Proteor's Hydracadence1 system) with the gait patterns of patients using other knee joints without a knee–ankle link and the gait patterns of individuals with normal gait. Prince et al. (1997) [35], reviewed spatio-temporal, kinematics, kinetics and EMG data as well as the physiological changes associated with gait and aging. Coluccini et al. (2007) [8] assessed and analysed upper limb kinematics of normal and motor impaired children, with the aim to propose a kinematic based framework for the objective assessment of the upper limb, including the evaluation of compensatory movements of both the head and the trunk. Ouerfelli et al. (1999) [26] applied two identification methods to study the kinematics of head-neck movements of able-bodied as well as neck-injured subjects. As a result, a spatial three-revolute joint system was employed to model 3D head-neck movements.

Existing tools and frameworks provide designers with the means for creating virtual humans with different capabilities and use them for simulation purposes. DANCE [38], for instance, is an open framework for computer animation research focusing on the development of simulations and dynamic controllers, unlike many other animation systems, which are oriented towards geometric modeling and kinematic animation. SimTk's OpenSim[1] is also a freely available user extensible software system that lets users develop models of musculoskeletal structures and create dynamic simulations of movement. There are also many tools such as JACK[2] from Siemens, RAMSIS,[3] Santos,[4] Human Builder is the virtual user model for CATIA, Enovia and Delmia from Dassault Systems,[5] offering considerable benefits to designers looking to design for all, as they allow the evaluation of a virtual prototype using virtual users with specific abilities.

With the explosion of the Web, and e-commerce in particular, several commercial user modeling tools appeared in the market with the objective of adapting content to users' preferences. Standards and recommendations in this area had to cope with the spread of service-oriented architectures in ubiquitous environments and to cover workflow and user interface aspects e.g. UsiXML, EMMA (Extensible Multi Modal Annotation mark-up language) and MARIA XML. All these frameworks contain a user model component but do not cover all user modeling aspects. Another major source for the development of user models was the e-learning sector e.g. IMS AccLIP (Access For All Personal Needs and Preferences Description for Digital Delivery Information Model) and AccMD, which have been internationalised in the ISO/IEC JTC1 "Individualised Adaptability and Accessibility for Learning, Education and specification for the User Modeling software Training" (ISO/IEC 24751-1:2008). The Universal Remote Console – URC Standard (ISO/IEC 24752) the goal of URC technology is to allow any device or service to be accessed and manipulated by any controller. Users can then select a user interface that fits their needs and preferences, using input and output modalities as well as interaction mechanisms that meet their individual needs and preferences.

---

[1] https://simtk.org/home/opensim

[2] http://www.plm.automation.siemens.com/en_us

[3] http://www.human-solutions.com/automotive/products_r_auto_en.php

[4] http://www.santoshumaninc.com/

[5] http://www.3ds.com/products/delmia/solutions/human-modeling/overview/#vid1

Even though significant effort has been made in physical user modeling, and many tools use virtual humans for simulation purposes, there is no widely accepted formal way for the description of the virtual users, being able to also describe users with special needs and functional limitations, such as the elderly and users with disabilities.

There was as well a plethora of systems developed in human computer interaction during the last three decades that are claimed to be user models. Many of them modelled users for certain applications – most notably for online recommendation and e-learning systems. There is a bunch of application-independent models which merges psychology and artificial intelligence to model human behaviour in detail. In theory they are capable of modeling any behaviour of users while interacting with environment or a system. This type of models is termed as cognitive architecture and has also been used to simulate human machine interaction to both explain and predict interaction behaviour. A simplified view of these cognitive architectures is known as the GOMS model [16] and still now is most widely used in human computer interaction though it does not consider people with disabilities or non-expert users in detail. Existing user models focussed on inclusive interaction like CogTool[6] or SUPPLE [12] does not yet cover a wide range of users with perceptual, cognitive and motor disabilities.

The existing standards related to User Modeling provide guidance to ICT (Information Communication Technology) and non-ICT product and service designers on issues and design practices related to human factors. They aim to help designers and developers to maximize the level of usability of products and services by providing a comprehensive set of human factors design guidelines and meta-models in machine-readable formats. Within the context of the VUMS cluster activities towards the development of interoperable and multipurpose user models, a comparative review of these standards has been performed, in order to understand their similarities and differences and also to examine their potential use in the user modeling procedures of the cluster. Table 15.1 presents a comparison of the standards according to the following dimensions:

- Focus on accessibility: indicates if the standard focuses on people with special needs (provides guidelines for developing accessible products/services, analyses special needs of people with disabilities, etc.).
- Tasks support: indicates if the standard introduces new task models or includes guidelines for developing task models.
- Workflows support: indicates if the standard introduces new workflow models or includes guidelines for developing workflows.
- Description of user needs/preferences: indicates if the standard describes user needs/preferences using models (meta-models, ontology-schema, UML class diagrams, etc.) or includes guidelines for covering user needs/preferences during products and services design and development. User needs/preferences include:

[6]http://cogtool.hcii.cs.cmu.edu/

Table 15.1 Standards related to User Modeling – Comparison

Standard/aspects covered	Focus on accessibility	Tasks support	Workflows support	Description of user needs/ preferences	Description of device characteristics	Description of user characteristics (physical, cognitive, etc.)	UI definition support	Guidelines	Implementation details
ETSI TS 102 747								✓	
ETSI ES 202 746	✓			✓					✓
ISO/IEC 24751-1:2008	✓								✓
ISO/IEC 24751-2:2008	✓			✓					✓
MARIA XML		✓	✓				✓ (Multimodal)		✓
W3C delivery context ontology					✓				✓
W3C CC/PP				✓	✓				✓
URC standard (ISO/IEC 24752)	✓	✓		✓	✓		✓		✓
IMS access for all personal needs and preferences description for digital delivery information model	✓			✓					✓
ETSI EG 202 116	✓				✓	✓	✓ (Multimodal)	✓	
ETSI TR 102 068	✓				✓	✓		✓	

ETSI EG 202 325	✓ (limited)							✓	
BS EN 1332-4:2007	✓			✓					✓
ISO 11228-2:2007						✓		✓	
ISO/DIS 24502						✓		✓	
XPDL		✓	✓						✓
WHO ICF	✓								
WHO ICD	✓								
FMA				✓		✓			✓
H-Anim		✓		✓		✓	✓		✓
ISO/FDIS 9241-129:2010				✓			✓	✓	

  - General interaction preferences
  - Interaction modality preferences
  - Multi-cultural aspects
  - Visual preferences
  - Audio preferences
  - Tactile/haptic-related preferences
  - Date and time preferences
  - Notifications and alerts
  - Connectivity preferences

- Description of device characteristics: indicates if the standard describes device characteristics or provides guidelines to be followed during the design and development of input/output devices.
- Description of user characteristics: indicates if the standard describes user characteristics including sensory abilities (seeing, hearing, touch, taste, smell, balance, etc.), physical abilities (speech, dexterity, manipulation, mobility, strength, endurance, etc.) and cognitive abilities (intellect, memory, language, literacy, etc.). A standard may include definitions of user characteristics, changes of these characteristics with age, analysis of user populations and their characteristics, etc.
- UI definition support: indicates if the standard provides guidelines for developing user interfaces or introduces a language for defining user interfaces.
- Guidelines: indicates if the standard provides guidelines/recommendations that have to be followed by designers and developers of products and services.
- Implementation: indicates if the standard provides meta-models, UML diagrams, ontology schemas, XML schemas, and machine-readable formats in general.

15.3 VUMS Cluster Standardisation Efforts

Considering all these approaches together, it becomes challenging to define what a user model actually is. This lack of definition also makes the interoperability of user models difficult. On the other hand, there was a plethora of standards about human factors, user interface design, interface description language, workplace ergonomics and so on that can be used to develop user models. In this context the VUMS cluster aims to develop:

- A standard user model considering people with different range of abilities
- Common data storage format for user profiles
- Common calibration/validation technique
- Collaboration on ethical issues
- Ensuring sustainability by making them available within a standard

15.3.1 Purpose

The VUMS model aims to achieve two main purposes derived and motivated from two major application areas for user models:

- Simulating users to help designers in designing more accessible products and services
- Adapting interfaces to cater users with a wide range of abilities

The VUMS cluster followed the following approach, in order to develop an interoperable user model:

1. Definition of a common vocabulary to avoid confusion among terms like user model, user profile, simulation, adaptation, and so on.
2. Description of the terms in accordance to the existing standards.
3. Definition of a set of user characteristics covering physical, perceptual, cognitive and motor abilities of users with a wide range of abilities.
4. Definition of a VUMS exchange format to store these characteristics in a machine-readable form.

The VUMS exchange format provides the means that will allow the exchange of user models between the projects of the VUMS cluster, as depicted in Fig. 15.1. More specifically, as the VUMS Exchange Format contains a superset of user variables defined by each project (defined in step 3), any user model expressed in every project-specific format will be able to be transformed into a model following the VUMS Exchange Format.

5. Development of a set of converters, able to transform a user profile following the VUMS exchange format into each project's specific user model and vice versa (Fig. 15.2). As the VUMS exchange format includes the superset of the variables

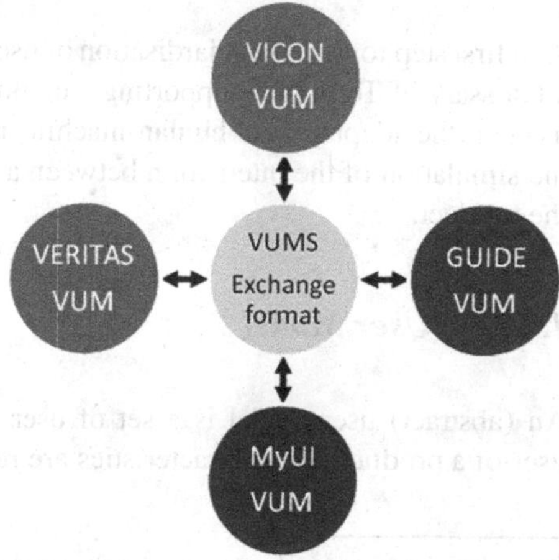

Fig. 15.1 VUMS exchange format

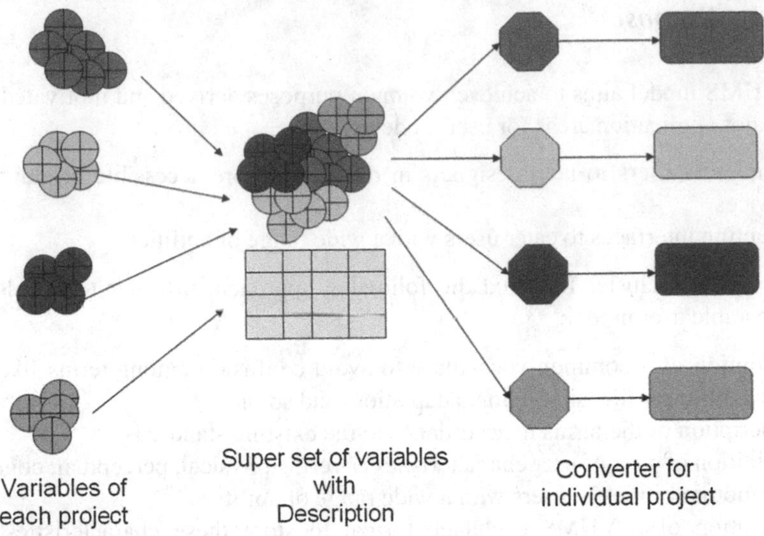

Fig. 15.2 VUMS converters

contained in each VUMS cluster project's user model,[7] the transformation of a project-specific user model into a VUMS user model is straightforward. Contrariwise, during the transformation of a VUMS user model into a project-specific user model, some information are not used, as some variables included in a VUMS user model may not be included in the project-specific user model.

The following sections describe these steps in detail.

15.4 Glossary of Terms

As a first step towards standardisation of user models, the VUMS cluster has defined a Glossary of Terms for supporting a common language. Its scope and contexts of usage is the adaptation of human-machine interfaces to the needs of the real user or the simulation of the interaction between a human and a product in order to design the product.

15.4.1 User Model

An (abstract) user model is a set of user characteristics required to describe the user of a product. The characteristics are represented by variables. The user model

[7]https://docs.google.com/spreadsheet/ccc?key=0AnAwpf4jk8LSdDd3TEJWLUtmN290YzVfTkNvcHYyMUE&authkey=CPOO65oE

is established by the declaration of these variables. It is formally described in a machine-readable and human-readable format. An instantiation of the user model is a user profile.

15.4.2 User Profile

A user profile is an instantiation of a user model representing either a specific real user or a representative of a group of real users. It is an instantiation of an (abstract) user model it is formally described in a machine-readable and human-readable format, compatible with.

15.4.3 Virtual User

A virtual user is a representation of a user based on a User Profile. The virtual user exists in a computer memory during the run time of an application. It includes components, which are able to interact with other virtual entities e.g. virtual products or software applications.

Virtual users intended for simulation purposes represent the human body as e.g. a kinematic system, a series of links connected by rotational degrees of freedom (DOF) that collectively represent musculoskeletal joints such as the wrist, elbow, vertebra, or shoulder. The basic skeleton of the model is described usually in terms of kinematics. In this sense, a human body is essentially a series of links connected by kinematic revolute joints. Each DOF corresponds to one kinematic revolute joint, and these revolute joints can be combined to model various musculoskeletal joints.

15.4.4 Environmental Model

An environmental model is formal machine-readable set of characteristics used to describe the use environment. It includes all required contextual characteristics besides the user model, the interaction model, the device model, the product and related user tasks.

15.4.5 Device Model

It is a formal machine-readable representation of the features and capabilities of one or several physical components involved in user interaction. It is important to carefully discriminate between user and device model as they are two kinds of models. Too often they are conflated together, with device properties sprinkled into user profiles and vice versa. The device model expresses capabilities of the device. A given device can be used by many different users and a given user could use different devices. By carefully separating the different functionalities of device modeling and user modeling in design scenarios it will be easier to enumerate the attributes for each model and from them develop the matching function and attributes of the adaptation process.

15.4.6 User Agent

A User Agent is any end user software (like browser, or other user interface component) that can retrieve and render application content and invoke requests to the User Agent Capabilities Model to modify the application content.

15.4.7 User Agent Capabilities Model

A User Agent Capabilities Model is a formal machine-readable representation of the capabilities of the user agent related to user interaction.

15.4.8 Application Model

An Application Model is a formal machine-readable representation of the states, transitions and functions of the application.

15.4.9 User Interaction Model

The interaction model is a machine readable representation of the interaction behaviour of an application. The interaction model is maintained UI-agnostic, which means it is independent of the concrete format of user interface output- and input data. Interaction model is often also referred to as abstract user interface model, like for example UIML, UI Socket, XForms, etc. It should be noted that the Interaction model can be used for adaptation of Human Machine Interfaces (HMI) and for simulating the use of an application/product with a virtual user.

15.4.10 Context Model

It is a machine-readable representation of information that can be used to characterize the situation of an entity. An entity is a person, a place, a device, or a product that is considered relevant to the interaction between a user and an application, including the user and applications themselves.

15.4.11 Simulation

Simulation is the process that enables the interaction of the virtual user with the application model within an artificial environment. The simulation can be real-time or off-line. Real-time simulation can be performed autonomously or manually, where the operator can interact with the environment from a 1st or 3rd person perspective. Accessibility assessment and evaluation can be performed automatically or subjectively by the operator.

15.4.12 User Model/Profile Validation

User Models are always simplified descriptions of the user. Validation is the process to determine whether the model is an appropriate representation of the user for a specific application. Mathematical then it needs a statistical validation process. If the model is non-mathematical then it should be validated through qualitative processes. We can standardize the type, process and metrics of validation.

15.4.13 Adaptive User Interfaces

User interfaces that adapt their appearance and/or interaction behaviour to an individual user according to a user profile. In contrast to adaptable user interfaces, which are modified by a deliberate and conscious choice of a user, adaptive user interfaces automatically initiate and perform changes according to an updated user profile.

15.4.14 User Interface Design Pattern

This is an approved user interface solution to a recurring design problem. User Interface Design has a formalized description. For the use in adaptive user interfaces, design patterns have a representation in form of reusable software components which can be put together to complete user interfaces during run-time.

15.5 Concept of Generic User Models

The discussions within the VUMS cluster revealed that a wide variety of user models are in use and will be in use in future. They all depend heavily on their specific use cases. There are a number of reasons for this:

- A full model of the user, meaning a model that includes facets according to the state of the art would be rather complex and inefficient in use for both simulation purposes and even more for implementation in a product's user interface.
- Existing devices might not be able to handle large user models
- Not all facets are needed for a specific use case. E.g. modeling some severe visual impairment is not relevant designing a car.
- Specific requirements might require modifications in existing user models.

Given that a user model can be seen as a set of variables or parameters which describe the human resources to fulfill an interaction task and their definitions, then an abstract user model can be defined by a set of parameters together with their descriptors. The following tree structure shows, how this can be illustrated graphically.

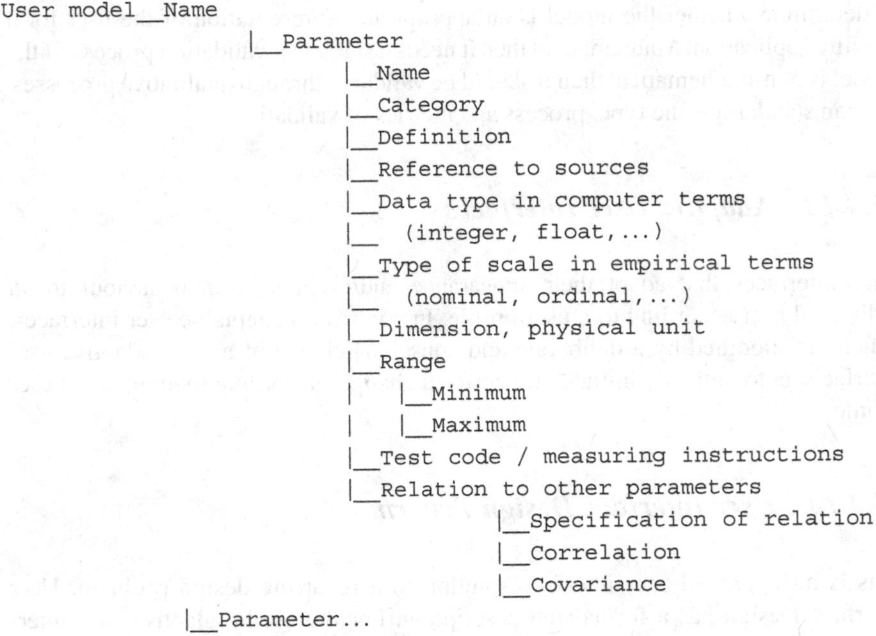

```
User model__Name
           |__Parameter
                 |__Name
                 |__Category
                 |__Definition
                 |__Reference to sources
                 |__Data type in computer terms
                 |__   (integer, float,...)
                 |__Type of scale in empirical terms
                 |__   (nominal, ordinal,...)
                 |__Dimension, physical unit
                 |__Range
                 |   |__Minimum
                 |   |__Maximum
                 |__Test code / measuring instructions
                 |__Relation to other parameters
                           |__Specification of relation
                           |__Correlation
                           |__Covariance
       |__Parameter...
```

Thus, a user model consists of a name and a set of parameters, which are specified by a number of descriptors. The descriptors are partly human readable information, which try to make the user model understandable (such as names, definitions, units, measuring instructions, references to more information, level of scale of the data). But they also include machine- readable information like data type.

In XML notation this can be formalized as follows. It is a pseudo code example, which shows the principle, not a language definition, yet.

```
<Abstract User Model>
    <Name>name</Name>
    <Reference>external references</Reference>
    <Parameter>
        <Name>name</Name>
        <Category>name of category in taxonomy</Category>
        <Definition>definition</Definition>
        <Reference>External references</Reference>
        <Datatype>from {character/string, enumeration,
          list/vector, integer, float, set}</Datatype>
        <Scaletype> from {nominal, ordinal, interval,
          ratio}</Scaletype>
        <Unit>unit</Unit>
        <Minimum>value</Minimum>
        <Maximum>value</Maximum>
        <Testcode>reference or definition how to
          measure</Testcode>
        <Relation>
              <Paraname>parameter name</Paraname>
              <Specification>spec of relation</Specification>
              <Corr>correlation coefficient float [-1;1]</Corr>
              <Cov>covariance float [-1;1]</Cov>
        </Relation>
    </Parameter>
</Abstract User Model>
```

There are two principles behind the design of the notation above:

1. Semi structured document
2. Tag-oriented definitions

Semi structured means that it stands between a strictly data-centred format, which focuses on machine-readability and a document-cantered format, which is optimised for human-readability. On the one hand all items are clearly labelled by standardised tags. On the other hand there is flexibility and freedom in defining the content/values between the tags.

Tag-oriented definitions means that each item is described by using the tag-syntax <Tag> content/value </Tag>. A competing way would be to write information as attributes. This syntax is not used, e. g. <Parameter min="20", max="180" unit="degrees">Range of motion</Parameter>.

A complete VUMS user profile in the VUMS Exchange format can be found in Appendix 1.

15.5.1 User Profile Converters

The proposed VUMS exchange format includes a large set of variables describing various human characteristics. The VUMS converters imports user profiles from the common exchange format to a project specific format. The converters parse the VUMS list of variables and select the appropriate set of variables after some simple arithmetic processing.

For example, The VERITAS project investigates automobile interface design and stores anthropo-morphic details of users including range of motions of different joints in VERITAS user models. On the other hand, the GUIDE project develops adaptable interfaces for digital TV interfaces and it uses the active range of motion of wrist to predict movement time for simulating interaction [Biswas et al. 2012] [3]. So, it reads the values of pronation and supination from a VERITAS profile stored in VUMS exchange format and uses them to derive active range of motion of wrist (Appendix 2). Similar case studies may also include other variables (visual, hearing, etc.) and projects like VICON and MyUI. Currently, all VUMS projects can import profiles from one project to other, and, thus, the simulation of interaction in different application domains (automobile, mobile phone, digital TV, adaptive interfaces) is achieved for any user profile.

15.5.1.1 VERITAS Converter

The VERITAS simulation platform can simulate a variety of human characteristics (motor, visual, hearing, cognitive), thus, almost all the variables contained in a VUMS user profile are also included in the corresponding VERITAS user model (with some differences in the syntax). Only a small set of variables included in a VUMS user profile are ignored during its transformation to a VERITAS user model, concerning mostly some general characteristics, such as user's name, e-mail address, language and some cognitive characteristics, like anxiousness, that are not currently supported by the VERITAS simulation platform.

The major difference between a VUMS user profile and a VERITAS user model lies to the fact that inside a VERITAS user model, the disabilities of a user as well as the affected/problematic tasks (due to the disabilities) are described, while a VUMS user profile does not include such information. This information is being lost during the transformation of a VERITAS user model into a VUMS user model.

As depicted in Fig. 15.3, the VUMS/VERITAS user model converter contains a simple graphical user interface (GUI) that supports the conversion between a VUMS profile to a VERITAS VUM and vice versa.

In the first case, the user loads a VUMS profile (Fig. 15.4a) and then provides a filename for the generated VERITAS VUM and selects where it will be stored (Fig. 15.4b). The opposite conversion is supported in a similar way.

Fig. 15.3 VUMS/VERITAS user model converter – main screen

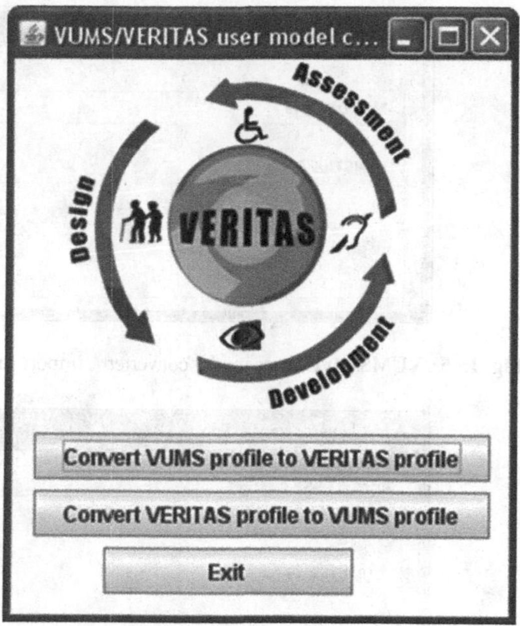

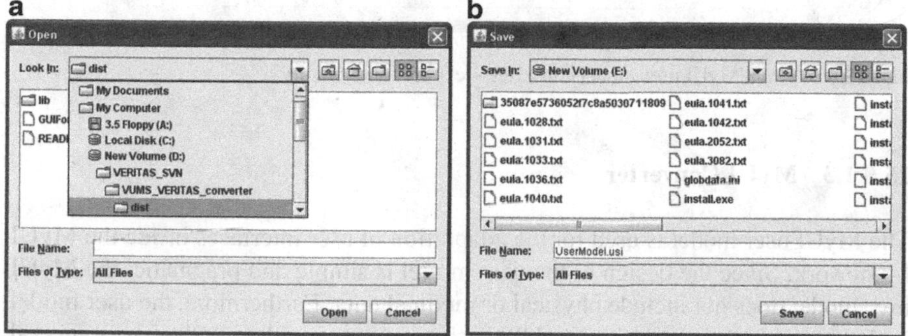

Fig. 15.4 Convert a VUMS profile to a VERITAS VUM. (**a**) Open VUMS profile (**b**) Save VERITAS virtual user model

15.5.1.2 GUIDE Converter

The GUIDE converter parses the VUMS list of variables and selects the appropriate set of variables after some simple arithmetic processing. For example, it adds up radial and ulnar deviation to evaluate the active range of motion of wrist.

The GUIDE converter is developed as a lightweight C++ application without any GUI so that it can be easily integrated to GUIDE framework and Simulator.

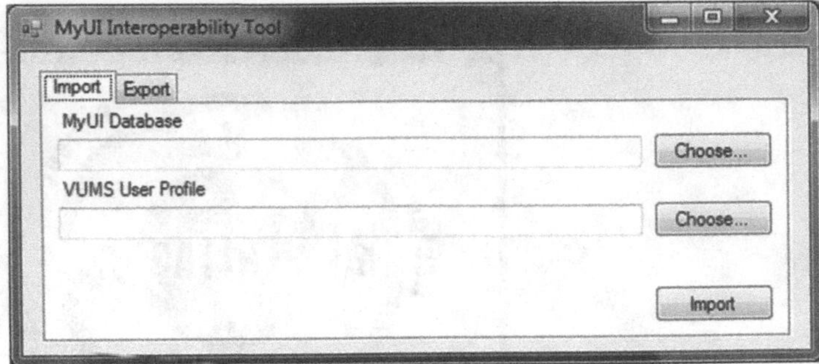

Fig. 15.5 VUMS/MyUI user model converter – import functionality

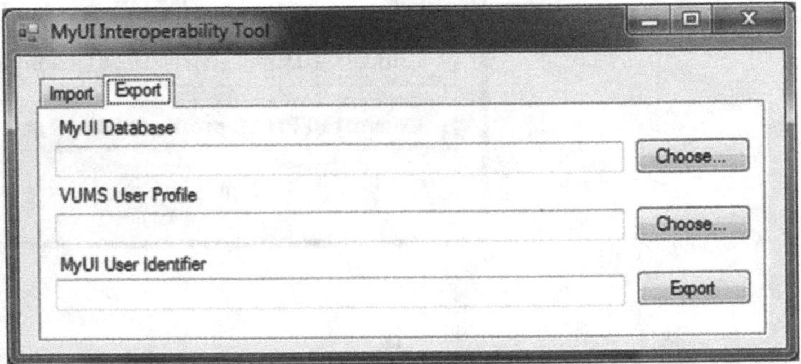

Fig. 15.6 VUMS/MyUI user model converter – export functionality

15.5.1.3 MyUI Converter

The MyUI user model is used for the adaptation of user interfaces inside the MyUI framework. Since the design of the user model is simple and pragmatic, the MyUI user model does not include physical or medical data. Furthermore, the user model includes covers the capabilities and limitations of a user and maps them to a interval between 0 and 4, where 0 means "not limited" and 4 means "very limited". Since the VUMS Exchange Format provides support for the variables in the MyUI user model the converter created inside the MyUI project, user profile variables can be imported (Fig. 15.5) and exported (Fig. 15.6) into the VUMS Exchange Format. Since the focus of the MyUI user model is not on medical measures or simulation, these information is lost whenever a VUMS Exchange Format file is transformed into a MyUI user profile.

15.5.1.4 VICON Converter

The VICON user models are used by the VICON platform for Simulation, evaluation and recommendation purposes to assess the usability and accessibility of

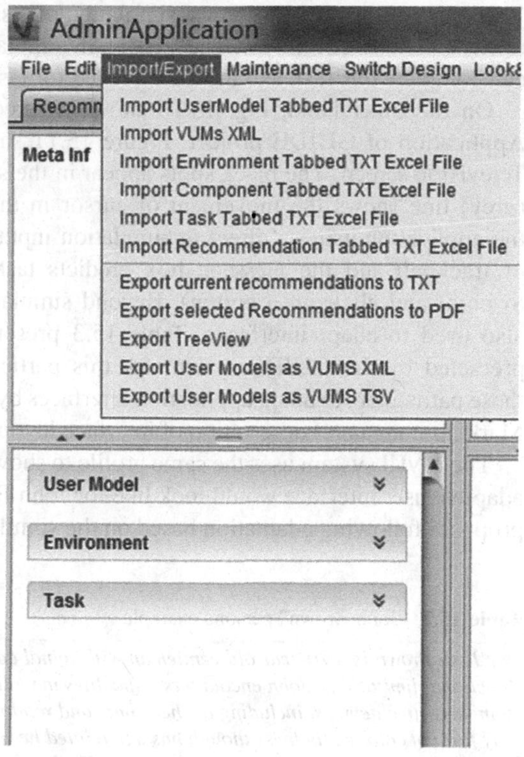

Fig. 15.7 VUMS/VICON user model converter – main screen

virtual prototypes. The VICON system can simulate a variety of user personae limited to physical characteristics e.g. visual and hearing. The VICON converter (Fig. 15.7) can import and export VUMS models beside other formats like excel or TSV. VICON uses only a subset of the VUMS variables. During the import process VICON imports all variables from the VUMS file and stores variables, which it does not need in a separate file and all variables it needs in the main repository. During the export process VICON creates a complete VUMS exchange format model; the variables which are not included in the VICON repository are filled with default values. The VICON converter is developed using the programming language Java.

15.6 Case Study

The VUMS exchange format enables all projects of the VUMS cluster to share a single profile and simulate and adapt interface based on this common profile. The following example considers a representative persona (Table 15.2) and shows simulation and adaptation examples for different applications. Appendix 1 presents his user profile in VUMS exchange format.

Figures 15.8 and 15.9 show a simulation of a situation while Mr Brown is trying to close the trunk of his car. The VERITAS simulation platform predicts whether he can complete this task and the time needed for task's completion.

On the other hand, Fig. 15.10 shows a screenshot of the Home Automation Application of GUIDE project. Figure 15.11 shows how Mr Brown perceives a Television screen. The black spots appear in the screen due to Glaucoma. The blue (grey) line shows the movement of cursor in the screen while the user operates the application using a direct manipulation input device like a gyroscopic remote or trackball and the message box predicts task completion time (time needed to point and click on a button). Beyond simulation, the common user profile is also used to adapt interfaces. Table 15.3 presents a set of interface parameters predicted by the GUIDE system for this particular user. GUIDE interfaces use these parameters to adapt application interfaces by updating a UIML (User Interface MarkUp Language) description of interface layouts.

The MyUI system uses the same profile to show how the main menu of the MyUI adaptive user interface would look like for John Brown. For him The MyUI system proposes following adaptation based on the simulation shown in Fig. 15.12.

Table 15.2 "John Brown" persona example

Mr John Brown is a 70-year old gentleman with spinal cord injuries and glaucoma. Due to his functional limitations, John encounters difficulties in walking, grasping and reading. John uses some assistive devices, including a wheelchair and reading glasses. He does not suffer from any form of colour blindness though has age related hearing impairment having higher threshold of hearing for high frequency tones. He does not also have any cognitive impairment as reflected by his scores in cognitive tests like Trail Making and Digit Symbol Tests.

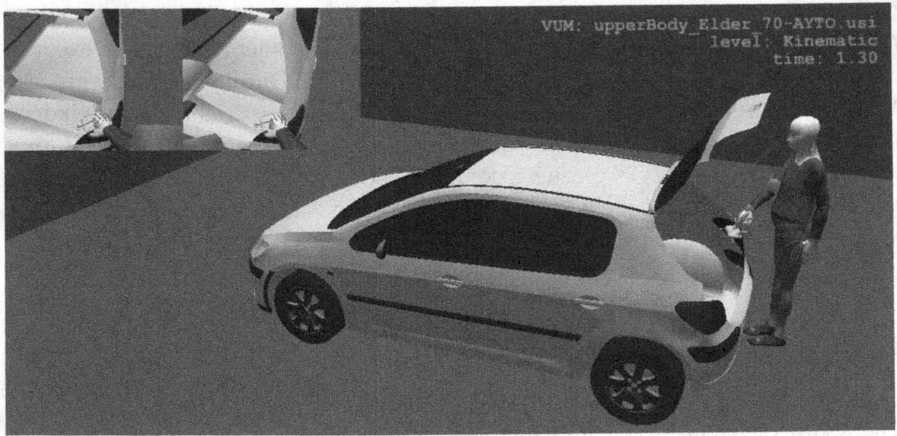

Fig. 15.8 Simulation for automobile interface in VERITAS project

Fig. 15.9 Simulation of a task of opening boot in VERITAS project

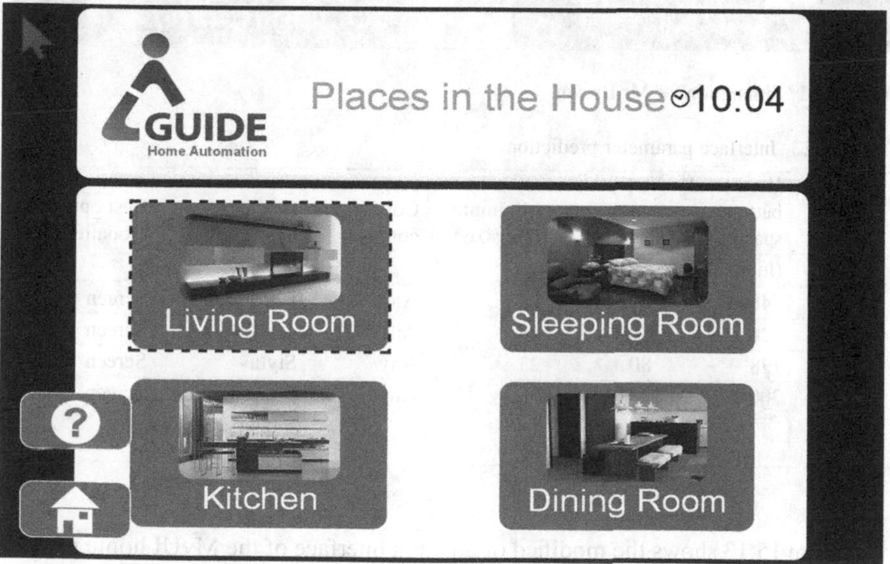

Fig. 15.10 GUIDE home automation application

- Font size is increased due to his perceptual problems (I guess your "reading" problems are not related to cognitive impairments)
- in addition to simple cursor navigation, numeric key navigation is enabled due to his motor problems ("grasping"). This results in displaying the respective numbers on every interactive element.
- as a consequence of enabling numeric key navigation, the number of displayed interactive elements (here menu buttons) is reduced to a subset of not more than ten options (keys #0 – #9)

Fig. 15.11 Simulation for Mr Brown

Table 15.3 Interface parameter prediction

Devices	Horizontal button spacing	Vertical button spacing	Minimum font size	Colour contrast	Best input modality	Best output modality
	(In pixel)					
Mobile	48	80	26	Any	BigButton	Screen
Laptop	128	80	24	Any	TrackBall	Screen
Tablet	128	80	23	Any	Stylus	Screen
TV	200	120	58	Any	Second screen bigButton	Screen

Figure 15.13 shows the modified or adapted interface of the MyUI home page.

15.7 Conclusions

This chapter presents a concept of a generic user model, which can be used to simulate interaction and adapt interfaces for a wide range of users, applications and platforms. It provides specification and examples of using the model as well as discusses ethical issues in developing user models. The VUMS user model has already been used in the VERITAS, VICON, GUIDE and MyUI EU projects and the list of user modeling variables is available online from the VUMS website. We

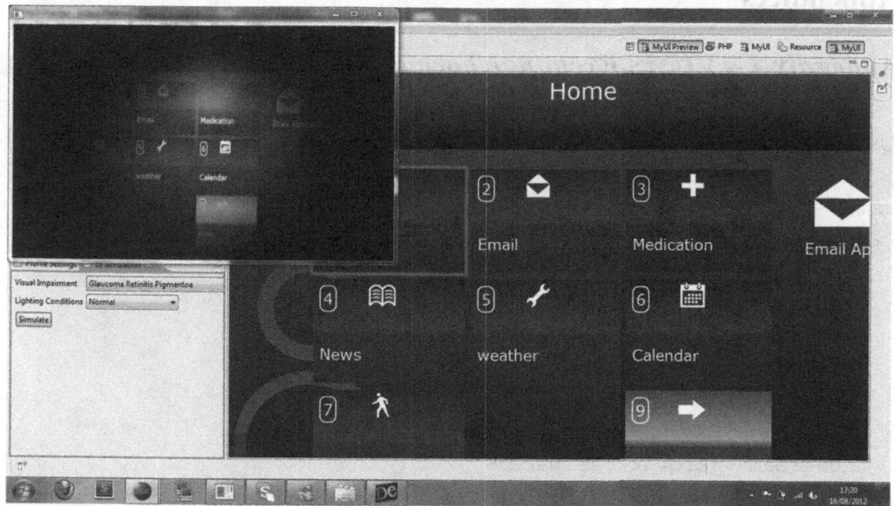

Fig. 15.12 MyUI home page and simulation

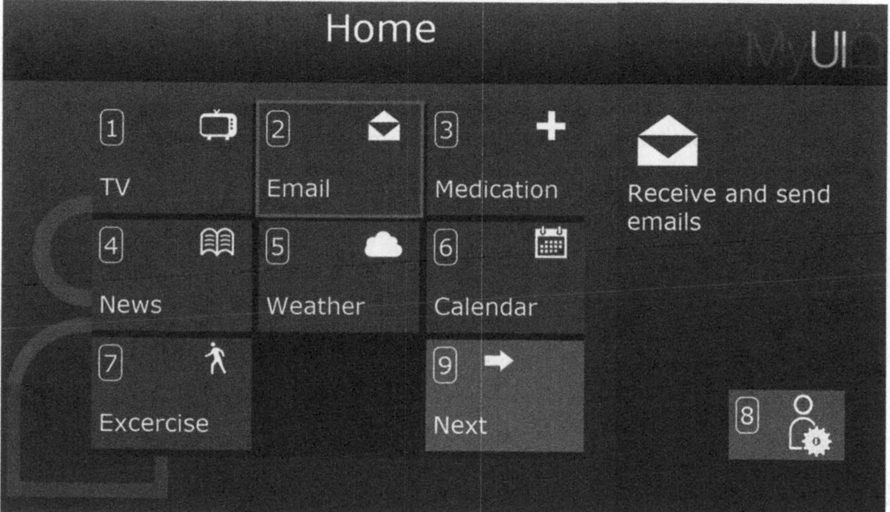

Fig. 15.13 Adapted interface in MyUI system

hope this chapter will help other researchers to follow this common user modeling format and enrich it further by using it in their applications.

Appendices

Appendix 1 – VUMS Exchange Format

User profile for Mr John Brown (common persona) in VUMS Exchange Format


```
<xml>
 <User>
  <ID>User_Model</ID>
  <General>
   <FirstName>John</FirstName>
   <LastName>Brown</LastName>
   <Email>jBrown@gmail.com</Email>
   <Language>EN</Language>
   <UserName>jBrown</UserName>
   <Password>jBrownPass</Password>
   <Age>70</Age>
   <Sex>Male</Sex>
  </General>
  <Preferences>
   <preferredInputModality>Pointing</preferredInputModality>
   <unsuitableInputModality>True</unsuitableInputModality>
   <preferredOutputModality>Screen</preferredOutputModality>
   <unsuitableOutputModality>Screen</unsuitableOutputModality>
   <microphoneVolume>2.0</microphoneVolume>
   <outputVolume>5.0</outputVolume>
   <brightness>5.0</brightness>
   <backgroundColour>Undefined</backgroundColour>
   <contentContrast>Undefined</contentContrast>
   <fontSize>7</fontSize>
   <fontColour>Blue</fontColour>
   <pointerSize>6.0</pointerSize>
   <pointerColour>White</pointerColour>
   <SuccessfulInteractions>1</SuccessfulInteractions>
   <StateTransitions>1</StateTransitions>
   <Experience>7.0</Experience>
  </Preferences>
  <AffectedTasks>
  <AffectedTask id="grasping_ID" type="motor"
    name="grasping" taskObject=""
    details="difficulty in grasping" failureLevel="2"/>
  <AffectedTask id="reading_ID" type="visual"
    name="reading" taskObject=""
    details="difficulty in reading" failureLevel="3"/>
```

```
<AffectedTask id="walking_ID" type="motor"
  name="walking" taskObject=""
  details="difficulty in walking" failureLevel="4"/>
</AffectedTasks>
<Anthropometric>
 <weight measureUnits="kgr" value="73.829723"/>
 <stature measureUnits="cm" value="169.906063"/>
 <headLength measureUnits="cm" value="19.01"/>
 <headBreadth measureUnits="cm" value="15.97"/>
 <sittingHeight measureUnits="cm" value="89.664626"/>
 <bideltoidBreadth measureUnits="cm" value="46.89837"/>
 <waistCircumference measureUnits="cm" value="96.169888"/>
<upperLimbAnthropometric leftRight="left">
 <shoulderElbowLength measureUnits="cm" value="32.80659"/>
 <forearmHandLength measureUnits="cm" value="46.17879"/>
  <bicepsCircumferenceRelaxed measureUnits="cm" value=
    "25.231592"/>
  <forearmCircumferenceFlexed measureUnits="cm"
    value="27.84888"/>
</upperLimbAnthropometric>
<upperLimbAnthropometric leftRight="right">
 <shoulderElbowLength measureUnits="cm" value="32.80659"/>
 <forearmHandLength measureUnits="cm" value="46.17879"/>
  <bicepsCircumferenceRelaxed measureUnits="cm" value=
    "25.231592"/>
  <forearmCircumferenceFlexed measureUnits="cm"
    value="27.84888"/>
</upperLimbAnthropometric>
<lowerLimbAnthropometric leftRight="left">
 <ankleHeight measureUnits="cm" value="7.49009"/>
 <hipBreadth measureUnits="cm" value="35.056997"/>
 <kneeHeightSitting measureUnits="cm" value="52.246091"/>
 <buttockKneeLength measureUnits="cm" value="58.542994"/>
 <footLength measureUnits="cm" value="26.3498"/>
 <footBreadth measureUnits="cm" value="10.18"/>
 <thighCircumference measureUnits="cm" value="51.327725"/>
 <calfCircumference measureUnits="cm" value="31.083029"/>
</lowerLimbAnthropometric>
<lowerLimbAnthropometric leftRight="right">
 <ankleHeight measureUnits="cm" value="7.49009"/>
 <hipBreadth measureUnits="cm" value="35.056997"/>
 <kneeHeightSitting measureUnits="cm" value="52.246091"/>
 <buttockKneeLength measureUnits="cm" value="58.542994"/>
 <footLength measureUnits="cm" value="26.3498"/>
 <footBreadth measureUnits="cm" value="10.18"/>
 <thighCircumference measureUnits="cm" value="51.327725"/>
```

```
<calfCircumference measureUnits="cm" value="31.083029"/>
</lowerLimbAnthropometric>
</Anthropometric>
<Visual>
<leftEye>
<visualAcuity>
<Value>-5.0</Value>
<Acuity1>6</Acuity1>
<Acuity2>10</Acuity2>
</visualAcuity>
<contrastSensitivity>80</contrastSensitivity>
<glareSensitivity>1.0</glareSensitivity>
<spectralSensitivity longValue="1.0"
   middleValue="1.0" shortValue="1.0"/>
<blindSpotArea minValue="0.0" maxValue="0.0"/>
<blindSpotSize minValue="0.0" maxValue="0.0"/>
<blindSpotOpacity minValue="0.0" maxValue="0.0"/>
<blindSpotCount>4</blindSpotCount>
<FieldLossP>0</FieldLossP>
 <FieldLossC>0</FieldLossC>
 <CB>0</CB>
<Distortion>0</Distortion>
</leftEye>
<rightEye>
<visualAcuity>
<Value>-5.0</Value>
<Acuity1>6</Acuity1>
<Acuity2>10</Acuity2>
</visualAcuity>
<contrastSensitivity>80</contrastSensitivity>
<glareSensitivity>1.0</glareSensitivity>
<spectralSensitivity longValue="1.0"
   middleValue="1.0" shortValue="1.0"/>
<blindSpotArea minValue="0.0" maxValue="0.0"/>
<blindSpotSize minValue="0.0" maxValue="0.0"/>
<blindSpotOpacity minValue="0.0" maxValue="0.0"/>
<blindSpotCount>4</blindSpotCount>
<FieldLossP>0</FieldLossP>
 <FieldLossC>0</FieldLossC>
 <CB>0</CB>
<Distortion>0</Distortion>
</rightEye>
</Visual>
<Auditory>
<leftEar>
<resonanceFrequency>10.0</resonanceFrequency>
```

```
<quarterK>5</quarterK>
<halfK>10</halfK>
<oneK>10</oneK>
<twoK>9</twoK>
<fourK>8</fourK>
<eightK>8</eightK>
<hearing>0.0</hearing>
</leftEar>
<rightEar>
<resonanceFrequency>10.0</resonanceFrequency>
<quarterK>5</quarterK>
<halfK>10</halfK>
<oneK>10</oneK>
<twoK>9</twoK>
<fourK>8</fourK>
<eightK>8</eightK>
<hearing>0.0</hearing>
</rightEar>
</Auditory>
<Cognitive>
<TMT>23</TMT>
<DIGSYM>43</DIGSYM>
<LanguageReception>0.0</LanguageReception>
<LanguageProduction>0.0</LanguageProduction>
<UnderstandingAbstractSigns>0.0
   </UnderstandingAbstractSigns>
   <Attention>0.0</Attention>
<ProcessingSpeed>0.0</ProcessingSpeed>
<WorkingMemory>0.0</WorkingMemory>
<LongTermMemory>0.0</LongTermMemory>
<ICTLiteracy>0.0</ICTLiteracy>
<ICTAnxiousness>0.0</ICTAnxiousness>
<HandEyeCoordination>0.5</HandEyeCoordination>
<visuospatialAbilities>Undefined</visuospatialAbilities>
<behaviour>
   <physiologicalArousal>
   <informationProcessing>Undefined</informationProcessing>
   </physiologicalArousal>
   <valence>Undefined</valence>
<emotionalIntelligence>Undefined</emotionalIntelligence>
   </behaviour>
</Cognitive>
<Speech>
   <phonation>
<voicePitch>120.0</voicePitch>
```

```
<fundamentalFrequency>135.0</fundamentalFrequency>
   <syllableDuration>-1.0</syllableDuration>
   </phonation>
   <prosody>
   <vocalStress>
<lipMovementCoordination></lipMovementCoordination>
   <jawMovement></jawMovement>
   </vocalStress>
   </prosody>
   </Speech>
   <Mobility>
   <upperLimb leftRight="left">
   <pullForce measureUnits="N" maxValue="335.0"/>
   <pushForce measureUnits="N" maxValue="335.0"/>
   <inForce measureUnits="N" maxValue="335.0"/>
   <outForce measureUnits="N" maxValue="335.0"/>
   <shoulderTorque measureUnits="Nm" maxValue="-1.0"/>
   <elbowTorque measureUnits="Nm" maxValue="-1.0"/>
 <GripStrength measureUnits="Kg" maxValue="30"/>
<StaticTremor measureUnits=" " maxValue="335"/>
<hand>
<finger fingerID="thumb">
<flexionA measureUnits="degrees"
   minValue="0.0" maxValue="35.0"/>
<extensionA measureUnits="degrees"
   minValue="0.0" maxValue="0.0"/>
<abductionA measureUnits="degrees"
   minValue="0.0" maxValue="35.0"/>
<adductionA measureUnits="degrees"
   minValue="0.0" maxValue="0.0"/>
<flexionB measureUnits="degrees"
   minValue="0.0" maxValue="35.0"/>
<extensionB measureUnits="degrees"
   minValue="0.0" maxValue="35.0"/>
<abductionB measureUnits="degrees"
   minValue="0.0" maxValue="35.0"/>
<adductionB measureUnits="degrees"
   minValue="0.0" maxValue="0.0"/>
<flexionC measureUnits="degrees"
   minValue="0.0" maxValue="90.0"/>
<hyperExtensionC measureUnits="degrees"
   minValue="0.0" maxValue="10.0"/>
</finger>
<finger fingerID="index finger">
<flexionA measureUnits="degrees"
```

```
   minValue="0.0" maxValue="85.0"/>
 <hyperExtensionA measureUnits="degrees"
   minValue="0.0" maxValue="0.0"/>
 <flexionB measureUnits="degrees"
   minValue="0.0" maxValue="90.0"/>
 <hyperExtensionB measureUnits="degrees"
   minValue="0.0" maxValue="0.0"/>
 <flexionC measureUnits="degrees"
   minValue="0.0" maxValue="90.0"/>
 <hyperExtensionC measureUnits="degrees"
   minValue="0.0" maxValue="10.0"/>
 </finger>
 <finger fingerID="middle finger">
 <flexionA measureUnits="degrees"
   minValue="0.0" maxValue="85.0"/>
 <hyperExtensionA measureUnits="degrees"
   minValue="0.0" maxValue="0.0"/>
 <flexionB measureUnits="degrees"
   minValue="0.0" maxValue="90.0"/>
 <hyperExtensionB measureUnits="degrees"
   minValue="0.0" maxValue="0.0"/>
 <flexionC measureUnits="degrees"
   minValue="0.0" maxValue="90.0"/>
 <hyperExtensionC measureUnits="degrees"
   minValue="0.0" maxValue="10.0"/>
 </finger>
 <finger fingerID="ring finger">
 <flexionA measureUnits="degrees"
   minValue="0.0" maxValue="85.0"/>
 <hyperExtensionA measureUnits="degrees"
   minValue="0.0" maxValue="0.0"/>
 <flexionB measureUnits="degrees"
   minValue="0.0" maxValue="90.0"/>
 <hyperExtensionB measureUnits="degrees"
   minValue="0.0" maxValue="0.0"/>
 <flexionC measureUnits="degrees"
   minValue="0.0" maxValue="90.0"/>
 <hyperExtensionC measureUnits="degrees"
   minValue="0.0" maxValue="10.0"/>
 </finger>
 <finger fingerID="baby finger">
 <flexionA measureUnits="degrees"
   minValue="0.0" maxValue="85.0"/>
 <hyperExtensionA measureUnits="degrees"
   minValue="0.0" maxValue="0.0"/>
```

```
<flexionB measureUnits="degrees"
   minValue="0.0" maxValue="90.0"/>
<hyperExtensionB measureUnits="degrees"
   minValue="0.0" maxValue="0.0"/>
<flexionC measureUnits="degrees"
   minValue="0.0" maxValue="90.0"/>
<hyperExtensionC measureUnits="degrees"
   minValue="0.0" maxValue="10.0"/>
</finger>
</hand>
<wrist>
<flexion measureUnits="degrees"
   minValue="0.0" maxValue="55.0"/>
<extension measureUnits="degrees"
   minValue="0.0" maxValue="47.5"/>
<radialDeviation measureUnits="degrees"
   minValue="0.0" maxValue="27.5"/>
<ulnarDeviation measureUnits="degrees"
   minValue="0.0" maxValue="35.0"/>
</wrist>
<forearm>
 <pronation measureUnits="degrees"
   minValue="0.0" maxValue="85.0"/>
<supination measureUnits="degrees"
   minValue="0.0" maxValue="85.0"/>
</forearm>
<elbow>
<flexion measureUnits="degrees"
   minValue="0.0" maxValue="142.5"/>
<hyperExtension measureUnits="degrees"
   minValue="0.0" maxValue="10.0"/>
</elbow>
<shoulder>
<flexion measureUnits="degrees"
   minValue="0.0" maxValue="86.0"/>
<extension measureUnits="degrees" minValue="0.0" maxValue=
  "40.0"/>
<abduction measureUnits="degrees"
   minValue="0.0" maxValue="21.0"/>
<adduction measureUnits="degrees"
   minValue="0.0" maxValue="30.0"/>
<internalRotation measureUnits="degrees"
   minValue="0.0" maxValue="80.0"/>
<externalRotation measureUnits="degrees"
   minValue="0.0" maxValue="12.0"/>
```

```
</shoulder>
</upperLimb>
<upperLimb leftRight="right">
<pullForce measureUnits="N" maxValue="335.0"/>
<pushForce measureUnits="N" maxValue="335.0"/>
<inForce measureUnits="N" maxValue="335.0"/>
<outForce measureUnits="N" maxValue="335.0"/>
<shoulderTorque measureUnits="Nm" maxValue="-1.0"/>
<elbowTorque measureUnits="Nm" maxValue="-1.0"/>
 <GripStrength measureUnits="Kg" maxValue="32"/>
<StaticTremor measureUnits=" " maxValue="305"/>
<hand>
<finger fingerID="thumb">
<flexionA measureUnits="degrees"
   minValue="0.0" maxValue="35.0"/>
<extensionA measureUnits="degrees"
   minValue="0.0" maxValue="0.0"/>
<abductionA measureUnits="degrees"
   minValue="0.0" maxValue="35.0"/>
<adductionA measureUnits="degrees"
   minValue="0.0" maxValue="0.0"/>
<flexionB measureUnits="degrees"
   minValue="0.0" maxValue="35.0"/>
<extensionB measureUnits="degrees"
   minValue="0.0" maxValue="35.0"/>
<abductionB measureUnits="degrees"
   minValue="0.0" maxValue="35.0"/>
<adductionB measureUnits="degrees"
   minValue="0.0" maxValue="0.0"/>
<flexionC measureUnits="degrees"
   minValue="0.0" maxValue="90.0"/>
<hyperExtensionC measureUnits="degrees"
   minValue="0.0" maxValue="10.0"/>
</finger>
<finger fingerID="index finger">
<flexionA measureUnits="degrees"
   minValue="0.0" maxValue="85.0"/>
<hyperExtensionA measureUnits="degrees"
   minValue="0.0" maxValue="0.0"/>
<flexionB measureUnits="degrees"
   minValue="0.0" maxValue="90.0"/>
<hyperExtensionB measureUnits="degrees"
   minValue="0.0" maxValue="0.0"/>
<flexionC measureUnits="degrees"
   minValue="0.0" maxValue="90.0"/>
```

```
<hyperExtensionC measureUnits="degrees"
   minValue="0.0" maxValue="10.0"/>
</finger>
<finger fingerID="middle finger">
<flexionA measureUnits="degrees"
   minValue="0.0" maxValue="85.0"/>
<hyperExtensionA measureUnits="degrees"
   minValue="0.0" maxValue="0.0"/>
<flexionB measureUnits="degrees"
   minValue="0.0" maxValue="90.0"/>
<hyperExtensionB measureUnits="degrees"
   minValue="0.0" maxValue="0.0"/>
<flexionC measureUnits="degrees"
   minValue="0.0" maxValue="90.0"/>
<hyperExtensionC measureUnits="degrees"
   minValue="0.0" maxValue="10.0"/>
</finger>
<finger fingerID="ring finger">
<flexionA measureUnits="degrees"
   minValue="0.0" maxValue="85.0"/>
<hyperExtensionA measureUnits="degrees"
   minValue="0.0" maxValue="0.0"/>
<flexionB measureUnits="degrees"
   minValue="0.0" maxValue="90.0"/>
<hyperExtensionB measureUnits="degrees"
   minValue="0.0" maxValue="0.0"/>
<flexionC measureUnits="degrees"
   minValue="0.0" maxValue="90.0"/>
<hyperExtensionC measureUnits="degrees"
   minValue="0.0" maxValue="10.0"/>
</finger>
 <finger fingerID="baby finger">
<flexionA measureUnits="degrees"
   minValue="0.0" maxValue="85.0"/>
<hyperExtensionA measureUnits="degrees"
   minValue="0.0" maxValue="0.0"/>
<flexionB measureUnits="degrees"
   minValue="0.0" maxValue="90.0"/>
<hyperExtensionB measureUnits="degrees"
   minValue="0.0" maxValue="0.0"/>
<flexionC measureUnits="degrees"
   minValue="0.0" maxValue="90.0"/>
<hyperExtensionC measureUnits="degrees"
   minValue="0.0" maxValue="10.0"/>
 </finger>
```

```
</hand>
 <wrist>
<flexion measureUnits="degrees"
   minValue="0.0" maxValue="55.0"/>
<extension measureUnits="degrees"
   minValue="0.0" maxValue="47.5"/>
<radialDeviation measureUnits="degrees"
   minValue="0.0" maxValue="27.5"/>
<ulnarDeviation measureUnits="degrees"
   minValue="0.0" maxValue="35.0"/>
</wrist>
<forearm>
<pronation measureUnits="degrees"
   minValue="0.0" maxValue="85.0"/>
<supination measureUnits="degrees"
   minValue="0.0" maxValue="85.0"/>
</forearm>
<elbow>
<flexion measureUnits="degrees"
   minValue="0.0" maxValue="142.5"/>
<hyperExtension measureUnits="degrees"
   minValue="0.0" maxValue="10.0"/>
</elbow>
<shoulder>
<flexion measureUnits="degrees"
   minValue="0.0" maxValue="86.0"/>
<extension measureUnits="degrees"
   minValue="0.0" maxValue="40.0"/>
<abduction measureUnits="degrees"
   minValue="0.0" maxValue="21.0"/>
<adduction measureUnits="degrees"
   minValue="0.0" maxValue="30.0"/>
<internalRotation measureUnits="degrees"
   minValue="0.0" maxValue="80.0"/>
<externalRotation measureUnits="degrees"
   minValue="0.0" maxValue="12.0"/>
</shoulder>
</upperLimb>
<lowerLimb leftRight="left">
<hip>
<abduction measureUnits="degrees"
   minValue="0.0" maxValue="37.5"/>
<adduction measureUnits="degrees"
   minValue="0.0" maxValue="25.0"/>
<flexion measureUnits="degrees"
```

```
   minValue="0.0" maxValue="135.0"/>
<extension measureUnits="degrees"
   minValue="0.0" maxValue="10.0"/>
<internalRotation measureUnits="degrees"
   minValue="0.0" maxValue="40.0"/>
<externalRotation measureUnits="degrees"
   minValue="0.0" maxValue="40.0"/>
<flexionTorque measureUnits="Nm"
   minValue="0.0" maxValue="58.62"/>
<extensionTorque measureUnits="Nm"
   minValue="0.0" maxValue="40.82"/>
</hip>
<knee>
<flexion measureUnits="degrees"
   minValue="0.0" maxValue="135.0"/>
<hyperExtension measureUnits="degrees"
 minValue="0.0" maxValue="7.5"/>
<flexionForce measureUnits="N"
   minValue="0.0" maxValue="162.42"/>
<extensionForce measureUnits="N"
   minValue="0.0" maxValue="783.0"/>
 </knee>
<ankle>
<dorsiFlexion measureUnits="degrees"
   minValue="0.0" maxValue="25.0"/>
<plantarFlexion measureUnits="degrees"
   minValue="0.0" maxValue="45.0"/>
<eversion measureUnits="degrees"
   minValue="0.0" maxValue="32.5"/>
<inversion measureUnits="degrees"
   minValue="0.0" maxValue="30.0"/>
</ankle>
<footToe footToeID="1">
<flexion measureUnits="degrees"
   minValue="0.0" maxValue="35.0"/>
<extension measureUnits="degrees"
   minValue="0.0" maxValue="35.0"/>
</footToe>
<footToe footToeID="2">
<flexion measureUnits="degrees"
   minValue="0.0" maxValue="35.0"/>
<extension measureUnits="degrees"
   minValue="0.0" maxValue="35.0"/>
</footToe>
<footToe footToeID="3">
```

```
<flexion measureUnits="degrees"
   minValue="0.0" maxValue="35.0"/>
<extension measureUnits="degrees"
   minValue="0.0" maxValue="35.0"/>
</footToe>
<footToe footToeID="4">
<flexion measureUnits="degrees"
   minValue="0.0" maxValue="35.0"/>
<extension measureUnits="degrees"
   minValue="0.0" maxValue="35.0"/>
</footToe>
<footToe footToeID="5">
<flexion measureUnits="degrees"
   minValue="0.0" maxValue="35.0"/>
<extension measureUnits="degrees"
   minValue="0.0" maxValue="35.0"/>
</footToe>
</lowerLimb>
<lowerLimb leftRight="right">
<hip>
<abduction measureUnits="degrees"
   minValue="0.0" maxValue="37.5"/>
<adduction measureUnits="degrees"
   minValue="0.0" maxValue="25.0"/>
<flexion measureUnits="degrees"
   minValue="0.0" maxValue="135.0"/>
<extension measureUnits="degrees"
   minValue="0.0" maxValue="10.0"/>
<internalRotation measureUnits="degrees"
   minValue="0.0" maxValue="40.0"/>
<externalRotation measureUnits="degrees"
   minValue="0.0" maxValue="40.0"/>
<flexionTorque measureUnits="Nm"
   minValue="0.0" maxValue="58.62"/>
<extensionTorque measureUnits="Nm"
   minValue="0.0" maxValue="40.82"/>
</hip>
<knee>
<flexion measureUnits="degrees"
   minValue="0.0" maxValue="135.0"/>
<hyperExtension measureUnits="degrees"
   minValue="0.0" maxValue="7.5"/>
<flexionForce measureUnits="N"
   minValue="0.0" maxValue="162.42"/>
<extensionForce measureUnits="N"
```

```
   minValue="0.0" maxValue="783.0"/>
</knee>
<ankle>
 <dorsiFlexion measureUnits="degrees"
   minValue="0.0" maxValue="25.0"/>
<plantarFlexion measureUnits="degrees"
   minValue="0.0" maxValue="45.0"/>
<eversion measureUnits="degrees"
   minValue="0.0" maxValue="32.5"/>
<inversion measureUnits="degrees"
   minValue="0.0" maxValue="30.0"/>
</ankle>
<footToe footToeID="1">
<flexion measureUnits="degrees"
   minValue="0.0" maxValue="35.0"/>
<extension measureUnits="degrees"
   minValue="0.0" maxValue="35.0"/>
</footToe>
<footToe footToeID="2">
<flexion measureUnits="degrees"
   minValue="0.0" maxValue="35.0"/>
<extension measureUnits="degrees"
   minValue="0.0" maxValue="35.0"/>
</footToe>
<footToe footToeID="3">
<flexion measureUnits="degrees"
   minValue="0.0" maxValue="35.0"/>
<extension measureUnits="degrees"
   minValue="0.0" maxValue="35.0"/>
</footToe>
<footToe footToeID="4">
<flexion measureUnits="degrees"
   minValue="0.0" maxValue="35.0"/>
<extension measureUnits="degrees"
   minValue="0.0" maxValue="35.0"/>
</footToe>
<footToe footToeID="5">
<flexion measureUnits="degrees"
   minValue="0.0" maxValue="35.0"/>
<extension measureUnits="degrees"
   minValue="0.0" maxValue="35.0"/>
</footToe>
</lowerLimb>
<neck>
<flexion measureUnits="degrees"
```

```
    minValue="0.0" maxValue="40.0"/>
  <extension measureUnits="degrees"
    minValue="0.0" maxValue="40.0"/>
  <leftLateralFlexion measureUnits="degrees"
    minValue="0.0" maxValue="45.0"/>
  <rightLateralFlexion measureUnits="degrees"
    minValue="0.0" maxValue="45.0"/>
  <leftLateralRotation measureUnits="degrees"
    minValue="0.0" maxValue="70.0"/>
  <rightLateralRotation measureUnits="degrees"
    minValue="0.0" maxValue="70.0"/>
  </neck>
  <spinalColumn>
  <flexion measureUnits="degrees"
    minValue="0.0" maxValue="90.0"/>
  <extension measureUnits="degrees"
    minValue="0.0" maxValue="30.0"/>
  <leftLateralFlexion measureUnits="degrees"
    minValue="0.0" maxValue="25.0"/>
  <rightLateralFlexion measureUnits="degrees"
    minValue="0.0" maxValue="25.0"/>
  <leftLateralRotation measureUnits="degrees"
    minValue="0.0" maxValue="30.0"/>
  <rightLateralRotation measureUnits="degrees"
    minValue="0.0" maxValue="30.0"/>
  </spinalColumn>
  <gait>
  <stepLength measureUnits="m" value="0.75"/>
  <stepWidth measureUnits="m" value="-1.0"/>
  <strideLength measureUnits="m" value="1.58"/>
  <footContact>-1.0</footContact>
  <gaitCycle measureUnits="s" value="1.07"/>
  <cadence measureUnits="steps/minute" value="112.0"/>
  <velocity measureUnits="cm/sec" value="82.0"/>
  <doubleSupport measureUnits="% gait cycle" value="20.0"/>
  <stepAsymmetry measureUnits="absolute" value="1.0"/>
  <weightShift measureUnits="degrees" value="-1.0"/>
  </gait>
  </Mobility>
  </User>
</xml>
```

Appendix 2 – GUIDE Profile Generated from VUMS Exchange Format

Example of a converter, GUIDE converter generates a shorter profile by parsing relevant fields for GUIDE project


```
<xml>
    <User>
        <ID>User_Model</ID>
        <General>
            <UserName>jBrown</UserName>
            <Password>jBrownPass</Password>
            <Age>70</Age>
            <Sex>Male</Sex>
            <Height>170</Height>
        </General>
        <Preferences>
            <outputVolume>5.0</outputVolume>
            <fontSize>7</fontSize>
            <fontColour>Blue</fontColour>
            <cursorSize>6.0</cursorSize>
            <cursorColour>White</cursorColour>
        </Preferences>
        <Visual>
            <Acuity>
                <maxValue>-5</maxValue>
                <Acuity1>6</Acuity1>
                <Acuity2>10</Acuity2>
            </Acuity>
            <CS>100</CS>
            <Scotoma>4</Scotoma>
            <FieldLossP>0</FieldLossP>
            <FieldLossC>0</FieldLossC>
            <CB>4</CB>
            <MD>0</MD>
        </Visual>
        <Auditory>
            <halfK>10</halfK>
            <oneK>10</oneK>
            <twoK>9</twoK>
            <fourK>8</fourK>
            <eightK>8</eightK>
        </Auditory>
        <Cognitive>
```

```
            <TMT>23</TMT>
            <DIGSYM>43</DIGSYM>
        </Cognitive>
        <Mobility>
            <GS>30</GS>
            <Tremor>335</Tremor>
            <ROMW>62.5</ROMW>
            <ROMFA>170</ROMFA>
        </Mobility>
    </User>
</xml>
```


References

1. Anderson, J. R., & Lebiere, C. (1998). *The atomic components of thought*. Hillsdale: Lawrence Erlbaum Associates.
2. Apkarian, J., Naumann, S., & Cairns, B. (1989). A three-dimensional kinematic and dynamic model of the lower limb. *Journal of Biomechanics, 22*, 143–155.
3. Biswas, P., Langdon, P., & Robinson, P. (2012). Designing inclusive interfaces through user modeling and simulation. *International Journal of Human Computer Interaction, 28*(1). doi:10.1080/10447318.2011.565718. Taylor & Francis.
4. Brusilovsky, P. (1996). Methods and techniques of adaptive hypermedia. *User Modeling and User-Adapted Interaction, 6*(2–3), 87–129.
5. Cappelli, T. M., & Duffy, V. G. (2006, July 4–6). Motion capture for job risk classifications incorporating dynamic aspects of work. In *Digital human modeling for design and engineering conference,* Lyon, SAE International, Warrendale.
6. Carmagnola, F., Cena, F., & Gena, C. (2007). User modeling in the social web. In B. Apolloni, R. J. Howlett, & L. C. Jain (Eds.), *Knowledge-based intelligent information and engineering systems* (Band 4694 in Lecture notes in computer science, pp. 745–752). Berlin: Springer.
7. Choi, J. (2008). *Developing a 3-dimensional kinematic model of the hand for ergonomic analyses of hand posture, hand space envelope, and tendon excursion*. PhD thesis, The University of Michigan.
8. Coluccini, M., Maini, E. S., Martelloni, C., Sgandurra, G., & Cioni, G. (2007). Kinematic characterization of functional reach to grasp in normal and in motor disabled children. *Gait Posture, 25*(4), 493–501. ISSN 0966-6362. doi:10.1016/j.gaitpost.2006.12.015
9. DeCarlo, D., Metaxas, D., & Stone, M. (1998). An anthropometric face model using variational techniques. In *Proceedings of the 25th annual conference on computer graphics and interactive techniques SIGGRAPH '98* (pp. 67–74). New York: ACM.
10. DiLorenzo, P. C., Zordan, V. B., & Sanders, B. L. (2008). Laughing out loud: Control for modeling anatomically inspired laughter using audio. *ACM Trans Graph, 27*(5), 125:1–8.
11. Eng, J. J., & Winter, D. A. (1995). Kinetic analysis of the lower limbs during walking: What information can be gained from a three-dimensional model? *Journal of Biomechanics, 28*(6), 753–758.
12. Gajos, K., & Weld, D. S. (2004) SUPPLE: Automatically generating user interfaces. In *Proceedings of IUI* (pp. 83–100).
13. Garner, B. A., & Pandy, M. G. (2003). Estimation of musculotendon properties in the human upper limb. *Annals of Biomedical Engineering, 31*, 207–220.

14. Hingtgen, B. A., McGuire, J. R., Wang, M., & Harris, G. F. (2003, September 17–21). Design and validation of an upper extremity kinematic model for application in stroke rehabilitation, Engineering in Medicine and Biology Society. In *Proceedings of the 25th annual international conference of the IEEE* (Vol. 2, pp. 1682–1685).
15. Holzbaur, K. R. S., Murray, W. M., & Delp, S. L. (2005). A model of the upper extremity for simulating musculoskeletal surgery and analyzing neuromuscular control. *Annals of Biomedical Engineering, 33*, 829–840.
16. John, B. E., & Kieras, D. (1996). The GOMS family of user interface analysis techniques: Comparison and contrast. *ACM Transactions on Computer Human Interaction, 3*, 320–351.
17. Kähler, K., Haber, J., Yamauchi, H., & Seidel, H. P. (2002). Head shop: Generating animated head models with anatomical structure. In *ACM SIGGRAPH/EG symposium on computer animation* (pp. 55 64).
18. Klyne, G., Reynolds, F., Woodrow, C., Ohto, H., & Butler, M. H. (Eds.). (2002). *Composite capability/preference profiles (CC/PP): Structure and vocabularies.* W3C Working Draft 08 November 2002. World Wide Web Consortium. Available at: http://www.w3.org/TR/CCPP-struct-vocab/. Accessed 12 Dec 2012.
19. Kobsa, A., Koenemann, J., & Pohl, W. (2001). Personalised hypermedia presentation techniques for improving online customer relationships. *The Knowledge Engineering Review, 16*(2), S. 111–S. 155. Cambridge University Press.
20. Komura, T., Shinagawa, Y., & Kunii, T. L. (2000). Creating and retargeting motion by the musculoskeletal human body model. *The Visual Computer, 16*(5), 254–270.
21. Koo, T. K., Mak, A. F., & Hung, L. K. (2002). In vivo determination of subject-specific musculotendon parameters: Applications to the prime elbow flexors in normal and hemiparetic subjects. *Clinical Biomechanics, 17*(5), 390–399, ISSN 0268-0033. doi:10.1016/S0268-0033(02)00031-1
22. Laitila, L. (2005). *Datormanikinprogram om verktyg vid arbetsplatsutformning – En kritisk studie av programanvändning*. Thesis, Luleå Technical University, Luleå.
23. Lamkull, D., Hanson, L., & Ortengren, R. (2009). A comparative study of digital human modeling simulation results and their outcomes in reality: A case study within manual assembly of automobiles. *International Journal of Industrial Ergonomics, 39*, 428–441.
24. Lassila, O., & Swick, R. R. (Eds.). (1999). *Resource description framework (RDF), model and syntax specification.* W3C recommendation 22 February 1999. World Wide Web Consortium. Available at: http://www.w3.org/TR/REC-rdf-syntax/. Accessed 12 Dec 2012.
25. Lee, S. H., & Terzopoulos, D. (2006). Heads up! Biomechanical modeling and neuromuscular control of the neck. *ACM Trans Graph, 25*(3), 1188–1198. Proceedings of ACM SIGGRAPH 06.
26. Ouerfelli, M., Kumar, V., & Harwin, W. S. (1999). Kinematic modeling of head-neck movements. *IEEE Transactions Systems, Man and Cybernetics, Part A: Systems and Humans, 29*(6), 604–615. doi:10.1109/3468.798064, URL: http://ieeexplore.ieee.org/stamp/stamp.jsp?tp=&arnumber=798064&isnumber=17313
27. Pai, Y. C., & Patton, J. L. (1997). Center of mass velocity-position predictions for balance control. *Journal of Biomechanics, 11*, 341–349.
28. Pai, Y. C., & Patton, J. L. (1998). Erratum: Center of mass velocity-position predictions for balance control. *Journal of Biomechanics, 31*, 199.
29. Pai, Y. C., Rogers, M. W., Patton, J. L., Cain, T. D., & Hanke, T. (1998). Static versus dynamic predictions of protective stepping following waist-pull perturbations in young and older adults. *Journal of Biomechanics, 31*, 1111–1118.
30. Paternò, F. (1999). *Model based design and evaluation of interactive applications*. Berlin: Springer.
31. Patton, J. L., Lee, W. A., & Pai, Y. C. (2000). Relative stability improves with experience in a dynamic standing task. *Experimental Brain Research, 135*, 117–126.
32. Patton, J. L., Pai, Y. C., & Lee, W. A. (1997). *A simple model of the feasible limits to postural stability*. Presented at IEEE/Engineering in Medicine an Biology Society meeting, Chicago.

33. Pennestrì, E., Stefanelli, R., Valentini, P. P., & Vita, L. (2007). Virtual musculo-skeletal model for the biomechanical analysis of the upper limb. *Journal of Biomechanics, 40*(6), 1350–1361, ISSN 0021-9290. doi:10.1016/j.jbiomech.2006.05.013. http://www.sciencedirect.com/science/article/pii/S0021929006001679
34. Porter, J., Case, K., Freer, M. T., & Bonney, M. C. (1993). Automotive ergonomics, Chapter. In *computer-aided ergonomics design of automobiles*. London: Taylor & Francis
35. Prince, F., Corriveau, H., Hebert, R., & Winter, D. A. (1997). Gait in the elderly. *Gait Posture, 5*(2), 128–135(8).
36. Rao, S. S., Bontrager, E. L., Gronley, J. K., Newsam, C. J., & Perry, J. (1996). Three dimensional kinematics of wheelchair propulsion. *IEEE Transactions on Rehabilitation Engineering, 4*, 152–160.
37. Sapin, E., Goujon, H., de Almeida, F., Fodé, P., & Lavaste, F. (2008). Functional gait analysis of trans-femoral amputees using two different single-axis prosthetic knees with hydraulic swing-phase control: Kinematic and kinetic comparison of two prosthetic knees. *Prosthetics and Orthotics International, 32*(2), 201–218.
38. Shapiro, A., Faloutsos, P., & Ng-Thow-Hing, V. (2005). Dynamic animation and control environment. In *Proceedings of graphics interface* (pp. 61–70).
39. Van Nierop, O. A., Van der Helm, A., Overbeeke, K. J., & Djajadiningrat, T. J. (2008). A natural human hand model. *The Visual Computer, 24*(1), 31–44.

Chapter 16
Standardization of Audiovisual Media Accessibility

From Vision to Reality

Peter Olaf Looms

Abstract The final chapter discusses role and utility of standardization of accessibility. Section 16.2 discusses the role of accessible media in the twenty-first century, in particular what we mean by 'media', 'computing' and 'accessibility'. Section 16.3 goes on to discuss the role of standardization in furthering media accessibility. Section 16.4 concludes with an account of the work of a focus group at ITU-T on Audio Visual Media Accessibility to produce a roadmap of actions covering legislation, regulation and standardization that can make Audio Visual (AV) media more accessible.

16.1 Introduction

In a book on accessible computing, a chapter on standardization and audiovisual media accessibility is potentially an intellectual minefield. The writer is unlikely to survive without first sketching out the context of the topic. This is what I intend to do with the aid of a few rhetorical questions:

- Which media are we talking about?
- What is the link between 'media' and 'computing'?
- What is meant by 'accessibility' in the context of audiovisual media?
- What is the purpose of standardization in the context of promoting accessible media?

In Sect. 16.2, I will address the first three questions by providing a personal view of the development of information and communication up to the present day to clarify 'media', 'computing' and 'accessibility' which lead on to Sect. 16.3 in which the standardization of digital audiovisual media is discussed.

P.O. Looms (✉)
ECOM-ICOM Programme, University of Hong Kong, Hong Kong SAR, China
e-mail: polooms@gmail.com

P. Biswas et al. (eds.), *A Multimodal End-2-End Approach to Accessible Computing*,
Human–Computer Interaction Series, DOI 10.1007/978-1-4471-6708-2_16

To conclude the chapter, I will explain what the International Telecommunication Union (ITU) 'Focus Group' on audiovisual media accessibility is doing at global level to make AV media accessible.

16.2 The Role of Accessible Media in the Twenty-First Century

16.2.1 From Oral Communication to Literacy

In a recent UNESCO report about communication, media and information and information literacy, Moeller [1] and her colleagues observed that "*Since the dawn of human civilization, in every sphere of human activity, the access to information, the creation and application of new knowledge, and the communication of such knowledge to others have contributed to the evolution of societies and the economic welfare of people. Knowledge about how to do things, how to communicate, and how to work with other people has therefore been regarded, since ancient times, as the most precious 'wealth' that humans possess*".

Some 50,000 years ago in Africa, our forebears used oral communication as the key means of sharing knowledge, supplemented by cave paintings. Forty thousand years later in places such as Egypt, Sumeria and China, writing emerged in the form of hieroglyphs, characters on oracle bones or clay tablets. These information media were joined by tallies such as the Inca Quipu for basic stocktaking and bookkeeping. For several thousand years, access to information and knowledge via such media was confined to the ruling classes. For the rest, communication was invariably face-to-face (presencial and 'real-time').

16.2.2 Mass Media

In the nineteenth century, the industrial revolution brought with it the option of making printing a mainstream technology, mass-producing posters, books and newspapers. Reading, writing and arithmetic were no longer skills that were confined to the elite but extended to the middle class. Analogue media were increasingly 'available'. Making them 'accessible' in the broadest sense of the word was based on the experience of publishers, editors and typographers. In certain societies, literacy and numeracy became competencies central to popular enlightenment and school education. Presencial, real-time communication was now joined by information media that allowed for virtual, asynchronous communication. Telecommunication such as the telegraph had the same qualities and reduced the barriers of distance.

The early twentieth century saw a shift from media design based on tacit knowledge to evidence-based media design. Systematic research into legibility and readability began to make a difference. In addition to studies on the importance of type size, type design and layout (line length, line spacing, colour contrast, justification and whether text is hyphenated), research revealed the importance of the saccadic rhythm of eye movement for readability.

Posters, newspapers and the paperback were joined by time-based media: silent movies, radio and television. As these audiovisual media became available and affordable, this gave them the potential to inform, educate and entertain even those who had little or no formal schooling. From a communication perspective, the telephone, radio and television were examples of virtual, synchronous communication, until radio and TV programmes could be pre-produced and archived for later distribution.

16.2.3 From Literacy to Digital Literacy

The period after the Second World War saw the ascendance of television and the emergence of computer processing and digital technologies that allow us to do more with less bandwidth. The move to digital first changed number-crunching, then word processing, audio, still images and finally TV and video. In the last decade of the twentieth century, the Internet moved out of universities into mainstream society. At least as significant was the meteoric rise of digital mobile telephones and networks.

Formal literacy and numeracy skills were still vital, but needed to be complemented by media and information skills – 'digital literacy' – to be able to use and benefit from the new means of communication.

16.2.4 Accessibility – Disability, Migration and Ageing

By the end of the twentieth century, the need to make information and communication technologies 'accessible' was being influenced by a number of factors. The three that I address here are changing perspectives on *disabilities and human functioning*, *migration* (both within countries and from one country to another); and *ageing* (shifts in the proportion of citizens over 60 in the industrialized economies).

The first factor is disability. In a paper written earlier in 2012 [2] I discuss the schools of thought on disabilities and human functioning, and how they have changed in the last 30 years.

One of the few widely used theoretical frameworks in this area is the 1980 International Classification of Impairments, Disabilities and Handicaps (ICIDH) from the World Health Organization, WHO. Arguably, this was the first global attempt to provide a coherent conceptual framework for disability. The ICIDH had three constituent dimensions – impairment, disability and handicap.

In the same period, the Union of the Physically Impaired Against Segregation, UPIAS, founded in 1972 worked for the acceptance of new definitions of impairment and disability [3].

New perspectives on the concept of disability emerged: the minority model (essentially a lack of equal rights as a primary impediment to equality between able and disabled populations) and the structural model (focusing on environmental factors as the cause of disability). Elements from the two were combined in the so-called social model in which disability is seen as a socially created problem and not at all an attribute of an individual. In the social model, disability demands a political response, since the problem is created by an unaccommodating physical environment brought about by attitudes and other features of the social environment.

The ongoing debate on disability led to a major revision of the ICIDH, the result of which was the International Classification of Functioning, Disability and Health (ICF) 2001. The WHO calls this amalgamation the *biopsychosocial* model.

A concerted effort was made in the drafting of the ICF to avoid terms with negative connotations by shifting the emphasis from disability to capability or 'human functioning'.

The term 'disability' was replaced by a neutral term 'activity'. Negative attributes of activity are described as 'activity limitation'. Similarly, 'handicap' was replaced by another neutral, higher order term, 'participation', that appears to cover the aim or the underlying communicative intent of the activities. Negative attributes are termed 'participation restriction'. An umbrella term 'disablements' was included to cover all the negative attributes of the ICF, i.e. impairments, activity limitations and participation restrictions.

The shift in the connotations of disability means that the scope of media accessibility is not longer limited to addressing the needs of persons with sensory impairments formally recognized by public administrations. Media accessibility now encompasses a wide range of disablements that constitute barriers to inclusion.

That leads to the second, related factor, '*migration*'. According to the UNDP [4]: "The overwhelming majority of people who move do so inside their own country. ... Approximately 740 million people are internal migrants... Most of the world's 200 million international migrants moved from one developing country to another or between developed countries." In countries such as Belgium, Finland, Switzerland, South Africa or India in which there are two or more officially recognized languages, or in states with significant immigrant or refugee populations, social cohesion requires media policies to address *linguistic* accessibility to prevent cultural and social exclusion.

The third factor – dealt with in Chap. 1 of this book – is demography and *ageing* populations. In addition to the challenge of age-related disablements, there is also the psychological and social dimension termed 'digital native' and 'digital immigrant' by Prensky [5].

16.2.5 *Inclusive Design for Both Digital Natives and Digital Immigrants*

Europeans below the age of 10 in urban, middle-class Europe are clearly digital natives who were born into a world where nearly everything is digital. They have grown up with computers, smartphones, games consoles and digital television.

Information and communication technologies (ICTs) in the industrialized world have made virtual communication widespread, contributing to the breakdown of the barriers of time and place.

Synchronous or asynchronous communication in the form of chatting, messaging, skyping, googling, multiplayer gaming and 'thumbs up' on social media are claimed to be at least as important for maintaining social relationships with peers as 'old-fashioned' presencial, real-time communication with friends and family.

Digital natives are not just 'couch potatoes' or passive consumers of media. They also zappers, voters, sharers of playlists, photos and videos, collectors, critics, conversationalists, co-creators (mash-ups) – changing role depending on the circumstances according to Li and Bernoff (2008) [6].

Many of those who are no longer young are 'digital immigrants'. Experience from the UK Switchover Help Scheme indicates that older people seem innately more distrusting of all technology. They grew up with analogue media that were prone to mechanical failure, but in some ways were easier to use (radio and TV receivers usually had simple, on-off interfaces).

Digital technologies for such digital immigrants – even mobile phones and digital TVs – may be unfamiliar and baffling to use and enjoy. Digital literacy for such persons requires them to recognize that using digital technologies is desirable and doable. It also requires unlearning old habits and learning new ways of doing things.

Designing digital media to make them 'accessiblc' requires an inclusive approach. Inclusion requires us to check the availability, affordability, accessibility and usability of what we do, summarised in the following figure as a pyramid – taken from Looms (2012) [2] (Fig. 16.1).

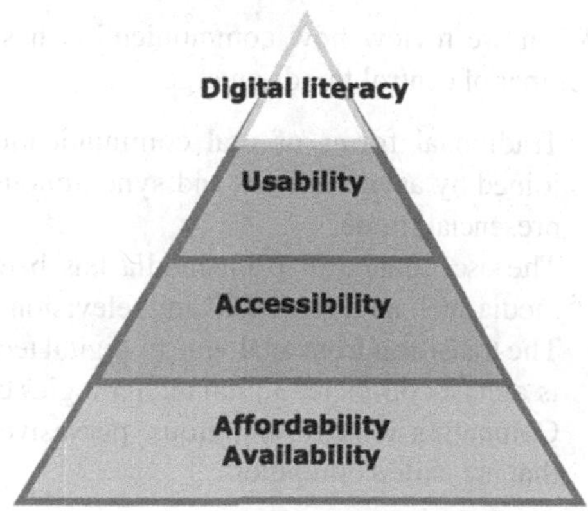

Fig. 16.1 The inclusion pyramid

Damodaran (2002) [7] provides a comprehensive review of such factors in a scoping document on the technological and business aspects of the switchover from analogue to digital television in the UK. Many of these potential barriers were revisited in 'Digital Britain', the final report on e-society for the UK government [8]. The report asserts that" ... there are several obstacles facing those that are off-line: availability, affordability, capability and relevance". Studies on Internet 'offliners' (those who have never used the Internet) such as Helsper (2011) [9] conclude that they are more likely to have lower education levels and no employment. Carter (2010) [10] suggests a loose taxonomy – three groups of persons who have most to gain from [digital] technologies:

> *Older people*: A substantial proportion of older people could be assisted by technology as a means of addressing their poverty, social isolation, health and need for support to live independently in the community.
>
> *The 10 per cent most economically deprived*: This group, as measured using the Index of Multiple Deprivation, are highly correlated with social housing /.../
>
> *Socially excluded and minority groups*: There are many smaller groups for whom the sources of exclusion are multiple and chronic – including factors like disability or learning difficulties, ethnic origin, location, culture or language. /.../ Other groups in this category include offenders, those with mental health issues, those out of work, early school leavers, looked after children and those with literacy and numeracy skills needs, homeless people or frequent movers, those living in isolated or rural communities, and families at risk from poverty, crime, addiction or poor health. This has a significant economic impact on those affected.

Cap Gemini (2012) [11] in their evaluation of the working of a UK campaign The Race Online 2012 present the business case for such an investment in broadband take-up by everyone. The report attempts to quantify the value for consumers of shopping and paying bills online, the educational benefits for children, improved employment prospects and lifetime earnings, and government savings in providing public services online.

16.2.6 Conclusions on Media and Accessibility

When we review how communication has changed in the last two centuries, a number of central trends emerge:

- Traditional forms of oral communication (face-to-face, real-time) have been joined by asynchronous and synchronous communication, in either a virtual or presencial mode.
- The ascendance of print media has been joined by audiovisual, 'time-based' media such as films, radio and television
- The transition from analogue to digital technologies that use computer processing is almost complete; digital technologies continue to change.
- Computing is now ubiquitous, pervasive and by no means confined to devices that are called computers.

- Digital literacy is to the twenty-first century what literacy was in the twentieth century – new competencies are required to complement the old ones.
- The connotations of 'disability' have broadened to encompass not only differently-able bodied persons with sensory impairments but also a broad range of factors (disablements) that can lead to exclusion.
- In a digital, globalized world, end-to-end computing accessibility requires us to look at 'access' from a broad perspective. Inclusive design needs to address the whole inclusion pyramid from availability and affordability at the bottom, through accessibility and usability to digital literacy at the top.

16.3 The Role of Standardization to Further Accessible Media

This second section looks at standardization. The rhetorical questions that I would like to address are:

- What are 'standards' and 'standardization'?
- In connection with media, what needs standardizing and at which level?
- How is media standardization currently done?
- What needs to be changed or added to improve media accessibility?

16.3.1 What Are 'Standards' and 'Standardization'?

The literature on the subject asserts that "standardization as a process of standard making, whereby "a 'standard' is to be understood, for the present purposes, as a set of technical specifications adhered to by a producer, either tacitly or as a result of a formal agreement"" David and Greenstein (1990) [12] discussed in Fomin and Keil (2000) [13]. Note the implicit assumption that standards are 'technical specifications'. The standardization landscape covers technical specifications but also legislation, regulatory guidelines and examples of good practice. Standardization can follow formal or informal paths. Taken together, they can all be agents of change.

Wood (2011) [14] in his paper on technical standards in digital television scopes the term in this way:

> The term 'technical standard' is used in different ways, and can mean different things. Broadly, it describes the common technological 'recipe' underpinning particular hardware equipment, or software interfaces and applications. Technical standards define the capability of the equipment or system, and the extent of the services it provides.
>
> Technical standards apply in many fields, including the media industry, and can be adopted at various levels. They may be applied to a particular company's products, or across an entire industrial sector. Equally, they may be adhered to or enforced regionally, nationally, or globally. Technical standards at all these levels are found in the media world today.

Theory/Model	Focus	Outcome	Explanatory Mechanisms	Deficiencies
A. Game theoretic: standard selection (Besen and Farrell 1994; Farrell and Saloner 1988)	Selection of type of standard: – committee – market – hybrid	Competing within vs. between standard(s). Fast vs. slow process	Rational (bounded rational) behavior of actors	Social forces are ignored. Determines outcomes, but can not account for process
B. Game theoretic: alliance formation (Axelrod et al. 1995)	Establishing alliances (selection of standard)	Joining in with: – collaborators – competitors – none	Rational (bounded rational) behavior of actors	Ignores timing of joining the alliance. Assumes acceptance of any member
C. Increased returns (Arthur 1989)	Selection/adoption of standard. Formation of dominant design	Dominant design. From competing between to within the standard	Adoption of technology increases attractiveness to third parties to support the technology	Points to complex socio-political processes, but does not answer "whys"
D. Bandwagon (Wade 1995, 1996)	Selection/adoption of standard. Formation of dominant design	Dominant design	Selection determined by organizational communities. Compatibility or sponsorship criterion	Processes within community are not addressed
E. Diffusion of Innovation (Rogers 1995)	Diffusion of innovation process	Character of innovation's adoption	Communication of information on innovation within a social ether	Assumes unlimited communication. Limited to micro level analysis
F. Power relations (Star 1991)	Decision making process	Explaining particular decision	Accounts for power and influences of individuals	Limited to micro level analysis
G. Knowledge creation (Cowan and Foray 1997; Michelis 1997)	Communication of knowledge	Expertise for standard creation. Information for decision on adoption	Knowledge distributed through personal and formal channels	Standard creation and diffusion are separated
H. Actor Network Theory (Callon et al. 1986; Latour 1987)	Analysis of choices/ paths. Passage points/ gatekeepers	Alignment of interests	Human and non-human actors have equal explanatory power. No micro-macro divide	Mostly descriptive

Fig. 16.2 Standardization models (From Fomin and Keil [13], p. 210)

Television is the most regulated media on most nation states when it comes to accessibility. It sets a precedent for the accessibility of other media, so it is a good place to start. The TV industry consists of a number of stakeholders each with their own interests. Wood also talks of 'the public interest' – "the provision of goods and services of the 'highest quality' at the 'lowest cost'". Public bodies through legislation and regulation influence the working of the market in the public interest.

Fomin and Keil provide a useful summary of standardization models: their focus, outcomes, explanatory mechanisms and deficiencies. These are summarized in Fig. 16.2.

The first column identifies eight of the main theories or models that can be used to analyze standardization. In media design, Roger's Diffusion of Innovation (E) is widely used but many of the others are used less frequently.

The second column summarizes the main focus of that model. In the case of Rogers, this looks at the take-up of innovations by early adopters, the early majority, the late majority and laggards.

Column three characterizes the outcome. Rogers leads to the characteristics of the take-up of innovation by various groups.

Column four covers the explanatory mechanisms invoked by the model, in Roger's case the communication of information about the innovation in a given social environment.

Column five summarizes the author's assessment of the main deficiency of the model in question. Rogers builds on the assumption that communication is unhindered and confines itself to analysis at the micro level.

The authors apply these models to the analysis of three different cases: 1st generation mobile phones, NMT, GSM and a wireless link. The cases involved *de facto* or *de jure* standardization committees, or an *ad hoc* alliance. The authors conclude that no one model could address all of the issues and suggest the use of multiple models to adequately explain the causal relations driving standardization:

Wood discusses the need for digital TV standardization, the main driving forces and the arguments for and against industry-wide technical standards. He looks at the related concept of 'technological neutrality' – that no regulation should specify particular technical solutions – at 'interoperability' and at the importance of interoperability for 'compatibility'.

16.3.2 In Connection with Audiovisual Media, What Needs Standardizing and at Which Level?

There are a number of stakeholders with interests in accessibility. First there are differently-abled persons who want to enjoy, say, television like anyone else. Then there are the various stakeholders in the value chain for television from those who create content all the way to those who use it shown in the next figure:

The value chain should be read from left to right, starting with (1), the production of content – TV programmes, access services spots/trailers and programme guides using metadata about the content.

The content is packaged as TV channels by broadcasters (2) and as a TV service (3) by platform operators (e.g. a Pay TV operator).

In many cases, the TV signals have to be delivered to multiple distribution platforms (terrestrial, cable, and satellite, IPTV, over-the-top (OTT) Internet). In the value chain shown above in Fig. 16.3, the signal is delivered via an internal, contribution system (4) to the organization that handles transmission (5). The signal is delivered to a TV receiver (6). In some cases this is a set-top box (STB) with a separate display (the box below). In others it is an integrated digital TV set with the receiver built into the screen – the dotted line around the top two boxes of (6). In both cases, the viewer (8) uses a remote control to interact with the TV service – programmes, access services and related information services – in order to enjoy the content without getting up from his chair. (7).

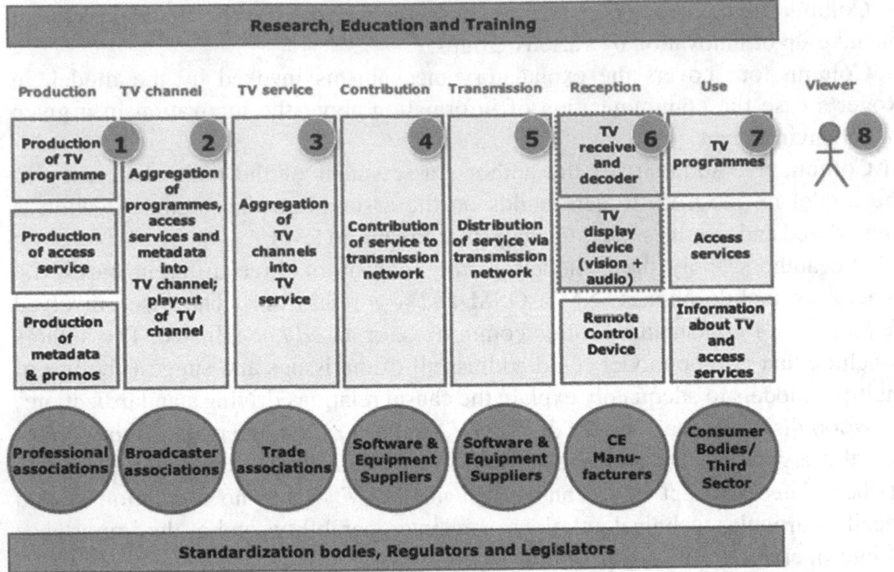

Fig. 16.3 A general value chain for digital television (Figure based on value chain in Looms (2011) [17])

From a technical perspective, interoperability means transporting the TV content all the way from (1) to (8). From an organizational perspective, there are both stakeholders directly associated with this value chain and those that have indirect interests and influence.

Below the value chain itself are a number of circles representing interest groups. At the bottom are standardization bodies, regulators and legislators. At the top are those who do research into media accessibility and provide education and training for those in the value chain.

When looking at media standardization, it is clear that the technical interoperability of the TV service needs to be in place. Traditionally, the focus has been on the receiver, the display and the remote control. I would argue that the value chain shows the need to focus end-to-end on the TV service and not just on the receiver (7).

In some cases, as hearing instrument manufacturers move to replace induction loop ('telecoil') wireless connections between television sets and hearing aids with digital wireless connections, we will have to include the interfaces between the primary receiver and assistive devices likely hearing aids in media standardization.

Standardization is important to facilitate some of the business processes that *lead* to a TV service, for example

- t- be able to archive the assets for later or other use
- t- ensure that access services can be delivered on multiple service platforms (not only digital TV networks using different systems but on broadband and mobile networks)

A typical example is the provision in Australia of Audio Description from August to November 2012 by the ABC. Some of the programmes are originally from the UK (for example *Midsomer Murders*, a TV detective series first sown on ITV in the UK) for which it makes sense to re-use the original AD if the audio recording is available and the rights have been cleared. This is a pointer towards legislation and ensuring that intellectual property associated with derivative works such as subtitles and audio description is adequately defined in legislation and production contracts.

16.3.3 How Is Media Standardization Currently Done?

As mentioned by Wood (op.cit.), standardization operates at different levels. This may involve formal standardization bodies or committees, or industry alliances that can be formalized or ad hoc initiatives.

The area with which I am most familiar is digital television, and Fig. 16.4 contains examples of the various entities active in digital television standardization:

The ITU is crucial for global and regional agreement on the use of spectrum -radio frequencies for wireless communication including radio, TV and mobile phone and wireless Internet. ISO and IEC play related but coordinated roles at global level.

As Wood explains, there are both standardization bodies and industrial alliances that work with technical specifications for digital TV. They may have their origins at global, regional or national level. The locus of action of national or regional alliances may change with time:

- The Digital Video Broadcast (DVB) family of standards was originally a European standardization project. Today it also underpins television interoperability outside European countries such as Australia, Columbia, India and New Zealand
- The US alliance called Advanced Television Systems Committee (ATSC) forms the basis of work on terrestrial digital television in the US, Canada, South Korea and in Mexico

Fig. 16.4 Digital television standardization

Level	Standardization bodies	Alliances
Global	ITU IEC ISO	MPEG
Regional	ETSI CE	DVB Digital Europe NorDig
National	ANSI BSI DIN	ATSC CMMB ISBD-T DTG

- Integrated Services Digital Broadcasting – Terrestrial (ISBD-T) forms the basis of digital television services not only in Japan where it was originally developed but also in Brazil and other countries in South America (with the exception of Columbia).
- China Multimedia Mobile Broadcasting (CMMB) is a digital television system developed in China.

All of these alliances have made use of global standards such as the Moving Pictures Experts Group (MPEG), yet in terms of digital broadcasting signals from each of these alliances are not 'comprehensible' by any single user device. Standards such as DVB can be regarded as a rich toolkit of techniques, somc mandatory and others optional, that allow for the design and delivery of TV services that are in line with regional or national circumstances. National and regional alliances in the first instance seek formal approval of their work from one or more standardization bodies at the same level (for instance DVB from European Telecommunications Standards Institute, ETSI).

Broadcast television in most countries is one of the most regulated media. National regulators commonly choose to adopt a technologically neutral stance. They prescribe objectives and targets but refrain from defining how those objectives should be met. This is left for market forces to decide. Digital standards such as DVB often contain both mandatory and optional requirements. This is certainly the case for the mechanisms for delivering access services that are often optional requirements – often with the aim of promoting innovation through competition.

If we take the case of digital television in the Nordic countries, the starting point is the DVB specification that has been submitted to ETSI. NorDig is the special interest group, an alliance of all the key stakeholders in the Nordic countries and Ireland. The NorDig executive committee receives suggestions for standardization initiatives from its members. This committee then asks the technical committee to prepare a business case for the initiative in question. Recent examples include an API, multichannel audio, Personal Video Recorders (PVRs) and access services for digital TV.

In the case of access services, the technical committee carried out a study on 16 of the most widely sold digital television receivers in the Nordic area that comply with the current NorDig specification. The products in the study account for a majority of receiver sales. Using a test transport stream, the receivers were evaluated using five different test scenarios to measure their performance in connection with Audio Description (AD). The scenarios included:

1. Being able to select AD (broadcast mix[1]) by signaling a 'virtual channel' so that the viewer just has to select the TV channel with AD on the EPG or by pressing the number keys on the remote corresponding to the TV channel ID
2. Selecting AD (Broadcast mix) by signaling the presence of AD broadcast mix

[1] AD Broadcast mix is an alternative 'ready-to-use' mix of the audio channels including the AD. It is produced by the broadcaster.

3. Selecting AD (Receiver mix[2]) by signaling the presence of AD receiver mix
4. Selecting the AD (Broadcast mix) by pressing the 'alternative audio' button.

All 16 receivers were able to handle the first scenario. Four responded correctly to the second scenario. Four responded in different ways to the 'receiver mix' signaling (differences in levels and fading). None of the receivers responded correctly to Alternative Audio. The receivers were also tested to see if the scenarios lead to interference with the normal operations of the receivers.

What is instructive to note here is that all receivers responded correctly to the first scenario that makes use of mandatory requirements in DVB. The other scenarios invoked optional requirements in DVB all of which were implemented in ways that the CE manufacturer had chosen.

The study provides the basis for the recommendation within NorDig that action is required to assure interoperability when providing services such as AD. How can this be done?

16.3.4 What Needs to Be Changed or Added to Improve Media Accessibility?

One approach to standardization that builds on existing standardization practices is the use of 'profiles' or subsets of the standard. Those involved in, say, NorDig can choose to agree on a specific implementation path, essentially making an optional requirement mandatory. NorDig has done this for TV channel identifiers and for mechanisms to accord top priority to DVB bitmap subtitles and a lower priority to subtitles delivered using DVB digital teletext, so that teletext will be suppressed if both kinds of subtitle are present. Such additions were submitted to DVB for consideration as an update and when approved they could then be sent to ETSI.

National regulators in the Nordic region can then choose to endorse the profile, subject to sufficient support from the stakeholders in the TV value chain. They retain technological neutrality while respecting consensus positions in the market. Regulation may not always be needed for access service provision. In Sweden, *Comhem* the main digital cable operator has no formal 'must-carry' obligations for AD from SVT, the Swedish public service broadcaster, but chooses to do so.

What emerges from the above account is that standardization involves end-to-end television service provision for each of the delivery platforms. It also involves the business process for exchange and archiving of content (programmes, access services and metadata). Standardization and regulation are prerequisites but not always a guarantee for access services provision

[2]AD Receiver mix delivers the AD as a separate audio track to the receiver. This track is mixed with the original programme audio in the receiver itself.

Compatibility needs also to be seen in relation to the effective lifetime of that standard in the marketplace.

Anecdotal evidence based on a cursory examination of media such as radio, TV, websites with rich media and electronic games suggests that:

- Life cycles for media are getting shorter (standards for analogue radio and TV lasted for many decades whereas their digital equivalents are evolving more rapidly; web browsers, games consoles, smart phones and computer tablets have life-cycles measured in years or even months)
- The number of delivery platforms for media continues to increase (the BBC's i-player for the asynchronous delivery and enjoyment of radio and television programmes is available on more than 40 different distribution platforms [15]).
- The effective life of audiovisual content – films, television fiction and documentaries – often exceeds the lifetime of the platforms on which it is delivered. The implication is that content assets (programmes, metadata and associated access services) need to be produced, packaged and delivered in ways that facilitate interoperability across platforms and over time. This requires a 'Create Once, Publish Everywhere' (COPE) strategy (also termed 'Author Once, Delivery Everywhere', or 'Produce Once, Publish Everywhere') for content commissioning, production and distribution [16].

This section demonstrates that standardization can be an important contributing factor to promoting media accessibility in well-regulated areas such as digital television. Standardization on its own is not necessarily a guarantee that end-to-end interoperability for a media service is in place.

16.4 The Work of the ITU-T 'Focus Group' on Audiovisual Media Accessibility

When the ITU explores a new area that may require a permanent forum to manage the work, the first step is to set up a so-called 'Focus Group' that allows for contributions from both ITU members and other interested parties. The activities of the Focus Group are self-funded, meaning that all those taking part do so at their own cost. ITU provides the secretariat and coordination.

Following a joint EBU-ITU seminar held on accessible media in November 2010, ITU-T with the support of ITU-R (that handles radio frequency allocation) decided to set up a Focus Group on Audiovisual Media Accessibility (ITU-T FG AVA). The group was set up in May 2011 with a mandate to conclude its work within 2 years.

The FG AVA takes as its starting point the 11 Objectives and 4 General Aims in its Terms of Reference (ToR) mentioned on the FG AVA website [18]:

Objectives

(i) Encourage the availability and use of access services taking into account the needs of all users, making "accessibility to all" a principle for universal design in line with the UN Convention on the Rights of Persons with Disabilities.
(ii) Determine how to involve all stakeholders, including potential users, in the development of digital audio-visual access systems. For users, the principle "nothing about us without us", must be applied to any system development.
(iii) Identify gaps in existing specifications that support the established service requirements in systems defined by both ITU-T and ITU-R.
(iv) Identify the challenges to interoperability and access service interoperability requirements. Consideration should also be given to testing and other compliance mechanisms.
(v) Actively to promote the use of systems for access services which apply internationally agreed standards for a given delivery platform.
(vi) Collect real-world problems from persons with disabilities and persons with age-related functional impairments.
(vii) Collect issues and problems related to implementation of the UN Convention on the Rights of Persons with Disabilities.
(viii) Suggest actions to be taken to resolve access-related problems if they are within the mandate of ITU.
(ix) Prepare clear guidelines on the application of the UN Convention on the Rights of Persons with Disabilities to the delivery of digital AV media.
(x) Collect examples of good practice through case studies and other means, and to prepare guidelines for the inclusion of access services in all new digital AV user devices.
(xi) Suggest actions to be taken to build awareness of accessibility and the concepts of universal design.

Further Aims

- Encourage people to become involved in the accessibility work of ITU.
- Encourage the participation of persons with disabilities.
- Encourage the participation of universities.
- Encourage the participation of company accessibility departments.

At the first meeting, a mission statement and a number of basic principles were agreed:

> We clarify what audiovisual media are, identify priorities and identify the options for making audiovisual media universally accessible and enjoyable.

The work emerging from a series of face-to-face and virtual meetings of the whole Focus Group and sub-groups will lead to 8 deliverables:

0. Produce a taxonomy of AV media (What is meant by the term "AV media"?)
1. Agree a subset of digital AV media for which actions are required (Which of these media do we address in the Focus Group? Do we also address television emergency alerts? Do we cover both analog and digital media, or should we concentrate on digital AV media?)
2. Produce operational definitions of AV media accessibility (Which persons have difficulty enjoying AV media? What is the nature of the challenge (public service emergency alerts, programs)? What can we do for these persons to make AV media easy to find, use and enjoy?)
3. Identify Key Performance Indicators for digital AV media accessibility (Which criteria can be used to assess the availability, use and enjoyment of digital AV media by everyone including persons with disabilities?)
4. Map the key stakeholders involved in accessible AV media creation, exchange, distribution, use and assessment (What is the "food chain" for various kinds of accessible AV media? How can each of them contribute to making AV media accessible?)
5. Identify the current accessibility provisions for AV media among signatories of the UN CRPD and examples of good practice (What is already being done? Which practices can be emulated by others working on accessibility?)
6. Identify actions that are needed to promote digital AV media accessibility
7. Recommend a sub-set of actions that should be followed up by the ITU to promote digital AV media accessibility

Deliverable 7 is relevant to this chapter, as a roadmap of actions would primarily concern frequency allocation and actions targeting legislation, regulation and standardization among its members.

FG AVA has focused on digital TV, IPTV, media on mobile networks and time-based media on the Web. Meeting 1 recognized that, given the role of computer games in industrialized countries, these should also be included if resources were forthcoming.

FG AVA consists of some 90 participants from a wide range of constituents, in particular universities. They take part in the 7 plenary meetings and – between plenary sessions – in innumerable *ad hoc* meetings of the FG AVA working groups that address issues to do with specific access services, platforms or regulation.

The Working Groups all use the same basic template using the 'gap' model for strategic plan to structure their work:

A. *Vision*. Where do we want accessibility to be in the medium to long-term?
B. *Current status*. Where are we now in relation to that vision? What is the gap between where we want to be and where we are right now? What prevents us from turning the vision into reality?
C. *Actions*. What actions are needed to break down the obstacles and barriers identified in B?
D. *Road map for ITU*. Which sub-set of actions can ITU promote to make audiovisual media accessible?

As can be seen from this chapter, FG AVA expects to complete its work on time. While it is premature to indicate the content of the Roadmap, what is clear is the need for concerted action at global, regional and national levels to raise awareness about the nature of the media accessibility challenge. Even in digital television, very few have a clear understanding of the nature of the challenge, what can be done, how little (in relative terms) accessibility costs and what the sustainable business models are to make AV media accessible. A part of this process is an understanding of how standardization can promote computing accessibility.

References

1. Moeller, S., Joseph, A., Lau, J., & Carbo, T. (2011). Towards media and information literacy indicators. Background document of the expert meeting, 4–6 November 2010, Bangkok, Thailand. Paris: UNESCO. Retrieved July 7, 2012, from http://www.ucm.es/BUCM/boletin/doc17043.pdf
2. Looms, P. O. (2012, October). Design models for media accessibility. *Journal of Designing in China*. Hangzhou, PRC.
3. UPIAS founding statement. http://www.leeds.ac.uk/disability-studies/archiveuk/UPIAS/UPIAS.pdf
4. UNDP. (2009). *Human development report 2009 human movement: Snapshots and trends*. New York: UNDP.
5. Prensky, M. (2001, October). Digital natives, digital immigrants. *On the Horizon, 9*(5), 1–6. Bradford: MCB University Press.
6. Li, C., & Bernoff, J. (2008). *Groundswell: Winning in a world transformed by social technologies*. Boston: Harvard Business Press.
7. Damodaran, L. (2002). Analogue to digital switchover: Human aspects of adoption (A scoping study for the Digital Television Project – CRSP456). http://www.digitaltelevision.gov.uk/pdf_documents/publications/scoping_study.pdf
8. Carter, L. (2009). Digital Britain – Final report. http://www.official-documents.gov.uk/document/cm76/7650/7650.pdf
9. Helsper, E. J. (2011). *The emergence of a digital underclass digital policies in the UK and evidence for inclusion* (Media Policy Brief 3). London: London School of Economics and Political Science, Department of Media and Communications. http://blogs.lse.ac.uk/mediapolicyproject/
10. Carter, L. (2010). *Delivering digital inclusion*. Annex 2: Who do we want to help? (pp. 4–5). London: UK Department for Business Innovation & Skills.
11. Cap Gemini Consulting. (2012). *6.2. The economic case for digital inclusion – Key findings* (p. 62). Evaluating the work of the UK Digital Champion and Race Online 2012 – An independent review March 2012 Race Online, UK.
12. David, P. A., & Greenstein, S. (1990). The economics of compatibility standards: An introduction to recent research. *The Economics of Innovations and New Technology, 1*(1/2), 3–41.
13. Fomin, V., & Keil, T. (2000). Standardization: Bridging the gap between economic and social theory. In *ICIS '00 proceedings of the twenty-first international conference on Information systems* (pp. 206–217). Atlanta.
14. Wood, D. (2011). *Mapping digital media: Technical standards in terrestrial television* (Reference Series No. 9). Open Society Media Program. Open Society Foundations. http://www.soros.org/reports/mapping-digital-media-technical-standards-terrestrial-television
15. Wikipedia. BBC iPlayer. http://en.wikipedia.org/wiki/BBC_iPlayer

16. Looms, P. O. (2006). Public service media: All things to all people – On all platforms, anytime? In: C. S. Nissen (Ed.), *Making a difference – Public service broadcasting and the media landscape in Europe*. Published in English, French, Italian and Estonian for the European Broadcasting Union by John Libbey Publishing, UK.
17. Looms, P. O. (2011). *Mapping digital media: Gatekeeping in digital media* (Reference Series No. 8). Open Society Media Program. Open Society Foundations. http://www.soros.org/reports/mapping-digital-media-gatekeeping-digital-media
18. ITU-T FG AVA website. http://www.itu.int/en/ITU-T/focusgroups/ava/Pages/default.aspx

Index

P. Biswas et al. (eds.), *A Multimodal End-2-End Approach to Accessible Computing*, Human–Computer Interaction Series, DOI 10.1007/978-1-4471-6708-2

Printed in the United States
By Bookmasters